THE YEAR BOOK OF WORLD AFFAIRS 1975

VOLUME 29

Editors:

GEORGE W. KEETON

AND

GEORG SCHWARZENBERGER

Managing Editor:

C. G. BURNHAM

AUSTRALIA
The Law Book Company Ltd.
Sydney : Melbourne : Brisbane

GREAT BRITAIN
Stevens & Sons Ltd.
London

INDIA
N. M. Tripathi Private Ltd.
Bombay

ISRAEL
Steimatzky's Agency Ltd.
Jerusalem : Tel Aviv : Haifa

MALAYSIA : SINGAPORE : BRUNEI
Malayan Law Journal (Pte.) Ltd.
Singapore

NEW ZEALAND
Sweet & Maxwell (N.Z.) Ltd.
Wellington

PAKISTAN
Pakistan Law House
Karachi

U.S.A. AND CANADA
Praeger Publishers, Inc.
New York

THE YEAR BOOK

OF

WORLD AFFAIRS

1975

Published under the auspices of
THE LONDON INSTITUTE OF WORLD AFFAIRS

PRAEGER PUBLISHERS

New York

All editorial communications should be addressed
to the Director, London Institute of World Affairs,
Thorne House, 4–8 Endsleigh Gardens, London
WC1H 0EH

*Published in 1975 by
Stevens & Sons Limited of
11 New Fetter Lane, London
and printed in Great Britain
by The Eastern Press Limited
of London and Reading*

*Published in the United States
of America in 1975 by Praeger
Publishers, Inc., 111 Fourth
Avenue, New York, N.Y. 10003*

Library of Congress Catalog Card Number: 47 29156

ISBN 0 275 33500 3

Printed in Great Britain

CONTENTS

page

TRENDS AND EVENTS   1

AN EXPEDITION TO THE POLES   4

By ALASTAIR BUCHAN
*Montague Burton Professor of International Relations
in the University of Oxford*

NEW TASKS FOR THE ATLANTIC ALLIANCE   22

By HELMUT SCHMIDT
Chancellor, Federal Republic of Germany

THE IDEA OF CONCERT AND
    INTERNATIONAL ORDER   34

By R. J. VINCENT
*Research Associate, International Institute for
Strategic Studies (London)*

ARGENTINA IN TRAVAIL   56

By H. S. FERNS
Professor of Political Science in the University of Birmingham

THE COUP IN CHILE   72

By G. W. HUTCHINSON
Professor of Physics in the University of Southampton

TOWARDS A NEW PACIFIC ALLIANCE   88

By COLIN CHAPMAN
Staff Correspondent, The Observer (London)

SINO-AMERICAN RAPPROCHEMENT AND THE NEW
    CONFIGURATIONS IN SOUTHEAST ASIA   106

By USHA MAHAJANI
*Professor of Political Science and Southeast Asia Studies,
Central Washington State College, Ellensburg*

NATURAL LAW AND THE RENEWAL OF THE
    PHILOSOPHY OF INTERNATIONAL RELATIONS   121

By BRIAN MIDGLEY
Senior Lecturer in Politics, University of Aberdeen

JUST WAR, THE NIXON DOCTRINE AND THE
    FUTURE SHAPE OF AMERICAN
    MILITARY POLICY   137

By JAMES T. JOHNSON
*Assistant Professor of Religion,
Associate, Graduate Department of Political Science,
Rutgers University, New Jersey*

v

vi   *Contents*

                                                                    page
THE WORLD COUNCIL OF CHURCHES AND RACISM   155
   By DARRIL HUDSON
   Associate Profesor of Political Science,
   California State University

INTERNATIONAL ORGANISATION IN FOREIGN
      POLICY PERSPECTIVE   173
   By MARGARET DOXEY
   Associate Professor of Politics, Trent University, Ontario

RECENT NORTH-SOUTH RELATIONS AND
      MULTILATERAL SOFT LOANS   196
   By JOHN SYZ
   Research Associate, London Institute of World Affairs

THE ANDEAN COMMON MARKET   208
   By L. D. M. NELSON
   Lecturer in Law, London School of Economics and Political Science

THE ECONOMIC SYSTEMS OF SOCIALIST EASTERN
      EUROPE: PRINCIPLES, DEVELOPMENT,
      AND OPERATION   222
   By A. NUSSBAUMER
   Professor of Economics in the University of Vienna

THE SOVIET CONCEPT OF SOCIALIST
      INTERNATIONAL LAW   242
   By IVO LAPENNA
   Professor of Soviet and East European Law
   in the University of London

EQUALITY AND DISCRIMINATION IN INTERNATIONAL
      ECONOMIC LAW (V):   265
      THE EUROPEAN COMMUNITIES AND THE WIDER WORLD
   By PETER GOLDSMITH
   Barrister-at-Law
   and FRIEDRICH SONDERKÖTTER
   Research Associate, London Institute of World Affairs

THE INTERNATIONAL LAW COMMISSION   283
   By B. G. RAMCHARAN
   Barrister-at-Law

MULTINATIONAL ENTERPRISES AND THE
      INTERNATIONAL LAW OF THE FUTURE   301
   By IGNAZ SEIDL-HOHENVELDERN
   Professor of International Law in the University of Cologne;
   Associé de l'Institut de Droit International

Contents

page

IMPERIALISM: PAST AND FUTURE   313

By STANISLAV ANDRESKI
Professor of Sociology in the University of Reading

THE CONCEPT OF WORLD ORDER   320

By RONALD J. YALEM
Associate Professor of Political Science, University of Alabama

CIVITAS MAXIMA?   337

By GEORG SCHWARZENBERGER
*Professor of International Law in the University of London;
Director, London Institute of World Affairs*

Index   369

TRENDS AND EVENTS

THIS annual survey is intended to serve three purposes:

(1) With every additional volume of this *Year Book* it becomes increasingly difficult for new readers to derive the fullest benefit from the material available in earlier volumes. This survey brings together references to themes examined in the past which have particular current relevance.

(2) The specific object of an annual publication is to make possible analyses in a wider perspective and on the basis of more mature reflection than may be possible in a quarterly or monthly journal. Thus, it is not the object of this *Year Book* to provide instant information on current issues of world affairs. Yet, international affairs have a stereotyped and largely repetitive character, so that, frequently, a " new " happening or " modern " development has been anticipated in one or more of the earlier volumes of the *Year Book.* " Trends and Events " provides evidence of some such continuity as may be traced over a span of years.

(3) References to earlier contributions also offer readers an opportunity to judge for themselves the adequacy of the conceptual and systematic frameworks chosen or taken for granted in the papers selected:

(A) TOWARDS A POLITICAL WORLD ORDER?

Aaronson, M.: *Political Aspects of International Drug Control* (9 Y.B.W.A., 1955)

Beloff, M.: *Problems of International Government* (8 *ibid.*, 1954)

Brennan, G. A.: *The United Nations Development Programme* (24 *ibid.*, 1970)

Cheng, Bin: *The First Twenty Years of the International Court of Justice* (20 *ibid.*, 1966)

Engel, S.: *The Changing Charter of the United Nations* (7 *ibid.*, 1953)

Falk, R. A.: *The Logic of State Sovereignty Versus the Requirements of World Order* (27 *ibid.*, 1973)

Frankel, J.: *The Soviet Union and the United Nations* (8 *ibid.*, 1954)

Goodspeed, S. S.: *The United Nations Conference on Trade and Development* (19 *ibid.*, 1965)

Green, L. C.: *The Double Standard of the United Nations* (11 *ibid.*, 1957)

Groot, E. H. U. de: *Great Britain and the United Nations* (8 *ibid.*, 1954)

1

Harrod, J.: *Problems of United Nations Special Agencies at the Quarter Century* (28 *ibid.*, 1974)

Miller, A. S.: *The Organisation for Economic Co-operation and Development* (17 *ibid.*, 1963)

Northedge, F. S.: *America, Russia and Europe* (28 *ibid.*, 1974)

Ogley, R., and Smith, M.: *Insiders and Outsiders* (28 *ibid.*, 1974)

Schwarzenberger, G.: *From Bipolarity to Multipolarity?* (21 *ibid.*, 1967)

Toussaint, Charmian E.: *The Colonial Controversy in the United Nations* (10 *ibid.*, 1956)

Winkler, R.: *The United States and the United Nations* (8 *ibid.*, 1954)

Yalem, R. J.: *Tripolarity and World Politics* (28 *ibid.*, 1974)

Yturriaga, J. A. de: *Non-Self-Governing Territories: The Law and Practice of the United Nations* (18 *ibid.*, 1964)

Zemanek, K.: *The United Nations and the Law of Outer Space* (19 *ibid.*, 1965)

(B) THE WORLD ECONOMY

Alexandrowicz, C.: *The Study of International Economics* (4 Y.B.W.A., 1950)

Desai, R. R.: *World Monetary Reform* (20 *ibid.*, 1966)

Fisher, A. G. B.: *The Future of International Economic Institutions* (1 *ibid.*, 1947)

Goodwin, G. L.: *GATT and the Organisation for Trade Co-operation* (10 *ibid.*, 1956)

James, A. M.: *The UN Economic Commission for Asia and the Far East* (13 *ibid.*, 1959)

Mahajani, Usha: *Foreign Aid at the Operational Level in South-East Asia* (19 *ibid.*, 1965)

Paenson, I.: *The Problem of East-West Trade* (10 *ibid.*, 1956)

Ross, L. W.: *The Washington Monetary Agreement 1971* (26 *ibid.*, 1972)

Strange, Susan: *The Economic Work of the United Nations* (8 *ibid.*, 1954)

(C) THE LAW OF THE SEA

Alexander, L. M.: *Off-shore Claims and Fisheries in North-West Europe* (14 Y.B.W.A., 1960)

Brown, E. D.: *Deep-Sea Mining: The Legal Régime of Inner Space* (22 *ibid.*, 1968)

Johnson, D. H. N.: *The Geneva Conference on the Law of the Sea* (13 *ibid.*, 1959)

Smith, H. A.: *The Anglo-Norwegian Fisheries Case* (7 *ibid.*, 1953)

(D) Humanising Armed Conflicts?

Dinstein, Y.: *Another Step in Codifying the Laws of War* (28 Y.B.W.A., 1974)

Radojković, M.: *Les Armes Nucléaires et le Droit International* (16 *ibid.*, 1962)

Schwarzenberger, G.: *Neo-Barbarism and International Law* (22 *ibid.*, 1968)

—: *The Law of Armed Conflict: A Civilised Interlude?* (28 *ibid.*, 1974)

(E) The Re-emergence of Japan

Green, L. C.: *Making Peace with Japan* (6 Y.B.W.A., 1952)

Grieve, M. J.: *The Foreign Policy of Japan* (28 *ibid.*, 1974)

Ireland, G.: *Uncommon Law in Martial Tokyo* (4 *ibid.*, 1950)

Mendle, W. M. L.: *Japan's Defence Problems* (22 *ibid.*, 1968)

Nish, I. H.: *Is Japan a Great Power?* (21 *ibid.*, 1967)

—: *Japan Among the Powers* (28 *ibid.*, 1974)

Northedge, F. S.: *The Divided Mind of Japan* (11 *ibid.*, 1957)

(F) Australia's New Image

Archdale, H. E.: *Lessons of Australian Federalism* (9 Y.B.W.A., 1955)

Teichmann, M.: *Australian Dilemmas in Asia* (22 *ibid.*, 1968)

(G) The Churches and International Relations

Chirgwin, A. M.: *The World Church* (1 Y.B.W.A., 1947)

Grubb, Sir Kenneth, and Booth, A. R.: *The Church and International Relations* (17 *ibid.*, 1963)

Ivanyi, B. G.: *Church and State in Eastern Europe* (6 *ibid.*, 1952)

Wood, J. D.: *The World Council of Churches* (26 *ibid.*, 1972)

It may also be helpful to remind readers of the cumulative index to Volumes 1 to 25 in the 1971 volume of the *Year Book of World Affairs*—Managing Ed., Y.B.W.A.

AN EXPEDITION TO THE POLES

By

ALASTAIR BUCHAN

I—THE INEVITABILITY OF MODELS

THE complexity of the international system has long forced those who sought to analyse its nature or to predict its course to seek refuge in analogy, to use a model of interactions found in some other series of relationships than those between States and societies. One may agree with Hedley Bull that models are no advance over generalisations or insights deduced from empirical study of the evidence [1]; nevertheless for generations men have used them, and the models devised by scholars have had a profound effect on the conceptions of statesmen. During the long ascendancy of physics and astronomy after Newton and Keppler, the structure and the character of international politics were generally described by reference to the laws of gravitation and dynamics; the coining of the term " the balance of power " at the beginning of the eighteenth century is one such use and both Hume and Rousseau made use of models derived from the behaviour and properties of stars and planets which seemed adaptive to the European system. Much of the early analysis or justification of imperialism was cast in terms of models drawn from engineering; descriptions for instance of power flowing into a " vacuum." The intellectual excitement caused by the advances in biology just over a century ago, when coupled with a greater awareness of the sociological factors in the relations of States, led in turn to a vogue for anthropological models, not only among intellectuals but politicians. The conception of international politics as a perpetual struggle for survival of the fittest had a disastrous effect on the attitudes and assumptions of leaders and on the general climate of educated opinion in Europe in the years before 1914 [2]—and indeed in the United States also, though there the most fervent Social Darwinist, Theodore Roosevelt, escaped the consequences of his views.[3]

---

[1] See " The Case for a Classical Approach " in K. Knorr and J. N. Rosenau (eds.), *Contending Approaches to International Politics* (1969).

[2] This subject is lucidly explored in J. Joll, *1914: The Unspoken Assumptions* (1968).

[3] See *The Strenuous Life* (1899), p. 200: " The twentieth century looms before us with the fate of many nations. If we stand idly by, if we seek merely swollen, slothful ease and ignoble peace, if we shrink from the hard contests where men must win at hazard of their lives and at the risk of all they hold dear, then the bolder and stronger peoples will pass us by, and will win for themselves the dominions of the world."

The study of international politics in the inter-war years was influenced partly by a reaction against Darwinian models, partly by a sense of the growing universalisation of communications and political interactions, partly by the existence of the League as a universal institution. The consequence was a greater use of models based upon domestic politics or municipal law, or on the behaviour of social groups like the family. Those who theorised about the evolution of the British Empire into the Commonwealth were particularly fond of familial models and, as Australian and Canadian writers have pointed out, this often prevented them from observing what was actually occurring; namely, the gradual transformation of an organic, ethnic relationship into a genuinely international one.

The model making of the immediate post-war decade was, to put it mildly, confused; the statesman's attempt to create a concert of Powers had no sooner been enunciated than it broke down and the subsequent decade presented too swift a pace of change for either the theorist or the politician to think in terms more profound than " them " and " us," although Hans Morgenthau attempted to apply the tenets of imperialism to the expanding influence of the two super-Powers.

It was, I imagine, Morton Kaplan (for I do not know of an earlier author) who introduced the analogy from electro-magnetism,[4] namely " polarity," into international relations theory with the publication of *System and Process in International Politics* in 1957, and it quickly came into general use and has remained so. Kaplan, and those who support him in the belief that the natural sciences can provide insights into the nature of political behaviour which empirical study alone cannot achieve, have always contended that the modal behaviour of the units of the international system can be deduced from its structure. I think this is to a certain extent true. But my concern is that a model based on the concept of polarity is now becoming inadequate for either descriptive or predictive purposes, just at a time when it has become firmly planted in the heads of a generation of students and their teachers, many of whom are now reaching positions of authority. There may be as much danger in this situation as there was in the existence of a generation of political leaders in 1914 who had absorbed the Darwinian model in the 1870s and 1880s, when the industrial Powers were less highly militarised than they were a quarter of a century later.

---

[4] Polarity has another meaning in the language of mathematics or physics, namely, the poles of the axis on which a body in motion rotates. But by this use of the term, there never could be more than two poles.

II—The Properties of a Pole

When it first gained coinage, that is at the end of the 1950s, the concept of " bipolarity," the notion that the Soviet Union and the United States were the negative and positive (or vice versa, if one were a Russian) terminals of the whole current of world politics, was a graphic and accurate description of reality. At that time and for some years afterwards, those two States were the core Powers of the international system. Although the Soviet Union had an economy only half as productive as that of the American, her military strength overshadowed that of every country except the United States; although she had only some nine allies where the United States had over forty, they included the world's most populous country; and the leadership of Khrushchev imparted a dynamism to her external policy which hid many internal weaknesses and divisions. By the same token the United States at that point in time wielded a combination of strategic and military strength, and political, economic and technological influence which made Washington in every sense the capital of the West. British and French influence had declined markedly throughout the 1950s and Germany remained highly vulnerable, so that the Atlantic Alliance which had started as a genuine coalition of reciprocal interests had become a more and more tightly controlled American military command system: Japan was still almost as much an American dependency as the other Pacific allies of the United States. One could argue about the extent to which the so-called Third World was outside or inside the magnetic field of the super-Powers but there could be no argument about the industrial world, including distant outposts of it such as Australia.

In the late 1950s and early 1960s there was still a considerable fear of great Power conflict and it was natural that scholars and analysts of all kinds should place considerable emphasis on the strategic or deterrent properties of the super-Powers. This was the period when the conception of the " adversary partnership " was born, the recognition that in such a situation of influence and strength, super-Power competition was not entirely a zero-sum game, that the dynamism of the international system would be less liable to produce dangerous static if the two poles were connected in some way—hence the rapid blooming of the concept of arms control, and the welcome given to such initiatives as the Atmospheric Test Ban or the installation of the Hot Line [5]; hence also, however, the

---

[5] In his " Bipolarity, Multipolarity and the Future," *Journal of Conflict Research* (1968), R. Rosecrance suggests that this represented a confusion between bipolarity and *détente*. This was not, I think, the common view among policy-makers a decade ago, who saw bipolarity as a model of the distribution of power.

general support for defence expenditure especially in the United States. It was developments in this range of State power that seemed to determine the nature of the international system.

The weaknesses of bipolarity as a working model, or as an abstraction sufficiently close to empirical truth to be a useful or durable guide to policy, seem, in hindsight, to have been threefold. First, it tended to attribute too much of the polar characteristics of the super-Powers to their strategic and military strength. Secondly, and in consequence, the model made no provision for a redistribution of relative power at levels other than the strategic. Thirdly, it assumed that the structure of the international system was a function of the interaction of governments, or of the power wielded by States as such, to a greater extent than was in fact the case. The consequence was that its predictive, and eventually even its descriptive value, was impaired.

The first consequence of the acceptance of the model of polarity was that discussions about system stability or transformation became very largely centred around the ownership of nuclear weapons and the issue of nuclear proliferation. It is true that proliferation seemed a somewhat more likely prospect ten or twelve years ago than it does today. Its likelihood diminished partly because three of the existing nuclear Powers, the United States, the Soviet Union and the United Kingdom, insisted on the negotiation of an international instrument, the Non-Proliferation Treaty of 1968, which brought proliferation as nearly under international control as such an instrument can. It is true that China and France refused to sign it, as did two significant potential nuclear Powers, Israel and India. But the fact that about one hundred countries have signed it, including Japan and Germany, suggests also that possession of nuclear weapons had by the end of the 1960s to a certain extent ceased to be considered the touchstone of autonomy or security.[5a] The diminishing significance of the British and French nuclear forces as factors even in their own governments' estimation of their interests, the fact that China's possession of a nuclear capability has had only regional significance—in her deterrence of Soviet attack—and has had little bearing on her re-entry into the mainstream of world politics, suggests that we had a decade ago, too narrow a definition of power. This does not mean that nuclear proliferation may not become an issue again, though the strategic difficulties confronting any new entrant to the nuclear club become more formidable every year: but proliferation has not so far been the agent of systemic change that both governments and academics

---

[5a] India's recent underground detonation of a nuclear device suggests, however, that considerations of status still affect the possibilities of participation.

(myself included) thought it would be. Nor, by the same token, has the rise of the Soviet Union to a position of parity in strategic weapons with the United States; this has put the credibility of an American nuclear response to an attack on one of her allies that was not an attack on herself in some doubt, but this has always been in some doubt ever since the Soviet Union first acquired the means of delivering nuclear weapons on North America nearly 20 years ago. And the penumbra of obscurity that surrounds the whole question of when and in what circumstances nuclear weapons might be used, is accepted by many, though not all, strategic analysts as a factor that increases their deterrent power.

This relates to the second and third lacuna in most people's conception of the nature of the assets which the two super-Powers wielded when it became widely accepted that they were the two terminal poles of the international system. Their power was seen as deriving from the actions of their governments and the force they controlled, and insufficient attention was paid to their economic and political influence or the magnetic properties of their societies; in other words the electro-magnetic analogy was not pushed far enough. Of course there was an asymmetry in this form of influence. The United States was not only an open society but one which had for thirty years been undergoing a great social and economic revolution. Her leadership on the whole commanded respect and its judgment had not yet been impugned by the Vietnam *débâcle*; she had absorbed Keynesianism; she had changed in twenty years from a second rate scientific Power to the world's pioneer; her currency was the unquestioned basis of the international monetary system. So powerful was the United States in comparison with either adversaries or allies 10 or 12 years ago that some Americans [6] described the structure of the international system as " unipolar " though this always seemed to me, and to American policy-makers, for that matter, a considerable exaggeration.

It is true that the Soviet Union did not possess the same range of magnetic properties as the United States. The ranks of its intellectual admirers in Europe had been decimated by the 1960s and popular support for Communism had become reduced to a hard core of party faithful who were animated more by a quarrel with their own society than Russophilia. Nevertheless to the leaders of poor or new States, struggling to free themselves from Western political or economic dominion, the Soviet Union could still serve both as a magnet and a model. She had gifts to offer; she still had a confidence in her own ideology though this began to evaporate

---

[6] *e.g.* Z. Brzezinski in *Bulletin*, United States Department of State (July 3, 1967) or George Liska, *Imperial America* (1967).

during the 1960s under the hammer blows of Chinese criticism, and she had achieved industrialisation by a process of iron discipline which many governments in the Third World would have liked to emulate.

It is the period between 1957 and 1963 to which, in my view, the term bipolar can be most accurately ascribed, a period when—whether a smaller country needed a steel mill, a loan or a nuclear guarantee—it had little option but to send its emissaries to either Washington or Moscow. But even then there was considerable debate as to whether and for how long this situation would continue; some writers like Hedley Bull, Raymond Aron and Leonard Beaton, among non-Americans, and Henry Kissinger among Americans argued that a diffusion of power and the appearance of new poles was inevitable; others disputed this. Still others like Kenneth Waltz argued that the retention of a bipolar structure of power was not only probable but desirable; because it made the handling of the political or inter-State crises that were inevitable in an ideologically divided world more manageable and less dangerous; because, with growing Soviet interest in the Third World to match the interest increasingly shown by the United States since the 1950s, the bipolar balance now knew no boundaries; and because super-Power dominance made it easier for the international system to absorb a rapid pace of political, economic and technological change without degenerating into major conflict.[7]

This was also the view, implicit or explicit, of the political leadership of the two super-Powers. In the case of the Soviet Union any other view implied the recognition of China, with whom its relations had steadily deteriorated and which had exploded its first nuclear device in 1964, as an equal partner in the Communist system and an autonomous great Power in its own right. On the American side, it created an ambiguity in foreign policy goals which first became apparent in the summer of 1962 and which has never been properly resolved. On July 4, 1962, President Kennedy expressed strong American support for a United States of Europe, meaning an autonomous European Community that included the United Kingdom and other countries besides the original Six and with a political as well as an economic role, the two great power centres on either side of the Atlantic closely linked. Yet only a few weeks earlier his Secretary of Defense, Mr. Robert McNamara, had made a speech at Ann Arbor, Michigan, in which he had attacked the British and French nuclear forces as redundant and dangerous and had made explicit his view that the United States would insist on centralising control of any European crisis in its

---

[7] See " The Stability of a Bipolar World," *Daedalus,* Summer 1964.

own hands. Mr. McNamara's words had the ring of actuality while those of his President were more those of aspiration. Nine months earlier the President had acted unilaterally and not as the leader of a coalition to sustain the bipolar balance during the Cuban missile crisis.

III—THE EROSION OF BIPOLARITY

In the decade between 1964 and 1973 it became increasingly difficult to be satisfied that a model using the physical analogy of bipolarity continued to be a useful mode of analysing the structure or predicting the development of the international system. In the first place, two significant countries, France and China, and several smaller ones such as Roumania and Venezuela, North Korea or Pakistan, began to pursue policies independent or critical of the super-Power to which they were allied. Yet during the 1960s it was very hard to assert that they themselves were acquiring the characteristics of poles. It was true that both France and China had leaders of great personal charisma and that their declarations of independence from Washington and Moscow found a distinct echo in many other capitals. But neither became strategic Powers—which had originally been regarded as the hallmark of a pole—in the same category as the United States or the Soviet Union: nuclear Powers they might be but their ability to sustain a confrontation with either super-Power without exposing their own much greater vulnerability was low and still is low. Moreover, their ability to exert military influence at any distance from their borders was clearly limited. Nor was economic power of decisive significance, and the policies that France and China pursued in the developing world showed, by their selectiveness, that both recognised that their influence was very far from being universal.

In counterpoint the United States during this same period augmented her very considerable military strength but this did not increase her ability to influence world politics. By 1968 her military budget was nearly double what President Eisenhower had regarded as an acceptable upper limit of expenditure and she had more men in uniform than the Soviet Union. Yet her inability to bring a small Asian Power to terms should have disposed of any illusion that there was any direct relationship between strategic polarity and the exertion of force. The Vietnam War made clear that in the new international system, different as it is in the quantity of sovereign States and in the quality of international politics from any previous one, military power did not necessarily translate into influence or magnetism. Ironically enough, those responsible for American decisions about intervention and the escalation of military force in

Vietnam—President Johnson, Mr. Dean Rusk and Mr. McNamara in particular—were heavily influenced in their decisions by the need to sustain American credibility and therefore influence in those parts of the international system of which she was a strategic pole, namely her alliances, and also with her twin pole, the Soviet Union. In fact, the Vietnam War had the reverse effect of creating new strains in her relations with her allies and did not strengthen her position in relation to the Soviet Union.

What the Vietnam War and other developments of the 1960s proved, just as the arresting of Khrushchev's attempt to liberalise the Soviet political system had done, was that polarity implied another dimension than the strategic or political, namely the social or ideological dimension. It is difficult to generalise about this, still less to quantify it; but no European who was involved in the discussions and analyses of this period could fail to be aware of the declining social magnetism of both super-Powers, and of the United States in particular, as Vietnam led to increasing divisions in American society, as problems like urban decay, ethnic antagonism, student alienation, came to dominate the headlines, and as the reputation of the United States as the most successful experimental society in the democratic world declined accordingly. This did not seriously impair the credibility of American strategic power but I think it is fair to say that by the end of the 1960s the United States had ceased to be regarded as the magnetic pole that it had been a decade earlier, and much more as the generator of crude strategic power, however necessary this might be still regarded to the security of her allies. Allied statesmen felt decreasingly inclined or able to take risks in following American leadership, or in adjusting the interests of their own countries to those of the United States, because of the decline in popular respect in their own countries for American society. Anti-Americanism ceased to be simply a product of jealousy on the part of élites in other States of the enormous wealth or power of the United States and became tinged with a more widespread distrust of American society. The decline in respect for Soviet society has not been so marked because, as I said earlier, it was never as great, but it has occurred and is still occurring as the autocratic characteristics of the régime become more publicised.

It will be difficult for the historian to disentangle this aspect of the erosion of bipolarity in its full or tight (to use Morton Kaplan's word) sense, from the marked changes that have occurred in the distribution of economic power. In the early 1960s the centrality of the American economy to the functioning of the whole system of trade and payments was still an important component of its role as a polar Power. A decade later the American economy was still the largest and in most ways the strongest in the world, but it had ceased—perhaps only temporarily—to have the polar characteristics of the post-war era. For a complex series of reasons, which it would be pointless for a non-economist to try and analyse, the United States ran into increasing balance of payments difficulties in the later 1960s, culminating in a crushing deficit of nearly $30,000 million in 1971 and of $10,000 million in 1972. Its causes were primarily two: a marked increase in the rate of American overseas investment from 1964 onwards, and a decline in competitive power of American products, except in certain industries, by comparison with those of Western Europe and Japan. The American share of monetary reserves held by countries of the non-Communist world had dropped from 60 per cent. in 1946 to 20 per cent. in 1966 and to under 15 per cent. by 1971. On the plane of economic interaction the United States had become only the largest of several large trading partners and had also ceased to be the dominant monetary power, though neither the European Economic Community nor Japan possessed the ability to take its place, so that the dollar has remained the basic international currency.

The apparent declining relevance of the model of polarity, at any rate of bipolarity, appeared to be ratified by the American opening of relations with China, which was initiated by Henry Kissinger's visit to Peking in July 1971 and formalised by the President's visit of the following February, as well as by China's admission to the United Nations in the intervening months. One could, and still can, argue whether China has the characteristics of a pole in the sense that the post-war super-Powers were poles, but there was no denying that by a decision that was largely that of the United States alone, even though it was solicited by China, the world's largest Power had been encouraged to enter into an active role in world politics.

IV—THE FRUSTRATION OF MULTIPOLARITY

In this new situation, there was a tendency to abandon the model of polarity in the general sense in which it had been used in the Cold War years in favour either of the classical model of the multiple balance of power or to distinguish different forms of polarity at different levels of interaction. Certainly it is true, as Hedley Bull predicted over 10 years ago, that " the system of polarisation of power will cease to be recognisable: that other states will count for so much in world politics that the present great powers will find it difficult, even when co-operating, to dominate them."[8] But what had emerged by the early 1970s was not a multipolar world in the sense that American and other analysts (such as Pierre Gallois in France) had envisaged, namely, a system in which a number of Powers, greater than two, possessed the essential characteristics, or most of them, of the original super-Powers.

China is an embryonic strategic Power in the sense that she is slowly acquiring a nuclear capability of limited range. But she possesses little naval or air power which would enable her to exert military influence at a distance. Though the quality of her civilisation and her adaptation of Marxism to the needs of a poor country give her some polar characteristics in relation to the developing countries, her economic assets are limited and are likely to augment, like her military influence, only slowly. Japan had had, until 1973, twelve years or so of dynamic economic expansion which endowed her with limited polar characteristics in certain fields of trade. Yet she is not only virtually without military power, but also extremely vulnerable to the decisions of others since her economic strength depends on a very high level of imported raw materials. Her social or political system is not a charismatic one, and if she were to attempt to become a pole, in the sense of a strategically independent nation with its own sphere of economic and political influence, this would arouse reactions based on memories of her behaviour a generation ago, which might well make such an effort self-defeating. The European Community, as enlarged in 1973 to include the United Kingdom, has some polar characteristics: it contains two nuclear Powers, though of a very limited nature; it accounts for over a third of world trade, and it has certain polar characteristics too in that it has powerful links with parts of the developing world, and, like Japan, technological and other assets to offer these countries and those of Eastern Europe. But unlike Japan it is only a Community which at present shows no signs of advancing to the status of a Power while its component countries are individually, and even collectively, strategically and economically vulnerable.

A country like India which a decade ago was being discussed as a potential pole of a multipolar system, has now detonated a nuclear device, but this does not make her a nuclear Power, still less a pole, given her increasing economic difficulties. Canada lacks the aspirations to become a pole, and it is not yet clear that the rising wealth of Brazil is matched by sufficient internal cohesion to make her a polar Power even within her own régime. And what is true of Brazil in Latin America is true of Nigeria in Africa.

If the model of a multipolar world, of a number of Powers more

[8] See Rosecrance, *op. cit.* in note, 5, above.

than two, endowed with the ability to guarantee their own security
and that of their neighbours, to project their influence and to sustain
their interests globally, has so far failed to materialise, other attempts
to devise alternatives that reflect and elucidate the reality of the
international system have so far been unsuccessful. One such attempt
was made by no less a person than the President of the United
States when at the beginning of 1972 he suggested that the classical
model of a pentagonal balance should be a goal: " We must
remember that the only time in the history of the world that we
have had any extended periods of peace is when there has been a
balance of power. It is when one nation becomes infinitely more
powerful in relation to its potential competitor that the danger of
war arises. So I believe in a world in which the United States is
powerful. I think it will be a safer world and a better world if we
have a strong, healthy United States, Europe, Soviet Union, China
and Japan, each balancing the other, not playing one against the
other, an even balance." [9]

I will not belabour the weaknesses of this concept partly because
I and others have done so elsewhere,[10] partly because it was clearly
only a *ballon d'essai* which quickly disappeared from American
policy statements. Any such concept overlooks not only the disparity
of the assets of the five power centres which the President named,
by comparison with other participants in earlier multiple balances
of power, but several other factors too: the continuing, if diminished,
role of ideology in world politics which makes re-alignments and
re-adjustments difficult, the changed nature of power, and above
all the intractability of the international system in which the major
power centres pursue their interests. It ignores also the fact that,
although we may live in what is now a single international system,
the realities of classical factors like distance have not disappeared.
It is true that economic decisions taken in Tokyo or Brussels can
affect employment or prosperity on the other side of the world, but
it is doubtful if any but the two original super-Powers can take
political decisions whose consequences are felt universally.

This point has been clarified by the limitations on the influence
of the most enthusiastic proponent of a multiple balance of power,
namely China. It is possible, though it cannot be proved, that Sino-
Soviet hostility had a bearing on the willingness of the Soviet Union
to reach certain specific agreements with the Federal Republic and
with the Western Powers in Berlin in 1970 and 1971. But strong
Chinese diplomatic pressure on the countries of Western Europe

[9] See *Time*, January 3, 1972.
[10] See S. Hoffman, " Weighing the Balance of Power," and my " A World
Restored?," *Foreign Affairs*, July 1972.

to convert the European Community into a fully independent power centre, so as to reduce Soviet pressure on her, or to resist any agreements with the Soviet Union on force reductions in Europe, has had no effect because China is not in a position to offer Europe any material assistance if it were to embark upon an independent course. Nor could Europe come to the aid of China in the event of some Sino-Soviet *débâcle*. The world is still a very big place, and to attempt to apply to it models derived from epochs when the international system was dominated by a group of Powers who lived cheek by jowl, who had a common diplomatic parlance, and who could use force to readjust imbalance without catastrophic consequences, can lead only to confusion and disappointment.

The other model which the evolution of the international system has suggested in recent years is that of the double triangle. It is predicated on the assumption that national power can no longer be considered as a single entity and that the major Powers have different interests or coadjutors at different levels of interest. By this view the United States has deliberately developed a triangular relation between herself, the Soviet Union and China but the content of it is overwhelmingly strategic and political. I will not elaborate on this, partly because this new situation of tripolarity has been explored in the previous volume of this *Year Book*.[11] The second triangle governs economic and technological relations and its angles are the United States, the European Community and Japan.

This model is closer to reality than that of a pentagonal balance, and it is not surprising that it should be well received in the United States since it assumes that that country is the apex of the two principal relationships that govern the course of international politics. But it is open to certain serious criticism as a guide either to comprehension or to policy.

In the first place, it seems to me still unproven that the bipolar strategic and political relationship of the old super-Powers has in any comprehensive fashion become tripolar, or that either regards China as a pole in the sense that they regard each other. However, it may be too soon to pass final judgment on this. A second weakness of such a concept is its assumption that economic and strategic relations can be divorced. Indeed Dr. Henry Kissinger and other American leaders have done their best to resist it by their assertion that monetary, trade and security relationships between the major components of the Western or economic triangle are inherently

---

[11] R. J. Yalem, "Tripolarity and World Politics," in this *Year Book*, Volume 28 (1974), pp. 23–42. It has also been examined by M. Tatu, *The Great Power Triangle: Washington-Moscow-Peking* (1970), by W. E. Griffith, *Peking, Moscow and Beyond*, Washington Papers Nr. 6 (1973), and by others.

related.[12] It also assumes that there is no economic content in the relationships of the United States with the Soviet Union and China, an assumption which is not accepted either in Peking or Moscow. Finally, it suffers from the same weakness as the pentagonal balance of power model, namely, in assuming that issues of peace and war, conflict and co-operation between the other 120 or so States in the world is primarily a factor of the relationships of the major Powers.

V—BI-MULTIPOLARITY?

It was the developments of the last three months of 1973 that made both these models questionable before their assumptions had been accepted or their implications fully explored. For the outbreak of the fourth Arab-Israeli war, and the precipitation of a crisis in the relations between the oil-producing and consuming States which was partly related to it, have, each in their fashion, made it necessary to reconsider recent models or empirical generalisations about the way in which the international system is developing.

The behaviour of the United States and the Soviet Union after the outbreak of the war through the attack of Egypt and Syria on Israel on October 6, 1973, tended to dispute any proposition that the structure of real power of crisis management has ceased to be bipolar. First, the two super-Powers regarded their interests as more closely affected from the very beginning of the conflict, though it took both Washington and Moscow by surprise, than other Powers. As the fortunes of war fluctuated and as its intensity consumed large stocks of armaments in the hands of the belligerents, both Powers felt obliged to re-supply their clients. Secondly, the United States refused to let its principal allies, the United Kingdom and France especially, assume any significant role in the achievement of a ceasefire. A final ceasefire was in fact accomplished partly by a process of super-Power bargaining which was entirely bilateral, and which involved the alerting of American forces in Europe and the movement of military supplies from European bases without serious consultation with European NATO Powers. Thirdly, China played no significant role in the bargaining process and in fact abstained from the Security Council's resolution which formalised the ceasefire. Fourthly and finally, the subsequent negotiations between the super-Powers and the belligerents which in the succeeding three months converted the ceasefire into an armistice,

---

[12] H. A. Kissinger in a speech to the Associated Press in New York on April 23, 1973, said: "The political, military and economic issues in Atlantic relations are linked by reality, not by our choice nor for the tactical purpose of trading one off against the other."

at least between Egypt and Israel, and led to a conference with wider prospects of a settlement, were conducted almost single-handed by the American Secretary of State, acting, it seemed, not only on behalf of his own government but that of the Soviet Union as well.

One can argue that there were special factors in this situation, or that the Middle East has long been a special case, which makes it rash to make broader deductions about Great Power relations from crises that arise there. For nearly 15 years both Israel and her neighbours have been dependent on the super-Powers for their armaments; Israel arouses special emotions in the United States; Egypt has been since 1971 a formal ally of the Soviet Union. In terms of communications and of their own positions as world Powers, it is an area to which both countries ascribe a crucial significance.

The accident of personalities should also make one chary of making the events of late 1973 the basis of a final judgment. The new American Secretary of State, Dr. Kissinger, is a man not only of remarkable energy, but is possessed of great skill in personal diplomacy; and, moreover, has a temperamental liking for it. The constitutional crisis in Washington, moreover, caused by the Watergate scandal, made it particularly important to achieve a diplomatic success for the Nixon Administration at that time. " A common soldier, a child, a girl at the door of an inn, have changed the face of fortune and almost of nature," wrote Burke in emphasising the role of casual as well as causal factors in history. If Mr. William Rogers had still been Secretary of State (as he was six weeks before the Arab-Israeli war broke out) and if Dr. Kissinger had been laid low with shingles or a broken leg, the United States would probably have sought to act in concert with her European allies and would also have been less readily accepted as the partner and sometime agent of the Soviet Union, for this situation was a product of the considerable personal respect in which Dr. Kissinger is held in Moscow.

But, while these special considerations are important, the Middle East crisis has in some ways only served to confirm other indications not only of the continuing bipolarity of the structure of power, but also of changes in the character of the bipolar relationship itself.

For the other development of late 1973, a near quadrupling of the price of Middle Eastern oil, a severe cutback in production by some of the Gulf States, and a boycott of supplies to the United States introduced new factors into the equation. True, the energy crisis was not unexpected: since 1971 it had been apparent that the Organisation of Petroleum Exporting Countries (OPEC), which includes Venezuela, Indonesia, Iran and the Arab oil States, had acquired an effective unity of action when, by the Teheran agreement, it forced a significant increase in the price of crude oil on the Western companies. A year later, by the Riyadh agreement, OPEC laid the foundations for control over the rate at which their asset would be extracted. Western governments had been expecting steady increases in prices throughout the 1970s and had been planning for the possibility that the rate of production would not conform to their demands, which would, on normal assumptions, have doubled between 1972 and 1980. The fourth Arab-Israeli war simply accelerated what might otherwise have been a slower process of change in the relations between producer and consumer States.

Nevertheless, the economic disruption to which the action of the OPEC States has led, the extent to which they have succeeded in splitting the Western alliance system, the court that individual countries, France, the United Kingdom and Italy in particular, have paid to the major producers, make me wonder whether, in terms of earlier definitions, they should not be credited with the characteristics of a " pole " in the evolving international system. If the capacity to harm or benefit the interests of major States, if the possession of bargaining power, are the characteristics of a pole, then the OPEC States are poles to a greater extent than China is a pole. Yet OPEC is simply a functional agreement among a number of disparate nations who are not in any sense politically allied or linked by ties of race or ideology (although all with the exception of Venezuela are Moslem). And even the two most powerful, Iran and Saudi Arabia, have no other polar characteristics, except in their own region. They are not strategic Powers, although they can affect the strategic power of others; the magnetism of their societies is limited (though Saudi Arabia possesses the Holy Place of the world's largest religion); their general economic influence is limited although their financial weight is likely to grow considerably. Either one has to accept that there is yet another plane of interaction in international relations than the politico-strategic and the general economic planes, although the structure of relationships on it is not yet fully determined (it may become either multipolar between different producing and consuming countries or bipolar between a coalition of OPEC and OECD Powers) or one must broaden one's definition of polarity still further.

To complicate the theorist's problem, the emergence of energy supplies and costs as a major factor in world politics has added a new dimension to the characteristics of the original polar Powers, the United States and the Soviet Union. The Soviet Union is self-sufficient in oil and an important potential exporter of natural gas. The United States is now an importer of oil to the tune of some 15 per cent. of its consumption, and in the normal course of events might have become dependent on imports to the extent of a third or more of consumption by the end of the decade. But it is already apparent that if she takes reasonable measures to conserve a very wasteful public attitude to the consumption of energy, exploits her own and Canadian oil resources, and accelerates the development of nuclear energy, she has the economic and scientific base to retain a fair measure of independence. Europe and Japan by contrast are very much more vulnerable. Europe is dependent on imports for some 80 per cent. of its energy and Japan for 100 per cent., a situation which can only be altered very slowly by the development of nuclear and other resources. China has a very small amount of oil to export and would find it difficult to import significant quantities, for purposes of economic growth (as other poor countries like India are finding it), at today's prices.

It is too early to judge how significant or permanent a part energy relationships are going to play in affecting the structure or nature of the international system. It may well be that in a few years' time measures to conserve consumption plus the energetic exploitation of energy sources under the direct control of the industrial Powers may have modified the polar characteristics of the OPEC States or the vulnerability of Europe and Japan. On the other hand, there can be little argument that the scarcity and value of a number of raw materials, and not oil alone, are likely to increase, phosphates, copper and iron ore, for instance. This is likely to have two consequences. First, it will involve various parts of the developing world in the interplay of great Power relations, in a different fashion than they were involved in the Cold War years, as the exerters of power and leverage in their own right rather than the object of ideological or political competition between the Communist and the Western Powers. Secondly, the significance of raw materials is likely once again to increase the polar characteristics of the super-Powers and of the Soviet Union in particular, because their command of indigenous raw materials is greater than that of China, Europe and still more of Japan.

CONCLUSIONS

What I have said suggests that we have lived through a period in which it was difficult to argue that the international system was

either remaining bipolar or tending towards a multipolar structure,'
and are now emerging into a situation in which some of the characteristics of bipolarity are becoming more pronounced again. But
the original model of bipolarity which envisaged the super-Powers
as the great buttresses of a Gothic apse, stability being imparted
to the whole structure by their mutual antagonism, is now misleading. This is partly because they have succeeded in identifying
a widening range of common interests, not merely on problems like
arms control where the attempt to control de-stabilising innovations
such as MIRV forces them into a position of increasing mutual
trust, but also, say, on the exchange of American cereals and
technology for Soviet oil and raw materials. The increasing community of interests between the Soviet Union and the United States
has also been evident in the preparatory discussions on the Law
of the Sea Conference where they emerge as *status quo* Powers
standing shoulder to shoulder against the pressures of the developing world for a new régime of the oceans. The Gothic model is also
misleading because their influence over the rest of the international
community has weakened and the peripheries of their competition
have narrowed. When they try to act on the assumptions of an
earlier age, as the Soviet Union did over Czechoslovakia in 1968
and the United States did over the Middle East in 1973, the limitation of their influence within their own sub-systems becomes
apparent.

A more constructive thinker should be able to seize this opportunity to develop an entirely new model of the contemporary State
system, based perhaps on some biological analogy, perhaps with
those strange forms of plant life that are found in tropical waters
and which assume a different shape or colour according to the
kind and degree of external stimulus. The attempt has eluded me
and for the time being I find the most useful model that which
Richard Rosencrance has called " Bi-multipolarity " [13] in which
the original polar States have an ambiguous relationship, part
co-operative, part competitive, while the lesser Powers are divided
on many issues but have a common interest in resisting the pretensions of the greater. It is, as he points out, a situation in which
policy-making and calculations of system equilibrium are much
more difficult than in the simpler structures of the past, but in
which the prospect of serious conflict may be less, partly because
the original poles can be less sure of the loyalty of allies while
retaining sufficient influence to restrain conflict between them.

---

[13] " Bipolarity, Multipolarity and the Future," *Journal of Conflict Resolution*
(1966). Reprinted in J. N. Rosenau (ed.), *International Politics and Foreign Policy*
(1969).

But the empirical evidence is changing so rapidly that the time is coming when we must either abandon structural models altogether, something that academics find easier to do than policymakers, or devise a new taxonomy of power that illuminates rather than obscures the new realities of action and interaction in the international system.

NEW TASKS
FOR THE ATLANTIC ALLIANCE

By

HELMUT SCHMIDT

I—CHANCES FOR A NEW STABILITY

IN contrast to what the founding fathers of the Atlantic Alliance had in mind, the main problem of our days is not so much to maintain security as such but to bring security and peaceful change into accord. Various statesmen and scholars have proclaimed during recent years, what has come to be called the end of the post-war period. Today, we are not only discussing the most important of these changes; we are looking at the dilemmas they pose, at the chances for a new stability and at the possible dangers resulting from new instabilities. The East-West relations have been, since 1945, the dominant element of tension in world politics. These relations have been changing their character for a number of years, and the changes constitute an important transformation in international politics. That process raises new problems while solving old ones. For both Europe and the United States, the tasks ahead will not be easy. In the area of security as well as in the economic field, our common main effort has to be to reconcile the goal of Western European unity and a peaceful change of East-West relations in Europe with a new and viable relationship between Western Europe and North America.

Europe has been—despite crises over Cuba, the Middle East and Southeast Asia—the most important region in the struggle between East and West for the last quarter of a century. It has been an issue producing enormous tensions. Today, it is the object, partner and theatre of enormous diplomatic activities instead. The future of our continent is deeply involved in the conference for security and co-operation in Europe, in the negotiations on Mutual and Balanced Force Reductions (MBFR), in the Strategic Arms Limitation Talks (SALT), in the world-wide negotiations within the General Agreement on Tariffs and Trade (GATT), in the deliberations on a reform of the international monetary system, and in the manifold mutual summit meetings between leading political figures of East and West.

In this "era of negotiations," the *dramatis personae* have to overcome the era of confrontation. They also have to secure two or three decades " of moderation," of absence of war and of peaceful change. And they have, at the same time, to avoid a new phase of political or economic instability.

22

For the European countries, the changes of the international politics must result in three intertwined dimensions: First, the necessity of a balance of power; secondly, the structure of peaceful relations between the States which are involved in this field; and thirdly, the freedom of one's own decision without interference from outside.

II—THE BALANCE OF POWER

Balance of power will continue to be the most important factor affecting global security, because the universal order will continue to be governed by rivalry, competition and the juxtaposition of States, peoples and ideas. Balance in the political sense of the word is non-static; rather it is marked by dynamic changes and fluid zones of transition, embracing objective structures as well as subjective valuations, ideals and moral forces.

In an analysis of the prospects of how peace and freedom of decision can be preserved, more than a slide-rule is needed to pass judgment. Commenting on the question of the significance of declining defence efforts on the part of the West, I summarise the results of my evaluations.

The West, comprising all the North Atlantic Treaty nations and, to some extent, also Japan, will for some time to come have at its disposal a power potential—*i.e.* labour, capital and land, which is larger in quantity, higher in quality and more diversified than that of the Warsaw Pact. The West will, therefore, retain its capability to activate extensive sources of power in order to attain goals or to satisfy other needs.

It is, on the other hand, incontestable that the Warsaw Pact nations are spending a larger share of their gross national product for military purposes. Expressed in US-dollars, however, their expenditure—in absolute figures—is less than that of the West. But if one compares the military capabilities of both sides under the aspect of equal cost standards, the expenditure by the Warsaw Pact is probably only a little below that of the West.

During the past ten years the West has gradually stepped up defence spending, expressed in real value, though less so than the Soviet Union and the other nations of the Warsaw Pact. This implies that in fields where the West enjoyed military preponderance, such as the strategic nuclear sphere and on the high seas, this advantage has been surpassed or at least equated. Where the Soviet Union possessed a military lead, for instance in the conventional land forces in Central Europe, the West has been incapable of reaching a numerical balance. The conclusion derived from a global comparison of the capabilities of both sides still places the West in a relatively more favourable position, but this is not true if we look at Europe alone. It is in Europe that the West is inferior.

The adverse geographical and political conditions render deterrence and the defence of western interests difficult in Europe and in the Middle East, to say nothing of an independent European policy in these fields *vis-à-vis* the Soviet Union—a possibility that cannot be realised, anyway for the foreseeable future. Because of the continuing national motivation and organisation of the western nations, their defence efforts, particularly in Western Europe, cannot as yet be put to optimum use.

New centres of power are emerging; they might exert a de-stabilising influence on security policy while at the same time serving to increase the readiness of the two world Powers to counter such trends by intensifying their efforts at consolidating the existing security structures. We should not overlook the fact that ideological conflict and political rivalry are to continue. This means that the rivals will exploit any vacuum of power, including one in the military force ratio.

Both East and West are endeavouring to counter-balance weaknesses of their military capabilities and their politico-military situation by employing different kinds of measures. The Soviet Union is bolstering up the Warsaw Pact countries' loyalty to that alliance by way of a centralised command structure, military standardisation and ideological control. The West European allies and the United States are toning down the weaknesses of their defence efforts by military integration in planning, command and control as well as through political consultation in security matters. The Alliance's relative weakness in Western Europe is to some extent offset by a multinational composition of the deterrent and defence forces in the threatened areas; this implies that in regional or local conflicts an enemy would be subjected to the risk of an immediate qualitative and geographic expansion into a world conflict, involving the United States.

III—ALLIES AND RIVALS

There are a number of political conflicts and tensions that determine the contemporary foreign and security policies of the allied partners. The principal cause of uneasiness and uncertainty which can be observed today lies in the fact that the United States is re-appraising its role in all important fields which have a global impact: security, the international monetary and financial system, trade, and energy. In the fifties, the United States possessed the lead in all these areas. While it is true that the United States still retains its position as the largest and strongest Power, there are now other centres of power that have developed into impressive competitors and rivals in the monetary field, in trade and energy.

Strategic nuclear parity with the Soviet Union; the need for considerable imports of crude oil; the decline of confidence in the dollar as a reserve currency; competition in world trade with Western Europe and Japan: these are determining factors of America's position in the world today. The change in America's role in the world of necessity involves the West European countries in this process. Three questions must, therefore, receive special emphasis in my survey:

1. How will the relationship between the United States and Western Europe develop in the future?
2. Of what consequence to Europe is the new relationship between the United States and the Soviet Union?
3. What are the prospects for European co-operation?

IV—THE UNITED STATES AND EUROPE

The developments of the past few years have strengthened the conviction that changes are emerging in the relations between the United States and Europe—changes that are bound to be accompanied by difficulties and tensions. We shall be able to solve these problems only if we examine, with great candour, all aspects that are related to this question. The—at times—nine different European viewpoints, no less than the peculiarities of the decision-making process in the United States, complicate this operation. Some of the tensions are caused by misunderstandings, prejudices or a lack of communication. However, I firmly believe that we should not allow to call into question the fundamentals of our alliance nor to loosen the vital bonds of partnership and friendship with the United States. This point cannot be repeated often enough. Nevertheless, the rearrangement of the bonds between Europe and America will continue to be a central problem of our policy in the time ahead and it will have a significant impact on world politics outside the Atlantic area.

Defence and Security

These are the principles of a lasting Alliance across the Atlantic Ocean:

(a) We must adhere strongly to the goals we have in common. We must look ahead and maintain a determination jointly to handle and solve security problems; the defence of America will continue to begin in Europe; and the Europeans will remain to have an inherent interest in the effectiveness of the North Atlantic Alliance. We must be aware of the fact that even a unified Europe will need the Atlantic Alliance, for this will be the only way of keeping an adequate balance with the Soviet Union in the strategic nuclear field for long years to come and, thereby, to make up for a conventional deficit in the European theatre—also for a long time to come. This Alliance, in future, must eventually have room for a vigorous Europe imbued with a strong will and the capability of acting on its own. The United States has to realise that its analysis of the changes in the global balance is correct only if it accepts this premise with all its consequences.

(b) In this connection the existing military force ratio must be borne in mind. All the games with numbers cannot deny the fact that the Soviet Union is capable of reinforcing, rapidly and effectively, its troops in Central Europe. On our side, the combat-ready divisions are not backed by any substantial reserves that could be committed to battle in sufficient time. The Soviet Union could, with some prospects of success, seek to arrive at military decisions having a strong political impact at a point of its own choice, since it is convinced of its ability to confine the conflict. Now as before, the West is forced to seek protection through a credible threat of escalation, and that threat must remain inescapable.

The financial element in our common security policy is a troublesome nuisance, but it must not become the cause for a fundamental political reorientation. What the United States President stated at the close of his visit to Europe in Limerick, Ireland, in October 1970 was true then and will remain true. In substance, he said: A strengthening of European defence is the prime requisite for maintaining the American troops in Europe. I admit that—while looking at the various European countries—it seems to be rather difficult to actually draw the practical conclusion from this insight against domestic political pressures.

Monetary Policy

The relations between Western Europen and the United States are by no means confined to the aspect of security; they also involve the monetary system, problems of trade and the energy policy. The " de-coupling " of the currencies of most industrial countries from the US-dollar following the monetary crises in 1973 and the formation of a European zone of stable exchange rates (so-called snake) have been first steps in a " long march " towards a more balanced international monetary system. Basically, this is a matter of reducing both the role of the United States as the " financier dominant " of the currency reserves of other countries and also the role of the United States as the greatest borrower and, thereby, as the greatest source of superfluous international liquidity.

With the predominant position of the dollar as an intervention currency there was no need for the United States to balance its international payments. For several reasons, the dollar has lost much of its former strong position during the past five years: one is that the financing of the war in Southeast Asia has even developed into worldwide inflation. Another reason is that American industry has not been so very keen on exporting goods, but has rather concentrated on investment abroad. As a result, a huge dollar surplus developed both in the international markets and in the currency reserves of other countries, and international confidence in the dollar dwindled.

In international discussions, the deterioration of the United States balance-of-payments position has too long been looked at with " benign neglect " by United States officials, a term that was first used in 1971. This attitude added severely to the already growing irritation over the US-dollar in Europe, Japan and elsewhere. As a result of the neglect, the system of fixed exchange rates began to weaken and crack in a world of increasingly frequent imbalances in international financial and money relations.

The frequent changes in exchange rates in recent years have been signs of the necessity to move towards a new international monetary system. The United States has, meanwhile, abandoned its neglecting attitude of selfishness and is successfully seeking to improve its balance-of-payments position. What gives us reason to cherish hopes for the future is the fact that Japan, Germany and to a lesser extent others, too, have undertaken serious sacrifices to help the Dollar, that rigid positions have been abandoned and that most countries involved are now prepared to contribute to the process of restructuring the monetary and financial relations. But new dangers loom large in the wake of the oil-price explosion which has put most industrial countries into deficit. The problem of financing the deficits, of the re-cycling of the surpluses derived by oil-exporting countries, of adapting the international capital markets and banking system to the sudden changes do require a much greater degree of international co-operation than heretofore. At the same time a long-lasting phase of floating is going to be a menace to both the trade and political structure of the free world. It could also develop into a new source of tension and rivalry within the West. In this field, there is, therefore, an urgent need all over the world for renouncing national obstinacy, for single-mindedness and for political and economic *Augenmass* in the sense in which Max Weber used that word.

Trade

Just as important to the future relationship between Europe and the United States as the reform of the world monetary and financial system are the multilateral negotiations in GATT. President Nixon's Trade Bill of 1973 has met with a mixed reaction in Europe and Japan. Some regard it as a double-edged sword designed to defend American interests against the undesirable effects of both greater liberalisation and increasing protectionism in international trade. Others see the Bill as staking out the field of negotiation to the disadvantage of the European countries which have themselves not yet agreed on a common negotiating position. Both views appear justified since, apart from authorising protectionist reprisals, the Bill also contains sensible provisions that are worthy of applause. The goal to be accepted by all should be maximum liberalisation of international trade and complete and global reciprocity.

In the field of industrial tariffs a reduction appears possible. Beyond that, the negotiations should lead to a firm agreement to abolish all tariff barriers completely in the long term. Such an agreement would make it much easier to solve other problems, *e.g.* in the field of preferential arrangements.

Nobody should expect tariff reductions alone to bring about any fundamental improvements. This would be a rather biased view, as is immediately clear to anybody who compares the numerical effects of a reduction in tariffs with those of changes in exchange rates. The external tariffs of the European Economic Community (EEC) average 8 per cent.; in the United States a similar rate applies. However a 50 per cent. tariff reduction on both sides of the Atlantic would have a far less noticeable effect, both economically and politically, than had the recent changes in monetary parities or central rates.

The problems of agricultural trade seem to require even greater patience and imagination for their solution than those of tariff and non-tariff trade barriers. Both in the United States and in the European Community agriculture is protected to guarantee appropriate incomes to those employed in agriculture. In the United States this is achieved by subsidising incomes and imposing quantitative restrictions on imports. The European Community practises a system of guaranteed agricultural prices with no limits to production.

As we all know, the European agricultural market is an essential element of the European Community. Therefore, only someone who intends to disrupt the Community will demand that it give up its common agricultural policy. The arguments put forward by the United States in this field are less compulsive than those of the consumers in the EEC. The United States agricultural exports to the EEC are far greater than its agricultural imports from the Community and it has, therefore, much less reason to complain.

Both parties will have to make concessions in this field, and this requires patience and understanding on both sides.

The preferential treatment granted by the European Community to many Mediterranean and African countries—among them many former colonies of European States—that are now associated members of the Community and the opening of associated membership even to the Caribbean countries have somewhat clouded European Community-United States relations. Americans are afraid of European trade imperialism seeking to dominate world trade by establishing a huge trading bloc.

The Community has begun to grant general preferential treatment to developing countries. However, the United States Trade Bill also provides for preferential treatment of such countries. Thus, this problem should have been somewhat alleviated for the future.

Before I pass on to energy policy, a particularly important and controversial element of United States-European relations, I should like to point out a further potential source of tension. I refer to the competition for Soviet trade which is assuming entirely new dimensions—something the West can only welcome from a political point of view. It would be an unnecessary complication if America and Europe tried to outbid each other in offering Moscow credits on favourable terms.

Energy Policies

The energy gap of the 1970s and 1980s already loomed large in all industrial countries and received dramatic aggravation in connection with the conflict in the Middle East. The oil-producing countries have successfully begun to follow a common strategy towards the oil-importing countries and, as a result, these are faced with a selling monopoly in the Middle East. In my view, it is vital that the industrial countries in this situation should seek to avoid cut-throat demand competition between themselves. The breakdown of energy supply can lead to a general economic crisis which would affect not only the industrial countries but the developing countries as well.

Up to now, the United States, Japan and the European States have been pursuing independent energy policies. Within the EEC, regrettably, it is much the same picture. This is potentially very dangerous. So far, there are not even the beginnings of a common Western concept of energy policy. My concern is growing as governments keep standing aloof, leaving this domain to the big multinational corporations, which are no longer capable of handling the complex of problems, the political, monetary and investment problems especially. I think this topic ought to be placed high on the agenda of the American-European dialogue and should include

Japanese participation. The Washington Energy Conference therefore was an important step in the right direction; but the follow-up is still inadequate.

V—THE ALLIANCE VIS-à-VIS MOSCOW

Some Europeans live in the fear of United States-Soviet agreements being concluded at the expense of European interests. This fear is kept alive by trends which are apparently unavoidable in United States-Soviet relations. It became apparent again after the United States had concluded with the Soviet Union the Agreement on the Prevention of Nuclear War in June 1973, without satisfactory prior consultation with the Europeans—though the text of the agreement satisfactorily takes account of European interests—and again in the course of the United States crisis management during the latest Arab-Israeli armed conflict. However, there are ways of effectively obviating that fear as long as the common interests of the United States and Europe are emphasised by the political leaders on both sides of the Atlantic.

The negotiations on SALT II and on MBFR must take into full account the risks inherent in these negotiations. The Europeans must be given an early opportunity to get information about the preparation of decisions in the United States; they must be given ample opportunities to make their own voice heard. There must be give and take, and consultation must not be confined to trimming fixed American positions so that no corrections in substance can be made.

One must avoid the possibility of limiting MBFR to the United States and the Soviet Union exclusively. Where tactical nuclear weapons—*i.e.* the so-called forward based systems—and American force levels are concerned, European interests are directly affected, for it is only *all* allied forces and their equipment together that make up the counterbalance to Soviet capabilities. To say that the only thing that matters is the balance between Soviet and American forces in Europe would be wrong. If it were correct, we Germans would really be spending our money in pursuit of a totally unreasonable defence policy.

In these matters, one must say, it is primarily for the United States to ensure the degree of clarity called for in the relations among allies. And the Europeans will have to suppress their academic arguments and nation-State outlook on matters that have world-wide implications. This remark does not only apply in the case of Germany alone but of others also, especially the United Kingdom and France.

VI—EUROPEAN CO-OPERATION

The members of the European Community have undertaken to settle, by 1980, their entire interrelations in a European Union. I shall not attempt to anticipate the results of this endeavour. What does appear to be feasible is a close network of arrangements involving the co-operative application of national policies in order to eliminate potential conflict, to harmonise discord, and to make preparations for a political change of the West-European nation-State outlook.

In the field of security and defence, however, it is unjustifiable to limit participation to the members of the EEC. Rather it is a question of intensifying co-operation of all European NATO partners in matters pertaining to security and defence. This is being strived for in EUROGROUP with the aim of harmonising the viewpoints of the Europeans in the fields of security and defence, within the Alliance and in its best interest, of improving the defence efforts through rationalisation and, finally, of diminishing the burdens of the United States continued stationing of forces in Europe.

Noteworthy successes have already been achieved: but the past and present divergencies between France on the one hand and the NATO partners on the other in questions of security and defence are retarding progress: it seems to me that the new French government might wish to give the matter some second thoughts while parallels between United States and Soviet security interests increase. In that case France might gain from greater co-operation among Europeans in the fields of defence and weapons production. The main effort of European co-operation in NATO today is being made in such activities as planning, defence technology, procurement, logistics, supply and training. It does not by any means touch so far the question of independent nuclear deterrents and their effect in the years to come. I do not believe that this question is to be answered with the affirmative. Therefore, I am again convinced of the necessity of maintaining the Alliance with the United States.

EIGHT CONCLUSIONS

I summarise my conclusions in the following arguments:

1. Regardless of any existing, and even conceivable, political and international agreements on the limitation of freedom of action in foreign policy, and regardless of the developments of economic interdependence, a real balance of power (including a balanced military force ratio) continues to be an important and effective instrument of preserving peace.

2. Any armed conflict, any threat of the use of force in the East/West relationship is fraught with the risk of self-destruction. Consequently, war also in the future is an unsuitable way of reaching political objectives. This is why the struggle for changes in the balance of power, for spheres of influence and for reaching political objectives is shifting to other fields—to the political, economic, energy, and ideological spheres. Nevertheless, even in East/West relations there continues to be a risk of armed conflict—at least in the form of political pressures based on military power.

3. The balance of power is governed by a wealth of measurable and immeasurable, objective and subjective factors. These factors include military, geographical, economic, political and psychological elements. In the field of security the point of balance is never a static one—balance is rather a dynamic state with a wide variety of dimensions where changes are taking place constantly and inevitably.

4. In terms of the military resources available to NATO, the Western defence effort has not slackened—in real terms there is even an increase in comparison with 1962—but this increase is less than that found in the Soviet Union. Consequently, the assumption that the defence resources available to the West are on the decrease is only true with regard to the Soviet capabilities confronting the West and with regard to the share of defence expenditure in the gross national product and in the public budgets.

The Western defence capabilities are subject to weaknesses which must be overcome by suitable measures if the balance of power is to be maintained.

5. What the changed world situation—in particular the changed situation of the United States—implies for Western Europe in terms of strategy and security policy is quite clear. We must proceed on the assumption that the Soviet capabilities, which are essentially undiminished, and are indeed continually modernised, will continue to be deployed immediately at our doorstep. Together with ideological elements and with the Soviet self-interest in foreign policy, which is not necessarily in harmony with ours, this fact confronts us with the necessity to maintain a compensatory ratio of strengths. This ratio of strengths must include all fields—from the capability of conceiving and pursuing a collective foreign and security policy to the capability of achieving nuclear deterrence and the capability of financing the next technological-industrial stage and of digesting this next stage mentally.

Balance in the strategic field is the prerequisite for an effective nuclear deterrence in particular when this deterrence must function NATO-wide and must be provided by only one, or at most by only a few, partners in the Alliance. This necessity involves requirements and conditions for any theoretically conceivable European developments.

6. Steps towards political unification will precede any decision by Europe on its future nuclear policy. For the foreseeable future the identity of security interests of Western Europe and the United States, faced with the danger of Soviet predominance in Western Europe, continues to be a vital condition for the nuclear capability of the Alliance. Of necessity, this fact has consequences for the conventional role of the United States in Europe and for the function of tactical nuclear capabilities as a link between the conventional forces and the strategic weapons.

7. We are faced with a situation in which matters of security policy are increasingly regarded more lightly by citizens of all alliance countries and by the political authorities in governmental institutions, as well as within the institutions of society. We will have to endeavour to keep alive in the minds of our citizens the sense of necessity to tackle the aforementioned tasks.

8. The devastating effects of any nuclear conflict and the shifting of the power-political struggle to fields other than the military are important motives for the Western concept of persuading the Soviet Union and the East European countries to continue to normalise the mutual relations, to refrain in earnest from the threat and use of force, and to consent to partial co-operation, especially in the fields of industry, trade, and perhaps energy. This policy is a prerequisite for a balanced mutual reduction of the military forces of all countries on either side. None of us is able to predict which side will be the winner in the struggle for the ultimate form of the future economic system in Europe. What I consider important is, however, that we concentrate our powers on the development of concepts which are in keeping with our valuations of freedom, of the dignity of the individual and of the balancing of the forces which influence the structure of our governmental system.

THE IDEA OF CONCERT
AND INTERNATIONAL ORDER

By

R. J. VINCENT

THE idea of a concert of great Powers has in recent years re-entered the discussion of international politics.[1] One of its more celebrated ushers has been President Nixon, who has spoken to Mid-Western newspaper editors of a world whose future will be determined by five economic super-Powers, and to *Time* of an even balance of power among them.[2] And recent developments in world politics have made the notion of concert more than just a subject for a Presidential blueprint: the Soviet-American *détente*, China's joining the international community and her *rapprochement* with the United States, Japan's economic success, and the promise, however remote, of a unified Western European community of nine. In addition, the recent war in the Middle East has returned the world's attention not to a speculative concert of five but to a concert which is held to be actual between two. The purpose of this paper is primarily to discover the extent to which (if any at all) there is a concert of Powers discernible in the international politics of the present, and to give a central place in this inquiry to the concept of order, so that the question whether a concert can be said to uphold order in international relations will be the instrument for the measurement of how closely the Powers are acting together. A second and subsidiary purpose is to consider some arguments for and against a concert as an arrangement of international politics.

I—CONCERT

Two or more Powers acting together in any circumstance is one version of what is meant by concert in international relations. There is also a more formal version, as in " the Concert of Europe," which means an enduring diplomatic arrangement by which the great Powers of Europe made a habit of consulting, and less frequently acting, together.[3] The version used here will be that of co-operative

---

[1] An earlier version of this paper was written under the auspices of the Center of International Studies at Princeton University, and read there in a series of colloquia on Great Powers and International Order in May 1973.

[2] See extracts from speech of July 6, 1971, in Department of State, LXV Bulletin, Nr. 1674, July 26, 1971, pp. 93–97; and *Time*, January 3, 1971.

[3] See C. Holbraad, *The Concert of Europe: A Study in German and British International Theory* (1970), pp. 3–4.

34

management of international politics by the great Powers. Co-operative management, and its objectives, will be the focus of interest, not the number of managers co-operating, so that condominium, for example, will be treated as a variety of concert and not as something to be set apart from it. As to the notion of management in international relations, it will be part of the purpose of this paper to decide, in the course of examining whether a concert maintains order, in what precisely it consists.

So long as this management is confined to great Power relations, it might be said, a concert is a benevolent enough institution designed to accommodate the interests of those Powers, and of no great concern, though they may be curious, to States remaining outside it. But no such confinement is possible. In the nuclear age, the super-Powers have not provided for the imperative of avoiding a direct confrontation between them by confining their activities within their own frontiers. Indeed, to the extent that proxy wars have become an accepted means of carrying on great Power rivalry in the nuclear age, that rivalry has been directly foisted upon lesser States. Thus, even a concert restricted to the minimal object of avoiding direct confrontation between the super-Powers involves the small States intimately. A theory that would justify the establishment of a concert must then address itself to the situation in which great Powers impose their will on small States as well as to that in which the strong make arrangements among themselves.[4] And the concern here is not merely with such arrangements as would avoid super-Power confrontation, but with control or management that would bring about and maintain order in international relations.

II—ORDER

The notion of order has become a disreputable one. At best it is taken to indicate a mindless adherence to the *status quo*. At worst it is regarded—as in the slogan " law and order "—as a codeword for oppression. If it is to be rescued from these ideological clutches, and at the same time made intellectually respectable as a tool for analysis, it must also be saved from the imprecision of its friends. World order is sometimes defined as the complex of norms and procedures existing in international relations, or, more generally, as the characteristic modes of behaviour, structures of authority, types of conflict, and methods of resolution relied on by actors in pursuing their goals in world politics.[5] Order in this conception is not a particular pattern of relations arranged according to some principle

---

[4] I shall return to the question of justification in considering argument for and against concert in sections IV and V below.

[5] See R. A. Falk, *This Endangered Planet* (1971), p. 215.

(and only a pattern at all by the inclusion of the adjective " characteristic "), but merely the shape taken by what exists, or who prevails, in international politics. To think of order in this descriptive and general way does not facilitate an answer to the question whether any particular norm or procedure or mode of behaviour *contributes* to world order in a more substantial sense than being by definition a part of it.

Order as a value which might be upheld or impaired is a pattern of a particular kind. That pattern might be said to exist in any society if relations within it display a degree of conformity to rules, and we might think of orderly behaviour simply as obedience to rules, and of disorder as their infraction. But this definition also would fail to show how order might or might not be enhanced by a particular rule or rules, and we may approach the idea of order more closely by remembering that rules themselves exist to make possible the achievement of certain purposes, and that among these some are more fundamental than others. Indeed, we may isolate three purposes without whose achievement, in some degree, social life would not be possible, and think of order as the particular pattern which provides for that achievement. Accordingly, order may be defined as that circumstance in which, in a measure that it is impossible precisely to specify, life is secure against violence, possession remains stable, and contracts are honoured.[6]

Of this conception of order it might be said that while its intention is to state general requirements for social life, it can be tied too easily to the existing arrangements, so that this particular distribution of property is the one to be upheld, or that particular contract is the one to be honoured. To guard against this, it may be argued, we must add as an ingredient of order some measure of justice, requiring that life not be intolerable, or that possessions be shared according to some principle of fairness, or that promises not be extorted—or at least not regarded as binding if they are. And this argument might be pushed further into the proposition that it is only an order legitimised by attention, again in some degree, to the claims of justice, that can be maintained over time.[7]

---

[6] For the contemporary adoption of this notion of order for the study of international relations, see H. Bull, " Order vs. Justice in International Society," XIX *Political Studies* (1971), pp. 269–272. For its part in a modern author's " minimum content of Natural Law," see H. L. A. Hart, *The Concept of Law* (1961), pp. 189–195. The history of the idea can be traced back to Hume, *Treatise of Human Nature*, Bk. III, Pt. II; Hobbes, *Leviathan*, Chaps. XIV and XV; and ultimately to the Stoics. On the last see S. I. Benn and R. S. Peters, *Social Principles and the Democratic State* (1959), p. 27.

[7] And if not justice, then at least change, might be held to require accommodation if order is to be made dynamic. Thus Hume has the transference of possession by consent as one of the three fundamental laws of nature: *Treatise of Human Nature*, Bk. III, Pt. II, sections IV and VI.

The difficulty with arguments of this sort is that they do not rest, as does our notion of order, on an account of what is necessary for social life, but on an ultimately subjective judgment about the form that life should take. And in thus moving beyond a minimalist conception of order, particularly in a society so rudimentary and culturally heterogeneous as that formed between States, such controversy might result as to undermine rather than contribute to international order. Even if it is conceded that a dynamic order is to some extent dependent on the achievement of justice, assuming for a moment sufficient solidarity in international society to make sense of such a general notion, then this still cannot obscure the more fundamental fact that justice is an idea which presupposes society, and is thus dependent on order defined as the conditions necessary for social life. Of interest here is the degree to which this minimum order is or might be maintained by a concert of Powers.

III—CONCERT AND ORDER

At the beginning of this century, Oppenheim observed, as though there were little controversy about it, that " [a]ll arrangements made by the body of the Great Powers naturally gain the consent of the minor States, and the body of the six Great Powers in Europe is therefore called the European Concert." [8] But while he took the view that past progress in international law had been the result of the political hegemony of the great Powers, their predominance was not based on law, and to be a great Power was not to enjoy special legal rights. By the Covenant of the League of Nations and, after it, the Charter of the United Nations, the great Powers acquired special rights and duties in the area of maintaining international peace and security. There was now a legal basis for concerted action (and due to the veto the Powers were to act in concert or not at all), but the new doubt was about the possibility of any arrangements being made by the body of great Powers, not their lawfulness. In reference to the management of international order, have these doubts been dispelled, or might they be?

That imperative of order which requires that life be secure against violence might be said to apply, in a society populated by States not individuals, only to those individuals who are entitled to protection as the accredited representatives of States. Moreover, it might be added, the environment of the international anarchy is one in which the lives of individuals, far from being protected, are laid down on behalf of the State or a group within it. The reason it remains possible to speak of order in international relations despite these limited expectations about diplomats, and dismal ones about

---

[8] L. Oppenheim, *International Law: A Treatise,* 2nd ed. (1910), Vol. I, p. 170.

soldiers, is that the imperative of protecting the lives of individuals against violence is a responsibility delegated to the several States making up international society, and the focus for the investigation of order in that society is thus not the lives of individuals but the security of States. The achievement in some degree of this goal of international society has been attributed traditionally to the attention paid by States to maintaining a balance of power among them. The heir, or at least one of the legatees, to this principle in contemporary international society—the balance of terror—has made, because of the devastating weapons involved in its maintenance, our distinction between the goals of providing for security and protecting life rather theoretical. To what extent may a concert of Powers achieve them?

The stark relationship of deterrence, by which each super-Power is supposed to prevent an attack on itself by means of a capacity and will to strike second with aim sufficiently unimpaired to inflict unacceptable damage on its opponent, is hardly a relationship of concert, or even of limited co-operation. But when a *détente* between the Soviet Union and the United States allows them to seek agreement about arms control, and to extend that control outside their relationship, the question arises of order (in our first sense of " security ") as something which is managed, aimed for, as opposed to being the more or less accidental and approximate result of a struggle for strategic superiority. Thus the Nixon administration's espousal of a doctrine of " sufficiency," rather than superiority, in strategic weapons, the acknowledgment by both super-Powers at their talks on the limitation of strategic arms of the principle of " equal security " (or perhaps " equal insecurity " for the hostages of assured destruction), and the real, if limited, measure of arms control achieved at the first round of those talks, might all be taken as evidence of a recognition on the part of the super-Powers of a balance of nuclear power as a goal of their relationship, and of a joint attempt to approach it. Moreover, the purpose which the principle of balance is designed to serve—the discouragement of aggressive behaviour and of adventurism in foreign policy by any of the participants in the balancing system—itself finds expression in Article I of the June 1973 Agreement between the Soviet Union and the United States on the Prevention of Nuclear War: " . . . the parties agree that they will act in such a manner as to prevent the development of situations capable of causing a dangerous exacerbation of their relations, so as to avoid military confrontations, and to exclude the outbreak of nuclear war between them. . . ." In addition, the establishment of a standing consultative committee to promote the objectives and the implementation of the strategic arms limitation agreements, and the reaffirmation in the Joint Soviet-

United States communiqué issued on June 24, 1973, after the Moscow meeting of Nixon and Brezhnev, that regular consultations should continue at the highest level, might be taken as parallels to that congress system of diplomacy which was a feature of the European Concert of the 19th century. But the large loopholes in the arms limitation agreements, allowing an acceleration in the qualitative if not the quantitative arms race, are a warning against dwelling at greater length on the partnership than on the adversary aspect of the relationship between the super-Powers—their willingness to continue consulting each other notwithstanding.

These consultations have been, and look forward to being, bilateral. What is the outcome if control is sought not within, but outside, this relationship, as in the case of the Non-Proliferation Treaty sponsored by the two super-Powers together with the United Kingdom? This treaty might generally be welcomed on the basis of the hypothesis that the fewer the States armed with nuclear weapons, the safer the world is, but at the same time suspected as an attempt by the great Powers to kick down the ladder behind them, making their temporary superiority permanent and institutionalising thereby their role as managers of world order. Although this prospect might not be an unattractive one for the super-Powers, it is hard to sustain a view of the Non-Proliferation Treaty either as an excursion into joint control by the United States and the Soviet Union, or as a bid to make it permanent. For, in the first place, if the Non-Proliferation Treaty is a piece of great Power management, then the United Kingdom too is a member of the board. Secondly, the United States has been as anxious in recent years to reach an accommodation with China as with the Soviet Union despite the Chinese disdain for the treaty; a curious lapse if the treaty is the instrument of a concert of two. And in the third place, States have been invited to sign the treaty; they have not been coerced into doing so.

If one of the reasons why a nuclear peace managed by a concert of two is neither currently very visible, nor much in prospect, is that it would leave out the lesser nuclear Powers, might the concert be extended to include them? Writing in 1962, John Strachey looked forward to a possible " concert of the world " in which the nuclear super-Powers would among them arrange humanity's affairs, keeping the rest of the world in order.[9] He found it not hard to imagine that by the 1970s half a dozen nuclear super-Powers might constitute this authority, which would have a form of collective security arrangement operating within it, and would be united by an agreement to prevent the spread of nuclear weapons beyond it. In the

[9] J. Strachey, *On the Prevention of War* (1962), pp. 296–298.

1970s, President Nixon—although he has not gone so far as to
speak of a concert of powers,[10] and has conceived of a class of
economic rather than nuclear super-Powers—seems not to have
dismissed altogether the Strachey vision.

The difficulty with the Nixon vision of a return to a balance of
power if not to a concert of it, lies in his notion of an " even "
balance, each Power " balancing the other." For the Powers are
neither equal, nor comparable, nor even, in the case of Europe, a
" Power " at all, and in these circumstances the idea of their
balancing each other is an odd one. If approximate equality among
the Powers is a conspicuous absentee from the contemporary international system compared with that of 18th and 19th century
Europe, nor is the use of force functional to the maintenance of the
central balance as, we are told, it was in balance of power systems
of the past, and that flexibility of alliance held to have been a
characteristic of them has not been a feature of the comparatively
rigid relationship of deterrence. There are then grounds for doubt
about the existence of or potential for an " even " balance of power,
and if such a balance has been historically the base on which a
concert might rest, we may question the potency of a concert of
five or six as an institution which might order the contemporary
world. To lump the nuclear Powers together into a group which
might act in concert merely because it is made up of all the nuclear
Powers, is perversely to overlook the hostility between the United
States and the Soviet Union when they alone formed that group,
and also to be led astray by a preoccupation with the question of
avoiding a nuclear exchange characteristic of the time at which
Strachey was writing.

If the advent of nuclear weapons has not given rise to a concert
of Powers either as manager of the central balance or as preventer
of the spread of nuclear weapons, there is at least evidence that their
coming has encouraged the super-Powers to avoid confronting each
other directly, lest any conflict in which they both became involved
should escalate into a nuclear exchange.[11] The Soviet Union and the
United States have allowed one another a free hand within their
respective spheres of influence in Eastern Europe and Latin
America.[12] The force of this free hand has been felt by the lesser
Powers within each bloc through their economic and ideological

---

[10] Except to the extent that his notion of Powers evenly balanced, " not playing
one against another," is one of concert.

[11] We have seen above such a policy made explicit in the Soviet-United States
Agreement on the Prevention of Nuclear War.

[12] Also, the Vietnam experience might be interpreted as showing that a super-
Power carries around with it its own sphere of influence—the Soviet Union not
getting directly in the way of the forcible expression of an American interest.

subservience, and also, for the more recalcitrant among them, through being put in their place by armed intervention. In this way, the principle of State sovereignty, the rule which has traditionally rendered possession to some extent stable in international relations, stands modified—overridden by inter-bloc norms which do not extinguish the independence of the weaker States within them, but which do prevent them from seeking a remedy outside the bloc: counter-intervention is not available to uphold the principle of non-intervention.

To speak of " inter-bloc norms " is perhaps to go too far. The degree of co-operation implied by the establishment of norms in a relationship, which might entitle us to point to an incipient concert of super-Powers, seems to require between them more than a but recently avowed agreement to avoid confronting each other directly. And this might consist in each Power welcoming the other policing its bloc (though not perhaps enthusiastically) as a reinforcement of the principle of order by which it does its own policing. There would seem to be in such an agreement an acceptance, jointly, of a responsibility for keeping order, and not merely a separate expression of interest which is acquiesced in grudgingly for the sake of nuclear peace. There are some grounds for the view that the relationship of the super-Powers has taken a step in this direction. There is a sense in which the intervention of one super-Power in its sphere of influence is the issue of a licence authorising the other to behave in the same way towards its subordinates.[13] And though each super-Power continues to object to the intervention of the other, these objections have the character perhaps of ritual noises, and protests on behalf of the sovereignty of States against a system of intervention become but homage paid by vice to virtue.[14] Certainly

---

[13] For a persuasive presentation of this view which has the " Johnson Doctrine " for the Dominican Republic in 1965 authorising the " Brezhnev Doctrine " for Czechoslovakia in 1968, see generally T. M. Franck and E. Weisband, *Word Politics: Verbal Strategy Among the Superpowers* (1971). The authors do not, however, endorse this situation as one to be defended on the ground of order. On the contrary, their argument is directed at the dismantling of the " dual-ghetto system," and the restoration of the independence of the lesser States within the blocs. Given the importance of mutual authorisation, they argue, the licence the United States issues should be a radically different one.

[14] The protest itself has become, suspiciously, a joint one. At Moscow, in May 1972, the United States and the Soviet Union took it as the eleventh of the general principles governing their relations that they " make no claim for themselves and would not recognise the claims of anyone else to any special rights or advantages in world affairs. They recognise the sovereign equality of all states." Department of State, LXVI *Bulletin*, Nr. 1722, June 26, 1972, pp. 898–899. Speaking for the United States, as Secretary of State, Dr. Kissinger told the United Nations General Assembly on September 25, 1973, soon after his appointment: " We have not been asked to participate in a condominium; we would reject such appeal if it were made."

the practice of the super-Powers is consistent enough in this area for a good case to be made for the explicit recognition at least of the legitimacy of " hegemonial jurisdiction " as a ground-rule of contemporary international politics, on the argument that continuing refusal to recognise this pattern of State practice would " cast the entire enterprise of law and order in world affairs into cynical disrepute." [15] And if the recognition of such legitimacy were recognition of an emerging concert, it is not absurd, referring strictly to the principle of stable possession and not to our other goals of order, to conceive of its extension to include China. For if the entrance of China into the international community as a member of the Security Council, and the *rapprochement* between her and the United States can be said to indicate an acknowledgment of the Chinese position as at least an apprentice super-Power, then these developments might sooner or later be accompanied by recognition of her predominant position in Southeast Asia, and of a claim on her part to behave in relation to that area as the other Powers have behaved in their areas of special interest.

A concert is least visible in regard to that goal of order which requires that promises be kept. The very contract which established the formal concert of great Powers in the modern world—the United Nations Charter—is not one we can confidently point to as evidence either that obligations of treaties are being observed, that their breach is being punished, or that the great Powers are acting together to enforce them. The doctrine of collective security as espoused by the framers of the Charter and of the Covenant before it did not, as is often said, make all States *equally* responsible for holding the line against aggression: it imposed primary responsibility on the great Powers whose lead was then to be followed by the lesser States. Where this lead has not been given the record of collective security has been a cheerless one. The view which takes the cases of Manchuria, Ethiopia, and Korea as " successive landmarks in the development of international organisation," and Korea in particular as a " significant, and one may hope, a

---

[15] See Falk, " Zone II as a World Order Construct," in J. N. Rosenau, V. Davis, and M. A. East (eds.), *The Analysis of International Politics* (1972), pp. 187–201. If, however, a central place is given to " gradations of dependency " within the blocs, and to the extent of independence still enjoyed by bloc members, rather than to patterns of super-Power activity, then we might decide that the recognition of inter-bloc at the expense of inter-State norms is too hasty; a selective positivism. Moreover, one author has pointed out that a balance of five might have as one of its principles a right of free access to blocs in a political and economic sense: " mutual acceptance of tacit rules of conduct in security matters does not constitute a spheres-of-influence agreement, since it does not exclude the effort to extend political influence in each other's security sphere." M. D. Shulman, " What Does Security Mean Today? ", 49 *Foreign Affairs*, July 1971, p. 615.

decisive, stage in the evolution of collective security," [16] includes
Manchuria and Ethiopia as promising examples of international
organisation when they may fit better into an account of its failure,
and places the Korean case on a pedestal it hardly deserves. The
fortuitous absence of the Soviet Union from the Security Council
made the exercise possible as one under United Nations auspices;
security perhaps but not wholly collective. And when the United
Nations forces crossed the 38th parallel into North Korea, this was
perhaps collective action (at least of a Western coalition), but not
security in the sense of simple repulsion of aggression. Chapter VII
of the Charter assigning special responsibility to the great Powers
for action with respect to threats to the peace, breaches of the
peace, and acts of aggression, has not been the object of malign
neglect, or of a conspiracy of great Powers against it. It assumes
a solidarity in international society which does not exist, and its
provisions are the weaker for this assumption.

Might a concert operate not so as to uphold this or that contract,
or part of a contract, but to defend the principle *pacta sunt servanda*
itself? The particular undertakings of great Powers to lesser allies,
attached as they are thought to be to the prestige and credibility
of those Powers, have been, by their very existence, potent arguments for a response when challenged. This is the province of
" America keeps her word," which recurred as a tedious public
defence of the United States intervention in Vietnam, but featured
too as an important, even the overriding, argument deployed
privately within the government for the continuing commitment.[17]
It is not a province for concert. Neither the United States nor the
Soviet Union is much concerned to defend the reputation of a class
of States called great Powers by demonstrating jointly that they
keep their word (even though both have an *interest* in seeing contracts honoured in international relations). Each of them separately
is concerned for its own prestige: and this applies also to the junior
great Powers.

If willingness to consult each other, and anxiety to follow a
common policy are two tests for the existence of a concert of Powers
in international relations, then the behaviour of the Soviet Union
and the United States during the war of October 1973 in the Middle
East might be described as concerted. Moreover, we might detect
in their joint endeavour activity which could be held to satisfy in

[16] C. Wilfred Jenks, *A Common Law of Mankind* (1958), pp. 192 and 194.
[17] " Why we have not *withdrawn* from Vietnam is, by all odds, *one* reason:
(1) to preserve our reputation as a guarantor, and thus to preserve our effectiveness in the rest of the world." From Assistant Secretary J. T. McNaughton's
memorandum " Some Paragraphs on Vietnam," January 19, 1966, in Neil Sheehan,
et al., The Pentagon Papers (1971), pp. 491–493.

some degree each of our three goals of order. Thus, the concern of both super-Powers for an early cease-fire and their striving together to achieve it at the United Nations and elsewhere, might be held to demonstrate an anxiety on their part to protect the central balance between them from the danger presented to it by their support for opposite sides in the war. As to the goal of stable possession, we might discern a common aspiration to achieve it in the desire of both super-Powers, expressed in Security Council resolutions, to return to the territorial distribution which obtained before the 1967 war. And the frequency with which both super-Powers proclaim Security Council resolution 242 as the instrument of a lasting order in the Middle East might be held up as an example of their mutual concern that such resolutions should indeed be binding on members, and not be mere pieces of paper.

Although we might interpret the recent behaviour of the super-Powers towards the Middle East from the standpoint of order, it is not with the value of order so much as with that of peace that they have been commonly associated. And while it may be argued that a peace raised up on a foundation of a just order is a condition more exacting than that of mere order, it can be argued also that a peace founded upon no more than the absence of fighting is a value less demanding than that of order. That it is a fragile peace of this latter kind which a concert was concerned to and has produced in the Middle East is suggested by the " minimalism " of the United States position throughout the war—the concern above all to stop the fighting deferring the problem of order, and the anxiety that no nuclear Power should commit its troops in a peace-keeping role. There is in this a limit to the means of a concert as well as to its objectives. Thus, when the Soviet Union overstepped the limits of the United States concept of concert by responding positively to an Egyptian request that United States and Soviet troops should police the cease-fire, and by showing an apparent willingness to do so unilaterally, she tipped the relationship between the super-Powers back from one of concert to one of conflict. So a concert that would produce order in our first sense led to the very danger of disorder that it sought to avoid. As Dr. Kissinger himself pointed out, the relationship between Washington and Moscow is an inherently ambiguous one.[18] Moreover, the notion that an imposed peace is possible in the Middle East because of the client relationship between the contestants and the super-Powers has received an ironic twist as the Arab States themselves seek to impose their terms by wielding the oil weapon.

It cannot be said then that to the extent that order prevails in

[18] *The Times*, November 22, 1973.

contemporary international society it is the achievement of a concert of Powers, whether of two, three, five or six.[19] Order is more the result of the recognition by States of reciprocal interests—in the keeping of the nuclear peace in which all share a concern but for which the great Powers alone are responsible, in the principle of State sovereignty by which most States grant that their rights over their own domains are made legitimate and to some extent stable by acknowledgment of the right of the others to a comparable jurisdiction, and in the convention that covenants are to be kept, a convention without whose observance in some degree co-operative international and transnational relations would cease to be possible.

If order is thus approximate, and concert unreliable if there at all, ultimately we may trace both conditions to the same source. Although there might be special reasons, derived from a comparison with the conditions that underlay the 19th-century Concert of Europe, which can be adduced to show the poor outlook for a concert of the contemporary world, such as the absence of an immediately post-war opportunity for radical change, or of a stable balance of power among more than two, or of a common enemy strong enough to frighten the Powers into alliance,[20] there is reason too for thinking that the barriers in the way of the establishment of a concert are the same as those which obstruct the path of orderly international relations in general. If the international anarchy can be taken as a prime cause of disorder in the relations of States, the great Powers (as well as their inferiors) may be the beneficiaries of, but are also caught in, this absence of government. Separately they cannot impose their authority on the whole of the globe. Though they might do so together, their rivalry as competing States prevents the degree of co-operation such imposition would require. In the same way, that cultural and ideological heterogeneity in international society which leads some to doubt whether it is possible to speak at all of a society displaying order is also an obstacle to the establishment of the authority of a concert. The great Powers are not homogeneous islands in a heterogeneous sea, but are themselves culturally and ideologically diverse. For this reason among others

---

[19] The tendency here has been to think either of two, or of five or six. For thinking in threes about traditional great Powers, the United States, China and the Soviet Union, see Holbraad, "The Triangular System," VIII *Cooperation and Conflict*, 1973. For thinking in threes about great Powers defined economically, the United States, Japan and Europe, see J. Chace, "The Concert of Europe," 52 *Foreign Affairs*, October 1973, pp. 106–107, and Z. Brzezinski, "United States Foreign Policy: The Search for Focus," 51 *Foreign Affairs*, July 1973. For general treatments see A. Buchan, "A World Restored?" and S. Hoffmann, "Weighing the Balance of Power," 50 *Foreign Affairs*, July 1972.

[20] For such a comparison, see Holbraad, "Condominium and Concert," in Holbraad (ed.), *Super Powers and World Order* (1971), pp. 18–22.

the great Powers have been unable to take advantage of the piece of international theory embodied in the Charter of the United Nations which gives them collective predominance in the area of international peace and security. The theory which does retain a universal legitimacy is the competing one of the sovereign equality of all States. If a hierarchy is no less necessary for order to obtain in international politics than it is for any other area of social relations, it is a system that is constantly bumping up against this doctrine of equal sovereignty, and it has yet to gain ascendancy over it. Although we may doubt then whether a concert of Powers describes the contemporary condition of international politics,[21] it remains a possible arrangement of them. What historically has been the sort of case made for concert, and what objections have been raised against it?

IV—ARGUMENTS FOR CONCERT

Metternich's case for a concert of Powers stemmed from his view that order in European international relations was a social as well as a political matter, and that it made no sense to separate them. While not derived with quite the mysticism of the Tsar, it was a view that drew strength from the old notion of a unified Christian European community with a legitimate monarch enthroned in each part of it. The dynastic arrangements made at Vienna after the Napoleonic Wars were as important as the territorial settlement. It was not possible to safeguard the one without attention to the other, for revolution, when it occurred and its occurrence and spread were not accidental or dependent on local conditions but were the result of a conspiracy against all thrones, would undermine the political as well as the social order. It followed that it was the duty (though, unlike the Tsar, Metternich tempered observance of it with a concern for the European balance of power) of the great Powers of Europe to concert together to preserve the fabric of the Vienna Settlement, and their right to act together to extinguish revolution wherever it broke out.

Gladstone's appeal to the Concert of Europe, like Metternich's, was based on a conception of European society more extensive than that described by the political order of States. His " public law of Europe " was not merely a law of States (justifying, for example,

---

[21] This is a judgment about the traditional inter-State order with which this paper is concerned. President Nixon's criterion for identifying super-Powers, it should be remembered, was (however misleadingly) an economic one. A judgment about concert in an economic or transnational order would require analysis going far beyond the present purpose. I merely note here that for example, an enquiry into the triangular relationship between the United States, Europe and Japan would be a candidate for such an analysis.

British participation in the Crimean War to right a Russian wrong); it arose too from a civilisation of Europe that was concerned with conduct within States as well as among them. The pillar of this civilisation was not dynastic, but moral, and it was a morality informed not by the imperatives of crowns as it had been for Metternich but by a common European opinion or sentiment, a sense of modern civilisation shared by the people of Europe. And it was that this sense should not be outraged that Gladstone invoked the Concert of Europe on behalf of the liberty of small States, or to uphold the principle of national self-determination, or against inhumanity within States. The function of the Concert was not to protect the old order, nor simply to maintain the peace of Europe, but to be the instrument of a new order based on justice.

For both Metternich and Gladstone, the case for a concert of Powers was made more attractive by membership in it, and more again perhaps by their anticipated leadership of it. What reaction might be expected from those that are neither of these things—the excluded led? It is not necessarily a hostile one, and we may distinguish a weak and a strong sense in which a concert is acceptable to those remaining outside it.

Even the more militant States of the Third World have in an indirect way (and this is our weak sense of acceptance) asserted an interest in a solidarist international society presided over by a concert of Powers. When a resolution of the General Assembly sponsored by African States condemns the North Atlantic Treaty Organisation (NATO) Powers for contributing to the " creation in Southern Africa of a military-industrial complex aimed at suppressing the struggle of peoples for their self-determination and at interfering in the affairs of the independent African states," [22] the concert of Powers that is taken to make up NATO is singled out for abuse. But the abuse is meant to hit home by appealing to the consciences of the people of those Powers; it is not mere mindless invective. It is as though a government were being made the target of a demonstration. Appeals to conscience and demands for recompense of this kind, as generally directed at the haves by the have-nots, assume a concert which is not there in order to make the appeal more potent.[23]

A stronger sense in which the States excluded from a concert nevertheless find it an acceptable arrangement of affairs lies in that tradition of thought which has the interests of the small best served

---

[22] Res. 2787 (XXVI) of December 6, 1971.

[23] In the same way Sisir Gupta has a large body of reformist opinion in the Third World as that of trade unionists in a Welfare State, not of a revolutionary proletariat: " Great Power Relations and the Third World," in Holbraad, *op. cit.* in note 20 above, p. 116.

by the co-operation of the great, and not by discord among them.[24] If a concert is at least a partial solution to the problem of the international anarchy in which the weakest suffer the most, then it is possible to argue that its formation might alleviate rather than aggravate the predicament of the small in a number of ways. In the first place, if peace among the great Powers is made more dependable by their co-operation, this is of benefit to the small as well as to the great. Peace, and particularly the nuclear peace, is not something that matters to the great alone. Secondly, the establishment of a concert among the great might mean that the small States no longer risked enlistment on the side of one great Power in its conflict with another [25] (although they would by the same token forgo the opportunity of playing off one great Power against another). Thirdly, it has been argued that the less the world was concerned with East-West issues, the more it would occupy itself with North-South problems, as declining defence expenditure released resources and as Northern populations looked outward from their preoccupation with the nuclear peace to a welfare-oriented international order.[26] Fourthly and finally, it has been said that if *détente* were to lead to the super-Powers clinging less tenaciously to their ideologies, and even moving towards each other, the small might find themselves the occupants of the area of doctrinal overlap between them, enhancing their influence and that of the only forum in which they might make a difference in international relations—the United Nations.[27] If Nehru's vision, and the sanguine expectations attached to the growth of *détente*, have faded with its advance, enough has been said here to raise doubts about any automatic assumption that a concert of great Powers is an undifferentiated menace to the small.

V—Objections to Concert

The famous objection to Metternich's design for a concert of Powers came from Castlereagh. The alliance among the great Powers formed after the Napoleonic Wars was to subdue France and to uphold the Vienna Settlement. It was meant neither as a union for the government of the world, nor as a superintendent of the internal affairs of other States. It should assume no general collective jurisdiction for

---

[24] For a short account of this pattern of thought, see W. T. R. Fox, *The Super-Powers* (1944), pp. 140–143.

[25] And indeed might invoke the concerted action of the Powers against a local opponent. Witness the recent Egyptian invitation to the super-Powers to intervene in the Middle East to preserve " the peace of the world "; *The Times*, October 25, 1973.

[26] This was a favourite argument of Nehru's. See Gupta, " Great Power Relations," p. 117.

[27] *Ibid.* p. 117.

unanimity or concurrence on all subjects was not possible or desirable. The Powers were essentially different. Europe, as we should say today, was a plural society. It should behave as a unity only when there was actual danger to the territorial system, and refrain from action on abstract and speculative principles of precaution.

In opposing this notion of minimum order to Metternich's more inclusive conception, Castlereagh was not objecting to the idea of concert. He sought merely to set limits to its pretensions by restraining from within. He was a much less reluctant European than his successor, Canning, who delighted in separating Britain from the Europe of the Holy Alliance. For " reluctant Europeans," in the 20th century, and for reservations about concert from a conservative standpoint, we might look to the United States, bearing in mind that it is in America that a modern concert of great Powers would be likely to have its origin. It was to Castlereagh's doubts about the Holy Alliance, and particularly to Canning's convictions against it, that Henry Cabot Lodge looked back to find arguments with which to oppose American participation in the League of Nations on President Wilson's terms. Addressing the Senate in August 1919, he observed that the combination of Powers cursed throughout history as the Holy Alliance had grown out of the " ingenuous " and " praiseworthy " provisions of Article VI of the 1815 Treaty of the Quadruple Alliance, which had looked forward to periodic meetings of the signatories for consultation upon their common interests, and for the " consideration of the measures which at each of those periods shall be considered the most salutary for the repose and prosperity of nations and for the maintenance of the peace of Europe." If the infamous Holy Alliance could spring from so innocent a statement, he feared the monster that might be spawned by the far more sweeping provision of the Covenant by which the " Assembly may deal at its meetings with any matter within the sphere of action of the League or affecting the peace of the world." [28]

That Lodge should refer to the annals of British foreign policy for ammunition to use against the League Covenant bears witness to the lack of an indigenous American tradition of speculation about the nature and limits of a concert of Powers in international relations. Neither the Farewell Address counselling against the United States involving herself with any part of Europe, nor the Monroe Doctrine proclaiming a principle of inter-hemispheric non-intervention, could give much guidance in the matter of the management of international order. An anarchical conception of order which went little further than this idea of America separate from Europe took no

---

[28] See test of speech in H. C. Lodge, *The Senate and the League of Nations* (1925), Appendix V, pp. 380–410.

greater notice of the idea of concert than it did of any of the other
devices, like the balance of power, by which the countries of the old
world sought to run their affairs.[29]

It was in this register of isolationism that Lodge pitched his most
telling arguments against Wilson's League. His references to Castlereagh and to Canning were, in the last analysis, an elegant aside. In
his opening blast against the League on February 28, 1919, Lodge
saw it contravening all the tenets of the isolationists' creed: it
abandoned the Farewell Address and the Monroe Doctrine; its
tenth article had " the youth of America ordered to war by other
nations without regard to what they or their representatives desire ";
and the extension of the control of its executive council or its court
to every possible international dispute (particularly over immigration) would mean the United States parting with " the most precious
of sovereign rights, that which guards our existence and our
character as a Nation." No gain for peace in the Americas was to
be found by annexing the Americas to the European system. The
United States was being invited " to move away from George
Washington toward the other end of the line at which stands the
sinister figure of Trotsky, the champion of internationalism." [30]

If these were the pronouncements of a convert to isolationism, it
was Senator Vandenberg's conversion from isolationism, and his
search for the " middle ground " between it and internationalism,
which was applauded towards the end of the Second World War as
the development that had brought to an end that arid polarity which
had parched American foreign policy for so long. His inspiration
in 1943 of a Republican charter favouring " responsible participation by the United States in postwar co-operation among sovereign
nations to prevent military aggression and to attain permanent peace
with organised justice in a free world," and the speech in January
1945 expressing his disbelief that any nation hereafter could " im-
munise itself by its own exclusive action," [31] represented a repudiation of the old doctrine of separateness while stopping short of
Willkie's " One World." This middle ground was not taken, however,
on the basis of a coherent theory of foreign policy containing an
account of the limitations of a concert of power in international
relations. Vandenberg battled through the San Francisco Conference
on a mixture of doctrines derived more from the domestic experience

---

[29] Or at least, in the case of the balance of power, to think no further than
balancing European interests in the Americas in assessing the problem of foreign
policy. See Hamilton, *Federalist*, Nr. 11.

[30] From the text of the speech in Lodge, *op. cit.* in note 28 above, Appendix I,
pp. 344–369.

[31] A. H. Vandenberg Jr., with J. A. Morris, *The Private Papers of Senator
Vandenberg* (1952), pp. 58 and 135.

of politics than from thought about relations among States: standing up to the Russians, creating a " town meeting of the world," justice for Poland, the sanctity of regional arrangements.[32] After Vandenberg had his town meeting, with the onset of the Cold War, conservative thought on international relations turned to the conflict of one super-Power with another and away from any concert between them, and the idea of co-operative management of the world remained, until recently, neglected by it.

It is no accident perhaps that these conservative objections to a concert of Metternich's designing, or to any kind of international organisation, took shape either in an island off the European shore, or in a continent across the Atlantic which felt that it had shaken off the dead hand of European history. We might look to the same sources for the radical objection to the idea of concert in general, and to the Gladstonian conception of it in particular. Thus, to Gladstone's schemes for protecting human rights or for establishing the liberty of nations, stands opposed the Cobdenite doctrine of non-intervention with its emphasis on self-reliance for those striving to be free and self-restraint for outsiders. Against Gladstone's notion of the great Powers as the custodians of European civilisation, embodying and acting on behalf of the moral sentiment of Europe, stands Cobden's, and before him Tom Paine's, dismissal of all foreign policy as a conspiracy of aristocratic government against nations and people. And opposed to the Gladstonian view of the virtues of a concert of all great Powers as an institution that would bind up the selfish aims of each, stands Cobden's conviction that " [w]hatever may be the future state of the world . . . at present it would be to the last degree inexpedient to bring the representatives of the different nations together for the purpose of inducing them to *agree* to *anything*. They would be far more likely to sow the seeds of war than to plant the olive tree throughout Europe." [33]

These arguments against concert might be heard within States which have the option of joining it or remaining outside it. What of the States that are excluded whether they would be members of a concert or no? Are they especially suspicious of a concert in a way not shared by those States that have chosen not to join? China, until recently a State isolated from the international community, partly because she chose to be but partly too because she was unwelcome in it, has expressed the outsider's attitude to concert. Claiming to be the sole repository of the true ideology of Marxism-Leninism, China has set herself apart from and vilified a Soviet Union taking the capitalist road and colluding with the United

[32] *Ibid.* Chap. 10.
[33] Quoted in D. Read, *Cobden and Bright* (1967), p. 113.

States in what is described as a last desperate attempt to obstruct the inevitable revolution. But the concert thus arranged between these disparate Powers is seen as a rickety structure, and the collapse of what order it establishes is thought to be foreshadowed by Chinese support for the war of national liberation, the bearer of the revolution.[34]

The Chinese assertion of doctrinal purity and distance from the Soviet Union is not, however, the result of a theoretical disquisition upon the reality of international politics from a revolutionary standpoint; it is the formulation of an aspirant super-Power whose strength has been its psychological magnetism for the Third World. The Chinese surrender of this moral high-ground in recent years, in the Indian sub-continent and in her *rapprochement* with the United States, is perhaps an indication of the strength of the aspiration, and of the dispensability of purism. For the most pungent criticism of concert in the near future we might look to the lesser nuclear States of Europe, and indeed to Japan, the Powers which have had their moorings shaken in the new world of limited co-operation between erstwhile ideological rivals. Though China was the State most critical of super-Power collusion during the recent October War, it was not from she alone that the criticism came.

Beyond the States that might criticise a concert today but join it tomorrow are those that are likely neither to receive an invitation to join nor to become powerful enough to select themselves for membership whether invited or not. We have looked earlier at some of the reasons inclining the States of the Third World to an acceptance of their lot. But at the United Nations it is nevertheless the States included in this group that make the most extensive claims of sovereignty, assert the widest duty of non-intervention, and at the same time endorse the most enthusiastically the right of self-determination.[35] The suspicion of the great Powers, separately or together, which these claims can be said to show (though not only of the great Powers) has found its most recent and sharp-edged expression in the sayings of Colonel Gaddafi of Libya: in his refusal to make a servile obeisance to the will of the great Powers or of the Security Council; in his criticism of the neo-colonialism of the super-Powers and particularly that of the Soviet Union; in his threat, by use of the oil weapon, to destroy the temple with everyone inside

[34] C. P. Fitzgerald, "Chinese Reactions to Tendencies Towards Condominium," in Holbraad, *op. cit.* at note 20 above, pp. 74–75.

[35] See my *Nonintervention and International Order* (1974), Chap. 7, sections IV and V. For the observation that it is the States of Eastern Europe and Latin America that are the most insistent about the principles of State sovereignty and non-intervention (though not of the right of self-determination), see R. Rosenstock, "The Declaration of Principles of International Law Concerning Friendly Relations: A Survey," 65 *American Journal of International Law*, October 1971, p. 726.

it, and in his suggestion of an African-Arab-European alliance against the super-Powers.[36] An extravagant rejection of concert perhaps, but one in a tradition of championship of the liberty and independence of States, that the small should not be made by their weakness the pawns of the great.

Finally, not from any particular political standpoint, we may question the habit of thought which links the great Powers separately, and more still a concert of them together, to order rather than to disorder, and show towards it the same sceptical attitude that we took up earlier towards the association of small Powers with objections to concert and to an order based on it. Even when those who rely for order on the great Powers address the criticism that the great Powers might in fact be the agents of disorder rather than order, they are inclined to shrug off the suggestion by observing that if power were held by others, by Sweden or Switzerland or Third World States, things might be better but they might also be worse, and by the argument that the critical small have never in fact been tested by power.[37] But even granting authority to the great Powers in circumstances where there is no alternative to it, and therefore granting also that any disorderliness on their part is in the category of the policeman who overreacts, or who in some other way exceeds his authority, it is quite possibly the case that behaviour of this kind is more destructive of the whole fabric of order in world society than is trouble made by small States—the " demonstrators " of international politics. Whether this is true or not, the United States intervention in Vietnam can be regarded as having impaired, rather than upheld, each of our three goals of order outlined above. The manner and extent of American bombardment of both South and North Vietnam was not an impressive defence of the value of protecting the lives of the non-communist South Vietnamese. And if we transpose the goal of " protecting life " to that, in international relations, of maintaining the balance of power, there is a good case to be made that American intervention was not a checking of the overweening power of another in Southeast Asia, but the creation of an imbalance favourable to herself. The goal of stability of possession, in either of its modes— that of State sovereignty or that of hegemonial jurisdiction—was not upheld by the United States intervening in the internal affairs of Vietnam and at the same time trespassing within a sphere of influence, however inchoate, of another great Power.[38] And though

---

[36] Interview with *Le Monde* reprinted in *The Times,* October 25, 1973.

[37] See, *e.g.* Bull, " World Order and the Super Powers," in Holbraad, *op. cit.* in note 20 above, pp. 143–144.

[38] I put these conclusions thus baldly to illustrate disorderly conduct on the part of a great Power in terms of the definition of order used here. I do not mean to

the sanctity of promises was a goal which America sought ostentatiously to uphold in Vietnam (the choice of which promises to keep, however, being sometimes of critical importance), order in one of its senses being maintained thereby, we may count it disorderly when the complete sum of order is done—since it became a disproportionately exacting obligation, the necessity of whose fulfilment justified too much.[39] Simple goals though they may be, our principles of order require a fine political judgment for them to be upheld in any circumstance, and such judgment was not conspicuous towards Vietnam. A concert of great Powers might of course inspire more confidence than the great Powers acting separately, since in it, as Gladstone thought, their mutual antagonisms might be muted, and their individual excesses balanced. But it might also aggravate differences and multiply excesses. A concert is not an institution which should be above suspicion merely because it is a joint authority any more than great Powers should be above it because they are authorities.

CONCLUSIONS

It seems from the examples we have looked at that the argument for concert accompanies a conception of the solidarity of World society uninterrupted by State frontiers, while doubts about concert seem to go along with a notion of the plurality of international society with but a slender tie binding one national society to the next. The possession of a design grander than mere minimum order seems to be a characteristic common to all exponents of concert, while its opponents, where they are not motivated by a grander design of their own, seem ready to make do with the world as it is from fear that the profligacy of the concert-builders would make matters worse.

This essay has not provided an exhaustive account of all those systems of order that would enlist a concert for their achievement.

---

overlook a complex debate in arriving at them, but merely record here my greater sympathy with the Falk view rather than that of J. N. Moore as they formed the most impressive statements for and against the legality of American participation in the war. The debate, carried on in the pages of volume 75 of the *Yale Law Journal,* is reprinted in Falk (ed.), *The Vietnam War and International Law* (1968), Vol. I, pp. 362–508. Lest it should still be held that this is a tendentious view, I think it possible to argue that the manner of American participation was disorderly even if it could be shown that the principal defence of counter-intervention to uphold non-intervention was a sound one.

[39] J. T. McNaughton, in the Pentagon Paper referred to in note 17 above, while arguing that the principle " America keeps her word " was the most important reason for continuing intervention, showed his awareness of this point by observing: " At the same time, since it is our *reputation* that is at stake, it is important that we not construe our obligation to be more than do the countries whose opinions of us *are* our reputation."

Metternich and Gladstone went beyond minimum order, but so too did Tom Paine's notion of a concert of democratic Powers, and Woodrow Wilson's league of collectively secure States whose membership in international society was to be determined by the principle of national self-determination. The architects of the characteristically modern grand design are the environmentalists. Falk would endow a Concert of Principal Actors (not just States) with the mission of overseeing the task of understanding and organising responses to "the endangered-planet emergency." [40] Each of these departures from minimalism deserves separate attention. We might simply point out here that the barriers in the way of an effective concert in these areas are the same as those that prevent the achievement of a concert maintaining minimum order. There is no reason to suppose that, in the actual practice of States, maximalism shall be rewarded but not minimalism. In particular, States are likely to remain as deaf to the declaration that they are an ecological nuisance, as they were blind 15 years ago to Herz's demonstration of their strategic obsolescence.[41]

With regard to a concert that would maintain minimum order, we may detect hesitant movement in each of the three elements that Gladstone thought of as the procedural aspects of concert: "the definition of a common objective, consultation by diplomatic discussion or conference as to a programme of action, [and] execution of plans by concerted diplomatic pressure or by a mandatory." [42] We should, however, make a more confident judgment about a concert forming in the area of consultation and discussion than in the design of a joint programme for action or in the formulation of common objectives, and more confident, in turn, about the concerted making of plans than about their concerted execution. Observing this uneven development, and observing too that the development is not taking place across the whole range of super-Power, or great Power, relationships, we may conclude that limited co-operation is not yet management of world affairs, and that this is particularly true as the management would apply to States outside the concert. Of the curiosity that the super-Powers are adversaries at the same time as being partners, it is some years now since Aron prompted us to think of this situation as banal rather than paradoxical.[43]

---

[40] Falk, *op. cit.* in note 5 above.

[41] See J. H. Herz, *International Politics in the Atomic Age* (1959).

[42] As summarised in W. N. Medlicott, *Bismarck, Gladstone, and the Concert of Europe* (1956), pp. 314–315.

[43] R. Aron, *Peace and War* (1966), p. 536.

ARGENTINA IN TRAVAIL

By

H. S. FERNS

IN his book, *The Conditions of Economic Progress*, published in 1940, Colin Clark classified Argentina among the rich nations of the world, occupying a position in terms of wealth comparable with the United States, Canada, Switzerland, Sweden and the United Kingdom.[1] In a world table of Gross National Products *per capita* published in *The Times* of London in September 1972, Argentina occupied a lowly position: poorer in these terms than Spain or Venezuela. Measured in terms of *The Times*' table Argentina may have been fifteen times as rich as the poorest nation in the world, but it was only one-sixth as rich as the richest. Richer than most European nations in 1930 Argentina by the 1970s was poorer than any of them except Portugal, Albania and Yugoslavia.

Without supposing that a high Gross National Product (GNP) is the equivalent of social and political well-being or the cause of it, economic performance is nonetheless a social variable of which account must be taken in describing and analysing modern community life. Economic expectations are a part of socio-political consciousness. What these expectations are and the degree to which they are satisfied are part of the substance of political life. Economic expectations, like ideological enthusiasms, are communicated from community to community. The demonstration effects of the material wealth of one community on other communities are social and political solvents which cannot be ignored. Economic expectations and demonstration effects, often in contradiction to ideological preconceptions, have been particularly important factors in Argentine politics, perhaps always, and certainly since the 1930s.

I—THE ARGENTINE STANDARD OF LIVING

Two observations must be made about the high standard of living in Argentina on the eve of the depression which engulfed the world in 1929. It was not a high standard of living equally distributed regionally over the whole Republic. Standards of living in terms of income *per capita*, life expectancy, infant mortality and observed standards of housing and clothing were higher generally in the Litoral and in provinces like Mendoza than in the areas where plantation crops like cotton and sugar were grown, and where the

---

[1] Colin Clark, *The Conditions of Economic Progress* (1940), p. 2.

population was more Indo-American than Euro-American. The second point to notice about the Argentine standard of living was its composition. It was a traditional high standard inasmuch as the important components were food, clothing, house-room, leisure and civic amenities. For the rich there were the added components of superabundant house-room, luxurious artefacts, travel and prestigious pastimes like polo, opera-going, gentlemanly scholarship and horse racing.

By 1930 the components of a high standard of living were beginning to change as a result of industrial and commercial developments, principally in the United States and to a lesser degree in Western Europe. In the United States Henry Ford was well established as the prophet of a new conception of popular well-being. The gospel of Ford consisted of two interdependent promises: power for everyone in the shape of a petrol driven motor vehicle produced at a price consistent with the power of the people to purchase, and industrial wages high enough to give the worker the power to purchase. Henry Ford was a materialist messiah who did deliver the goods. Through technical innovation and the investment and re-investment of profits he succeeded in reducing the selling price of a standardised motor vehicle from over $850 a unit in 1908 to under $300 a unit by 1925. At the same time he raised wages to the point where $5.00 a day was the minimum wage in Ford plants.[2]

The Ford gospel powerfully affected both the popular imagination and the commercial and industrial practices of entrepreneurs in the United States and in Western Europe. Morris and Austin in Britain aimed at putting people on wheels with power at their disposal. One of the master mass psychologists of the 1930s, Adolf Hitler, took up this gospel, and, had he not allowed himself to be seduced by other and more evil gospels, the Volkswagen, whose design he authorised, would have put continental Europe on wheels by the early 1940s in the same way that the United States had been by 1930.

If we assume that the ratio of motor vehicles to people in a community is an indicator of changes in standards of living, and of the capacity of communities to satisfy economic expectations, then it would appear that the United States, Canada, Australia and New Zealand in 1930 were the communities in which the change of emphasis in consumption patterns from the traditional elements of well-being towards consumer durables using power was most advanced. In 1930 there were, for example, in the United States

---

[2] A. Nevins, *Ford: the Times, the Man and the Company* (1954), p. 646; and A. Nevins and F. E. Hill, *Ford: Expansion and Challenge* (1957), p. 386.

23 million privately owned motor vehicles including taxis for a population comprised of 30 million households; or one motor vehicle for every 4·5 people. Very few American households except those of the very rich and very poor were spending less than 10 per cent. of their income on motor cars.[3]

In Argentina, as in Western Europe, the revolution of consumption patterns in the direction of consumer goods using power was nothing of this magnitude, but, on the other hand, it was changing in the direction of that taken in the United States. With the onset of depression the trend in all the advanced communities was arrested—even in the United States. The total of motor vehicles fell slightly everywhere between 1930 and 1935, and ratios fell even more, but after 1935 the trend towards higher ratios resumed. In Germany between 1932 and 1939 there was a dramatic change which resulted in an increase of privately owned motor vehicles from under half a million to 1,100,000. Argentina, on the other hand, ceased to follow the trend in changing patterns of consumption. The ratio of motor vehicles to people fell from 1930 onward: 1 : 28 in 1930, it fell to 1 : 40 in 1933. Although the ratio improved slightly after 1933 it never reached 1 : 28 again until 1958.[4] By this time Western Europe had long overtaken Argentina, and, in spite of changes which raised the ratio to 1 : 11 in 1969, Argentina is now far below European standards of motor vehicle availability, and very far below the ratios of the United States, Canada, New Zealand and Australia.

Neither observation nor *a priori* reasoning suggests that popular economic expectations in the Argentine community differ radically from those which have developed in North America and in Western Europe. Communication and travel being free, Argentine people generally, particularly the great majority living in the Litoral, have experienced the demonstration effect of changed material standards of living in other advanced countries. They do not derive their economic expectations from the examples of their neighbours in Bolivia, Chile, Paraguay and Uruguay and not, until recently, from their neighbours in Brazil. As in much else their economic expectations have long been admittedly European and, not admittedly, but actually North American. The source of much political malaise over the past forty years has been failure, or only limited success, in satisfying powerfully felt economic expectations. Repeated failure or small success has so ruined and perverted social and intellectual energy that it has been romantically trans-

---

[3] *Historical Statistics of the United States* (1961), pp. 15 and 462.
[4] Asociación de Fabricas de Automotores, *Industria automotoriz Argentina* (1971), p. 22.

formed into a bewildering variety of non-material expectations of an ideological and metaphysical kind. Rationally achievable dreams have been converted into irrational day-dreams.

II—THE ARREST OF ARGENTINE DEVELOPMENT

A number of massive generalities have been advanced to explain the arrest of Argentine development. Two of the most massive and general are interconnected: the notion that Argentine industrialisation has been wilfully halted by the agricultural and pastoral interests, and the companion hypothesis that international capitalist-imperialists have robbed Argentina of the means of enjoying a higher standard of living. There are, however, a few general facts which cast some doubt on these hypotheses. For example, New Zealand, which is an almost totally agricultural and pastoral community living almost entirely by processing and exporting the products of the countryside has not experienced the frustration of unsatisfied economic expectations. Using the motor vehicle to population ratio as an indicator, we observe that New Zealand in 1972 ranked next to the United States in motor vehicles *per capita*, and the New Zealand patterns of consumption are no more limited to food, clothing, house-room and leisure than those of Sweden or Canada.

Theories of class conspiracy provide no explanation in the Argentine case. It is possible, however, to attribute to the commercial policies of the United States some degree of responsibility for Argentina's failure in the mid-1930s to resume the trend towards modern patterns of satisfying economic expectations. During the 1920s the United States was increasing its share of the Argentine market, and this expansion was attributable to increasing sales of motor driven vehicles, tractors, farm machinery, electrical equipment, cinematic equipment and films: nearly all significant components in the evolution of the standard of living. But the United States was not matching sales in Argentina with the purchase of Argentine products in the United States. The American market was closed absolutely to chilled and frozen meat from Argentina in spite of the fact that American-owned meat packing firms controlled between 50 and 60 per cent. of Argentine meat processing and export industry. The sale of Argentine wool in the United States was heavily burdened with tariffs and so was another major Argentine export, linseed. Less than 10 per cent. of Argentine exports went to the United States, whereas upwards of 30 per cent. of Argentine imports came thence.

The strains created by American commercial policies were the subject of much discussion in the late 1920s. The British, who were losing their share of the Argentine market, encouraged the Argentines to think in terms of " buying from those who buy from us." A special mission from the United Kingdom in 1929 under the leadership of Lord D'Abernon negotiated an agreement with the government of Hipolito Yrigoyen, by the terms of which the balances generated by the sale of Argentine produce in the United Kingdom would be spendable only on British products or for the satisfaction of British claims on Argentina. This agreement never came into effect, but its principles were given a practical expression in the Roca-Runciman trade agreement signed in 1933.

Between the time when Argentina signed its first bilateral trading agreement with Finland in 1931, and 1937, Argentina had negotiated bilateral agreements with Belgium, Luxembourg, Germany, the Netherlands, Spain, France, Italy, Rumania, Austria, Brazil, Uruguay and Peru as well as with the United Kingdom, her biggest customer. On the other hand, trade with the United States was limited and controlled through the operation of the Exchange Control Commission and tariff policies. While imports of necessary capital equipment like tractors, farm machinery, lorries and grain handling equipment were permitted, the import of passenger motor-cars was severely reduced, and automotive imports were mainly of replacement parts. During the 1930s the number of passenger motor vehicles in Argentina fell absolutely.

The policy of " buying from those who buy from us " had the effect of reinforcing the patterns of consumption of the past. Real consumption rose by 25 per cent. in the 1930s, and capital investment diminished.[5] Bilateral trading agreements were aimed at conserving established patterns of economic relations not only in the minds of the Argentines, but of the parties with whom they negotiated. The British, for example, wrote into the Roca-Runciman agreement a provision insuring the free and unimpeded export of coal to Argentina, and the limitation of Argentine tariffs on textiles imported from the United Kingdom. These were provisions which reinforced past patterns of consumption and technology. No special attention was paid to expanding the market for consumer durables such as motor-cars or for new capital equipment.

Judged in terms of price stability, the maintenance and improvement of real standards of living, the expansion and improvement of the technology of agriculture, and the improvement of the infrastructure of roads and urban amenities, Argentine economic management during the 1930s was very good: better than that of the United

---

[5] United Nations, I *El Desarrollo Economico de la Argentina* (1959), p. 114.

States, and Canada or France.[6] But it was unexciting conservative management with little popular appeal capable of countering the political agitation about electoral frauds, personal corruption among the politicians and xenophobic suspicion of " foreign imperialism."

III—THE EFFECTS OF WORLD WAR

When war disrupted the Argentine bilateral system of trading the government contemplated two new departures in policy. The Pinedo Plan, which for political reasons came to nothing, was an imaginative, well thought out scheme for mobilising the capital surpluses of the country through the sale of national bonds bearing interest at 2 per cent. This was a feasible proposal made so by the extraordinary success of the Argentine Government in maintaining price stability, low levels of taxation, balanced budgets, and the steady reduction of the rate of interest. The Pinedo Plan proposed the expenditure of the funds borrowed on low cost housing, the further improvement of cereal storage facilities and the encouragement of industrial development. The Plan was modest and conservative inasmuch as it sought to strengthen existing trends towards popular welfare based on housing, food, civic amenities and leisure.

The other new departure, also rendered abortive by political action, was the negotiation of a trade treaty with the United States. The treaty, negotiated but never ratified, opened the United States market to Argentine produce in a way that had never existed since the imposition of high wool tariffs by the United States in 1866. The agreement negotiated in 1941 was by no means a free trade agreement, nor a proposal to integrate the American and Argentine economies, but it did represent a new departure which offered some hope of solving an extremely difficult problem of economic intercourse. Promising as the prospects were, it is unlikely, however, that American industrial interests with a stake in the Argentine market would ever have been strong enough in the domestic politics of the United States to beat down the interests opposed to the free import of Argentine meat and cereals. Without opening the American market to the strong competition of the Argentine food industry, the American exporters of consumer goods could not gain free entry into the Argentine market.

There was never any hope of a complete or even a partial integration of the American and Argentine economies once the Argentine government decided, as it did at the Rio Conference in 1942, not to support the United States in its war against the Axis Powers. After January 1942, the United States Government refused to supply

---

[6] C. F. Díaz Alejandro, *Essays on the Economic History of the Argentine Republic* (1970), p. 95.

Argentina with industrial equipment, and the United Kingdom was obliged under the terms of its Lease-Lend Agreements with the United States strictly to limit its export to Argentina. In any case the United Kingdom's conversion to a war economy made it impossible for the one source of capital goods in Western Europe to meet any demand from Argentina for industrial equipment. Argentina did not lack capital. By 1939 Buenos Aires had become a capital market. The stability of the Argentine currency, the accumulative capacity of the Argentine community and low rates of interest made Argentina a good source of spendable funds. Lacking, however, was the opportunity to purchase capital goods for the industrialisation of the country and the strengthening of its infrastructure, particularly the production of electrical energy.

Argentina continued to supply the United Nations with food products paid for, not with the means of improving the Argentine capacity to produce, but with gold, promises to pay in the shape of blocked sterling, and by the redemption of bonds and by the sale of foreign assets in Argentina. The result of these arrangements was the steady and heavy depreciation of the capital equipment of the country, the development of labour intensive industries to supply consumer goods and a further expansion of the agricultural and pastoral industries to supply the war demand of the United Nations. The agricultural sector was further relied upon to provide some of the energy used in production. For example, in the absence of coal, and the inability to convert to oil and electric traction, the railways began to burn cereals in the deteriorating steam locomotives.

In some respects the productive plant of Argentina suffered more from the war than countries like Germany and the Soviet Union which had been devastated by military violence. In those countries industry had been running flat out, steadily improving its technology and expanding its labour force in response to the demands of war. Bombing had killed people and destroyed housing, but it had only marginally reduced productive capacity. In Argentina, on the other hand, nothing was destroyed but much was worn out and nothing had developed. Six to seven years' exclusion from the stimulus to industry provided by war had serious effects on Argentina, not the least of which was the reduction of autonomous capacity to diversify and strengthen the industrial infrastructure.

During the years of the Second World War a paradoxical economic situation developed. On the one hand, there was a high level of economic activity in terms of employment and productivity and, on the other, the economy was running down and its physical capital was wearing out. At the same time the spending power of the community was mounting rapidly in terms of wages and incomes and in terms of capital accumulation in the form of gold, and blocked sterling balances. Argentina was moving from being a net debtor to being a net creditor nation. The agricultural and pastoral sector was working flat out to supply the United Nations with food and to provide substitutes for coal. The industrial sector was likewise running flat out to provide such consumer goods as could be produced by the existing industrial equipment. Inevitably in the circumstances of deficiencies in industrial capital equipment, industry was growing in labour intensity, and wages were rising. At the same time those bidding for political leadership, and particularly Perón and his companion Eva Duarte, were adding impetus to the natural economic forces pushing up wages and mass spending power. Given the productive capacity of the Argentine economy at that time, higher wages could be matched with higher consumption of food, clothing, welfare, amusements and more leisure. In the early 1930s Argentina was consuming approximately half of its agricultural and pastoral products and exporting the other half. By 1949 the rates of exports to home consumption was 30:70. The *per capita* consumption of meat in 1949 was 10 per cent. higher than in 1940–44.

IV—THE FIRST PERÓN PERIOD

Looked at in terms of economic expectations and the demonstration effect of the changing components of rising standards of living in the United States and Western Europe, Perón could well have rallied support by describing the Argentines as *desautomovilizados.* As it was he chose the term *descamisados.* This term, although a piece of sentimental rhetoric in national circumstances, served to focus the consequences of what was happening as a result of running the traditional economy to its limits. At the same time it constituted an inducement to the poor outside the Litoral, in the Argentine northwest, in Chile, Paraguay and Bolivia to seek betterment in the labour-intensive industries of Argentina where high standards of living based on food, clothing, housing and urban amenities really were improvements for them.

By stating the problem in terms of shirtlessness, Perón was able to attract not only the comparatively few shirtless in Argentina into the urban economy of the Litoral but also the many more numerous shirtless of the limitrophe countries. Thus he was able to build one wing of a solid political movement based on satisfied or partially satisfied expectations. For the majority of the Argentines, who were anything but shirtless, he offered to meet their expectations by two means: industrialisation and income redistribution.

This second part of his plan for political mobilisation was much harder to realise than his promises to the shirtless. The economy of Argentina had been meeting the economic expectations of the shirt-less of Europe for nearly a century, and it was organised to do this up to a point for the shirtless of the Argentine northwest, Chile, Bolivia and Paraguay. But to realise the expectations of a new high standard of living, which included consumer durables, involved policy decisions of a very difficult kind, ones which Perón and his successors have failed to make with a sufficient degree of the real effectiveness necessary to produce satisfaction and the possibility of political contentment.

In the circumstances in which Argentina found itself at the close of the Second World War, the economic policy required to satisfy the expectations of both the *descamisados*, drawn into the Argentine economy by the industrial expansion of the war years, and the *desautomovilizados*, who had for nearly two generations experienced rising real standards of living, involved deliberately and carefully choosing between two possibilities: one, which may be called the New Zealand option, was to continue along traditional lines investing heavily in pastoral and agricultural activity and its supporting industrial structure in order to buy consumer goods from the major low cost producers of automobiles, electrical equipment, and the like. The other option was industrialisation with the object of producing the major items of a modern high standard of living in Argentina itself. Both of these options were practical, rational possibilities, and the political outcome of both would have been the satisfaction of economic expectations of the poorest and, likewise, the expectations of those who already had achieved a traditional high real standard of living.

As it was, when Perón was elected President in 1946, he chose neither option. To the burden of six years of heavy depreciation of physical capital Perón added four to five years of decapitalisation and mistaken investment policies.

At his inauguration as President, Perón proclaimed a policy of positive State intervention in the economy. There was nothing new about this. The State always had intervened in the economy and directed its functioning. Perón's conception of State intervention was, however, new to Argentina. State intervention to Perón meant State ownership and control of key economic organisations: railways, docks, telecommunications, energy production, the central bank, insurance, the oil industry, and new industries such as steel making. Nationalisation of key industries in Argentina had, however, a different consequence than in countries in Europe where similar policies were being pursued. Nationalisation with compensation to the owners in the United Kingdom, for example, meant that capital assets were transferred from the State to private capitalists, and that the private capitalists were able to deploy those assets for other purposes to their own and the economy's advantage. In the Argentine case, nationalisation with compensation meant the export of capital to the foreign owners with no guarantee that this capital would be employed to the advantage of the Argentine economy. The Argentine State acquired what was often worn out physical plant, and paid out spending power which the former owners of the nationalised enterprises were free to use to their own advantage elsewhere.

On the face of it this was an act of folly and imprudence. It must be borne in mind, however, that Perón and his policy makers were not entirely free agents. In 1940 the Argentine Government had agreed to sell produce to the United Kingdom for promises to pay (IOUs) in the shape of blocked sterling balances. These were secured on British investments in Argentina, where the Argentines had power and control. The United States had at first bought what it needed from Argentina and paid in gold. In August 1944, the United States Government stopped paying in gold, and henceforward Argentina began to accumulate American IOUs. Thus, the Argentine Government in 1946, when Perón came to power, could not take over foreign assets without compensation unless it wished to lose its stock of IOUs which the foreign capitalists could simply fail to honour as a reprisal for uncompensated seizures of capital stock. On the other hand, uncompensated nationalisation of foreign-owned enterprises was not the only alternative to nationalisation with compensation. If Perón had not been imprisoned by his own rhetoric about imperialism and nationalism, he and his advisers could have worked out arrangements by which urgently needed fresh investment in the transport industry, energy industry and telecommunications could have been effected without the heavy outflows of capital which his actual policies involved. Altogether, during the years 1945–49 more than 4 per cent. of the Gross National Product (GNP) was dissipated on the purchase of railways telecommunications systems, and there is no evidence that any part of this expenditure benefited the Argentine economy.

The Argentine economy was probably strong enough to stand the waste of 4 per cent. plus of the GNP on compensating foreign capitalists, had the government used the rest of its investment resources to strengthen the infrastructure and lay the foundations of industrial growth on a scale sufficient to produce the consumer goods necessary to satisfy popular expectations. But it did not do so. Nationalisation of major sectors of the economy important for growth and for reducing costs in all other economic activities placed a new and heavy responsibility on the government as a source of capital. Government investment grew from 6·9 per cent. of the GNP in 1935–39 to 12·9 per cent. in 1945–49. This was an inadequate expansion having regard to the needs of the energy industry, transport and communications, not to mention the steel industry. But even this expanded public investment was not devoted sufficiently to essentials: 50·8 per cent. of public investment during the years 1945–49 was non-economic; 29·3 per cent. was spent on the armed forces and 12·4 per cent. on public buildings.[7] Even investment in productive enterprises was devoted to activities having few or no saleable end-products such as an aviation industry and an abortive nuclear energy industry.

Although the terms of trade during the years 1946–48 were more favourable to Argentina than at any time in history, the Argentines were consuming more of food stocks at a time when these were extremely expensive in terms of world prices. The traditional real standards of living rose during the years 1945–49, but at the expense of equipping the community with the means of making the transition to modern high standards of living.

A crisis in the Argentine economy developed in 1949. The extremely favourable terms of trade between Argentina and the rest of the world began to shift as agricultural and pastoral production improved elsewhere. The consequences of decapitalisation and mis-investment began to bite home. As if this was not enough, one of the most serious droughts in modern Argentine history hit the country in 1951. In spite of severe economic crises, Perón was, however, still able to command popular political support. By a combination of popular appeals and suppression of criticism and anti-government activity, he won the election of 1952. With his political base seemingly assured, Perón then embarked upon a new economic policy, which aimed with some success at correcting the errors of his economic leadership during his first administration. He increased investment, and directed investment to feasible projects calculated seriously to strengthen the industrial infrastructure and to build up industries capable of satisfying real consumer expectations.

Increased investment came from two sources. As a result of severe wage restraint and severe restraint of government expenditure, real consumption was cut, real wages were reduced, the rate of inflation was brought down, and a balance of payments surplus achieved. During the years 1950–55 fixed capital formation rose from 114 billion pesos (at 1960 prices) in 1950 to 140 billion pesos in 1955. This was reinforced by turning to a second source of

---

[7] United Nations, I *El Desarrollo Economico de la Argentina* (1950), p. 82.

capital: foreign investment. Perón signed a number of agreements which introduced or expanded the role of foreign capital and expertise in the petroleum, automotive, chemical and electronics industries. Energy production expanded and strengthened so that by 1955 the production of electrical energy was nearly 60 per cent. greater than it had been in 1949.

The economic revolution which Perón initiated after the economic crisis of 1949, the material evidence of which began to manifest itself during his last three years of office, was achieved at a heavy political cost to his leadership. Perón's technique of political mobilisation from 1943 onwards was a materialist one: to produce or be seen to produce material benefits for the wage-earning majority. Support for Perón was generated by rhetoric backed with benefits and reinforced with organisation and control at the trade union and party political level. After 1949 the flow of benefits diminished. Urban real wages fell from 181 (1943=100) in 1949 to 143 in 1952, and indeed, Perón initiated a long trend towards a diminishing share of wages in the GNP. In 1950–52 the share was 39·4 per cent.; in 1953–55 38·8 per cent. and this fall continued so that in 1959–61 it was only 33·8 per cent.[8] As real benefits diminished and the cost of the new economic policies began to weigh more heavily on the wage workers, Perón was obliged to depend more and more upon organisation and control to insure the degree of political support and mobilisation necessary for retaining office and leadership.

Perón's solution of the mobilisation problem was more totalitarian than authoritarian, an almost inevitable development in view of the demagogic, adventurist and highly personal political style he had fashioned for himself since his first entry into politics as a young officer during the *coup d'état* of 1930. Having regard for his dependence upon foreign investment for part of his programme of economic development, there were limits to the lengths he could go in the direction of a totalitarian solution, but, as Stalin had amply demonstrated, totalitarianism at home is quite compatible with doing business with industrial interests abroad. In Perón's case he appears to have believed that successful political mobilisation could be achieved, once the flow of benefits had ceased, by stimulating rather than diminishing antagonisms between the government and the important secondary organisations of the community like the Church, the universities, the social organisations of the traditional élite and rival political parties. Raising the temperature of political life proved, however, to be a mistake. The anti-Perónist elements in the Armed Forces, which had hitherto failed in their

---

[8] Díaz Alejandro, *Essays,* p. 129.

endeavours to overthrow him, this time acted without generating any serious counter-response either within the Armed Forces themselves or in society at large.

V—THE INTERREGNUM

The departure of Perón as an individual did not involve any serious change in the direction of the industrial revolution he had inaugurated; nor did it result in any improvement in economic management. The growth of industry directed to the provision of a wide range of consumer goods satisfied two kinds of popular demands: the demand for jobs and the demand for modern consumer goods. Unfortunately the satisfaction of these demands was limited in two ways. In the first place the growth of industry was slow compared with growth in comparable countries like Canada and Australia and even in comparison with not entirely comparable communities in Latin America like Brazil and Mexico. Moreover, growth was erratic. The result was not a steady absorption of labour into industry but frequent periods of high rates of unemployment. In the second place the products of industry were costly. Motor-car production, for example, expanded from less than a thousand vehicles in 1952 to 207,570 in 1969. But these motor vehicles cost anything from 185 per cent. to 250 per cent. more than the same vehicles produced in Italy, France or the United States. What was true of motor vehicles was generally true of most consumer goods. Ironically, it was in the production of machine tools, which is a labour-intensive industry, that Argentine industrial production compared more nearly with costs in other industrial countries than in the production of the goods satisfying popular economic expectations.

Argentine industrialisation did increase *per capita* income: from United States $407 in 1950 to $703, but this was poor compared with, say, Australia where *per capita* income increased from United States $604 to $1,945 during the same period.[9] Poor economic performance in terms of overall productivity translated into reduced popular welfare and disappointment of expectations. The old Argentine high standards of living were eroded as housing provision declined, civic amenities deteriorated, and *per capita* food consumption declined. At the same time, modern high standards were not being achieved by the population generally. The content of welfare and satisfaction changed, but only to a degree that tended to evoke frustration and create an atmosphere of discontent. This was not a good material basis for political harmony and solid support, not just for a leader or a party but for the system generally.

---

[9] *The Review of the River Plate*, April 20, 1972.

The Armed Forces had been responsible for the overthrow of President Perón in 1955. From that time onward, until with their agreement he returned to power by a popular election in 1973, the Armed Forces were the decisive factor in Argentine political life. The uncertainties, internal conflicts and ambiguities among the officers about their role in the community produced an ever-present atmosphere of insecurity and unsettlement in society. Argentina might have done better in terms of economic performance under a *laissez faire* market régime; and it might also have done better under a strongly *dirigiste* socialist or semi-socialist régime. As it was, Argentina enjoyed the benefits of neither. At the level of politics as well as economics several types of leadership and management were tried, but none for long enough to work for the public benefit.

In terms of production those enterprises most insulated from the uncertainties of politics and public economic policies, notably the large multinational corporations in the motor, chemical and electronics industries, performed best and grew most steadily.[10] Industries in the public sector with the exception of the petroleum industry tended to perform least well, for those were the ones most liable to political pressure to maintain and make jobs and to keep down prices. The continuous inflation, less than 10 per cent. per annum during only two years out of fifteen, and exceeding 100 per cent. during one, imposed on private investors and entrepreneurs a pattern of activity not conducive to sustained and balanced development. Inflation provoked investment in hedges against inflation such as land, buildings and foreign assets and in enterprises with short cycles of production in which the recovery of capital is quick and susceptible to moderately successful estimation of risks. Workers' organisations were naturally impelled to seek constant increases in money wages and the maintenance and extension of regulations and legislation insuring job security and high rates of severance pay. Over staffing and under financing of public services bred corruption, administrative sadism and public inefficiency.

VI—THE RETURN OF PERÓN

Given these circumstances it is not surprising that political bitterness and incoherence developed strongly during the period between Perón's fall and his resurrection, and that this had a serious feedback into the economy. Confused and dark as the situation seemed when Perón returned to power, there were, however, some bright features

---

[10] J. H. Dunning, " Investment in Argentina," CXXII *The Banker* (1972), pp. 735–740.

in the Argentine situation. Perhaps, the most important feature was the parlous nature of the situation itself. The possibility of a total breakdown of public authority and the outbreak of an anarchic civil war among factions and classes provoked a great fear which expressed itself in a willingness once more to accept the leadership of Perón. The return to power of Perón was no guarantee of a successful public policy either politically or economically, but it created the possibility of one which might transcend all private and sectoral interests and command the assent of a majority drawn from the several classes and regions of the country.

A second favourable feature was the alteration of the terms of trade between the suppliers of primary necessities, like Argentina, and the great industrial States of Western Europe and Asia. The world economy in the 1970s seems to be moving towards a situation resembling that which developed from 1896–97 almost without interruption until 1929–30 when food and raw material producers were in an advantageous trading situation *vis-à-vis* the advanced industrial nations. If the trend of the early 1970s persists, Argentina will have more leeway for beneficial development than at any time since 1930. Whether or how Argentina will take advantage of this situation is by no means clear, but the possibility seems likely to persist for some time.

For nearly thirty years from the close of the nineteenth century to the onset of the great depression, Argentina enjoyed great prosperity and a very considerable measure of political peace within a constitutional framework, the democratic nature of which tended to grow. An important element both in the prosperity and the peace was the parallelism of interest among the major socio-economic groups in society: landowners, industrial and commercial interests, wage workers and foreign investors. The economy grew and all interests benefited in some measure, so that political rivalries were more struggles among personalities than the antagonisms of diverse interests groups. The catastrophic decline in the price of primary products in 1929 shattered this parallelism of interest, and no politician since has succeeded in finding a way of restoring this parallelism. Many have contributed to intensifying antagonisms rather than mending them.

Basic to restoring a parallelism of interest is the recognition that the agricultural and pastoral sector of the economy is the key to economic progress, and that investment in this sector is the means of reducing the cost of living, increasing capital accumulation and financing industrial growth, and so contributing to the improvement of standards of living not only in Argentina, but in the poor communities which predominate in South America. The fact that the rich communities are once more having to pay more for their food and raw materials is an enormous advantage to the poor nations. Argentina is not a poor nation in an absolute sense. It is in fact developed enough to provide what the Third World needs: cheap industrial products necessary for Third World development towards the standard of living which Argentina achieved forty years ago.

THE COUP IN CHILE
AND ITS IMPLICATIONS

By

G. W. HUTCHINSON

ON September 11, 1973, the constitutional Government of Chile was overthrown violently by the country's armed forces and its President, Dr. Salvador Allende, died by machine gun fire. The *coup* was undoubtedly one of the most expert, ruthless and bloody in the sad history of Latin America. The number of dead may never be known, but it is certain that the military junta which took over the control of Chile proceeded systematically and efficiently to remove the possibility of opposition by killing, imprisoning and expelling prominent sympathisers of the Allende Government, and by a programme of terror and victimisation of working people.

As a *coup* it was not novel in history: only a particularly unpleasant example of a well known type of event. It was not even the first time that an avowedly socialist Government had come to power constitutionally and had been removed unconstitutionally. Dr. Cheddi Jagan, a Marxist, was elected constitutionally in British Guiana in 1953 and was removed 133 days later by the suspension of the constitution by the British Government. Neither was it new for those who executed the *coup*, and their sympathisers, to feel the need to justify the action. If there was something new in this event it was because of two things.

The first was that for nearly three years, from November 3, 1970, Chile under the socialist administration of the Government of Unidad Popular had " appeared to present a unique prospect, that of a highly democratic policy, long accustomed to constitutional stability and orderly rule, seeking to apply Marxist methods to the solution of fundamental problems without recourse to coercion and violence." [1] Thus, the *coup* appeared to come as an unambiguous conclusion to something very rare; an experiment and practical test of the political theory of reform. The other was that it was some of those who consider themselves most devoted to democracy and constitutionality who found themselves among the apologists. The veneer of polite civilisation was rudely torn away from that view of politics for which the basic aim is to maintain the *status quo* of privilege, and the ultimate sanction is armed force. For those of us

---

[1] H. Blakeman, " Chile: the Critical Juncture? " in this *Year Book*, Vol. 27 (1973), pp. 39–61.

outside, though not for the nine million Chilean people, it is this novel impact on political and sociological thought which is of primary interest. In order to understand them it is necessary to see the *coup* in the setting of the situation which went before it.

I—EXTERNAL TRADE BALANCE

Dr. Allende and his government had been struggling to maintain order and carry out their promises of social progress in a continuing atmosphere of crises. They had taken over the country with " an immense foreign debt " [2] which stood, at the beginning of 1973, at over $4,000 million. The annual short term credit granted by American banks had been drastically cut from $240 million to $32 million. This was especially serious because much of the copper mining and agricultural machinery on which the economy depended was of United States origin. Dr. Allende visited the Soviet Union in December 1972 and reached agreement on Soviet assistance to Chile in building industrial enterprises, in power production, agriculture and fisheries and in a technical training programme. The Soviet Union agreed to provide credits of $355 million, of which $185 million would be in sterling and other " hard " currencies, and food worth $30 million, but this was only a small part of what was needed.

By far the largest part of Chile's earning power for foreign trade derived from copper. Its value was 80 per cent. to 85 per cent. of all exports. In the January after Dr. Allende's election the world price of copper fell to 56 per cent. of what it had been in April 1970, and it fell again during the following year causing a further loss of $200 million to Chile. This blow to the national economy was aggravated by strikes in the mines and by actions of the American Kennecott Copper Corporation which, with the Anaconda Company, had once controlled most of the Chilean copper production. The mines had been partially nationalised by the Christian Democratic Government between 1966 and 1969 under a generous agreement for compensation. Allende's Government completed the nationalisation " by a unanimous decision of Parliament, in which the Government parties [were] in the minority, with scrupulous regard for domestic legislation [and] with the norms of international law " [3] but with provisions for compensation much less favourable to the companies. Deductions from the amount of compensation were to be made corresponding to the amount by which the profits had exceeded 12 per cent. per annum since 1955.

---

[2] Allende, January 18, 1973.
[3] Allende, address to the General Assembly of the United Nations, December 6, 1972.

Profits had indeed been large (for Kennecott in 1969 they reached 205 per cent.[4]), but this did not reconcile the companies to the arrangements by which no further compensation was owing to Kennecott and only the relatively small amount of about $10 million to Anaconda. Their appeal to the Chilean courts was rejected on September 7, 1972, but on September 30, 1972, Kennecott obtained from a French court an " attachment " on payment to the Chilean Government in respect of a cargo of copper due into Le Havre. The French dockers refused to unload the cargo, the ship sailed to Rotterdam and Kennecott brought an unsuccessful action through a Dutch court. Similar action was taken in the Swedish courts. Although these actions did not end unfavourably to the Chilean Government, they did help to disrupt the normal flow of copper exports, especially to Europe to which some 65 per cent. of the sales had been made.

II—The Internal Economy

The copper miners had been among the highest paid of Chilean workers. The Government's policy was to increase the wages of the lowest paid workers: the proportion of the national income going to wage earners increased by some 5 per cent. during 1970 and 1971. This increased their demand for consumer goods, and especially high protein foods, and the prices rose, so that the miners were left at a relatively less advantageous position. Discontent followed (fostered, it was rumoured by opposition inside and outside Chile) and there were serious strikes.

The stoppage at the Chuquicamata mine by supervisors in August 1972, was followed by an even more damaging strike of miners at El Teniente, the largest underground mine, in April 1973. They claimed a 41 per cent. wage increase beyond that agreed by the government. Since their union, under Christian Democratic influence, was supported by the opposition parties, this developed into a major political confrontation. It was settled in July by the granting of a substantial down payment to the miners and a monthly increase of 3,000 escudos backdated by three months, but cost the country an estimated $1 million a day and the stoppage of all copper exports in June and half of those in July.

At the same time that its overseas earnings and credit were being thus drastically reduced, Chile was forced to import more food. This was partly because food production decreased about 10 per cent. because of disorganisation occasioned by the greatly increased rate of redistribution of the land. Wheat production was worst

---

[4] Allende, *ibid.*

affected and fell from 1·36 million tons in 1971 to below 0·7 million tons in 1972. It was claimed by Luis Corvalan, secretary general of the Communist Party in August 1972, that much of this apparent decrease arose from "petty corruption," *i.e.* the disappearance of supplies on to the black market. The cost of importing this deficit was over $60 million.

Even so, the most important factor was the increased buying power of the working classes. According to the National Institute of Statistics, taking into account inflation, this increased by 80 per cent. between December 1970 and May 1972. In the same period, the buying power of "white collar" workers increased by 23 per cent. according to the same source. The foreign exchange rate of the escudos was, by mid-1973, chaotic, being variously quoted at between 20 and 350 escudos per United States dollar depending on the nature of the transaction, and the black market rate was up to 1,300. Internally, the inflation, which had been running at about 30 per cent. per annum under the previous government of Eduardo Frei Montalves, had soared to 85·6 per cent. during the first six months of 1973 (compared with 27·5 per cent. during the first half of 1972).

Difficult as such inflation may be to live with for the richer part of the community, it must be realised that it did not very much affect the majority of wage and salary earners. Their remuneration was annually increased by legal "reajuste" to bring it into line with the previous year's inflation. The reajuste due in January 1973 was brought forward to October 1972, family allowances were increased and a lump sum bonus was paid. It was the middle and upper classes, the business man, and above all the large corporations involved in international trade who stood to lose under the increasing socialism of the Government's programme. The great majority of the people were undoubtedly better off; better fed, better housed, healthier and better educated. For instance in 1971, 43 million kilos of powdered milk were delivered to pregnant mothers and children (80 per cent. of them receiving it free). Under the Frei government a similar distribution was made but reached less than 13 million kilos. The infant mortality rate decreased 10 per cent. in 1971. Total consumption of food increased by 13 per cent. in 1971 and 12 per cent. in 1972.

On January 10, 1973, the Minister of Finance, Senor Fernando Flores Labra, announced, to counter the black market, the establishment of a quota of about 30 essential foodstuffs for each family, to be administered through local committees—the *junta de abasteccimientos y presios* or J.A.P.—and through local retailers who would be assured of their supplies from the government wholesalers in return for a promise to sell at prices not exceeding an authorised maximum. This measure was needed because real inflation existed: demand had outstripped supply, and queues and black markets were the inevitable result in a " free " economy. These quotas seem to have been successful in many of the poorer communities. Perhaps they should have been started much earlier. Certainly in 1973, it was not the working people who complained.

III—POLITICS AND ITS EXTENSION

Indeed political support for the Government coalition, Unidad Popular (UP) continued to increase. Congressional elections were held on March 4, 1973, for all 150 seats of the Chamber of Deputies and half of the 50 seats of the Senate. The UP was opposed by an alliance of parties known as the Federation of Democratic Parties (CODE). An independent socialist party (USOPO) also stood but achieved less than 0·3 per cent. of votes for the lower house, with no representative elected, and less than 2 per cent. of votes for the Senate, with one successful candidate. It was the hope of CODE to get an overall two-thirds majority in the combined Congress so that, under the Chilean constitution, the President could successfully be impeached.

The actual swings have to be interpreted with caution because the voting age had been decreased from 21 to 18 since the previous election. Overall, the UP representation increased in the Senate from 16 to 19 and in the Chamber of Deputies from 57 to 63. Their voting strength actually increased from 54 to 63 because three Communist Deputies had resigned since the previous election in order to join the Cabinet. The CODE representation decreased respectively from 32 to 30 and from 93 to 87.

There could be no doubt that, in spite of a vitriolic campaign of propaganda against President Allende, he and his policies had gained in popular support, though he had not matched the spectacular success of the municipal elections of April 1971, and continued to govern against the attacks of a majority of Congress. An analysis of the swings among different sections of voters showed that UP had gained most in areas of agriculture and small industry and less in mining areas. In 1964, when the land re-distribution was administered by Christian Democrats (a member of CODE) it was they who had gained voters in agricultural areas. On both sides the more militant parties, the Socialists within UP and the National Party within CODE, roughly doubled their representation in the Chamber at the expense of their more cautious colleagues.

There is little doubt that their failure to oust the President in these elections caused desperation among many of the middle classes and was for them the turning point beyond which they regarded politics as something not to be performed only through the ballot box. The extreme left, represented by the *Movimiento de Izquierda Revolucionaria* (MIR) which was not part of the Government, were equally frustrated that the Government socialist legislation would still be impeded by a hostile majority in Congress. Violence increased on both sides, and the Minister of the Interior, Gerardo Espinoza (a Socialist), issued a warning on March 31, 1973, that the Government would " strictly apply the law in regard to the maintenance of order " with reference especially to illegal occupation. On April 5, 1973, police clashed with MIR members trying to occupy a food distribution centre in Santiago. On April 27, a worker was killed and seven other people injured by shots said officially to have come from the building in which was the Christian Democratic Party headquarters.

Dr. Allende said in his May Day speech: " Our first task is to avoid the civil war which our country's enemies are trying to provoke." At the opening session of Congress on May 21, 1973, he said the country's crisis was due to " economic aggression by the large international monopolies " supported by the " internal aggression of those who have lost power " and appealed to the Christian Democrats to " fight against the civil war favoured by certain sectors of the Opposition." Meanwhile the right-wing *Patria y Libertad* announced that the traditional parties had " exhausted " their chances of action and " direct action " was needed. Even the National Party, from within CODE, advocated " civil disobedience " and called for Government orders to be ignored. Its executive was arrested on June 21, 1973.

A state of emergency was declared in Santiago province on May 5, 1973, and in O'Higgins province (including El Teniente mine, where the strike had started within a month of the election) on May 10. This followed clashes including at least two deaths. Many more violent clashes followed. On June 21, in the midst of a general strike which paralysed the country, the Trade Union Federation (CUT) called a mass demonstration in support of Allende. About 700 thousand people took part in Santiago and there were large demonstrations in other cities. A state of emergency was again declared in Santiago on June 27 following an attempt on the life of General Carlos Prats Conzales, Commander in Chief of the Army, known to uphold the traditional, non-political role of the military as the servants of legal government. Two days later, on June 29, he showed his loyalty. The presidential palace was surrounded and shelled by tanks under the command of Colonel Roberto Souper Onfray. It was under General Prats' command that they were defeated and dispersed in a three-hour battle. Twenty-two people were killed, but euphoria followed among Allende supporters: the crunch had come and the Army had remained loyal. Allende had a further success in ending by negotiations the miners' strike. Perhaps he could go to the country on a plebiscite to remove the obstructionist Congress.

Euphoria was short lived. The country was outwardly calm under a curfew and a general state of emergency, but throughout August terrorism was an almost nightly occurrence. Oil and gas pipe lines were destroyed; bridges attacked, railways dynamited, and *Patria y Libertad* (which had been involved in the attack on the palace) announced at a clandestine press conference at a mountain hide-out that it had " gone underground " and would " fight to the last to finish off Salvador Allende's Régime." Transport was disrupted by the lorry owners striking again on July 31, 1973, as they had done during the previous October. The extension of politics into war had effectively taken place. Only the loyalty of the armed services could maintain constitutionality.

But the armed services were divided in their loyalty. It was rumoured that the Air Force and Navy favoured a coup. On August 7, 1973, the Navy arrested a group of ratings sympathetic to the UP. On August 24, General Prats ceased to be Commander in Chief of the Army in order, so he said, to maintain its unity, and left the cabinet. Allende, who had stood against right and left for the Chilean—the constitutional—way to socialism, stood alone, supported by millions of his people, but not by the ultimate power: armed force.

IV—The Textbook Coup d'Etat

The Times of September 13, 1973, in its leading article described the situation at the time of the *coup* as one in which " a reasonable military man could in good faith have thought it his duty to intervene." Suppose we accept that assessment of the military mind without implying that it is properly considered " reasonable " by the rest of society, and consider what should be the nature of the " intervention," according to military logic.

The first and absolutely overriding criterion must be that the *coup* should succeed. The will to win is the most essential requirement in the mental equipment of a soldier or of any competitive sportsman. The difference is that there are no man-made rules for the soldier by which, if he breaks them, he can effectively be disqualified from winning. He obeys only the laws of physics and psychology. Therefore, once the soldier has taken over and law and the constitution are in abeyance, there must be no silly squeamishness about human dignity, suffering or life. The eye witness reports gradually coming out from Chile make it quite clear that the military fell into no error of logic in this respect.

How then should " he "—the reasonable military man—proceed? He should make sure that overwhelming force is solidly with him. The first communiqué by the Junta on the morning of September 11 was signed by General Pinochet (Commander in Chief of the Army since August 24), Vice Admiral Toribio Menno (Navy), General Leigh Guzman (Air Force) and General Cesar Mendoza Duran (Carabineros). General Prats who had shown himself too constitutional was out of power and left the country on September 15. Some possible dissidents in the Navy had been dealt with on August 7, reportedly with exemplary brutality. A journalist on the spot (Jorge Timossi) reported that some soldiers were shot and non-selected troops confined to barracks. Some officers were arrested, including Admiral Paul Montero, Commander in Chief of the Navy and General Alberto Bachelet of the Air Force. According to Pinochet (in a statement on September 17), there were large arsenals in the power of the Marxist elements, but they certainly did not compare with the destroyers, submarines and cruisers with which the Navy took control of Valparaiso and other ports from 2.00 a.m. on September 11, the tanks which dominated the streets of Santiago from 8.30 a.m. or the Hunter fighter planes which bombarded La Moneda Palace at 11.30 a.m.

In many factories where the workers had stayed at their places of work at the instruction of the CUT there was the will to resist but no physical resistance because no arms were available. Many arms had been confiscated by the armed forces during July in searches made to enforce the law controlling the possession of arms. On October 11, the only serious armed resistances seem to have been at the Moneda Palace. Even at the Technical University, the chief centre of student support for the UP, where most resistance was attempted, no amounts of arms were available to make it effective. It must be concluded that Pinochet was, for public relations purposes, making too modest a statement of his generalship: he had overwhelming forces, and he used them.

Having secured this dominance, the *coup* must be conducted with the tactical advantage of surprise and speed. Rumours of a *coup* were inevitably rife, but both its date and its ferocity were unsuspected. The Navy had left harbour, ostensibly to rendezvous with units of the United States Fleet for exercises. It returned by night. President Allende was informed of action in Valparaiso at 2.00 a.m., but, even at 5.00 a.m., he rejected advice that his supporters should be alerted for civil war. By 9.00 a.m. when he made his last broadcast condemning the insurgents, but still urging calm, he was already besieged in the palace. The snipers had been silenced by about 4.00 p.m.

Of course, some warning had to be given to friends in case of any unfortunate misunderstandings. The White House was informed via the United States embassy in Santiago, of the impending *coup* ten hours before it took place. The United States government did not relay this information to President Allende; it merely diverted four United States Navy ships from Chilean waters. The Junta could rely completely on discretion from this quarter. The involvement of the Central Intelligence Agency (CIA) and of the American based International Telephone and Telegraphy Corporation (ITT) in efforts first to prevent Allende's election and then to create every possible difficulty for his régime had been well known, largely due to the work of the *Washington Post's* columnist, Jack Anderson.[5] The sympathy of the White House itself was evident from the Congressional hearings concerning the murky internal politics of the United States.

Next, the enemy must be deprived of information and leadership and cowed into submission. The " enemy " must be taken to be the majority of the population, and not only UP supporters, for many Christian Democrats in opposition to UP including three prominent members Bernardo Leighton, Renau Fuentealba, and their presidential candidate of 1970, Radomiso Tomic repudiated the *coup*.

All broadcasting stations sympathetic to the UP had been silenced by about 10 a.m. on the day of the *coup*. From then on the Junta were in control of all means of mass communication.[6] All newspapers and periodicals favourable to the UP were suppressed and all others subjected to military censorship. Books found in libraries and private houses were burned if considered by the military to be subversive. The country's frontiers were closed, air traffic stopped and outgoing dispatches censored for two days.

On September 13, 1973, the Junta issued a statement accusing Allende's Government of having violated the fundamental rights to freedom of expression and of education. The outrageous irony of this statement seems to have escaped its authors. The majority of the organs of press and broadcasting had been in the hands of his opponents during the whole of Allende's rule.

As to education, the Junta placed all institutions of higher education under military control, evicting their rectors. The technical

---

[5] See M. Cushman (ed.), *Subversion in Chile, a case study of U.S. Corporations in the Third World* (1972).

[6] A clandestine paper entitled " Aranco " was circulated secretly later.

university and most faculties of Social Science, History and Philosophy which had given courses considered undesirable were closed down. Students considered to have unsatisfactory records were expelled from universities. Many Chilean academics were dismissed because of their sympathy with the UP: many were arrested, some assassinated (including some foreign postgraduate students) and many left the country. They found refuge in some Latin American countries, and readily in Sweden. In the United Kingdom an organisation under the name Academics for Chile was formed on October 13, 1973, to supply support for them and disseminate information about the victimisation, but officialdom was much less helpful. A group of seven Chilean refugee students was denied entry to England, for instance, in December of that year on the grounds that they had omitted to apply formally for political asylum.

All " Marxist " political parties were declared unlawful on September 14. The CUT was declared unlawful on September 26, and on the following day the activities of all political parties were " suspended." All provincial governors and mayors were dismissed and replaced by Junta nominees. Both houses of congress were dissolved. The new Minister of Foreign Affairs Rear-Admiral Huerta, said on September 13, that the Junta would remain in power as long as circumstances demanded it. General Pinochet was proclaimed President and his cabinet was named on September 11: all but two of its fifteen members had military titles. Even one of these two was later replaced by an Admiral.

Thousands of people were arrested on the day of the *coup* and later during systematic, house to house searches by the military, both in Santiago and in the provinces. It was officially stated on October 10, that 5,400 UP supporters had been detained; but by very many reports from reliable unofficial sources, that number was a ridiculous understatement. The number of people *killed* has been estimated at up to six times that figure by some observers. It was obviously the policy, and the perfectly logical policy, of the Junta to deprive of any opportunity for activity, and especially of any leadership, all active supporters of the UP and the MIR. The National Stadium in Santiago was turned into a detention centre and 60 teams of interrogators were employed there.

There are so many eye-witness accounts of the brutalities which occurred there, and elsewhere, that, even allowing for some exaggeration, it must be concluded that the military jailers of Chile have nothing to learn on the subject of atrocity from their counterparts in Nazi Germany, Japan, Brazil or others whose inhumanity we have at various times been invited to abhor. The accounts range from deprivation of food and warmth and decency of sanitation, which could have been due merely to inefficiency, through beatings, strippings, indignities such as vaginal " searches " and forced holding of uncomfortable postures, which could be due to the individual sadism of subordinates, to deliberate use of beatings, electrical goads and other tortures during interrogation, from which the official command of the operation cannot be absolved. Indeed, the official use of torture was confirmed by Amnesty International after an investigation in January 1974. As an act of terror, designed to discourage opposition to the Junta, it was clearly most efficiently carried out.

The fate of many leaders and intellectuals of the Left is still in doubt, but some have been killed: a very logical extension of the use of military force. After all, it is only if one intends to negotiate with him that there is any political advantage in keeping an adversary alive.

It is, however, possible to question the logic in the way in which Victor Jara was killed. After all, he was not a politician; only a popular singer of international repute. Was it really advisable to break his wrists and torture him before killing him? There are limits beyond which terror is counter productive by driving the population to desperation. Pablo Neruda, winner of the 1950 Peace Prize, of the 1971 Nobel Prize for literature and of Lenin and Stalin Prizes, Chilean Ambassador in Paris 1970–72, poet of the left of Chile and of the Spanish speaking world, relieved the Junta of the embarrassment of a decision about his future. He died naturally on September 24. His funeral became an occasion for the only large, informal, demonstration against the Junta.

Allende did not die naturally. He was killed by machine gun fire during the fighting in the Moneda Palace after refusing to surrender. Officially he was stated to have killed himself. This may be true, although, since it might be the account most acceptable to the Junta, it must not necessarily be believed. There are other stories that he was shot by his attackers. They had bombarded both his home and his palace so they could certainly not be absolved from his death however it eventually occurred. His failure to surrender certainly marred a little the textbook smoothness of the *coup*. But then even the best general cannot avoid making his opponent into a martyr if he is brave enough. Certainly his death must absolve Allende from much adverse criticism of history. He atoned for any failure in political ruthlessness. The worst that can be said of him is that in politics he was too good to be great.

V—After The Coup

If anyone expected things to improve quickly in any way in Chile after the *coup*, they were wrong. If inflation was bad before, it has been much worse since: the cost of living rose by 87 per cent. in October alone, and it is rising far faster in later months. The JAPs were dissolved on September 13, 1973, and prices soared, even though the produce hoarded by traders started to appear in the shops. Even the right wing paper, *El Mercurio*, warned of impending bankruptcies in many smaller companies unable to cope with the rigours of a free economy. The plight of both working and professional classes is made worse by the very large numbers who have lost their employment. In many firms wholesale dismissals occurred of those whose names were on prepared lists of UP supporters. In such circumstances the fear of dismissal is a most potent weapon in keeping the people at work and in sullen quiet.

Even so it is evident that all is by no means quiet. Reports filter out of small scale guerrilla actions, especially from the mountains, and even of some unrest in the armed forces. Thus, an atmosphere of fear continues in which left sympathisers fear repression and right sympathisers fear reprisals of which some have certainly occurred. The denouncer of Luis Corvalan was found shot. A woman who had denounced several left wing people in Valparaiso was found hanged. The *Tribuna* of September 26, 1973, carried a headline offering E°500,000 reward to anyone " who gives up 16 traitors to Chile." There does not seem to have been much response.

The Supreme Court recognised the Junta on September 13, 1973. The leader of the right wing National Party called for support for the new régime. The *Patria y Libertad* movement dissolved itself on September 17, stating that its aim was achieved: its members who had been detained were released on September 26. The Christian Democrats were very much divided. Ex-President Frei, in an early message, appeared to favour the *coup*, probably hoping in due course to find himself again in a position of influence; but any hope of this kind which he had must by now have been dashed. The Roman Catholic Church wrung its hands plaintively in its concern for human rights and the spilling of blood, but has yet to produce any evidence that it contains the stuff of saints and martyrs within its official hierarchy. There is no prospect of any return to democratic government for the foreseeable future. A new constitution has been promised by the Junta, but not for ratification by any vote of the people of Chile.

VI—INTERNATIONAL RELATIONS

The first indication of the attitude of other governments came from the actions of the embassies in Chile. Relations with Cuba were immediately broken off by the Junta. The Swedish Embassy was especially notable in giving shelter to refugees from arrest. The courage of the Ambassador Haraid Edelstam in several instances of confrontation with the forces of the Junta earned him their displeasure to such an extent that he was declared *persona non grata* on December 4, 1973, but, in the meantime, at least 500 refugees had found shelter and escaped from the country through his embassy. In contrast, the British Embassy maintained a strictly formal attitude in sheltering only British nationals who appealed to it. Those of other nationalities were left to the tender mercies of the agents of the Junta. In the House of Commons on November 28, 1973, Mr. Amery, Minister of State for Foreign and Commonwealth Affairs, said, " British missions should not be used as sanctuaries. [Embassies] were not places where opponents of the Government with whom Britain was trying to establish or maintain relations should take refuge." Presumably if, in default, they died under torture, that was a matter for the washing of hands. The embassies in Chile of all European Economic Community (EEC) countries except the United Kingdom felt no need to stand so strictly on protocol and sheltered refugees who were not their own nationals.

The United Kingdom recognised the Junta 11 days after the *coup*: but already, before that, Victor Santa Cruz (a former Chilean Ambassador to Britain) and Sergio Vergara (representing Chilean industrialists) had come to London to explore the prospects for finance and credit for the Junta. They had meetings with, among others, the Bank of England, the Department of Trade and Industry, the London Chamber of Commerce, the Confederation of British Industry (CBI), city banks and the Shell Company. It was clear that big business and conservative government in the United Kingdom found it very easy and congenial to resume business relations with the friends of the Junta.

In the meantime, on September 12, 1973, Sweden cancelled its £4 million aid for Chile, and Denmark suspended its state loan of $7 million. Belgium and the Netherlands also suspended aid to Chile. So did West Germany, on September 21, 1973. Naturally, the *coup* was condemned in the Soviet Union and Socialist countries of Eastern Europe; it was also condemned by all political groups of the Argentine Congress. An international conference on " Solidarity with the People of Chile " was held in Helsinki on September 29 and 30. A secretariat of UP in exile was set up in Rome on September 18.

The governments which had recognised the Junta by September 19, 1973, were those of Argentina, Brazil, El Salvador, France, Guatemala, Nicaragua, Paraguay, Portugal, Spain, Switzerland and Uruguay. British recognition on September 22, 1973, was announced against strong opposition from Labour Members of Parliament and from the Trades Union Congress (TUC) and several of its constituent unions. In the United States, Senator Edward Kennedy said on September 28, " the U.S. Government has given no aid to the freely elected Government of President Allende and has even prevented any initiatives in this direction. It should not hasten to give economic aid to a régime which has seized power in a brutal military *coup*." Nevertheless, there were probably few tears in the offices of ITT, and the United States had recognised the Junta on September 24, 1973.

Very large rallies, demonstrations and public meetings were held in many cities of Europe to protest against the *coup* and express sincere but impotent sympathy with the people of Chile. The principal demonstration in London took place on November 4, 1973, with a meeting filling Trafalgar Square and addressed, among others, by President Allende's widow.

The press in Britain gave less news about the *coup* than seemed to be available in continental Europe. The *New Statesman* of September 14, 1973, headed its leader " Disaster in Chile " and saw the likelihood that, from that disaster, " the trail will lead back to the Pentagon." The *Daily Telegraph* was predictably complacent and even exultant. The *Guardian* offered sympathy. It was *The Times* in its leading article of September 13, 1973, which perhaps gave most food for thought. Briefly paraphrased, it argued that it was all Allende's fault. He had failed to prevent the polarisation of left and right, though almost in the same breath he was accused of leaning over backwards to conciliate the middle classes. Though middle class and international interests had sabotaged the economy, it was his failure and the " reasonable military man " was justified in taking over.

After a few weeks Chile disappeared from the headlines, obscured by the war in the Middle East and then by domestic issues. On December 10, 1973, the BBC television programme " Panorama " was devoted to Chile. The report was factual and the horror of the *coup* was not hidden; but, inevitably, the majority of the interviews were with middle class people supporting the Junta and the general impression was of a people looking forward to a return to normality after an excursion into " extremism " under Allende. By January 21, 1974, the BBC had evidently decided the serious chapter on Chile was closed. Its news bulletin contained, unusually, one item from Chile: it concerned a monkey sentenced by a Chilean court after being maddened by eating red peppers. Thus, the soothing ointment was applied over an ugly scar of history.

VII—IN PERSPECTIVE

But the scar will not be hidden. It will only become less conspicuous because it takes its place with so many others. It has been shown again that politics is about power and the power is fundamentally ruthless military force. Morality has not entered into the final equation. Self interest is the driving force and since power is in the hands of a small fraction of the population, it is their narrow interpretation of self interest which prevails. On this interpretation, change from the *status quo* can only be violent and can only occur when military force changes hands. On this interpretation, too, the democratic and constitutional process is merely a facade to be manipulated as long as possible but overridden when necessary. That is the more honest way of writing *The Times* leading article: it is the " reasonableness " of the military man.

If we are to attribute blame it should not be to him. He does the job he is trained to do. If we, in Britain or anywhere else, train and pay military men, we can blame them only if they are not effective in what they are trained to do. We can blame no one but ourselves if we do not like what they do when we are obliged to see it.

In Chile, the democratic, constitutional process produced a situation which, if it was allowed to continue, would not be in the self-interest of those who had power, and privilege: the owners of property, the large international corporations, the military men themselves; the cultivated people of the professional classes. The situation was therefore changed unconstitutionally, first with propaganda and economic sabotage—both by international intrigue and by political strikes—then by physical sabotage, and, finally, claiming the resulting disruption of society as the excuse, by military *coup*. Whether, in early 1973, Allende could successfully have used military, unconstitutional power himself we shall never know. Whether he should have done so, if he could, must be the crux of any analysis of the happenings in Chile, or of the politics of the world in the twentieth century.

For we do not live in a world which accepts the *status quo*, or even in which it is stable enough to be maintained. Technology has given the opportunity for mass education, and education has produced a world population no longer content to be exploited in the same way as in the past, though far from knowing what it does want or how to achieve it. Since 1917, we have been in a world in which an irreversible change in social structure is seen to be possible, and the clock will not go back. The basic differences between this century and the ones before it is that for the first time the rate of change in the way people live is fast enough for a change in kind, in priorities, to be seen in one generation. Thus, for the first time the wisdom of the father is not even appropriate, let alone acceptable, to the son. Political change would be even more rapid than it has been but for the basic weakness of progressive politics; that there is only one way of going on doing the same thing but innumerable ways of doing something different.

Once it is accepted that changes in social organisation will come the important questions are how they will come and what effect the manner of their coming will have on the resulting society. Either we praise Allende for his gentleness and constitutionality, or we blame him; and whichever we do for him, we must do everywhere, and here.

Those who condone the way he was overthrown are driven to agree with the British Communist Party in stating that " The ruling class will not easily surrender wealth and power. On the contrary, it will strive by every means direct and indirect, constitutional and unconstitutional, to restrain the popular movement, to break its strength and sap its unity. There will be particular dangers of such resort to force at crucial stages of the struggle, for instance when a general election is likely to result in a socialist majority; or even more when a socialist Government has been returned and is taking essential measures to break the economic and political power of the monopolies." [7] If that is right and we have to learn the lesson that the only way to change society is through blood, it is not likely that changes will quickly converge towards a much better society.

The British establishment has shown itself, in the official attitude to the events in Chile, to be one of the most reactionary in the world. Many people here obviously and sincerely want the *status quo* in social organisation to continue. Even supposing it could continue indefinitely, are they really wise to condone unconstitu-tionality to maintain it? But, in the long term they cannot be right, for some time, in some way, changes will come. In Chile there was an attempt at a gentle revolution. The establishment there has crushed it and the next revolution will—predictably—not be gentle, nor will it lead to a gentle, constitutional society. If the establish-ment here associates itself with the *coup* by condoning it, they risk driving those working for change here to despair of the possibility of producing change constitutionally. That is a grave responsibility.

---

[7] Programme document, " The British Road to Socialism."

TOWARDS A NEW PACIFIC ALLIANCE

By

COLIN CHAPMAN

THE trade of journalism is such that those who practise it live so close to day-to-day events and politicians' rhetoric that they often overlook long-term trends of significant importance. For four years now newspaper foreign coverage on both sides of the Atlantic has been a cameo of the movements of Dr. Henry Kissinger. When Kissinger's principal concern was Indo-China, reportage from Vietnam and Cambodia was thorough. When he pronounced 1973 as the "Year of Europe," editors dutifully warmed to the theme. The Middle East hostilities forced a change of plan for the American Secretary of State, and the result was the international energy crisis and the Kissinger plan for dealing with it, once again, seen and reported through Western eyes.

This is not to deny the vital importance of Washington in international affairs, and Dr. Kissinger's role on the world stage. But, less heralded, without the publicity associated with a *force majeure*, there have been other developments that perhaps should not be overlooked. Some of the most significant have taken place in Oceania, that least populated of all sectors of Earth that stretches from Australia on the West to the islands of Tahiti in the East.

I—ATLANTIC OR PACIFIC WORLD?

A prerequisite for appreciating the significance of developments in Oceania is to reject, at least for the moment, the notion of the Atlantic with its centre of gravity built round North America and Western Europe, and substitute instead the Pacific world. The Pacific Ocean is the common denominator for the world's most populated country (China), the largest industrial Powers (the United States, the Soviet Union, Japan), and three resource-rich industrialised countries (Australia, Canada and Chile). A third of the world's population look to the Pacific rather than the Atlantic, and most of the major studies that have been carried out on developing countries have concluded that those that are situated in the western Pacific, that is in Southeast Asia, are most likely to take-off.

This is more than wishful thinking. Vast natural resources, inexpensive labour, growing markets, and relatively stable political and economic systems in Southeast Asia make the region one of the most attractive in the world today in terms of trade and investment. Its resources include most of the items that are becoming

88

increasingly scarce in world markets: petroleum, metallic minerals, forest products, and certain foodstuffs.

According to Arthur D. Little Inc., the United States management consultant and research company, the region's greatest natural resource is likely to be petroleum, with crude oil production expected to range between 765 million and 1,350 million barrels by 1980 and to between 1,020 million and 1,835 million by 1990.[1] The total value of Southeast Asian metallic mineral exports is expected to grow from $578 million in 1970 to more than $3,000 million by 1990, with more than half coming from copper deposits in the Philippines and Indonesia. " In contrast to South America and Africa, where many of the most valuable and accessible sources of hardwood have already been tapped, there are still many opportunities for large-scale, mechanised logging operations in South-East Asia," one researcher said.[2]

Other important reasons have been cited for Southeast Asia becoming the world's fastest growing development region. The United States, Japan, the World Bank and the Asian Development Bank are pouring more funds into Southeast Asia than anywhere else in the world. The aid will near $25,000 million during the 70s and reach $50,000 million over the next decade, to lift the gross national product from $29,000 million in 1970 to nearly $54,000 million by 1980, an average growth rate of 7·5 per cent. per year, or more than double the estimated population growth rate.

Military activity in the region is subsiding, and while fighting in some parts, particularly Indo-China, is likely to continue for many years, the nations of the region do seem to be moving into a period of evolution, rather than revolution. Arthur D. Little gives one further reason for incipient development. " The countries in the region have achieved a reasonable degree of fiscal and political stability, and, for the most part, the private sector is dominant." [3] It is important to add that even those countries under totalitarian régimes, notably China, North Vietnam and the Soviet Union, are pursuing resources policies which do not preclude partnerships with non-Communist countries. For example, China is now trading freely with the United States and Japan, North Vietnam is encouraging Western off-shore oil exploration of the Gulf of Tonkin, while the Soviet Union is anxious to persuade outsiders to invest risk capital in the Tyumen oil fields in Western Siberia.

---

[1] Survey of the economic potential of the Southeast Asian region by Arthur D. Little Inc., *South East Asia: Economic Survey* (1973).

[2] *Ibid.*

[3] *Ibid.*

II—Australia's Place in the Sun

Just to the south of Southeast Asia lies Australia, a thinly populated subcontinent whose own natural resources are almost as boundless as its empty spaces. Because so many British and American speculators burnt their fingers in the 1969–70 nickel rush, dupes in a game where the only winners were a few lucky gamblers and many unscrupulous stockbrokers, the true story of Australia's vast mineral wealth has not been fully grasped. Australia is self-sufficient in most important minerals, including aluminium, copper, coal, lead, zinc, iron ore, nickel, manganese, silver. The export value of mineral primary products has risen from the 1968 level of around A$543 million to over A$1,000 million, and this figure is expected to double by 1978.[4] Australia also is 70 per cent. self-sufficient in petroleum.

Across the Tasman Sea is New Zealand, also rich in resources, and with the best and most efficient agriculture in the world.

Until a few years ago both these countries were political eunuchs, with little or no independent thinking of their own, chorusing in unison, for the first half of this century with the views of successive British governments, and then, in the 60s with the Kennedy and Johnson administrations in the White House. The other countries in Oceania, New Guinea, New Caledonia, Fiji, and the other islands had no voice of their own at all. Almost the only time they penetrated the international consciousness was when the Queen of Tonga, jolly and smiling, journeyed to Westminster Abbey for the coronation of Queen Elizabeth II.

There were times when the sycophancy of Australian and New Zealand leaders reached a point of embarrassment, at least to the intellectual, if not all, subjects of Her Majesty's Dominion. Sir Robert Menzies, for seventeen years the Prime Minister of a moribund right-wing post-war government, once said of Queen Elizabeth II: "As I watched her passing by, I knew I'd love her till I die." A few years later Harold Holt was to tell President Lyndon Johnson: "Australians are all the way with LBJ," a reference to the decision to commit ground forces to the war in Vietnam.

It was not, therefore, surprising that images of Australia were largely confined to kangaroos and sun-tanned sportsmen. Donald Horne, the Australian writer most in tune with his country and its changing times, wrote in 1966: "Except for those places where it is still seen as a migrants' opportunity and a hope for the future, the world is not very interested in Australia—mainly because its intellectual life is second rate, and it is intellectuals who cast images of the world (however much other kinds of people then purvey

---

[4] L. Parker, *Australia in the Seventies* (1973), p. 73.

them) " [5]; and on another occasion: "Australia has not got a mind. Intellectual life exists, but it is still fugitive. Emergent and uncomfortable, it has no established relation to practical life. The upper levels of society give an impression of mindlessness triumphant. Whatever intellectual excitement there may be down below, at the top the tone is so banal that to a sophisticated observer the flavour of democratic life in Australia might seem deprived, the victory of the anti-mind."

Over the past five years both Australia and New Zealand have reached political and intellectual maturity, and now speak with minds of their own. Partly this is because threats of external aggression, from China or the Soviet Union, appear to have receded. But the catharsis of the new Antipodean nationalism was the election, in late 1972, of Labour Governments in both Australia and New Zealand, and, even more important than that, the appointment of strong minded, strong willed Prime Ministers both prepared to lead their countries with a sense of purpose and adventure. But disillusionment with the United Kingdom and the United States began in the mid-1960s. In the case of the latter, it was American prosecution of the war in Vietnam which first of all divided Australians, and then later produced a massive wave of anti-Americanism that led Canberra to pursue more independent policies. The break from Britain—because so many blood-ties existed and still exist—was much more complicated.

Sir Winston Churchill was perhaps the first to bring about a sense of disillusionment with the United Kingdom, when, in 1941, he tried to stop the return of Australian troops from the Middle East to defend their own country against the Japanese onslaught. John Curtin, one of Australia's more memorable Prime Ministers bluntly refused Churchill's demand. It was the first time the British had been rebuffed by their erstwhile colony: shortly afterwards Australia became the first country of the contemporary world to be saved by the Americans, and the ANZUS (Australia, New Zealand and the United States) alliance was born. Since the Second World War, Anglo-Australian relations have been little better than lukewarm. In 1966 Donald Horne described them thus: "It's like growing away from one's parents, and seeking new patterns of identity with them, looking for common hobbies and topics of interest, so that one can keep up a connection." [6] Horne named the Queen, Westminster Abbey, snobbery, and the West End theatre as the features of British life Australians thought about most.

There are some areas that still extract wisdom from London.

---

[5] D. Horne, *The Lucky Country* (1964), p. 17.
[6] *Ibid.*

The press is one, and so is television. Many newspapers prefer to pay substantial sums to publish secondhand the foreign reports and feature material of London and New York newspapers to having their own foreign correspondents. (This is certainly not due to lack of funds; Australian newspapers are among the most profitable in the world.) In addition, BBC television programmes like *Dad's Army* and *Softly Softly Task Force* feature prominently in Australia, largely because television talent, especially in production, is thin on the ground.

In most other respects Australia's connections with London are in decline, so much so that in 1974 Sir Robert Menzies awarded a prize for improving Anglo-Australian relations. The great British migrations of the post-war years have eased: now settlers from the United Kingdom represent less than half of the total arriving each year. The large increase in non-British immigrants has been a major factor in making Australian cities less stultifying and more cosmopolitan. The United Kingdom has been superseded by Japan as Australia's most important trading partner. British cars are increasingly rare on the roads as more and more Toyotas, Mazdas and Datsuns join the queues of traffic on the principal commuter routes. Britain's defence arrangements with Australia appear increasingly as a useful vehicle for conducting joint manoeuvres rather than as an effective force against any threat, real or imagined.

In both trade and defence, the initiative for the break came from the United Kingdom. It was the British Labour Government of 1964–71 that, against Australian wishes, all but ended British presence East of Suez, and pulled out of Singapore. It was the British Heath administration that pursued a policy of Europe at all costs, allowing relationships with both the white and black Commonwealth to suffer by default.

Yet once the breaks had been made, both Australians and New Zealanders indicated there was no going back. Having been forced to find new markets by the United Kingdom's decision to abandon a cheap food policy and New Zealand farm products in favour of the Common Farm Policy of the European Economic Community (EEC), the New Zealanders treated with derision a plea, in 1973, from the Heath government to " send over " more lamb to help the hard-up British housewife. New Zealand responded by calling a press conference to announce that more lamb was being sent to America, and to advise producers not to help out Britain. In Australia British exporters who could not deliver goods on time were shown the door, and the Government, abandoning knighthoods and other social trimmings of the British way of life, announced that " God Save the Queen " would no longer be the National Anthem.

III—CUTTING THE STRINGS

Both the Australian and the New Zealand Governments have set out to take their countries on a new course as Powers in their own right, not world Powers attempting to exercise a major influence internationally, but as countries giving high priority to a regional role. Both Mr. Whitlam and Mr. Kirk were conscious that their countries are of vital importance to the developing nations of Southeast Asia and Oceania, who see Australia and New Zealand as important counterweights to the industrial might of Japan.

In order, however, to attain credibility both Whitlam and Kirk had to cut the puppet strings that tied them to Washington and Western Europe. They did this within days of taking office. Both ended conscription, recognised the People's Republic of China, pulled troops out of Vietnam, and ordered their United Nations representatives to line up with African and Asian nations on a number of important issues. They began to accept the independent policies and economic nationalism sown several years earlier in Canada by Pierre Eliot Trudeau.

The first brush came with the United States. In December 1972, President Nixon ordered a *blitzkreig* of North Vietnam. The normal reaction in Australia and New Zealand would have been student demonstrations outside American buildings, with effigies of the President being burnt. The students did nothing, but Mr. Whitlam despatched a sharp note to the White House in which he also included a criticism of an American diplomat in Canberra for allegedly failing to reflect accurately Australian opinion. Mr. Kirk also made a protest about the bombing, although he said publicly that he had done it " more in sorrow than in anger." Both Antipodean leaders received curt replies from the President: Kirk described his as " waspish." There followed months of acrimony between Washington, Wellington and Canberra. Mr. Whitlam went to Washington, but the President did not see him, and subsequently the Australian leader made no attempt to hide his pique. Finally, Mr. Whitlam virtually requested a meeting with Mr. Nixon by announcing publicly that he would be in Washington on a certain day, and hoped to be able to talk with the American leader. The two met, but little light was thrown on their meeting. However, the Australian Prime Minister did subsequently announce that it had been fruitful and suggestions that key United States bases in Australia might be shut down dissolved.

It is perhaps worthwhile at this point considering just how critical are the United States bases in Australia to American defence. The most secret, and by far the most important, of the installations are those in remote areas, at Pine Gap and Woomera in Central Australia and at North West Cape near Exmouth in Western Australia. The first two provide earth links with America's IMEWS (Integrated Missiles Early Warning System). Giant satellites poised above the Equator monitor Soviet and Chinese military activity in Central Asia and North Vietnam: this is relayed to Australia and then to the United States. Were Australia not to provide a home for these bases, it is hard to see where else they could be. North West Cape is involved with monitoring the activities of the Soviet navy and directing the United States *Polaris* submarine fleet in the Indian Ocean. United States bases in Australia are also involved in electronic countermeasures and weapon research, especially on lasers.

One *quid pro quo* for providing these bases is the American nuclear umbrella, part of the shield provided by the ANZUS treaty, though it is a highly debatable point just where United States protection begins and ends. There is no doubt that some parts of Australia—particularly the city of Adelaide, which provides a great deal of the back-up facilities for Pine Gap and Woomera—are prime nuclear targets and there is equally no doubt as to what Mr. Whitlam means when he insists that " ANZUS remains the cornerstone of Australian defence." But Mr. Whitlam has found that the ANZUS treaty does not mean that Australia has to play the part of America's pawn: there is no reason to believe that the State Department does anything but welcome Mr. Whitlam's more independent line in the region, with recollections from the recent past in Europe of the way in which Willy Brandt's *Ostpolitik* became a catalyst for the improving relations between the United States and the Soviet Union.

The whole posture of the Whitlam Government has been always to listen politely to what the United States has to say, and then to pursue its own policies. This is what most of the Governments of Western Europe have been doing for several years; but the White House found it hard to get used to the idea of listening to independent voices from Canberra and Wellington.

One example will serve as an illustration. As a result of the non-aligned conference in Algiers in 1973, Algeria proposed a resolution at the United Nations calling for a General Assembly debate on the restoration of the lawful rights of the royal Government of the National Union of Cambodia in the United Nations: in other words the return of Prince Norodom Sihanouk in place of the man who ousted him in a bloodless *coup*, General Lon Nol.

The resolution was opposed by the United States, Japan, Malaysia, the Philippines, Indonesia, and 10 Latin American countries. Australia was lobbied heavily to join in the opposition, but instead joined the list of 29 nations who abstained. As Maximilian Walsh reported in the *Australian Financial Review*: " The Cambodian issue involved the first really public break in Australia's usually automatic alignment with the US, Japan and Indonesia on major questions concerning South East Asia. By standing out against the pressure of these three nations, the Whitlam Government demonstrated that it was indeed carving out an independent foreign policy. Axiomatically, an essential ingredient of this policy is a downgrading of Australia's relationship with the US." [7]

IV—Senses of Difference

At this point it should be said that it is wrong to assume exact identities of interest between Australia and its neighbour across the Tasman Sea, New Zealand. In New Zealand there was no cooling of enthusiasm for the United States—because there had never been much enthusiasm in the first place. The three million New Zealanders had never fallen for the American way of life, preferring their egalitarian, classless Welfare State. The Kentucky Fried Chicken Shops, the hamburger bars, and the large American cars that are so much part of Australian suburbia have just not found their way across the Tasman Sea.

Planned obsolescence, an integral part of the United States economy and of so much of the rest of the Western world, does not yet exist on any sizeable scale in the small towns and cities of New Zealand. A drive across the country is like watching one of those popular recreated movies of previous decades—*The Last Picture Show, Paper Moon, Summer of Forty-Two*. More than half the cars on the roads are more than eight years old. Many families are still running, apparently without problems, the same vehicles that they bought, shining new, in the early fifties.

In Australia Texas cattle ranchers hold hundreds of square miles of the country's Top End, the rich beef country. But in New Zealand those Americans who have purchased land for other than their own use as homes are being asked—not ordered—to sell it back. Australia is enmeshed in the United States defence network because of its active involvement in the IMEWS and OMEGA systems, but New Zealand stoutly refused to participate in either, and the American military presence is quite minimal. New Zealand has not gone as far as Australia, as has been noted in an official communiqué to " the importance of effective and reliable deterrents

---

[7] *Australian Financial Review*, October 1973.

for the promotion of stable relations among the major powers, for the maintenance of international security, and for the security of the US and its allies, including Australia."

Another important difference is the style of the two governments, as reflected in the personalities of the leaders. Norman Kirk, perhaps the most notable of all New Zealand leaders until his tragic death in August 1974, appeared as a self-made man, warm and humane, and with a deep concern for people rather than institutions, and an insistence that life must be built round the family. His life had been tougher than most. He left school at the age of 12 to become a roof painter, earning one United States dollar for a 44-hour week. He later joined the railways, spending his apprenticeship scouring out the boilers of steam engines. Kirk married at the age of 20; the next few years were spent trying to fend for his young family by eking out a meagre existence from a succession of dead-end jobs. His luck changed when he established himself in the south island city of Christchurch, and entered local politics. He built with his own hands his own home, and then educated himself by reading seven works of non-fiction a week. By the time he was 30 years old, he was New Zealand's youngest mayor, in charge of a suburban municipality. His reputation for getting things done led to the Labour Party persuading him to enter national politics, and in 1964 he was the natural choice for leader.

He was very different from Australia's Gough Whitlam, a university educated, somewhat arrogant, sometimes abrasive lawyer, who does not suffer fools or little men gladly and who speaks with the air of a lawyer defending a client picking his words carefully and cleverly. But Whitlam showed himself as more adventurous and more decisive, sometimes to the point of being impetuous, and believed he lead the people. Kirk preferred time for consideration, and was slow to take important decisions, preferring government by consensus. Thus, where Whitlam, within a few days of taking office, had barred South African sporting teams from Australia, Kirk refused, believing that government directives interfere with individual freedom. Whitlam abruptly ended Australian aid to South Vietnam; Kirk stepped it up to more than US$ 10 million, but channelled the money through the United Nations for rehabilitation. Whitlam abolished the Australian New Year's honours list: Kirk let it stand. Unlike Whitlam, Kirk believed the Five Power defence arrangements had some value, and had promised to keep New Zealand forces in Malaysia and Singapore as long as they were wanted there. It is only a token presence but it has done much good for the New Zealand image. Whitlam has said repeatedly that he believes SEATO (South East Asia Treaty Organisation) is a dead duck; Kirk acknowledged that the pact may have little military future, but felt it could be the basis for an agreement on regional co-operation. On the other hand, New Zealand seems less inclined to support the idea of a new regional body as proposed, unsuccessfully, by Whitlam on his visit to Jakarta in mid-1973. Perhaps the greatest difference of all was that Mr. Kirk got on with businessmen and industrialists to the point where he established a reasonable *rapport*: Mr. Whitlam, in contrast, has few allies in the commercial field.

A further divergence is evident in relations with Japan—for both countries now of critical importance. New Zealand diplomats have frequently indicated that their country would like to sign a trade and friendship treaty with Japan, and join with her in joint ventures in Asia. Australia, despite the fact that Japan is her most important trading partner, has shown reluctance to take such a step. This is not to say that the relationship is a bad one.

There is, furthermore, the relationship between New Zealand and Europe. New Zealand diplomats spent so many months lobbying their case for special treatment in the corridors of the Brussels commission that Wellington acquired a knowledge of the workings of the European Common Market that Canberra did not possess. At the same time New Zealanders—despite the scant regard paid to their problems by the Heath administration—retained their affection for Britain and the British. As Michael Southern reported in the *Financial Times*: "When the sun sets on the British Commonwealth, New Zealand will surely be the last outpost of loyalty to the Queen and of affinity to the British people . . . in spite of the perfidy of Britain, New Zealanders still cherish memories of better days and are prepared to continue with what is left of the relationship." [8] Even so, like Australia, New Zealand is running down the size of her High Commission in London.

Finally, there are the economic differences. Both are young countries who enjoy a standard of living close to the highest in the world. In New Zealand half the people are under the age of 25. On paper Australia is by far the richer country, because of its vast reserves of minerals discussed earlier, but New Zealand's highly efficient agriculture is finding new markets all the time, and wool and lamb prices have been high over the past two years. Beef production has also been increased. Wool and beef receipts have not been affected by United Kingdom entry into the EEC, because most New Zealand beef goes to the United States, and there are no barriers to trade in wool. In January 1974 the United States also lowered the cheese barrier, and so New Zealand stands to gain in

---

[8] *Financial Times*, October 1973.

dairy production too. High export prices received for New Zealand food exports have been more than sufficient to pay all import needs and still leave very substantial overseas reserves. In seeking new markets, such as those that have been found in Asia, Japan and South America, exporters have begun to look not only for direct outlets for dairy meat and wool, but also at means of converting these products into marketable forms. There are already factories established that convert dairy produce into dried forms which are reconstituted at point of sale overseas.

In contrast Australian agriculture is less efficient, except perhaps in beef production. The Australian economy has also had to come to grips with Labour policies, many of them expensive and in-flationary. Australia is having to find the money for a government health and welfare scheme: New Zealand has always had one. Mr. Whitlam has had to spend more than A$200 million on Australian schools to bring them up to New Zealand standards. He has had to spend millions of dollars on decentralisation plans; New Zealand is already decentralised with a good network of roads and adequate essential services. Whitlam has to budget millions of dollars on improving the lot of Australian Aborigines, the majority of them destitute, wandering nomads or despairing, city-fringe dwellers. It will take at least a decade to bring them to the equivalent level of the Maoris, who now have a significant and growing place in New Zealand society. New Zealand has Maoris in its cabinet, and Maori language and culture is taught in New Zealand schools. By social yardsticks, New Zealand—a Scandinavia in the southern hemisphere—is far ahead of Australia. Whereas one Australian in eight is said to be living on or below the poverty line, there is virtually no poverty in New Zealand. Equally there are few millionaires. It needed Whitlam's socialism to bring about a fundamental change to the structure of Australian society; his New Zealand counterpart has had only to expand on existing foundations, and keep the economy afloat.

V—DEFENCE OR DEFENCELESSNESS?

But whatever differences exist between the two countries are differences of detail. Both Australia and New Zealand share the common aims of a peaceful and prosperous Pacific, and both have the same ideas as to how this can be achieved.

These bear no relation to the policies of five years ago. The late Norman Kirk said in a speech to the Institute of International Affairs in August 1973: " There has been a complete review of foreign policy with the purpose of achieving a policy which is distinctly New Zealand in style, which reflects an individual viewpoint, and which is self reliant in character . . . we have sought to give more direction to this country's foreign policies, and to undertake a greater degree of forward planning, particularly in our aid programme. From the outset we have been guided by the principle of what is best for New Zealand's best interests, and this test has been applied to each decision we have made."

Both Governments have abandoned the fear of (Communist) "Asian hordes" descending from the "Near North" (Far East), and forward defence has been forsaken. Even the hawks who still believe in the idea, and have in the past advocated a strong Australian and New Zealand military presence in Southeast Asia, appreciate that the United States departure from Vietnam renders this no longer practicable. Some of them argue for "Fortress Australia," under which the country would increase defence spending, rely on the American nuclear umbrella for defence in a thermonuclear war, and strengthen missile defences and ground forces to combat an invasion. An extension of this—"Lifeboat Australia" —would increase the country's isolation in a political sense in that immigration would stop, thus preventing large-scale industrialisation and, in turn, environmental pollution. Australia, in effect, would cast herself off from the over-populated world, and repel, by force if necessary, all those who tried to join the lifeboat. It is an improbable prospect, but the people who advocate it would not like to be thought of as cranks.

In contrast to this is the serious school of thought who would like immigration to be abandoned altogether—and those who subscribe to it are by no means all "trendies" of the left. Dr. Peter King, of the University of Sydney, has argued in a paper called, appropriately, "The Defence of Defencelessness," [9] that spending should be progressively rolled back to 1973 levels with the savings diverted to foreign aid and domestic health, education and welfare programmes.

A newspaper made the additional comment: "A similar philosophy has recently been expressed by one of the Government's economic advisers, who said Australia's best defence policy was 'chipping off bits of Western Australia, and selling them freely to everyone.'" [9]

The Australian Government's attitude to all this is that it is not enough just to talk loosely about vague possibilities. Lance Barnard, the Minister of Defence, told the Returned Servicemen's League (RSL), a particularly influential pressure group who believe in a much larger defence posture, that, among the limitless range of possibilities, Australia had to identify what is more likely and

[9] *Australian Financial Review*, October 1973.

probable. " We have to ask who has, or is likely to have, a powerful enough motive and the will to attack us; in what circumstances is this likely to occur; where is the military capability; and when are these things likely to happen." [10]

Mr. Barnard, knowing his audience would be highly critical of anything he said, then went on to quote from a secret Defence Department document drawn up by the Chiefs of Staffs and the Secretaries of the Defence, Foreign Affairs, Prime Minister's and Treasury departments.

" Australia is remote from the principal centres of strategic interest of the major powers and, because of its location and size, is a difficult country to invade, conquer, and occupy. . . . It can be said that Australia is at present one of the more secure countries in the world. Many of the contingencies that preoccupied earlier strategic policy now appear remote."

The committee said: " The present strategic situation contrasts strongly with that which faced Australia 10 years ago and which contributed to the substantial expansion of Australian defence forces and capabilities in the 1960s. The present and likely trends identified have not indicated any likelihood of threat of direct attack on Australia. . . ."

" Threat of direct attack . . . would require fundamental changes beyond the developments assessed as likely. Australia would then be in a radically new situation . . . such a development would take time and would affect many countries other than Australia."

Mr. Barnard observed that, in its discussions of Southeast Asia and Australia's immediate neighbourhood, the defence committee stated: " Northeast Asia is strategically more important to the major powers than is Southeast Asia." He said that, apart from stressing the nuclear constraints among the super-Powers, the committee pointed to the increasing dependence of the large industrial economies of Western Europe, Japan, and North America on " an uninterrupted and very large flow of essential raw materials across a world-wide grid of producing, processing, and shipping facilities.

These developments are making the industrial countries more cautious about using military force, and placing increasing significance on the peaceful accommodation of problems."

This does not mean that Australia has decided to place itself in the trust of the international community, following the example of post-war Japan, where the level of self-defence forces is low, both in terms of population, gross national product, and trade. The Governments of both countries have rejected the " defenceless-

---

[10] *Ibid.*

ness " argument, and, notwithstanding the low-threat assessment of their own experts, intend to maintain a substantial force, and to adjust defence strength according to regular strategic surveys.

Accepting that the defence of continental Australia is the prime concern, the Whitlam government is maintaining strong land forces equipped with tanks and artillery capable of dealing with an invasion at home. Coupled with this is an air defence capability for Australian cities, bases, and ground forces, and a strong Navy consisting of reconnaissance elements, and highly sophisticated anti-submarine equipment. The Navy's key aims are to protect trade routes, deter a missile threat from the sea, and build up a coastal defence structure capable of protecting incursions below armed threat level—such as fisheries protection and environment monitoring.

Beyond this there is both Australia's and New Zealand's keenness to provide peacekeeping forces for the United Nations, and the provision of help to friendly nations. It is this last item that has been the object of much discussion in the last two years, particularly in view of the sudden move to home rule of the former Australian trust territory of Papua New Guinea.

VI—THE FUTURE OF THE REGION

Papua New Guinea, with 2·5 million people, is perhaps potentially the most volatile of the countries in the region and is also the nearest to Australia. It quietly gained self-government on December 1, 1973, after years as an Australian administered United Nations trusteeship territory. There was none of the fanfare normally associated with these occasions: the Government decided that a quiet weekend with no parades, no festivities, no meetings and no liquor was the best way of ensuring no friction.

It is potentially a very rich country and no longer a vast slumbering giant of an archipelago. It has large reserves of copper, timber, and tropical crops, and possibly oil and natural gas. Considering it is only a decade since most of its people emerged from Stone Age conditions, it has roads, communications and air services superior to many developing nations. But as Christopher Ashton, a resident journalist in Port Moresby, reported: " The danger for Papua New Guinea is that, whatever its investment guidelines, it lacks the expertise to evaluate investment proposals, and may end by either giving away too much or by frightening away worthwhile investment by asking too much." [11]

Then there are the political problems. The central one is similar to that faced in a number of African countries: coaxing the regions into an effective federation. Papua New Guinea is a country of vast

[11] *Ibid.*

ethnic, cultural, economic and political differences. As self-government has approached, so bitter fragmentation has spread. Although there are far fewer of them, many Papuans feel superior to the New Guineans. They were much better educated and treated with more sophistication by the Australians than were the New Guineans under pre-1914 German Rule and under the following Australian administration. Port Moresby, the administrative centre, is in Papua, and this has enabled Papuans to feel they have something, in terms of Melanesian prestige, that the other peoples of the territory do not possess. But the dominant area of the country is the highlands of New Guinea, where 800,000 still mainly tribalised people comprise a third of the island's entire population. These proud people are insular enough anyway, but they especially scorn the Papuans, and have been determined to establish political dominance by sheer weight of numbers.

As if this was not enough, there are then the attitudes of the peoples living on the rich outer islands of New Britain, New Ireland and Bougainville. In all these places there have been strong pressures for secession. When Prime Minister John Gorton visited New Britain in 1970, a crowd of 10,000 angry Tolai people gave him an extremely hostile reception, and helicopter gunships were hovering overhead ready to pluck him out of trouble had the riot police and barbed wire failed to do the trick. And the riot police have had, over the last three years, a very busy time at Bougainville Island because of major disputes over the development of the rich copper mine owned by Rio Tinto Zinc there. The Papua New Guinea Government owns a 20 per cent. equity in Bougainville Copper, but many local people feel this is insufficient, and have been encouraged by a report from a Harvard Professor, Louis T. Wells, who argued that urgent changes were necessary. Professor Wells pointed out that some agreements in Central Africa looked for a 75 per cent. return for governments, and put forward a scheme which would produce an extra $193 million in revenue over five years.[12]

It would be pleasant to think that these teething difficulties could be resolved peacefully, but that may be taking an over-optimistic view. Certainly in Canberra the Australian Government hopes for the best but is ready for the worst. A special defence squad has been on exercises where a violent uprising in a mythical country, " Cocoana," has to be put down. Prime Minister Whitlam is adamant that Australian troops should not be involved in action on New Guinean soil, and they would only be used as a last resort, and at the request of Mr. Michael Somare, the young lawyer whose careful

---

[12] *Ibid.*

blend of fire and statesmanship is bringing his country through a thousand years of civilisation in three years flat.

This, then, is a region bristling with change. Two affluent countries, Australia and New Zealand, self-confidently pursuing new and independent foreign policies, striking up a strong regional identity. Near them are newly emergent countries—like New Guinea, a resources and oil-rich Indonesia, and the Fijian archipelago. And there are hundreds of small islands, who are proud to be self-ruling, but look to Australia and New Zealand for leadership and guidance.

The critics may ask meanwhile, how change can be other than a sham and empty rhetoric when Australia and New Zealand, the " westernised " nations in the region are so strongly economically dependent on the world's large industrial nations? After all, is it not a fact that most of Australian and New Zealand industry, commerce and natural resources are under British, American or Japanese ownership? One favourite story of those who argue that Australia is just a giant granary and quarry is to tell how the annual production figure for one of the country's largest iron ore producers is determined once a year at a meeting between Tokyo, London and New York directors in Hawaii.

This may have been in the past, but the realisation that political independence can only be by economic independence has gained ground rapidly and is one of the principal driving forces for change in the region. It is this that has led to the dramatic rise in economic nationalism. This is why the Australian Government has lent so much verbal support for the Arabs and Third World countries, for it shares their belief that their raw materials and markets have been ruthlessly exploited by the big international cartels.

The Australian Liberal-Country Party Government who, for years, encouraged foreign ownership and even control of Australian business presided over a period of unparalleled take-over of natural resources. In 1972 it reversed this policy and, when Labour came in, the Government continued the new trend with Prime Minister Whitlam repeatedly expanding the concept of Australian ownership and control. Foreign take-overs of Australian firms are now subjected to special scrutiny, and at the start of 1974 legislation was planned to prevent take-overs in the banking, finance and insurance sectors.

But it is in the sector of energy resources explorations and development that the Labour Government's policy is most severe and a complete change from the past. Mr. Whitlam has proclaimed a policy of total Australian ownership and control of energy development and exploration projects. Direct foreign equity participation is to be excluded from four energy fields—uranium, oil, natural gas, and black coal. In other resources development in Australia will be more flexible, looking for partnerships with equity capital in a number of mining ventures. Prime Minister Whitlam enunciated his policy in Tokyo on October 29, 1973.

"No longer is there a wholly uncritical approach to foreign investment. We intend to ensure that foreign capital inflows are associated with productive investment which adds to Australia's real resources and brings us benefit. My Government has the firm policy objective of promoting control of Australian resources and industries. We also want to achieve the highest possible level of Australian ownership of our resources and industries. By this phrase we mean the highest Australian equity that can be achieved in negotiations, project, that are fair and reasonable to both parties and are within the capacity of our own savings to support." [13]

New Zealand shares many of the same sentiments, but approaches the problem of foreign ownership less publicly, and perhaps less forcefully. Because there are not the same large profits to be made in New Zealand because it is a more even society with heavy taxation of the rich and because it is so much smaller, New Zealand has found it easier to contain the spread of foreign control, while, at the same time, attracting sufficient development capital.

New Zealand's role in the region is very different to Australia's. New Zealand is perhaps slightly less concerned with Southeast Asia than is Australia, though Wellington would deny this. But New Zealand is much more closely involved with the affairs of the South Pacific islanders than is Australia. This is partly because New Zealand is a multi-racial society, with its large Maori population of 202,000 out of a total population of 2·5 million and heavy influx of island people year by year. There are more Polynesians in Auckland than anywhere in the Pacific; there are already 50,000 people from the Cook Islands alone, and more are coming.

New Zealand appears to be especially conscious of the problems which industrialisation, social progress, and rising expectations will bring to the islands in the years ahead. It sees the central problem as whether the islands' educational systems should lay emphasis on training people to work in an urban, industrial environment or bringing up people to live in a simpler, communal, island tradition.

New Zealand is by no means convinced that industrialisation is the answer. In an interview before he died Norman Kirk said: "The islanders may well have a better way of life. Perhaps we should copy them rather than the other way round." The interviewer, Peter Robinson, editor of the *Australian Financial Review*, added the comment: "The island concepts of community—of

[13] *Ibid.*

sharing work, responsibility and achievement—obviously appeal to him." [14]

New Zealand is keen on the development of South Pacific democracy through the establishment of a South Pacific Parliament, a political forum similar to the West European Union. Mentor countries, including Australia, the Cook Islands, Fiji, New Guinea, New Zealand, Tonga and Western Samoa would each nominate two parliamentarians, one of them a minister, which would build on the experience of the South Pacific Commission, a yearly gathering of administrators.

Yet it is hard to see what such a body could achieve without the support of French Colonies in Polynesia—Tahiti and New Caledonia. And there are other obstacles.

The most significant of these is the overwhelming sweep of Japanese business interests into the island regions. While the New Zealanders, and—with the exception of banking interests—the Australians, are cautious about taking over much of the commercial and industrial life, the Japanese have no such inhibitions.

Future Japanese influence is the great unknown. Ultimately Japan will come to control, or have a stake in, much of the economic life of Australia, New Zealand, and the rest of Oceania. But the assertive nature of the present political structures in the area should be strong enough to prescribe limits on that Japanese influence.

---

[14] *Ibid.*

SINO-AMERICAN RAPPROCHEMENT
AND THE NEW CONFIGURATIONS
IN SOUTHEAST ASIA

By

USHA MAHAJANI

THE growing accommodation between China and the United States
marks a turning point not only in their bilateral relations but also
in world politics. Its foundations were laid by Richard Nixon soon
after he became President in 1969. By 1971, China watchers had
begun to note a decline in the Sino-American mutual hostility.
They observed that " Chinese relations with the U.S. and USSR
seem to be at a point where China has more options open to it to
improve relations *concurrently* with *both* super powers than has
been the case in some time." [1] China chose only one option: to
foster a *détente* with the United States. The impact of this *détente*
has been felt in China's relations with several countries. Antagonism
with the Soviet Union and India has become accentuated, but
relations with several allies of the United States like the United
Kingdom, Canada, France and Japan have reached a marked degree
of cordiality and co-operation.

The impact of the Sino-American *rapprochement* on Southeast
Asia has not been visibly traumatic, but this should not lead us to
believe that the area is immune from the repercussions of the Sino-
American *détente*. The reason lies primarily not only in the proximity
of the region to China, but also in the fact that both China and
the United States regard it with close interest. It is hazardous for
scholars, in this age of dramatic disclosures and stunning " punches,"
to attempt to adumbrate the shape of coming events. Nevertheless,
it is possible and purposeful to try to discern new international
configurations in Southeast Asia in the 1970s as a result of not only
the Sino-American *détente*, but also a number of other developments
within and without Southeast Asia.

I—A PROFILE OF THE REGION

Southeast Asia is unique in several ways. It is a truly heterogeneous
geographical region in the world with more languages, ethnic and
racial groups and religions than in any other comparable area. No

---

[1] D. Tretiak, " Is China Preparing to ' Turn Out '? : Changes in Chinese Levels
of Attention to the International Environment," *Asian Survey*, March 1971, p. 219.

other region has received so profound an impact from a combination of civilisations—Indian, Chinese, Arab and European. Above all, Southeast Asia has been under heavy political dominance of external Powers since the 16th century, a dominance which shaped its political configurations. Until then, Southeast Asia had its own international system characterised by extensive contacts, power politics, and wars of conquest among individual Southeast Asian kingdoms. China occasionally undertook military intervention, causing physical destruction and important political consequences, but the so-called relationship of vassalage between Southeast Asian kingdoms and China was a technicality rather than a reality, more a self-illusory myth created by China, just as she had assumed Japan, Portugal and even England to be her tributary States, than an actual state of political affairs. In pre-colonial days China was never able to impose its own order on Southeast Asia or create political configurations in its own image.

The naval expansion of West European States, beginning at the end of the 15th century, brought Southeast Asia under the purview of West European dominance and carved it into Spanish, British, French, Dutch and American colonies. European colonialism marked the prevailing political configuration in Southeast Asia until the outbreak of the Second World War when Japan conquered the entire region and established its own imperial order in the name of Greater East Asia Co-Prosperity Sphere. The defeat and retreat of Japan from Southeast Asia in 1945 also set into motion yet another two-fold process: the progressive withdrawal of the Western ruling Powers, and the rise of independent Southeast Asian States.

II—Southeast Asian Configurations:
1945–1971

These two mutually reinforcing processes would have created certain patterns of interaction and alignment among the former rulers and the ruled. But after the end of the Second World War, Southeast Asia became integrated into the emergent, universal, Global International System, marked by bi-polar politics between the newly emerged super-Powers, the United States and the Soviet Union. Southeast Asian States were caught in the vortex of that most sweeping and total politics of antagonism known as the Cold War. The rise of Communist China in 1949 as a military and ideological ally of the Soviet Union, and, therefore, an adversary of the United States, intensified Cold War politics in Southeast Asia to a degree unparalleled in any other region, except perhaps in Berlin. More than the Soviet-American conflict of interest, that between China and the United States now dominated the international politics in Southeast Asia.

Sino-United States antagonism had an added bad taste of a longtime close friendship turning sour. During the war President Roosevelt had even offered Indochina to Chiang Kai-shek to boost up his sagging spirit. The Potsdam agreement had provided for Nationalist Chinese armies to occupy Southeast Asia north of the 16th parallel for the purpose of disarming Japanese soldiers. In short, the United States had viewed Southeast Asia, at least partially, as a sphere of influence for China, then herself a member of the American camp. The establishment of a communist government in Peking radically altered the United States perspective on Southeast Asia. Henceforth, United States policy was to pry that region loose from any Chinese communist influence and bring it within the purview of its own anti-communist strategic, political and economic considerations. Communist China was branded as a satellite of Moscow and the Communist-led national independence struggle in Vietnam as a part of international communist expansion. Although United States support for the French reconquest of Indochina was categorically affirmed by Truman in his August 1945 meeting with de Gaulle and although United States assistance was given to the French long before communism triumphed in China, it was thereafter that the United States formalised and expanded its military aid to the French for the Indochina war. The Eisenhower Administration pondered direct air intervention in 1954, focussing on China as the arch foe. It warned China of " massive retaliation " and dispatched two aircraft carriers with nuclear weapons to the Gulf of Tonkin in May 1954, to be used in case the Chinese intervened with their " volunteers." [2] To complete the fortress of strength against China, the United States brought about the Manila Pact which called into being the Southeast Asia Treaty Organisation (SEATO).

The dominant configuration in Southeast Asia until mid-1971 was, therefore, the conflict between United States efforts to keep China out of Southeast Asia and the Chinese attempts to leap across the barrier to build up close relations with at least non-aligned countries. Both Powers had various degrees of success. Those countries that were militarily aligned with the United States rebuffed every Chinese overture for normalisation of relations. Several non-aligned countries, like Burma, Cambodia and Indonesia, forged close ties of co-operation and friendship treaties with China until *coups* in Indonesia in 1965 and in Cambodia in 1970 destroyed them. By mid-1971, China did not have a single good friend in

---

[2] C. Cooper, *The Lost Crusade, America in Vietnam* (1970), pp. 72–73.

Southeast Asia, including the Democratic Republic of Vietnam (North Vietnam), which has always harboured deep suspicion of China. As against this setback, China had gained some prestige in Southeast Asia even by 1969 insofar as few of the anti-communist regional countries regarded China as a major threat to their security. Some, like Malaysia, were even proposing China's entry into Southeast Asia as one of the major guarantors of a neutralisation plan.

Within the framework of the Sino-American Cold War, several external Powers were exerting influences in Southeast Asia commensurate with their interests and capacities. The United Kingdom had remained a colonial Power longer than any other Western country and had a highly deterministic role to play in the formation of Malaysia in 1963 and the subsequent five-power defence arrangements involving, besides herself, Australia, New Zealand, Malaysia and Singapore. France had lost her Indochinese empire and, with it, any substantial interest in the region, except the perpetuation of French culture in the former colonies. The Netherlands had sought to retain vestiges of her former empire but was impelled, under United States pressure, to surrender West New Guinea to Indonesia in 1962. However, since 1965, Dutch political and economic interests were revived in Indonesia with great fervour. Japan, crushed militarily and humiliated politically, had ceased to be a factor in Southeast Asia. Japanese caution and the lingering Southeast Asian bitterness had forced the Japanese government to adopt a virtually invisible, " low profile " in political and military spheres and an equally visible, expansionist policy in that of investment and trade, both calculated to bolster Japanese economy. India had no military and economic interests in Southeast Asia, except as a donor of aid under the Colombo Plan, but her political role was for several years one of leadership and influence among the non-aligned nations. That is why the neutral country chosen to become Chairman of the three International Control Commissions in Indochina in 1954 was neither Burma nor Indonesia, but India.

As a super-Power with global interests, the Soviet Union had not neglected Southeast Asia. Beginning with her membership in the Economic Commission for Asia and the Far East (ECAFE), the Soviet Union had initially engaged in a self-defeating diplomacy of denunciation of both the western Powers and the national bourgeois leadership of Southeast Asia for being stooges of western imperialism. After Stalin's death in 1953 the Soviet Union embarked on a policy of aid, trade and political friendship and forged close ties with several non-aligned countries, notably Indonesia under Sukarno. But the Soviet Union never regarded Southeast Asia as her vital sphere of interest and, unlike in the Middle East and South

Asia where she signed military alliance treaties with Egypt and India, she scrupulously refrained from any military involvement and intervention. Soviet military aid to North Vietnam has undoubtedly been substantial, but the motivation has been ideological, not strategic.

III—New Configurations in the 1970s

The most dramatic impact of the Sino-United States *détente* which, one must remember, had been developing even before mid-1971, has been on Indochina. It is here that Cold War propaganda and rhetoric from both China and the United States have proved to be of a hollow ring. China had stoutly called for total United States withdrawal from Indochina and made valiant but calculatedly vague pledges of resolute support for the Indochina people. The United States had justified her military intervention in Indochina as a move to stem Chinese expansionism. But as early as 1965, China subordinated her professed " revolutionary " opposition to the United States in Vietnam to her growing conflict with the Soviet Union and began obstructing the flow of Soviet aid to North Vietnam through the Chinese territory. China did not retaliate by counter-intervention after American bombing of Laos and North Vietnam began. In the spring of 1966, China reportedly told the United States privately that she would not intervene in Vietnam except in case of a United States (land) invasion of North Vietnam or an American attack on China, neither of which, the United States assured China, was intended. Once President Nixon's overtures to China began, the latter did not consider an end to the Indochina conflict and the withdrawal of United States troops from Indochina as a precondition for Sino-American *rapprochement*. As President Nixon instituted a blockade of Haiphong and renewed fierce bombing of North Vietnam, China merely murmured a weak protest that the United States was " wholly responsible for this complication," referring to the delay in signing the cease-fire agreement. There was not a hint of a threat of Chinese retaliation. Since the signing of the cease-fire agreement in Vietnam, China has ceased criticising the United States. She has welcomed the Laotian political settlement without echoing Pathet Lao's attacks on " United States imperialism." [3] China's championship of the Sihanouk government in exile is more rhetorical and diplomatic than militarily concrete.

The Guam Doctrine proclaimed by President Nixon in 1969 and

[3] H. Hinton, " China and Vietnam," in *China in Crisis: China's Policies in Asia and America's Alternatives*, vol. II, Tang Tsou, ed. (1968), pp. 208–222; *Renmin Ribao*, editorial, " A Major Step Towards National Accord in Laos," text in *Peking Review*, Nr. 38, September 21, 1973, p. 8.

the end to direct United States fighting in Indochina, coupled with Sino-American *rapprochement*, do not, however, signal United States withdrawal from Southeast Asia. In August 1970, Vice President Agnew was sent on a tour of Asia to assure allies that the United States, in President Nixon's own words, " is not withdrawing from Asia." Former Secretary of State, William Rogers, and Secretary Henry Kissinger have reiterated this stand, adding that the United States would remain a Pacific Power with full military, naval and air presence in East Asia and has no intentions of pulling out her troops from Taiwan or South Korea.[4] Even when moves for *rapprochement* with China were under way, President Nixon declared that over the next decade the United States must acquire a defence against China and *others* to make her foreign policy in the Pacific credible and secure against nuclear blackmail.[5] Now that the *rapprochement* with China has been effected, the " others " against whom a military posture is maintained is the Soviet Union.[6] The latter is acutely suspicious of Sino-American alignment and now views SEATO as being primarily an anti-Soviet pact. The United States has repeatedly emphasised that she would undertake all her commitments under SEATO and that United States interest in SEATO remains intact. In November 1973, SEATO decided to scrap its activities as a military deterrent since there is no "external threat" to the region and because of the "new situation of *détente* and relative peace in Southeast Asia," but, significantly, SEATO itself has not been abolished.[7]

United States military aid to Cambodia, Laos and South Vietnam is continuing and old commitments have been reaffirmed. The Thai government which was greatly worried about prospects of United States " withdrawal " has been assured to the contrary. In addition to South Vietnam, Thailand has been developed as a major United States base. The air base at Takli which was closed in 1970 was reopened in 1972 and two new squadrons of F-4 phantoms were stationed there. A new air base has been built in Nam Phong in the northeast as the first marine installation in Thailand. The number

---

[4] *New York Times*, August 23, 1970; Rogers' news conference in Tokyo, July 17, 1973, *Victoria Times*, Canada, July 17, 1973. Kissinger's visit to China, in November 1973, did not lead to any affirmation of United States intention to withdraw from Taiwan.

[5] *New York Times*, January 31, 1970.

[6] *Ibid.* April 22, 1971; *USSR and Third World*, April 26–June 1, 1971, vol. 1, Nr. 5, p. 221.

[7] *New York Times*, August 28, 1969, and July 2 and 3, 1970. Also Secretary Rogers' interview in Djakarta, June 30, 1972, on United States determination to " fulfil our obligations " in Asia. *Indonesian News and Views*, Indonesian Embassy [Washington D.C.], Nr. 8/72, July 15, 1972; *Seattle Post-Intelligencer*, November 27, 1973.

of B-52s has been doubled at Utapo from 40 to 80. Total United States plane strength in Thailand has risen from 450 to 750 planes, and the troops strength from 32,000 to 49,000, the same number as the United States troops strength in Thailand at the height of the Vietnam war under the Johnson Administration. In this " charade " of recreating a Vietnam in Thailand, the United States troops strength in Vietnam was " reduced " merely by transferring large sections of the Marine Air Wing from Da Nang to Thailand,[8] which is likely to remain a linchpin for continued United States military presence in Southeast Asia and possible renewal of military intervention in Indochina. Small-scale withdrawal of United States troops from Thailand has been halted since October 1973 when a civilian Thai government was installed.

The Philippine government claims to be reviewing the basic *raison d'être* of United States military bases in the contemporary context to examine whether they exist solely for mutual defence or whether they " perpetuate American participation in Philippine affairs and support American experiments in Asia." [9] But these seem to be merely ostentatious gestures. The Philippine government needs United States support to fight the growing insurgency; and to this day no threats to United States bases on Philippine territory would appear to be indicated.

Malaysia and Singapore, traditionally within the British military sphere of influence, have increasingly started looking to the United States for defence matters. The United States, for her part, has pledged full support in the event of an unprovoked aggression by enemies from without. Malaysia has warmly expressed gratitude that the Americans are prepared to " spread their umbrella for the security of the region." [10]

In Indonesia the United States has emerged as a military ally in fact if not in name. Ever since General Suharto's visit to Washington in May 1970, the " low profile " of the United States position has been abandoned in favour of open military co-operation. In fiscal year 1970, United States military aid to Indonesia was $5·8 million, including combat weapons. In fiscal year 1971, that aid amount was raised to $24·9 million. Since February 1972, following General Westmoreland's visit to Djakarta, military co-operation has been accelerated. Indonesia received $54 million in military aid for fiscal

---

[8] *Newsweek,* July 3, 1972, pp. 36 and 41.

[9] Speech by President Marcos, June 15, 1972, text supplied by the Philippine Embassy in Washington.

[10] Remarks by former Malaysian Prime Minister, Tengku Abdul Rahman, on the occasion of Vice-President Agnew's visit to Kuala Lumpur in January 1970, *Malaysian Digest* (Malaysian Embassy, Washington D.C.), January 14, 1970. See also *New York Times,* September 12, 1971.

year 1972, and this amount is to increase every year. Except for Australia's gift of sabre jets, the United States is the exclusive donor of military aid to Indonesia.[11] Indonesia's appointment on the new Vietnam Commission was not as a " neutral " nation, but as a United States ally.[12]

In the 1950s and 1960s, non-alignment meant opposition to the military presence of any foreign Power in the national and regional territory of the non-aligned nations. In the 1970s, at least in Southeast Asia, nations professing to be non-aligned want the United States to retain her military presence in the region. They even oppose North Vietnam's demand for United States withdrawal from South Vietnam and for unification of Vietnam. In fact, their foreign policy posture is predicated on continued divison of Vietnam.[13]

United States economic expansion in Southeast Asia is equally impressive. In the 1950s and 1960s, United States private investment was suspect in the eyes of non-aligned countries like Burma, Cambodia and Indonesia which took strict measures to curb it. Now, except for North Vietnam, all Southeast Asian countries welcome United States private investment which today exceeds $3 billion.[14] Thus, far from withdrawing from Southeast Asia or even losing its political influence, the United States remains by far the strongest and most deeply entrenched Power, enjoying high prestige and friendly relations with all Southeast Asian countries except North Vietnam. As such, it is likely to remain the single most dominant actor in the new configurations in Southeast Asia.

As a result of Sino-American *rapprochement* and the announced United States objective " not to deny China a growing role in Asia but to encourage it to be constructive rather than destructive," and in the light of softening attitudes of several Southeast Asian countries, China is expected to figure with increasing prominence in the new power alignments in Southeast Asia, in partnership with the United States and in congruence with her objectives. China has

---

[11] *New York Times*, July 13, 1971. Moscow Radio, March 25, 1972, charged that United States military bases are being built on Indonesia in Kalimantan and on Lombok Island, near Surabaya City in East Java. On Morotai and Biak islands radio tele-communications centres are being set up. A huge naval base is to be built on Bali. *USSR and Third World*, Vol. II, Nr. 3, February 14–March 12, 1972, p. 146.

[12] In a visit to Indonesia in 1972, Secretary of State Rogers stressed the importance attached by President Nixon to United States relations with Indonesia. *Indonesia News and Views*, Nr. 8/72, July 15, 1972.

[13] *The Mirror*, Government of Singapore publication, March 20, 1972; *Newsweek*, September 27, 1971, p. 53; *Malaysian Digest*, December 30, 1970 and February 28, 1971; *New York Times*, July 18, 1971.

[14] See below, note 33. United States investment in South Vietnam and Cambodia in industrial plants and in extractive industries is expanding steadily: *U.S. News and World Report*, November 1, 1971, pp. 71–72; also 53 *Survey of Current Business*, September 1973, Nr. 9, United States Department of Commerce, p. 26.

sharply reduced whatever little support she gave to local insurgent movements and has even withdrawn her military support for the communist and left-wing elements in Indochina.[15] Since 1971 China has not attacked SEATO, which, too, is no longer directed against China. United States " imperialism " is perfunctorily denounced, but a fight against it is not included in China's revolutionary tasks.[16] The *Peking Review* is no longer carrying attacks on United States imperialism in Indochina. China is also not averse to economic co-operation with the United States in Southeast Asia. She has joined ECAFE and has expressed interest in joining the Mekong River Project which was created in 1953 largely under United States leadership.[17] The United States is a major donor and is closely allied with its members, Laos, Cambodia, Thailand and South Vietnam. Thus, as one observer has noted: " China has come full circle from being rabidly anti-American to being a supporter of American foreign policy goals. It is a turnabout that will in one way or another affect the immediate political fortunes of Asia." [18]

China is not likely to remain content to be a partner of the United States and has already initiated a renewed form of the old Bandung diplomacy of friendship, solidarity and assurance towards Southeast Asian countries. But here China's approach is necessarily cautious, since she has to rebuild fences where they were broken in addition to building new ones. Above all, China must successfully convince Southeast Asian countries that she will not use Overseas Chinese as an instrument of her foreign policy. China has been trying assiduously to give such an assurance, but that might not be enough.[19]

It is, therefore, probable that China can play only that role which Southeast Asian countries are willing to assign to her and only to the extent that they wish. For China has none of the diplomatic, military and economic leverage in the region that the United States has. So far, many Southeast Asian countries have expressed preference for only trade relations with China. On the other hand, only Malaysia in Southeast Asia has rejected the idea of diplomatic

---

[15] " China reduces Support for Guerrillas in Southeast Asia," *Canberra Times,* July 7, 1973; text in *The Mirror,* July 30, 1973. A similar conclusion was drawn by M. Gurtov, *China and Southeast Asia: Politics of Survival* (1971).

[16] Editorial in *Renmin Ribao, Hongqi, Jiefangjun Bao,* text in *Peking Review,* Nr. 40, October 6, 1972, pp. 18–19.

[17] *The Asian Student* (published by Asia Foundation, San Francisco), October 28, 1972.

[18] Cheng Huan, " China Comes Full Circle," *Far Eastern Economic Review,* November 18, 1972.

[19] An Indonesian Chinese expressed his concern: " Even if future Chinese diplomats altogether ignore the Chinese communities in the region and pay attention to the indigenous peoples only—even that could create friction." " The Thaw Gathers Pace," *The Financial Times,* May 26, 1973. Also " Chinese Citizens—Vital Issue in China-Malaysia links," *ibid.* October 3, 1973.

relations with China. Moreover, Southeast Asian countries want China to be one of the guarantors of the plan for the neutralisation of Southeast Asia. This is one side of the coin. The other side is what China intends to do. Although a major Power, China cannot just pick and choose. Depending on the response of Southeast Asian governments, China is likely to make a selective rather than across-the-board approach. She may concentrate her benevolent diplomacy on some warmly reciprocative countries like Malaysia and Burma to heighten the sense of isolation of others like Thailand and the Philippines. This selective diplomacy might be effective against small nations but is not likely to be against Indonesia, the largest nation in the region and one that is getting considerable aid from Japan, the United States, the Soviet Union and Western European countries, not to mention United States military aid and Soviet offers of spare parts for military equipment and submarines given in the early 1960s. In such a case, China, not Indonesia, would be the loser.

Apart from bilateral approaches, China has already begun cautious and modest collective moves to obtain some leadership role in Asia including Southeast Asia. In May 1972, an Asian Table Tennis Union was inaugurated in Peking which Burma, Malaysia, and Singapore have joined, but not Indonesia, Thailand and the Philippines. China has sought to derive considerable propaganda gains by making this Union " a symbol of long-standing, close friendship between the Chinese and other Asian peoples and their common struggle." [20]

China is not likely to have a visible military presence in Southeast Asia for some time. In fact, she has withdrawn her military personnel from North Vietnam. But in a region so close to China, her military potential cannot be overlooked. China has already deployed missiles with a 2,500 mile range that bring Jakarta within range. It is expected to deploy a 3,500 mile missile very shortly and, by 1976, an intercontinental missile capable of delivering nuclear warheads nearly 7,000 miles, thus making Southeast Asia her military backyard. China is also fast developing a naval force with new longer range warships and submarines, intended as a counter to the Soviet naval presence in the Indian Ocean. [21] Thus, a Chinese naval presence in Southeast Asian waters may not be a distant event. China's swift seizure of the Paracel Islands and militant revival of its claims to Spratley and other islands arouses speculation that these might be used by China as a forward naval

---

[20] Peking Radio, May 5, 1972, and *Peking Daily* editorial, May 9, 1972, cited in *The Mirror*, May 22, 1972.

[21] *The Economist*, August 4, 1973; *U.S. News and World Report*, May 28, 1973.

base. The United States, it should be noted, refused to intervene against China in spite of South Vietnam's request. If the present trend in Sino-American friendship were to continue, this presence would be congruent with that of the United States.

China's growing presence in Southeast Asia must necessarily be at the cost of proportionate phasing out of Taiwan's relations with these countries. For China has never abandoned the triple principle (one China, represented by Peking, of which Taiwan is part). Several Southeast Asian countries have already started dissociating themselves from Taiwan. Even the Philippines, until 1971 a staunch ally, has initiated measures progressively to terminate its diplomatic relations. The United States is unlikely to try to reverse this trend. Already, two United States allies, Thailand and Australia, are proposing plans either to abolish Asian and Pacific Council (ASPAC), the largest regional political forum comprising countries in East and Southeast Asia, or to let it simply wither away. The latter proposal would involve upgrading the Ministerial Conference for Economic Development for Southeast Asia (MEDSEA) and transferring to it most of ASPAC's five practical projects. The move is designed to ease Taiwan out of East and Southeast Asian comity of nations, without actually expelling her, and to pave the way for China's collaboration with them.[22]

Since 1965 the Soviet Union has suffered heavy setbacks in Southeast Asia. The *coups* in Indonesia and Cambodia destroyed Soviet prestige and influence in addition to over $1 billion in Soviet bloc loans extended to Indonesia under Sukarno. During 1965–68, Indonesian and Soviet relations were only a little less aggravated than Sino-Indonesian ties.[23] In 1968, the Soviet Union expressed readiness to send spare parts for the military equipment supplied earlier and subsequently sent aid teams to Indonesia to discuss resumption of aid programmes.[24] But Indonesia has responded with scepticism. She opposes Soviet naval presence in the Asian waters and suspects that the Soviet Union views the Malacca Straits as the missing link in her chain of naval power stretching from the Pacific to the Indian Ocean, the Mediterranean and the Atlantic.[25] The Soviet Union is, thus, in the unenviable situation of having to plead with Indonesia to accept her aid and friendship—which the latter is reluctant to do.

Elsewhere in Southeast Asia, the Soviet Union has been making

[22] *Sydney Morning Herald*, September 18, 1973.

[23] Usha Mahajani, *Soviet and American Aid to Indonesia, 1949–1968*, Monograph nr. 14, Ohio University, Athens, 1970, pp. 36–37.

[24] *Antara News Service*, May 20, 1968; *New York Times*, August 25, 1971.

[25] *Chas*, an Indonesian Weekly, quoted in *The Mirror*, May 1, 1972; *New York Times*, August 13, 1972.

steady efforts to cultivate at least economic relations to recover her sagging diplomatic stature. Thailand and the Soviet Union signed their first Trade Agreement in December 1970 and have discussed joint ventures in mining.[26] The Soviet Union has promoted cordial relations with Malaysia, Singapore and the Philippines, and has fortified those with Burma with military assistance. She has applauded regional co-operation, but is unhappy about the position of some Southeast Asian countries on Indochina.[27]

On the whole, Soviet influence in Southeast Asia is virtually nil; Soviet pleas for an Asian Collective Security System sound like a broken record. Few Southeast Asian countries consider it seriously. Indonesia has rejected the scheme because it is " biased to one side " and excludes China, the United States, United Kingdom and France.[28] In the 1970s, therefore, the Soviet Union must limit her objectives in Southeast Asia to regaining some of the prestige she had in the previous two decades and not venture after a leadership role.

Japan will probably be impelled to retain her traditional low profile. She still has no diplomatic and military influence in Southeast Asian countries and they themselves are reluctant to assign to her a Great Power status. Indeed, they have been increasingly critical of Japan for not extending adequate aid for economic development. Indonesia has bluntly called on Japan to play down her military role, refrain from building a nuclear arsenal and then take the lead in developing Southeast Asian resources.[29] Japan has responded accordingly. Having developed a high stake in trade and investment in Southeast Asia, especially in Indonesia, she is actively participating in the Ministerial Conference for the Economic Development of Southeast Asia and has repeatedly pledged growing assistance on the terms acceptable to the local countries.[30] Japan is likely to count increasingly as an economic factor in the new configurations in Southeast Asia.

The United Kingdom's political stature and economic interests in Southeast Asia remain stable and secure, but her diplomatic leadership role has waned. The Sino-American *détente* has helped

---

[26] *Asian Recorder* [New Delhi], 1971, p. 10003; *Newsweek*, September 27, 1971, p. 50.

[27] *USSR and Third World*, vol. II, nr. 7, July 3–August 6, 1972, p. 367; *ibid.* vol. II, nr. 8, August 7–September 10, 1972, p. 426.

[28] Statement by Foreign Minister Adam Malik, quoted in *The Mirror*, September 10, 1973.

[29] Statement by A. Malik, *Straits Times* (Singapore), May 2, 1972; also *Malaysian Digest*, February 14 and 28, 1970, July 31 and August 14, 1970; February 28, 1971 and December 2, 1972; *The Mirror*, May 4, 1973 and August 20, 1973; and *The Times*, August 16, 1973.

[30] *The Straits Times*, October 13, 1973; *Japan Report* (Japanese Consulate in New York), vol. XVIII. Nr. 23, December 1, 1972.

" control " the Indochina conflict on the terms acceptable to China
and the United States, rendering the office of the Co-Chairmen of
the Geneva Conference virtually defunct. The United Kingdom's
military role is also being reduced. SEATO, where the British
military advisor served as Chief of Defence Staff since 1971, is
dismantling its military apparatus. The ANZUK (Australia, New
Zealand and United Kingdom force in Singapore) is jeopardised by
Australia's decision to withdraw at least 1,250 men, including all
combat elements, by February 1974 and additional 600 personnel
by April 1975. The United Kingdom contributes 2,000 men to
the total force of 4,500 but the Irish problem might force a reduction of that contingent. A future Labour Government might
effect total withdrawal. Thus, there may be no British servicemen
stationed in Singapore by the end of the decade.[31]

The United Kingdom does have an opportunity to exert diplomatic influence. She is the only country having friendly relations
with all other major Powers engaged in Southeast Asia, the United
States, Soviet Union, China and Japan, with no sharply conflictual
interests, whether military or economic. She has established friendship with the strongest regional Power, Indonesia, through aid and
investment.[32] The United Kingdom has no disputes with any regional
country. That over Sabah is strictly one between Malaysia and
the Philippines. The old-style military, " balance of power " politics
has no scope today. But the United Kingdom could become " a
diplomatic balancer " by assuming a more independent stance
vis-à-vis the United States than she has done so far.

India has retreated from Southeast Asia. The same developments
in Indochina that ended the United Kingdom's diplomatic role there
have terminated India's one-time dynamic influence in that region.
India has moved away from the United States, but the non-aligned
countries in Southeast Asia have drawn closer to her and welcome
her political, economic and military involvement in their region.
India, therefore, has no ideological ally in Southeast Asia nor seeks
one. She has fruitful ties with several great and major Powers and
prefers to exercise pre-eminence in her own subcontinent.

During the 1950s and 1960s, there was not a single Southeast
Asian association which was strictly regional in inspiration, member-
ship and co-operation. The Southeast Asia League, founded by the
Thai leader Pridi Phanomyong in September 1947, proved stillborn.
SEATO and ASA (Association of Southeast Asia, formed by

---

[31] " Changing British Attitudes," *Far Eastern Economic Review,* September 24,
1973.
[32] In July 1972, Foreign Minister Sir Alec Douglas Home held " very useful and
confidential " talks with Indonesian leaders who offered full guarantees for British
investments. *Indonesian News and Views,* Nr. 8/72, July 15, 1972.

Thailand, Malaya and the Philippines in 1960) proved unacceptable to Burma and Indonesia because of pro-United States orientation. MAPHILINDO, comprising Malaysia, the Philippines and Indonesia, was more an idea than an organisation. In 1967, under the lead of the Suharto government, a body, Association of Southeast Asian Nations (ASEAN), was formed, comprising Thailand, Malaysia, Singapore, Indonesia and the Philippines. Cambodia Laos and South Vietnam sent observers. ASEAN countries are anti-communist, welcome Western private investment [33] and closely co-operate with each other and the western Powers, notably the United States, the United Kingdom and Australia, who offer substantial military aid with or without a formal military alliance. Though pro-western and anti-communist in their foreign and domestic policies, collectively ASEAN members are resolved to shape their own destinies, oppose foreign interference and create a zone of Peace, Freedom and Neutrality in Southeast Asia.[34] No major Power can afford to ignore ASEAN in the pursuit of its diplomacy, although by dint of its economic and military orientation, ASEAN is an ally of the United States. At the same time, it is a hard-to-appease bloc for the rest of the big Powers.

CONCLUSIONS

This survey indicates that Southeast Asia is unlikely to remain free of external intervention and major Power conflict of interests. As in the global area, multipolarity will prevail in this region with the pre-eminence of the United States as the actor and a determinant factor. Sino-American competition has been replaced by tacit co-operation and congruence of interests. But two other distinct forms of rivalry and conflict have arisen. Japan and the United States are military and political allies in Southeast Asia, but the United States policy of the 1950s to restore Japanese economic interests in that region has made the erstwhile economic partners into arch rivals, each aggressively trying to push its own interests ahead. The United States forced Japan to revalue the Yen which improved the United States export position in Southeast Asia. Japan

---

[33] Several measures towards that end are described in *Malaysian Digest*, January 15, 1969, and February 15, 1969, and July 31, 1969; January 14, 1970, and November 14, 1970; and May 31, 1972. Thailand, Malaysia, Singapore and the Philippines have always welcomed foreign investment, to which Indonesia too has been most receptive since 1965. See Mahajani, *op. cit.* in note 23, pp. 34–40.

[34] ASEAN Joint Communiqué, November 27, 1971, *Malaysian Digest*, November 30, 1971. ASEAN co-operation is described in *ibid.* December 15, 1969; December 30, 1970; February 28, 1971; April 30, 1972; *Indonesian News and Views*, Nr. 3/68, March 1968, and Nr. 4/68, May 1968; *New York Times*, January 2, 1969 and August 14, 1969; March 8, 28 and 30, 1970; July 18, 1971 and January 13, 1972; *Japan Times*, April 15, 1973.

countered by establishing economic ties with North Vietnam in February 1972, to the acute displeasure of the United States.[35] This rivalry is likely to increase in the 1970s.

Of more serious proportion is the Sino-Soviet conflict which is being increasingly spilled over from South and East Asia into Southeast Asia. The Soviet Union has warned regional countries that Peking's role in ECAFE has merely " created new problems and obstacles to economic and social progress." [36] To counter China's nationalist appeal to overseas Chinese as a people, the Soviet Union is wooing the Chinese capitalist entrepreneurial class by denouncing the " British monopoly interests " for allegedly harming Chinese capital and keeping it out of several enterprises. The Chinese have ideological allies in the left-wing forces in Southeast Asia who have echoed China's denunciation of Soviet " social imperialism." [37]

In every respect, the Sino-Soviet conflict in Southeast Asia is likely to deepen into a Cold War style rivalry, but without involving the United States as deeply as before because China has, since October 1972, authoritatively pronounced the Soviet Union as her chief, in fact only, enemy: she has declared that her task is " to firmly oppose the policy of aggression and war of imperialism and social-imperialism, especially to expose the Soviet revisionist scheme of sham relaxation but real expansion." Much of the language, previously used against the United States, is now being directed against the Soviet Union.[38] Thus, Southeast Asia under the new configurations is still likely to remain an area of conflict and competition rather than peace and co-operation.

---

[35] *Christian Science Monitor*, February 17, 1972; *The Asian Student*, February 26, 1972; " New U.S. Edge on Japan Vital in Asian Markets," *Commerce Today*, May 15, 1972, p. 50; also United States Embassy reports from Burma, Thailand, Philippines, Malaysia, Singapore and Indonesia, issued from December 1971 to March 1972, circulated by United States Department of Commerce.

[36] Commentary in *Novosti Press*, quoted in *The Mirror*, July 2, 1973.

[37] *Ibid.* November 13, 1972; *USSR and Third World*, vol. II, Nr. 7, May 22, 1972–July 2, 1972, pp. 303, 305, 307, 308, 310, 313; *ibid.* July 3, 1972–August 6, 1972, pp. 426, 432–33, 437–38.

[38] *Peking Review*, Nr. 40, October 6, 1972, p. 19. Almost every issue of *Peking Review* since then carries an article or a quote from foreign journals on Soviet " imperialism " and attempts at hegemony in Asia.

NATURAL LAW
AND THE RENEWAL OF THE PHILOSOPHY
OF INTERNATIONAL RELATIONS

By

E. B. F. MIDGLEY

IN order to uphold the natural law as the true basis for the renewal
of political philosophy and the philosophy of international relations,
there are three tasks to be performed. First, it is necessary to survey
the diverse theories advanced over the centuries in the name of
natural law and to winnow the wheat from the chaff. Secondly, it
is desirable to show how it is that those modern doctrines of international relations which reject natural law are ultimately incoherent
or inconclusive *precisely because* natural law has been rejected.
Thirdly, it should be demonstrated how the authentic traditional
teaching on natural law is susceptible of homogeneous development
(and has, indeed, been so developed) to provide the fundamental
guide-lines for the discussion of those modern problems of international relations which are relatively new or even, in a sense,
unprecedented. I have undertaken the first of these three tasks—and
written something about the second and the third—in a lengthy
historico-critical study.[1] My purpose in this paper is not to summarise the main arguments of that study but rather to indicate
briefly how the modern debates on the theory of international
relations chronically fail to yield a synthesis because the necessary
philosophical foundation of natural law is lacking.

Fundamental theoretical discussion of international relations in
our own times (as in any other times) will commonly presuppose
philosophical or ideological positions which are adopted in other
spheres of intellectual activity. Even those writers who claim to be
adopting a so-called scientific approach to international relations
theory, will in practice find themselves presupposing something
which is philosophical or ideological unless they are content to
confine themselves largely to the statement of those facts which
are commonplace because they are not disputed.

Many writers on international relations theory would concede
that their thought presupposes (i) the rejection of the classical
philosophies of pagan antiquity (whether true or false), (ii) the
rejection of the Judaeo-Christian revelation (in all its interpretations

---

[1] E. B. F. Midgley, *The Natural Law Tradition and the Theory of International
Relations* (1975).

whether true or false), and (iii) the indiscriminate rejection of every tradition of natural law. (Even those writers who retain emasculated elements derived from one or more of these sources will commonly be influenced by the prevailing climate to such an extent that they will often write as though they accepted the modern scepticism.) This threefold rejection of the wisdom (together with many errors) of the past, has had an unhappy outcome. Since nature abhors a vacuum, modern scepticism has engendered a proliferation of mutually incompatible substitutes for true philosophy. Sometimes these substitutes may be designated as philosophical error insofar as some serious effort is still being made to discover philosophical truth even when that search does not meet with success. More commonly, perhaps, the serious search for philosophical truth is abandoned in favour of the adoption of some ideology or other which appears to suit, in some way, the short-term convenience of modern man in certain aspects of his life, including his socio-political life with its bearings upon international relations.

I—The Bearing of the Liberal Ideology and its Aftermath

One might single out David Hume as the philosopher who claimed to have shown the impossibility of any doctrine of natural law and who can certainly be said to have shown how the philosophical foundations of ideology (such as they are) were to be laid. Hume certainly demonstrated that his immediate predecessors (namely, the modern rationalist and voluntarist philosophers) had not sustained metaphysics as a philosophical science and that they had not offered any adequate basis for rational norms of human activity in any sphere. In effect, what Hume *really* succeeded in proving definitively was this: that once men abandoned the metaphysics of being and the Thomist doctrine of natural law, they could hardly avoid finding themselves driven along the road to scepticism. Then, as Martin pointed out, " if instead of rejecting the premises " (*i.e.* Hume's starting point in the decadent phase of the natural law tradition) " a person accepts the conclusions of Hume, thus denying all metaphysical truth, and then uses his reason as a slave of his feelings in order to construct a world in idea to satisfy some practical purpose, then that person becomes an ideologist and not a philosopher." [2] In the light of this analysis, it is appropriate to ask whether the various forms of the doctrine of liberalism, ought to be designated as philosophies or as ideologies.

Liberalism—especially in Britain and the United States—originally contained some emasculated elements of natural law and a

---

[2] W. O. Martin, *Metaphysics and Ideology* (1959), pp. 57–58.

certain orientation not uninfluenced by Christianity. Even in our own times, some of these vestigial elements remain especially in certain positions concerning human rights. Nevertheless, the attempted philosophical defence of a morality which claims to be true and of a rationality which claims to be right reason, has been, for long, largely abandoned by liberals. Accordingly, in most of its manifestations, liberalism ceased to be a philosophy. In most current expositions, it is merely one of the ideologies. Fortunately, it is true that men are often better than their ideologies would logically allow them to be. Certainly, in practice, the liberal ideology is, in most spheres, far less damaging to the common good than the totalitarian ideologies of the right or the left. However, in its more or less decadent forms, liberalism becomes an ideology of the subjective value-choice of the individual and the subjective value-choice of the State. The modern liberals have not succeeded, where their fathers had previously failed, in reconciling the more or less arbitrary norms postulated on behalf of the State with the more or less arbitrary norms attributed to the individual.

Moreover, if liberalism was, and is, ultimately untenable as a political philosophy of the State, it is, *mutatis mutandis*, untenable as a philosophy of international relations. In this field, as in the other, the substitution of ideology for philosophy has had its inexorable consequences. For the liberal ideologist cannot help finding himself in a position such that the science of international relations *without* ideology is blind whereas that science *with* ideology is perverse. There is thus envisaged a choice between a failure to solve the theoretical problems of international relations and a " success " which must concede that its " solutions " are without true intellectual foundations. Accordingly, the denial of right reason—with all its consequences—manifests itself today as it did in the Erastian ideology of Hobbes. Michael Howard will illustrate this when he advances his opposition to guerrilla warfare, not on the basis of the objective morality in this matter, but by means of a satirical gambit. He asks rhetorically: " How then does one deal with this, assuming that one is the kind of fascist beast who believes that the orderly structure of society ought to be preserved and that law is all the right reason we have? " [3] If we penetrate below the satire, we find Howard, like Hobbes, postulating an absurd world in which men are supposed to seek a necessary substitute for what is supposed never to have existed.

Similarly, we find in the post-liberal ideologies of communication, a doctrine of promiscuous communication whereby just any communication is an input which is allowed to play its role in the process

---

[3] *The Spectator*, June 17, 1972, pp. 932–933.

of generating an outcome. Such cybernetic systems are not non-ideological, as is sometimes claimed; it is rather that they imply an openness to indefinite ideological manipulation without regard to the norms of permanent truth or objective justice.[4]

Finally, it is instructive to observe that the neo-liberal system of Rawls is not only open to the criticism that its implications for international relations are indeterminate but also to the charge that this most secularised of liberal ideologies cannot help purporting, in the end, to achieve an intellectual objectivity which is foreign to its entire system. Indeed, Rawls indicts his own thought when he finds himself driven to re-define key words bearing upon human morality as terms of ideological art in his system. This process culminates in the incredible audacity with which Rawls goes so far as to suggest that his doctrine of the " original position " enables him to see the world *sub specie aeternitatis*.[5] So, as Pascal would say, there are men who have denied all the laws of God and nature and who are yet driven to invent an " eternal law " of their own which they seek rigorously to obey.

II—SUMMARISED ILLUSTRATIONS OF ANTINOMIES IN MODERN LEGAL AND POLITICAL THOUGHT ON INTERNATIONAL RELATIONS

Taparelli d'Azeglio, the 19th-century natural law theorist of national and international society, set forth one of the fundamental pre-requisites of legal and political thought in these terms: " There is no reign of law without unity of law; there is no unity of law without the unity of the doctrines which engender it." [6] In the present section of the paper, I shall not attempt to summarise the doctrines of the authors severally reviewed, but will merely extract certain philo-sophical or ideological elements which manifest characteristically the failure of these writers to meet the test prescribed by Taparelli.

(a) *Legal Rationality versus Extra-Legal Rationality in Sir Hersch Lauterpacht*

In an important article, Lauterpacht observed that, in the course of extensive discussions of various kinds of law, Grotius commonly failed to tell us what is *the* law governing a matter.[7] Lauterpacht's

---

    [4] See Midgley, *op. cit.* in note 1, chap. 10, for a discussion of J. W. Burton's general theory.

    [5] See J. Finnis's review of J. Rawls' major work in the *Oxford Magazine*, Vol. 90 (N.S.), January 26, 1973.

    [6] T. d'Azeglio: " L'Aristocrazia del Diritto," in XII *Civiltà Cattolica*, ser. II (1853–1855), p. 260.

    [7] " The Grotian Tradition in International Law," in XXIII *British Year Book of International Law* (1946), p. 5.

diagnosis of Grotius's failure to provide an adequate basis for the resolution of conflicts of laws is very significant. It points, in a rather general way, towards one of the basic philosophical deficiencies of the Protestant, Rationalist and Voluntarist tendencies in much modern natural law thinking from Grotius onwards. However, it is one thing to diagnose the symptoms of intellectual failure; it is quite another matter to understand the real nature of the failure and to find a remedy.

Certainly Lauterpacht himself failed to provide the philosophical synthesis which was lacking in Grotius. This fact is confirmed most strikingly in Lauterpacht's interesting paper entitled " The Limits of the Operation of the Law of War." [8] In this, Lauterpacht was certainly postulating a dual order of rationality: *legal* rationality in accord with positive international law and *extra-legal* rationality which is supposed to pertain to the necessity to preserve the political basis of the international legal order itself. Lauterpacht offers no philosophical basis for the reconciliation of these two orders of rationality. He simply leaves the reader with the crucial case in which there are alleged to be mutually contradictory duties both of which, each in its own order, constitutes a supposedly rational injunction.

(b) *Myres McDougal versus Juridical Positivism*

The policy orientation of McDougal's approach seems to have at least one point in common with natural law theory insofar as McDougal does not confine his legal thought to the mere fact of the enactment of the positive international law. McDougal seeks to overcome the dichotomy which is sometimes offered between a positivistic law, on the one hand, and the condonation of the random outcome of power politics, on the other. Rosalyn Higgins has rightly pointed out that the Yale School has not envisaged " law " and " politics " as hostile opposites and this fact could raise the expectation that McDougal and his disciples might be in a position to provide a harmonious synthesis. In borrowing from Scelle certain ideas about the reconciliation of the interest of the nation with the interest of the global community, McDougal develops an analysis which seems to approximately coincide, at certain points, with some of the themes of natural law thinking.

Unfortunately, it cannot be said that this partial coincidence points to a common philosophical foundation. Certainly, the juridical positivists are right to suspect that McDougal's broad juridical principles contain arbitrary elements. Moreover, they are correct in thinking that an insistence on such arbitrary elements—especially

8 See XXX *British Year Book of International Law* (1953), p. 243.

if it leads to the proliferation in various countries of diverse national preferences masquerading as law—must tend to bring the law into disrepute and must tend, therefore, towards the dissolution of positive international law. McDougal's doctrine seems to contain (whatever else it may contain) certain elements which ultimately belong to some kind of American ideology.

Nevertheless, in posing a positive legal order in whatever space is left unoccupied by the overriding operation of power politics, modern juridical positivism itself does not seem to have provided a sufficiently profound basis for the obligation of the positive law. A certain preoccupation with political realism seems to have led juridical positivism to adopt a dualism of legal and extra-legal operations for which no philosophical reconciliation is apparently available.

(c) *The "Classical" Ideology of Hedley Bull*

Bull has been associated with the plea for a classical approach to international relations.[9] The essence of this plea consisted in the argument that, at the centre of the subject, there have always traditionally been posed certain fundamental questions about morality and rationality in international relations which cannot be ignored by anyone who wishes to approach the subject with intellectual seriousness. Unfortunately, having made this point, Bull proceeded to suggest that the serious problems which occupy the very centre of the stage are, in fact, not susceptible of solution. Against this background, it could hardly be expected that Bull would be able to develop a coherent doctrine. In a more recent article, he postulated conflicting requirements of order and justice in international relations.[10] In doing this he is neglecting to follow the classical approach of such authorities as Vitoria who envisaged international relations in terms of a coherent hierarchy of common goods. In preference to this Vitorian approach Bull has chosen an international morality of contradictions which gives weight to—but is unable to resolve—the ideologies of the various actors on the international scene.

(d) *Neo-Machiavellian/Weberian Ideology in Raymond Aron*

Like Machiavelli and Max Weber, Aron explicitly postulates the heterogeneity of ethics.[11] It is not simply that Aron recognises

---

9 "International Theory: The Case for a Classical Approach," in XVIII *World Politics* (1966), pp. 361–377.
10 "Order versus Justice in International Society," in XIX *Political Studies* (1971), pp. 269–283.
11 See, for example, amongst many other references, "Qu'est-ce qu'une théorie des relations internationales?" in XVII *Revue Française de Science Politique* (1967), pp. 837–861.

the actual manifestation of a variety of ethical codes, legal codes, philosophies, religions and ideologies which are frequently incompatible with each other. Aron supposes that each one of us is tragically subject to ideological orientations and duties which are sometimes mutually contradictory. He seeks to deal with this inherently contradictory nature of human life by recourse to what he has chosen to call *praxeology*. He insists, however, that this praxeology is not based upon any truth which is philosophically superior to the competing ideologies. At the same time he claims that praxeology can achieve a " comprehension " of these ideologies and determine, in effect, the real bearing of each one. What is evident in all this is that Aron is attempting to have it both ways. He adheres to philosophical scepticism but he is unwilling to pay the price of scepticism. We shall return to draw the lesson which can be derived from Aron's unstable synthesis in our Concluding Remark.

(e) " *Christian/Machiavellian* " *Ideology in Reinhold Niebuhr*

Niebuhr's work reveals a sustained interest in the moral anxieties of the Protestant conscience. Niebuhr finds himself discussing moral claims made in the name of Christianity which are rejected in the name of realism. The paradox of Niebuhr's thought is simply this. He propounds incompatible duties and can offer no philosophical basis for resolving the dilemmas which he generates.

III—IDEOLOGICAL FACTORS
IN FUNCTIONALIST INTEGRATION THEORY

Although the writings of the functionalists have not escaped ideological distortion, it does not follow that they will always fail to say anything of importance. To illustrate this point, one might consider the parallel case of the French institutionalists. Certainly, the French institutionalists are not collectively committed to any one philosophy or ideology. Of the series of methodological and philosophical positions adopted by Maurice Hauriou in the course of his intellectual development, none could properly be dubbed as Thomist, or even, in any proper sense, as natural law positions. Accordingly, by the same token that Thomist doctrine is correct, Hauriou's philosophy was incorrect. Nevertheless, Georges Renard was actually indebted to Hauriou, although, as Broderick has pointed out, Renard struck out on his own beyond Hauriou in seeking to set institutional thought within the perspective of Thomist philosophy.[12] Similarly, it ought to be conceded that the functionalists

---

[12] A. Broderick (ed.), *The French Institutionalists* (1970), pp. xiii–xxv.

have made valid contributions to the discussion of integration theory despite their basic philosophical deficiencies.[13]

Characteristically, functionalism tends to prefer a co-operation model as an alternative to a conflict model. Consequently, it should be admitted that functionalism represents some kind of reaction against the more usual applications in the international field of the ideologies of power politics and of liberal individualism. Nevertheless, functionalism commonly seems, in some sense, to presuppose power politics and liberal individualism in the very process of seeking to go beyond them and to transform them. Indeed, everyone must " presuppose " power politics and liberal individualism in the specific sense that one must concede that—as a matter of fact—they operate as forms of behaviour and as ideologies, whether one accepts them as legitimate and valid or not. The peculiar feature of functionalism is that it appears, in a sense to accept them as quite normal even when functionalism itself is set upon side-stepping their inconveniences and avoiding their negative features.

One might take as an illustration of this theme the common acceptance by the functionalists of the *definition* of " politics " advanced by the exponents of power politics. Usually, the functionalists and the teachers of power politics seem to accept that " politics " is inherently about conflict. The latter embrace it; the former seek to move away from the field of " politics," thus understood, into some other field. The functionalists, accordingly, may prefer to think of other things. For this reason, there is the great emphasis in the thought of the functionalists upon the role of the " expert " who is supposed to be apart from " politics." This seems to result in a certain dualism of " politics " and " administration " which the functionalists do not seem to know how to resolve philosophically. For the functionalist feels himself driven to go beyond what he has accepted as " politics " and yet he does not feel able to reject that " politics " which he desires, as it were, to circumvent. How is he going to deal with all this?

In the field of social psychology, functionalism would wish to base itself on no mere empirical study of the existing situation. After all, functionalists desire, very often, to change the situation. On the other hand, their doctrine is not based on a truly philosophical psychology which would provide some of the guide-lines for the valid development of man's social and political life. Indeed, the functionalists find themselves unable to discard the pragmatism

---

[13] My criticism is applicable to the modern writings surveyed in P. Taylor, " The Functionalist Approach to the Problem of International Order: A Defence," in XVI *Political Studies* (1968), pp. 393–410, and in R. J. Vincent, " The Functions of Functionalism in International Relations," in this *Year Book*, Vol. 27 (1973), pp. 332–344.

and social engineering of the liberals. The pragmatic element participates in the intellectual deficiencies of the philosophy of pragmatism itself, namely, that it is concerned with what " works " without first having an adequate understanding of those ends in terms of which even *efficiency* (properly understood) can alone be rightly assessed.

The arbitrariness of " social engineering " (as of much that passes for " learning " or " communication ") results from the fact that, in using this concept, the functionalist cannot properly distinguish between the true exigencies of the common good and the various processes of amoral social manipulation envisaged in the liberal and post-liberal ideologies. The functionalists share the inability of the liberals to attain to a coherent doctrine of the common good because they have no coherent philosophy of man and consequently no coherent doctrine of political authority. They do not exclude the possibility that there are basically counter-rational elements in human nature as such and, consequently, they do not exclude the possibility that political institutions are basically necessary because of this human irrationality. Accordingly, there can be no adequate philosophical justification of the legitimacy of political authority insofar as the end of political authority, namely, the common good in the true sense, is not formulated within the framework of functionalism.

On the other hand, there can be no doubt that there are certain orientations in functionalist integration theory which urgently demand, for their ultimate justification, precisely that doctrine of the common good which the functionalists fail to uphold. Indeed, the paradox of functionalism, as an unstable synthesis, is that it can live neither with nor without the authentic concept of the common good. It is a corollary that functionalism can live neither with nor without the authentic Thomist concept of social reality.

We shall understand all this more clearly if we observe that functionalism seems to presuppose what are taken to be commonly accepted generalised ends of society. Yet, there is an ambiguity here and it is necessary to plumb the depths of this alleged consensus about ends. The question immediately suggests itself: Are we dealing here with the traditional Western concept of consensus (which is not unrelated to wisdom) or are we dealing with the modern concept of consensus as merely majority opinion in an aggregate? In other words, as Courtney Murray once asked: " Do we hold these truths because they are true or are these truths true because we hold them? " [14] Unfortunately, modern functionalism does not

---

[14] J. C. Murray, *We Hold These Truths* (1960), chap. 4, and his article " Natural Law and the Public Consensus " in J. Cogley (ed.), *Natural Law and Modern Society* (1966), pp. 48–81.

consistently maintain the first of these two incompatible positions. Sometimes a minimum natural law is presupposed but this invariably proves insufficient to sustain a coherent doctrine. Despite its impulse to overcome some of the defects of post-Reformation individualism, functionalism finds itself succumbing to this same individualism in the functionalist's confusion about the acceptance of pluralism in modern national and international life. After all, it is one thing to say that the common good (which embraces both the order of society and the exigencies of the dignity of the human person) requires acceptance of the co-existence of diverse philosophies and ideologies. It by no means follows from such acceptance that we ought to be committed to some kind of dogmatic agnosticism about what human life, embracing social and political life (including international affairs) is all about.

When we consider the more philosophically sophisticated formulations of functionalist doctrine, we find a three-fold scheme of function, purpose and powers.[15] In actual human history, all three are in many ways misconceived and perverted, but this is precisely the reason why a philosophy is required in order to show how, properly understood, they can be harmonised. Certainly, powers ought to be ordered to the true and legitimate functions and purposes of man and his societies. Yet how are the social functions of healthy societies to be reconciled with the deliberate purposes of those who participate in good government? Certainly, we ought to affirm, with St. Thomas Aquinas, that the *basic* socio-political inclination in man, when it operates rightly, operates in accord with a standard of right appetite which the practical reason (when thinking truly) can formulate. The Thomist doctrine that the natural inclinations in man are coherent with the precepts of the natural law, is the only basis upon which harmony is possible. Unfortunately, the functionalists fail to perceive that this is so. Moreover, this failure is one of the principal reasons for the paradoxes which continually afflict their work.

With regard to the role of authority in international life, the functionalists have commonly followed the fluctuating movements of opinion about current possibilities of achievement of federal power structures in the actual situation. Yet such purported realism does not excuse the functionalists from an examination of the objective exigencies of a properly ordered international life. It is possible, after all, to discuss such exigencies in general terms without claiming to prophesy whether or not the requirements of a properly ordered international life will be actually achieved. This necessary task has been undertaken consistently not by the functionalists but

---

[15] See D. Emmet, *Function, Purpose and Powers* (1958).

by the Thomists who have based their thought not on the mood of the hour, but on the objective exigencies of the common good dynamically conceived, that is, upon a hierarchy of common goods not excluding the common good of the global society of societies.

IV—AGGRESSION AND THE BIOLOGICAL IDEOLOGIES

It has long been supposed by the exponents of a psycho-analysis which derives from Freud that there are irrational drives in man which prevent any fundamentally ordered and harmonious solution of the problems of human conflict. Freud himself was committed to a position from which he was driven to call the human child a polymorphous pervert. Consequently, the Freudian ideology regarded the " normal " in human activity as a sub-class (as it were) of the " abnormal." Accordingly, whatever mitigation of the human condition Freud might have postulated in terms of his doctrine of sublimation, it is quite evident that his underlying ideology is subversive of any doctrine of the inherent unity of human nature and of the possibility of properly rational human activity.

More recently, the general ideological trend arising from Freudian psycho-analysis has received support from certain theorists concerned with the study of intra-species conflict, in animals and in man.[16] It is true that one of these theorists, Lorenz, appears to have begun some of his studies by way of a certain criticism of Freud. Nevertheless, there appears in some of his work on aggression—and notably in the theses of R. Ardrey—a series of axioms being developed which, if true, would be subversive of the very idea of the unity of human nature and of the possibility of truly rational human activity. These axioms of Ardrey and others are also in the broad tradition of those—including Machiavelli, Hobbes and Rousseau (to whose memory Ardrey dedicates a recent book)— who deny the applicability of right reason in political and international life.

In the debate between Ardrey and his opponents (effectively organised in a symposium edited by A. Montagu),[17] most of the writers claim in a general way to be proceeding on scientific lines by appealing to the results of the special sciences of animal and human behaviour. It is interesting to note, however, that each side tends to accuse the other of importing into the debate certain philosophical or ideological elements which each, in turn, tends to deny that he is using. When one looks at the debate objectively, however, it does appear that there are contenders on both sides

---

[16] See R. Ardrey, *African Genesis* (1961), *The Territorial Imperative* (1967), and *The Social Contract* (1970); and K. Lorenz, *On Aggression* (1966).
[17] A. Montagu (ed.), *Man and Aggression*, 2nd ed. (1973).

of the controversy who suffer from a certain failure to grasp what the controversy is about. Clearly, there are philosophical, as well as purely scientific, points at issue. The task is not to exclude philosophy as such but to exclude ideology and philosophical error. The failure to adequately recognise this point is no doubt one of the reasons why some of the contenders have employed erroneous ideology without fully appreciating what they are doing.

In order to understand correctly the ideological factors which are present in the debate, it is necessary first to observe that the positions of both Ardrey and Montagu are incompatible with the doctrine of natural law and that they are also incompatible with orthodox Christian doctrine. This is immediately evident in the case of Ardrey's theory of aggression. Although St. Thomas Aquinas envisages legitimate self-defence and a right of just war by legitimate authority, he denies that there is any right to undertake unjust violence or unjust war. In his general philosophy of human nature, St. Thomas taught firmly that no truly natural human inclination can itself be inherently ordered to evil. It seems evident enough that Ardrey would not accept the teaching of St. Thomas on these important points. Incidentally, it is sufficiently obvious that Ardrey's concept of aggression has nothing to do with the Christian concept of original sin. Ardrey holds not that human nature is merely wounded or weakened by original sin but that there is, inherent in human nature, a natural instinct of aggression which is subversive of ordered socio-political life. In the perspective of Christianity, Ardrey's doctrine constitutes, in effect, an implicit censure of God as the Author of human nature.

Accordingly, it is puzzling, at first sight, to find that Montagu is concerned to undertake a joint attack upon Ardrey and upon the Christian doctrine of original sin. Perhaps part of the explanation lies in the fact that whilst Ardrey might be supposed to follow in a tradition of " Social Darwinism," Montagu is anxious to show that he is as worthy a successor of Darwin as anyone, not merely by upholding a theory of evolution but also by sharing Darwin's ideological opposition to Christianity. This ideological orientation manifests itself in the very title of Montagu's article and, *inter alia*, in his discussion of a lengthy passage from St. Paul's Epistle to the Romans which he quotes. Montagu suggests that Ardrey and Lorenz stand in some sort of apostolic succession to certain believers, including especially St. Paul. It is difficult to grasp what Montagu is asserting here until we arrive at a passage in which he writes pejoratively of Jansenism. He does not actually assert that St. Paul was a Jansenist but the general thrust of the attack certainly gives the impression that Montagu supposes that there is a marked intellectual solidarity between the Pauline and the Jansenist doctrines of original sin. Since Montagu does not explain precisely where he stands on this matter, one can only respond by drawing attention to the traditional Christian teaching on original sin (including, *inter alia*, the interpretation of St. Paul), which is to be found in documents such as the Acts of the Second Council of Orange, the condemnations of the opinions of Baius by St. Pius V and his successors and in the Acts of the Council of Trent. Certainly, in these documents, there is no suggestion that it is compatible with Christian teaching to imagine that human nature is fundamentally put out of order by original sin. Indeed, that supposition was explicitly rejected by the Council of Trent. The thesis of Montagu—if it is to be thought applicable at all—is applicable (and only in a limited sense) to certain kinds of Protestant theological opinion which suggest that original sin gives rise to " total depravity."

Certainly, one must deprecate Ardrey's journalistic use of the expression " The Children of Cain " as a chapter heading in one of his books. It is not reassuring, however, to find that, although one of Ardrey's critics suggests that this reference to Cain is a misapplied cliché, Montagu himself proves to be no less journalistic than Ardrey whenever he touches upon matters of theology. Moreover, if Montagu's ideological excursions into theology are unsatisfactory, as I have shown, we can have no confidence that his philosophical presuppositions will be found to be in any better case. It is true that Ardrey's critics are on solid ground in rejecting—partly in terms of the empirical science of human behaviour—the thesis of Ardrey that the evidence points to the conclusion that man bears a nature which is inherently divided. Unfortunately, the majority of these critics seem to respond—at the philosophical level—by seeking to promote a view of man as having a nature which has no really specific teleological character. They replace Ardrey's ideological model of a basically disordered nature not with a true doctrine about man's basically ordered nature but with an alternative ideological model of a " nature " which is more or less indefinitely plastic, not only in fact, but even in principle.

Although the opponents of Ardrey's theses have shown that he has not been able to prove that there is an irrational aggressive instinct inherent in human nature, they have also commonly advanced an ideology about human nature which cannot be justified in science or in philosophy. In the course of denying that there is an aggressive instinct in man, some of Ardrey's opponents not only say that man is virtually " instinctless " but also suggest that his principal characteristic as man is to be widely open to polymorphous learning. Montagu says that man " has to learn his *human* nature from the human environment, from the culture that humanises him, and that therefore, given man's unique educability, human nature is what man learns to become as a human being." He goes on to say that the most important of man's genetic capacities is that for learning, educability, and concludes that " Man is capable of learning virtually anything." [18]

In a less extreme fashion, Eisenberg seeks to advance a similarly minimalist doctrine of human nature in terms of a discussion of the diversity of human cultures.[19] D. Pilbeam says of human behaviour, that " The appropriate or correct behaviour varies from culture to culture; exactly which one is appropriate is arbitrary." [20] In a revealing annotation in his bibliography, Omer C. Stewart suggests that " Anthropologists should return frequently to teach the concept that culture is entirely invented by man and is transmitted by learning." [21]

What is the ideological element which is obtruding itself in various forms in the quotations which I have just given? Some of the authors themselves might say that nothing is obtruding because they are merely reporting scientifically upon human cultural diversity—a diversity which, they might argue, can be confirmed empirically. But there is commonly something more. There is a tendency at least to minimise, if not to deny, the fact that there is a dividing line to be drawn between cultures which represent, on the one hand, the proper and legitimate cultivation of what is in man by nature and, on the other, the perverse, improper perversion of man's nature. They are minimising, if not denying, the distinction between that learning which is true learning in accord with man's nature and that " learning " which is possible but only at the cost of violating some basic good which is rooted in human nature itself. In seeking to refute Ardrey's thesis that irrational appetite is built into man, his opponents are commonly denying that there is any norm of right appetite. Without such a norm, they cannot really discuss what it might mean to say that man's appetite is inordinate or irrational.

V—HERMAN KAHN
AND IDEOLOGIES IN FUTUROLOGY

The philosophical deficiency of the thought of Kahn is exemplified in his use of the concept of " the rationality of irrationality " in nuclear strategy.[22] Recently, however, Kahn and Bruce-Briggs have

18 Montagu (ed.), *op. cit.* in note 17, p. 15.
19 *Ibid.* p. 63.
20 *Ibid.* p. 112.
21 *Ibid.* pp. 227–228.
22 See the analysis of this concept in Midgley, *op. cit.* in note 1, Chap. 12.

briefly developed a schema of possible ideologies for tomorrow.[23] They suggest that ideologies may be broadly classified in terms of two main types: the Augustinian and the Pelagian. They consider that the liberal tradition (including Marxism) is Pelagian whereas the Augustinians tend to be conservatives. They envisage here not a typology of philosophies and theologies (each of which claimed to be true), but a typology of (irrational) secular ideologies. Indeed, the authors explicitly state that neither of the two ideological types (as they have fabricated them) can prove its validity over against its opponent.

On might ask why Kahn and Bruce-Briggs did not choose to classify the ideologies with reference to a rather different theological typology, namely, the Thomists *versus* the Manicheans. The reason is perhaps not far to seek. The thought of St. Augustine (which, in philosophy, required the correction of St. Thomas) tends to be seen by American secular academics (through the distorting medium of their own culture) as a type of Protestant neo-orthodox theology of paradox (for example, Niebuhr), which is apt to be secularised as a, possibly conservative, ideology. If Kahn had considered the debate between Thomism and Manicheanism, it would not have been plausible (even in the modern Anglo-Saxon cultures) to " trans-value " this debate (in which Thomism is rather clearly the victor) into an intellectually inconclusive confrontation of ideologies. Since Marxism and most forms of liberalism can be said to have something in common with Manicheanism—at least, in whatever broad sense they have something in common with Pelagianism—the thought might have arisen that the liberal and Marxist ideologies (as well as the secularised " Augustinian " types of ideology), might all be shown to be erroneous. Accordingly, Kahn's schematisation exemplifies a general tendency of modern ideologists to utilise weak or unsatisfactory doctrines as the basis for a typology of subjective value-choices, instead of getting to grips with the authentic doctrine of natural law.

A Concluding Remark

Contemplating the competing ideologies on the modern international scene, Raymond Aron has concluded that there are antinomies inherent in human existence which no philosopher, ancient or modern, has ever been able to resolve.[24] One could reply that Aristotle and others, in pagan antiquity, did attempt to eliminate contradictions from their philosophies of human nature. It must be admitted, however, that these attempts were not wholly successful.

---

[23] H. Kahn and B. Bruce-Briggs, *Things to Come* (1972), Chap. XI.
[24] Aron, *op. cit.* in note 11, p. 860.

If it can be claimed that Aristotle laid the foundations for a perennial philosophy, he certainly was not able to perfect it. Again, in the modern world, we find countless philosophies which manifestly fail to achieve coherence and countless ideologies which do not even seek it. Nevertheless, Aron has exaggerated. For, among the mediaeval doctors, certainly, there is one, at least, who could claim, on good grounds, to have shown that although human life is mysterious, it is not absurd. Moreover, those who seek to conserve and to renew the tradition of the *Doctor Communis* not only remain; they remain undismayed (amid the proliferation of ideological magic on every side), waiting for the leaders and the teachers in our tormented and over-stimulated culture to resume the search for right reason.

Some years ago, I had the opportunity, in conversation with Aron, to suggest an approach to the modern ideological conflict of ideas which was utterly different from his own. I suggested that certain modern doctrines might sometimes at least refute each other. He responded immediately: " They are working for you? " I did not deny it. It is, after all, generally true to say that errors which refute each other may thereby serve unwittingly, in a certain measure, the cause of truth. My purpose in this paper has been to indicate how the modern world, which denies in so many ways the very existence of natural law, nevertheless betrays, in the midst of its antinomies, that it is natural law which alone can prescribe for that moral and intellectual malaise which the modern ideological doctors have vainly sought to cure with the panaceas of subjective value choice.

JUST WAR, THE NIXON DOCTRINE AND THE FUTURE SHAPE OF AMERICAN MILITARY POLICY

By

JAMES TURNER JOHNSON

DEFINITION and analysis of United States strategy and the policy underlying it appear at times to be yet another case of the old story of the blind men describing an elephant. A principal difference is that this particular " elephant " is not being described by men who are themselves " blind "; indeed, some extraordinary talent has been brought to this task in recent years. But one may suppose that the original three blind men were talented enough to perform adequately their respective tasks, for an elephant's trunk *is* like a snake, his body like a wall, and his leg like a tree trunk. These descriptions erred only in that none of the three blind men was able to grasp the whole; yet by putting together their various descriptions it is possible to get a reasonably accurate conception of what an elephant looks like and, moreover, what are the impressions conveyed by the experience of encountering him.

In the case of United States military strategy and underlying policy since the Second World War, one does not have to look far to find remarkably different appraisals. In his *Revolutionary War in World Strategy*, Sir Robert Thompson identifies the Truman Doctrine as stating a constant which consistently expresses itself in American strategy through the Eisenhower Administration, the years of Kennedy and Johnson, and into the Nixon presidency. Indeed, Thompson explicitly links the Truman Doctrine to the Nixon Doctrine enunciated in 1969; the latter is a reaffirmation of the former.[1] Thompson's analysis, of course, is directed to the specific case of revolutionary war, and he makes a good argument that so far as the United States has responded to Communist-inspired revolutionary activity over the last two and a half decades, that response falls within the scope of the policy announced by President Truman in 1947.[2] But since this analysis does not take account of the enormous differences between, for example, the massive retaliation strategy espoused by President Eisenhower and Secretary of State Dulles and the limited war strategy of the Kennedy Ad-

---

[1] Sir Robert Thompson, *Revolutionary War in World Strategy* (1970), pp. 162–163.
[2] For Thompson on the intent of the Truman Doctrine, see *ibid.* pp. 46–47.

137

ministration, it cannot be cited to prove that the whole of American military policy since the Second World War is somehow summed up in the Truman Doctrine.

The more broad-ranging and detailed analysis of the historian, Russell F. Weigley, in *The American Way of War* [3] does take such differences as those mentioned into account, as well as a great many more. Part Five of this book is a veritable compendium of strategies, both those urged by various military and civilian analysts and those actually adopted in successive administrations. But for Weigley there is a common undercurrent of policy which persists beneath American strategy during the 1950s, the 1960s, and into the 1970s: the policy of containment of Communist expansion. Weigley's opinion of the Nixon Doctrine, that it represents a look backwards to the strategy of deterrence of an earlier era, suggests that this policy too embodies containment in some fashion. [4]

Finally, to round out the circle of opinion, a number of writers have argued that American policy over the past 25 years has been so vague as to be no policy at all. On this view to speak of " containment " is to vocalise an abstraction; to argue for " stopping Communist aggression " is to adopt an ideological position as opposed to the further spread of Communism and not to enunciate a policy for effectively implementing that ideology. Even if " containment " is allowed as the name for a general national policy towards Communist countries, it has been insufficiently supported by more particular policies or statements of specific aims. Thus one of the most frequent criticisms of the United States presence in Vietnam was that American interests there were obscure and American aims announced in too general and vague terms. (It might have been added that United States strategy based on these interests and aims was too ill-formed and experimental to be effective as a base for war-making, but that is another matter.)

As a theological ethicist the present writer may only be grasping the leg or tail of this elephant, but my own position is closer to the last two mentioned above than to Thompson's. The United States has, as Weigley argues, adopted a number of strategic positions in the last 25 years, now facing the closing of the Iron Curtain, now fighting the Korean Police Action, now meeting the Cold War after Korea in the new circumstances of Soviet possession of atomic weapons, now responding to nuclear parity and the " missile gap," now fighting a counter-insurgency war in Southeast Asia which both was and was not a " limited war " in the Korean sense, and finally emerging from Vietnam to an era of increased communication

[3] R. F. Weigley, *The American Way of War* (1973).
[4] *Ibid.* pp. 468–469.

with the Soviet Union and China, no longer (if ever) a single " bloc " and enjoying rather testy relations with each other. Furthermore, as the Vietnam critics have argued, the various United States administrations concerned were singularly imprecise and poorly persuasive about American interests in Southeast Asia and American goals in South Vietnam in particular. All this suggests that definition of American military policy and strategy is a far more complex task than any simple, brief, or otherwise narrow-ranging analysis can encompass. It is not the purpose of this paper to attempt such a task.

If the moralist, whether theologically or philosophically trained, has anything whatever to say in this entire matter, it should not have to do directly with the definition of policy and of related strategy, but ought rather to focus on the moral content of the attitudes and interests which policy and strategy seek to embody and protect, and on the implications, morally construed, of particular policies and strategies. These twin concerns take this paper beyond the questions raised above as to how to define United States military policies and strategies in the period since the Second World War. It has been necessary, however, to venture into the edge of the briar patch of controversy over the nature of United States military policy and strategy to make clear the position from which this paper proceeds, and also to indicate that moral analysis of the entire matter, covering the past two decades and a half, is beyond reach here. I shall limit myself in this paper to moral analysis of the policy embodied in the Nixon Doctrine and of the strategy or strategies it implies. This will entail some looking backwards into recent and remote history, but the final concern throughout is this Doctrine. As an anchor for my analysis I shall employ the tradition of Christian just war thought, incorporated not only in Christian teachings but also importantly represented in the limits on war of modern international law. Finally, the point of such analysis is to suggest that some policies and strategies are morally preferable to others, and to place the Nixon Doctrine accordingly.

I—A Characteristic American Attitude towards War

Ralph B. Potter, an ethicist on the faculty of Harvard Divinity School, notes in his *War and Moral Discourse* a peculiar characteristic of the American people.[5] A generic pacifism, Potter observes, is clearly native to most Americans. As a people they do not like to go to war; they wish only to be left alone. (One might add that internationalism and the liaisons it implies have never had much grass-roots support in the United States. Washington's distrust of

---

[5] R. B. Potter, *War and Moral Discourse* (1969), pp. 58–61.

foreign entanglements and various forms of isolationism have been notable political expressions of the native desire to be left alone to which Potter refers.) But, Potter goes on, when war comes to the United States, the characteristic pacifist stance is transmuted almost instantaneously into that of the crusader, and the American is suddenly full of zeal for the right (his country's policies, as he understands them), and ready to carry the war home to the enemy as strenuously as possible. As Potter depicts it, the United States position appears to be curiously two-sided: as a nation Americans are pacifistic and yet crusaders, with no middle ground to be observed. How can this be? What does this analysis of the American character imply for the posture of the United States towards other nations, whether friendly or potential adversaries?

It should be noted that the " crusader " mentality which Potter associates with Americans at war has a strategic analogue. As Russell Weigley points out repeatedly, United States strategy has again and again throughout the history of the nation been a strategy of annihilation. Usually expressed in terms of elimination of the enemy's war-making power, this strategy has been used at different times to justify eradication of military forces and destruction of civilian morale; it was the basis of both the daylight air raids during the Second World War on German military production facilities and also the counter-city targeting of nuclear missiles which ex-pressed the strategy of massive retaliation.[6] The end of war as envisaged in a strategy of annihilation is quite different from that envisaged in a strategy of limited war; the former entails a notion of victory easily expressed as " unconditional surrender," while the latter implies a concept of victory as preventing the enemy from reaching his goals. By the standards of the former concept, this latter appears an unacceptable stalemate.

Now, so far as Potter and Weigley are, in their respective ways, correct about the kind of war-making for which Americans have a propensity, their observations suggest a considerable distance between American attitudes towards war and the attitudes expressed in the classic " just war " tradition. Just war doctrine, while it is not by any means identical with the United States limited war doctrine of the 1960s, is nevertheless a doctrine of limited war. Its fundamental rationale has three aspects: to prevent injustice from being done, to recompense victims of past injustice, and to punish perpetrators of injustice. All of these are inherently limited aims, and the traditional doctrine of the just war thus tends inevitably towards justifying only those wars which have something less than utter annihilation of the enemy as their goal. A prima facie argu-

---

[6] See Weigley, *op. cit.* in note 3 above; Chaps. 14–18, *passim.*

ment thus begins to emerge that characteristic United States attitudes towards war tend to produce policies and strategies at variance with the moral standards implied in the classic doctrine of the just war. That is to say, United States war doctrine, taken generally, stands outside the just war tradition.

But Robert W. Tucker, a political scientist teaching at the Johns Hopkins School of Advanced International Studies, has argued that the United States does indeed profess and adhere to a doctrine of just war. Tucker's book *The Just War* [7] defines this doctrine and its implications in some detail. Nevertheless, the doctrine which emerges under Tucker's scrutiny is not part of the classic just war tradition which has long been associated with Christian moral thought; rather it is one more version of the same phenomenon to which Potter and Weigley, in their different ways, are pointing. Since Tucker's treatment is more sustained than Potter's and more directed to the relation between attitudes (we might also at this point begin to say " moral orientation ") and policy than Weigley's, it deserves to be scrutinised here with some care. To do so will help move us beyond the prima facie case stated above for the non-relation of classic just war thought to American military policies and strategies.

Tucker's analysis in *The Just War* is intended primarily as a criticism of the massive retaliation doctrine of the Eisenhower-Dulles era, yet both by the intent of the author, and by implication, his arguments spill over into criticism of a more general American tendency to fight wars only in an all-out manner—the tendency already identified with the help of Potter and Weigley. But Tucker connects this tendency specifically with two more particular characteristics of the foreign policy of the Eisenhower Administration: ambiguity in policy formulation coupled with a high moral tone avowing that this nation's interests will always be that which is ultimately and essentially right. Neither of these latter characteristics, it should be noted, has been a monopoly of the Eisenhower presidency, though Tucker is correct that they are peculiarly obvious in the Eisenhower-Dulles policy era.

Tucker argues that two assumptions lay beneath the framing of United States policy in this Administration: first, that America has no goals different from those of humanity at large, and, second, that the United States will never begin a war. The first assumption is inherently utopian, for it denies the existence of specific national interests or goals which might conflict with those of the world at large, and moreover it defines the goals of humankind in the abstract terms of ideals " to be striven after though perhaps never attained in reality." [8] These ideals are presented only in the most general

---

[7] R. W. Tucker, *The Just War* (1960).   [8] *Ibid.* p. 23.

ways, as embodied in " co-operation," " consent " and " equality,"
and their more specific elaboration is resisted. Such is political
utopianism.

If the first of the assumptions identified by Tucker is accepted,
then a dilemma is posed. On the one hand, it means that the
United States calculations as to the amount of force it must exert
must *necessarily* be moral, in the sense that such force is always in
accord with the general good of mankind. But on the other hand,
these calculations can *never* be moral, for they admit no limits (such
as proportionality of evil done to good produced), since the good
of humankind is always indeterminate and unquantifiable. Indeed,
however, in United States policy this dilemma is resolved in favour
of admitting in principle the unlimited use of force in service of
the good of all mankind, an infinitely desirable end. The ground is
thus prepared, in principle, for the use of all force of which the
nation is capable.

If the second assumption identified by Tucker is accepted, an
equally serious conclusion follows. If the United States is to be
defined as, *per se*, a State which will never begin a war (" aggress "),
then any nation against which it fights is by definition a criminal
aggressor, not only towards the United States but also (by the
first assumption) against the rights of mankind at large. It must
be punished severely and the means of future aggression removed
from its grasp. Such a posture leads inexorably towards all-out,
no-holds-barred prosecution of war right up to the moment of
unconditional surrender.[9]

Tucker takes John Foster Dulles as the primary apologist of the
position he is describing, pointing to Dulles' identification of United
States goals with, not only the goals of the United Nations, but
also the end of moral rightness itself.[10] Other nations which would
instigate war (since the United States would never do so) are, in
Dulles' words, not just political and military adversaries but " moral
idiots." [11] Dulles' position is, according to Tucker, that the truth
is ours, and it has set us free—to fight wars, but only in defence

---

[9] I have elsewhere argued that the twentieth-century attempts to restore a *jus
ad bellum* to international law (something which had all but disappeared by the
end of the nineteenth century) have focused too narrowly on the aggressor-
defender concept and more particularly on the distinction between first and second
use of military force. [See " Ideology and the *Jus ad Bellum*," 41 *Journal of the
American Academy of Religion*, Nr. 2 (June 1973), pp. 212–228; and "Toward
Reconstructing the *Jus ad Bellum*," 57 *The Monist*, Nr. 4 (October 1973).] The
second assumption identified by Tucker is but the integration into the Eisenhower-
Dulles policy of the aggressor-defender *jus ad bellum* doctrine. Taken with the
first assumption, this position on the *jus ad bellum* leads to disintegration of all
in bello limitations. The strategy of massive retaliation is but the logical next step.
[10] Tucker, *op. cit.* in note 7 above; pp. 19–35.
[11] *Ibid.* p. 26.

of right against those who would practise aggression. This extreme reliance on a high moral standard of rectitude, coupled with the identification of United States interests with that standard, leads inexorably to a vision of the American military as soldiers of the right, always ready to serve in a holy crusade against those who by definition are aggressors against mankind. Tucker comments further:

" An extreme reluctance to resort to war has not implied restraint in the manner of employing force once war has been thrust upon us. This lack of restraint that we have shown in conducting war— and the lack of restraint with which we have threatened to conduct war should it once again be imposed upon us—has commonly been attributed to the indignation we feel towards the ' aggressor ' who initially resorted to armed force." [Tucker cites the explanation given by President Truman for the atomic bombing of Hiroshima.] " Nevertheless, the explanation of our behaviour by reference to its retributive motives does not resolve the moral ambiguities of that behaviour. Still less does it show how that behaviour can be reconciled with an allegedly profound moral aversion to the methods of violence." [12]

Thus Tucker comes round to a statement of the issue in terms which recall Potter's: as a nation, Americans are averse to war, but, nevertheless, we have a history of embracing its violence to the hilt whenever war comes. Tucker is correct that such behaviour poses a problem of consistency. But such inconsistency as this has been overlooked on numerous occasions in history by those who have transformed the idea of just warfare by assimilating its concepts to that of absolute national right, creating thereby a doctrine of national-henotheistic holy war. And herein lies the real problem for humanity: if such war is fought, how can humanity fail to be worse off?

One must ask again: is there in the American character indeed an all-or-nothing attitude towards war? So far as the policy and strategy of the Eisenhower-Dulles years are concerned, Tucker's tar and feathers would be extremely hard to remove. Massive retaliation in this case is but a clue to a much more profound and wide-ranging doctrine of war, largely enunciated by Dulles, and painstakingly delineated by Tucker. But sole reliance on the strategy of massive retaliation has not been American military policy since the beginning of the Kennedy Administration, though ironically the nuclear capacity of the United States now far surpasses that of the Eisenhower years. Still, the doctrine of massive retaliation is only a clue to a deeper syndrome, and other clues persist also. The enormous

---

[12] *Ibid.* pp. 21–22.

build-up of American troop strength in Vietnam under Lyndon Johnson, the pursuit of a military victory there throughout Johnson's presidency and into that of Richard Nixon, bombing raids on North Vietnam aimed at "warning" Hanoi of what would happen if attempts were made to escalate the war—these too are clues which point to the underlying United States attitude towards war, one which has not changed substantially since the Eisenhower presidency. Indeed, we need not stop with these examples. I shall argue below that the Nixon Doctrine also expresses this attitude. Moreover, Tucker suggests that Dulles must be regarded as merely giving precision and explicitness to a doctrine which is present in the United States attitude towards war long before him, certainly in the two world wars. As I have earlier noted, the traditional United States reliance on a strategy of annihilation, as identified by Russell Weigley, argues the same point.

Thus we are left with a number of questions. Granted that there is an all-or-nothing attitude towards war present among Americans as a kind of national characteristic, how can such a pairing of the pacifist and crusader themes persist? What, if any, relation can the concept of justified war contained in classic just war doctrine have to this attitude? And what does the existence of such an attitude imply for the military posture of the United States in coming years?

II—A HISTORICAL ANALOGUE: HOLY WAR DOCTRINE IN POST-REFORMATION ENGLAND

As a people Americans do not participate directly in the great medieval cultural tradition which produced just war doctrine in its classic form. Rather the intellectual roots of the American attitude towards war are to be found in the history of sixteenth- and seventeenth-century Europe, when the hoary just war doctrine broke down under the twin pressures of a profound split in the religious unity of Christendom and the emerging self-consciousness of nation States. To understand the crusading character of the United States attitude towards war we should not look to the medieval crusades, then, but rather to the crusades of Catholics and Protestants against each other in western Europe during the post-Reformation era. More specifically, I suggest that the intellectual heritage of the American people derives from a particular metamorphosis in classic just war doctrine that allowed the fighting of ideological wars of religion against non-co-religionists.[13]

This metamorphosis is nowhere found more clearly than in the writings of certain English Puritan figures on war. Here are present

---

[13] For fuller discussion of this point, see this writer, *Ideology, Reason, and the Limitation of War* (1975), Chap. II.

already the most prominent elements of the American attitude towards war to which Tucker and Potter refer; here also is avowal of a strategy of annihilation, even to the advocacy, in one case, of the utter destruction of all the enemy (who are, after all, seen as utterly in the wrong).

In the post-Reformation English holy war doctrine the provisions of classic just war doctrine are abandoned or modified. In the first place, the Puritan theorists are not concerned with justice conceived as a result of balancing the differing interests of nations. One of the criteria of the traditional just war doctrine is thereby abandoned. Secondly, the English holy war theorists have no interest in that justice which requires that war be fought only if the good to be secured outweighs the evil which war will produce; the traditional criterion of proportionality is replaced by the certainty of one's own righteousness and the enemy's unrighteousness. Thirdly, these writers hold only tenuously to the stipulation in the classic doctrine that all wars be fought only at the direction of legitimate authority. For them legitimate authority has always to be defined in terms of clear commission by God; it does not reside inherently in the office of prince or magistrate, who may be deposed by the righteous if he acts contrary to God's will. To such stalwarts of God as these, the term " legitimate authority " means ultimately that authority which God wields in their consciences through His Word, and all earthly authority must submit itself to that. We now need briefly to examine these claims more particularly as they are advanced by various writers.

For William Gouge, a celebrated Puritan preacher and author of voluminous works on numerous aspects of theology, the most just of all wars have been those " extraordinarily made by expresse charge from God." [14] He goes on to accept as just also all defensive wars and offensive wars waged for " maintenance of Truth, and purity of Religion." [15] The soldier who fights for any of these causes should not fear death on the battlefield, for he is fighting for God himself. " For a souldier to die in the field in a good cause, it is as for a preacher to die in a pulpit." [16] Even though Christians are normally men of peace, when they are fighting for the good they must not hold back in any way. " By slaughter of enemies, the land against which they are enemies hath rest, and security; as towns and high waies are safe and quiet by executing theives." [17] Gouge justifies this version of a strategy of annihilation yet further: " It

---

[14] W. Gouge, *Gods Three Arrowes* (1631), p. 215.
[15] *Ibid.*
[16] *Ibid.* p. 218.
[17] *Ibid.* p. 293.

is indeed a matter of pity, and ought to move our bowels of compassion that people should be so wicked and desperate, as to give occasion to have their bloud shed; but, the occasion being given, pity must be laid aside. God himself in such cases casteth off pity." [18] When the good are attacked, the attackers deserve to be the objects of the fiercest retaliation possible: this could well be no seventeenth-century Puritan speaking but an American apologetic for the massacre of the Sioux at Wounded Knee, the fire-bombing of Tokyo or the atomic bombing of Hiroshima and Nagasaki, or the strategy of massive retaliation itself.

Christians are men of peace who do not seek out wars, but when forced into them by the obstinate wickedness of others, they leave off their meekness, humility and pity and fight for the highest justice of all: the total eradication of wickedness. Thus, another Puritan writer, Thomas Barnes, cites Jeremiah xxxviii, 10, as warrant for just wars: "Cursed be he that keepeth backe his sword from bloud." "Jeremiah is not ignorant that peace is a better, yea a blesseder thing than war," Barnes continues. "But it seemes, he knew withall that a lawfull warre is to be preferred before an unlawfull peace." [19] As does Gouge, Barnes defines just or lawful war as having chiefly to do with matters of sinfulness versus righteousness.[20] This distinction has for them replaced the *jus ad bellum* of classic just war doctrine, whose justifications were couched in terms of men's transgressions against the rights and property of other men, not trespasses against the will of God.

The same point about the justification of war is advanced with great vigour by the Scottish Calvanist firebrand Alexander Leighton. Leighton has short shrift for the notion that war is simply an instrument of statecraft. Damning this idea with the epithet "Machiavellian," he insists to the contrary that the presence of God on one's own side is the most necessary element in any war. Without God clearly with you, you must refrain from going to war.[21] When secularised, this concept becomes precisely that of United States war doctrine: fight for the right, but for no other reason. When protection of national interest is impossible except when that interest expresses the right, it becomes necessary to define the right so that it is always in accord with the national interest—one charge Tucker explicitly makes against Dulles. But to return to Leighton, he takes no stock in the just war doctrine's limits on cruelty in war (its provisions on *jus in bello* by this time included both non-combatant

[18] *Ibid.* p. 295.
[19] T. Barnes, *Vox Belli, or, An Alarm to Warre* (1626), pp. 1–2.
[20] *Ibid.* pp. 29–30.
[21] A. Leighton, *Speculum Belli sacri: or the Looking-glasse of the Holy War* (1624), p. 45.

immunity and some limits on the amount of destruction to be admitted on land, buildings, and other property). For Leighton, once a war is begun, it must be fought with no quarter. Any limitation of one's own force advantages the enemy and hurts one's own side. To limit force in prosecution of war thus disadvantages the cause of righteousness and helps the forces of evil.[22] To proceed a bit further, Leighton's conception of the purpose of war is so abstract when viewed from a political or an historical perspective that it allows no calculation to be made as to the relative worth of alternative means to achieve desired ends. Since the end of war is for him nothing less than utter righteousness (or at least the eradication of sinfulness, which amounts to the same thing), every possible means must be used to achieve it. When an infinite end is sought, choice among finite means is unwarranted quibbling; *all* available means must be used. Leighton would probably also regard as quibbling the attempt to point out the impossibility of attaining an infinite good by use of even all possible finite means. What he and other writers of the same conviction, such as Gouge and Barnes, are arguing is, finally, the case for bringing the Kingdom of God to reality in history. Though they conceived the problem in terms of the conflict between Catholic Spain and righteous Protestant England, their arguments are much more generally applicable than this. In their writings these men, together with others elsewhere, have substantially discarded the just war doctrine as proclaimed throughout Christendom from the 13th to the 16th century, and replaced it with a doctrine of holy war. Yet they call their doctrine " just war."

Though this is no place to argue this point in detail, the intellectual ancestry of the United States attitude towards war is in this post-Reformation conception of war to be fought only in the cause of righteousness. The American doctrine of " just war " identified by Tucker does not spring into being with the appointment of John Foster Dulles as Secretary of State in the Eisenhower Administration; it has been nurtured throughout the long history of that self-conception by which Americans saw themselves as children of righteousness called to create God's Kingdom in their nation and so bring light to a darkling world. With the increased secularisation of the " Kingdom of God " ideal the cause of God has increasingly given way to the cause of the nation; it is this intellectual preparation which makes it possible for a Dulles to speak in tones of such high morality, and, more generally, it is this heritage which makes it extremely difficult for the United States today to move away from policies and strategies of total victory and absolute annihilation of the enemy to others which allow for more limited prosecution

---

[22] *Ibid.* pp. 50–51.

of war—though this latter would be closer to the standards contained in the classic Christian just war doctrine.

III—The Case of the Nixon Doctrine

If it had not already been explicitly indicated, the drift of this paper thus far would be enough to suggest that this writer is convinced that the Nixon Doctrine partakes importantly of the general United States attitude towards war discussed above. But the matter is complex, and it is not my intention to argue that the Nixon doctrine *necessarily* bodes ill for the future course of United States military policy and strategy. Though Richard M. Nixon was Vice-President in the administration which made the American " all-or-nothing " attitude into an official ideology and even transformed it into strategy, Nixon's policy has been shaped by Henry Kissinger, not John Foster Dulles—a fact which alone should give pause to those who would see in the Nixon Doctrine a return to the strategy of massive retaliation. This latter strategy was designed in such a way that its failure, as a deterrent to aggression, was a necessary implication if a massive retaliatory strike ever had to be made; that is, in a profound sense it was a strategy for a war that was never intended to be fought. Kissinger, on the other hand, has consistently advocated making nuclear weapons usable in combat, beginning with his argument for tactical nuclear weaponry in *Nuclear Weapons and Foreign Policy*.[23]

In the United States the Nixon Doctrine has been officially presented as a way to avoid future entanglements like that of Vietnam. It is pictured as a doctrine offering help to those who help themselves—with the proviso that United States help will extend only to military and other support, while the governments threatened will do the actual fighting themselves. Thus the doctrine had obvious political benefits when it was announced in 1969 to a nation weary of a war which many believed had gone on too long and which had become unpopular to an increasingly larger segment of the citizenry. These political benefits obscured the possible losses: strictly from a moral standpoint, for example, it is by no means clear that the United States should adopt a posture of non-intervention, and indeed classic just war doctrine justifies intervention in the cause of justice.[24] That is, leaving aside the possible political asset the Nixon Doctrine has been for the particular case of Vietnam, it is a moral (and perhaps also political) liability for possible future cases requiring some kind of response to aggression.

---

[23] H. A. Kissinger, *Nuclear Weapons and Foreign Policy* (1957).
[24] For a contemporary interpretation of this position, see P. Ramsey, *The Just War: Force and Political Responsibility* (1968), Chaps. 18, 22.

But the implications of the Nixon Doctrine go beyond the particulars of the domestic presentation of this doctrine. Russell Weigley states the total thrust of the doctrine concisely:

"In the Nixon Doctrine of 1969 [President Nixon] announced that even in limited wars of a non-guerilla character, the United States would expect the country under attack to provide the first line of defence, to hold off at least the first assaults of an aggressor, and to provide all the ground forces for the war. The Nixon Doctrine obviously implied a heavy reliance on air and sea power employing conventional explosives; but given the limitations of conventional air and sea power, either as deterrents or as weapons of decision, displayed since the North Korean invasion of South Korea in 1950, the doctrine also had to rely for its credibility on a suggestion of willingness to invoke nuclear war." [25]

The doctrine thus provides for a graduated range of response, with the airlift of *matériel* to Israel during the 1973 war an example of response at the lower end of the scale. Moving up the scale past bombing, shelling, and other such forms of air/sea support, one finds a gap where intervention with conventional ground forces would seem indicated. The next step, in order, after intervention by air and sea rather would be, as Weigley suggests, some form of nuclear war. The question, of course, is what kind of nuclear war is implied, and what can be said, from a moral standpoint, about such a possibility.

In spite of the fundamental differences between John Foster Dulles and Henry Kissinger, there are ominous signs that the era of massive retaliation has not been completely left behind. Indeed, in one sense it has never been, even during the presidencies of " limited warriors " like Kennedy and Johnson. So far as deterrence of the Soviet Union and China has been concerned, a massive retaliatory strike has remained the cornerstone of United States strategy. In this sense the Nixon Doctrine too has an ultimate reliance on this strategy. But the Eisenhower-Dulles doctrine went further than this: massive retaliation became a replacement for ability to fight conventional wars on a relatively small scale employing conventional weapons. Is the Nixon Doctrine reverting to this?

The first thing to be said is that, in so far as a graduated scale of military response is foreshortened by removal of one or more steps, the last step—massive nuclear strike—is that much closer to becoming a reality. In this way, at least, the Nixon Doctrine is closer to that of the Eisenhower presidency than to the presidencies of Kennedy and Johnson, when intervention with ground troops remained one step on the scale of possible military responses. The

---

[25] Weigley, *op. cit.* in note 3 above; pp. 468–469.

closeness of the ultimate step in the Nixon Doctrine is underscored
by a matter quite outside the doctrine itself, though having an
important effect on its implementation as strategy: the status of
preparedness of the military. Considerable concern is developing
that the Army is deteriorating under the all-volunteer concept, as
relatively highly-educated men who would formerly have been
drafted eschew military service. So far as this is true, the nation's
ability to employ ground troops in possible future conflicts is
lessened, and reliance on nuclear weapons becomes the alternative
to doing nothing at all. An analogy with the late 1950s is suggested,
when fatigue over the Korean War led to cutbacks in military
budgets and the " more bang for a buck " theory helped to promote
the strategy of reliance on nuclear weaponry. Although I cannot
here develop this idea fully, I suggest that the Nixon Doctrine
contains an implicit reliance on use of nuclear weapons far greater
than appears on the surface, and that this reliance approaches
that of the Eisenhower years implicitly, though not explicitly. It is
unrealistic to suppose that *any* fashioner of military policy and
strategy in either the United States or the Soviet Union could today
produce a doctrine which would not include ultimate reliance on
a massive nuclear strike. But two questions must be considered
before equating such ultimate reliance with the old massive retaliation doctrine of the Eisenhower-Dulles era: First, does the new
doctrine exhaust possibilities of military response farther down the
scale from the ultimate? And secondly, does the new doctrine rest
upon the idea that nuclear war, if fought, must be utterly non-
discriminating (in terms of its targets) and must involve the total
nuclear arsenal? I have argued that the Nixon Doctrine, in expressly
repudiating the possibility of use of land forces in a future case of
resistance to aggression, moves the United States just so much closer
to the possibility of nuclear war than did the defence policies of
the two previous administrations. But that alone does not argue
that the Nixon Doctrine is hiding beneath its cloak a massive
retaliation strategy like that of the 1950s.

Classic just war doctrine insists on the proportionality of means
to ends, the exhausting of less violent means before turning to those
more violent, and reasonable certainty that the total good done by
any war will outweigh the total evil done. The theological ethicist,
Paul Ramsey, has extensively developed the requirement of this first
criterion, proportionality, and I will not go into this matter here.[26]
It has to do with the fighting of a nuclear war and thus pertains
to the *jus in bello* of the classic doctrine. But the other two criteria

---

[26] P. Ramsey, *War and the Christian Conscience* (1961), *passim*. See also *The
Just War, passim*.

named require some attention. Both, as they are stated in the classic just war doctrine, belong to the *jus ad bellum*. But they also impinge upon the proportionality criterion of the *jus in bello* to require that any fighting which is actually done must be held to the minimum level of destruction necessary to achieve the justified ends for which the war is being fought. From this moral standpoint, then, the Nixon Doctrine receives poor marks—though not nearly so poor as those of the earlier massive retaliation doctrine. The critical point is that the relative violence of the means envisioned does not appear to be a consideration in the current doctrine. Air and sea power are notoriously destructive, and especially the employment of air power has been criticised as disproportionate from the Spanish Civil War to Vietnam. *Politically* to rely on air and sea forces to fight wars is an asset: the numbers of one's men killed or taken prisoner are lower than if ground troops are employed. But *morally* this cannot be the first or only consideration: ground troops are a weapon inherently more amenable to proportionate use.[27] A related question has to do with the use of nuclear weapons, whether tactical or strategic. Any number of modern-war pacifists have argued that nuclear weapons, whether tactical or strategic, are inherently disproportionate, and that any use of them is thus immoral. Although the argument has not, to my thinking, been totally convincing,[28] since the way these weapons are used has to be considered along with their inherent destructiveness, it is convincing enough to suggest that the likelihood of immoral use of nuclear weaponry requires that they be as far as possible down the list of available options. The Nixon Doctrine has foreshortened those options in the short-term interest of cooling dissatisfaction over loss of American lives in Vietnam.

There is much more that could be said on the matter of proportionality and the Nixon Doctrine, but it is also necessary here to look briefly into the question of whether the doctrine appears to be in accord with the just war criterion of discrimination. On this, Nixon's administration has moved significantly beyond that of Eisenhower. The critical difference is the re-targeting of some United

---

[27] One of the justifications of the atomic bombing of Hiroshima and Nagasaki, that use of the bombs saved the lives of countless American soldiers, is not a *moral* justification by the standards of classic just war thought. One problem is that it does not weigh the lives lost due to the bombs in the scale against the American lives likely to be lost in an invasion of Japan; this is one implication of the requirement of proportionality. Another is the indiscriminateness of the bombs, both inherently and in the way they were used: the victims were largely non-combatants. Though I am speaking here specifically of the atomic bombing of Japan, similar arguments can be made for strategic bombing using conventional explosives, and this suggests the problem with war by air power mainly.

[28] See my interchange with modern-war pacifist Gordon Zahn in 17 *Worldview*, Nr. 1 (January 1974), pp. 43–47.

States missiles away from Communist cities and towards their military installations. Paul Ramsey argued for this from a just-war perspective in his " counter-forces " (as opposed to " counter-force ") strategy as long ago as 1961 [29]; more recently it has been proposed by Yale political scientist Bruce M. Russett.[30] There are certainly positive and negative aspects to such re-targeting, especially since the Soviet Union appears to have done the same. On the negative side, this step would appear to make nuclear war more able to be fought, with its concomitant destructiveness. So far as those are correct who have argued that there is a " threshold " which obtains with nuclear weapons, so that once one is used an all-out exchange is likely, this re-targeting would appear to be morally dubious. But whether this " threshold " concept is right or not (and the arguments for it, too, have not been entirely convincing), the likelihood of great collateral damage to the persons and property of non-combatants living or working near the military installations which are now targets of missiles is enough to raise a question of the proportionality of nuclear weapons. These are important negative considerations. But positively, this re-targeting is in accord with the just war criterion of discrimination, better known as the principle of non-combatant immunity. War in the 20th century has tended to the breaking down of distinctions between combatants and non-combatants as recipients of the destructiveness of war. Part of the reason for this has been a tendency to regard not soldiers or governments but nations as friends or enemies, with the inevitable result that the civilian populations of enemy nations have come to be regarded as no different from their leaders or their armies. Again, one element of this tendency is the emphasis, which has been so strong in this century, on defining friends and enemies by their ideology. The United States entered the First World War " to make the world safe for democracy "; the Spanish Civil War and the concurrent civil strife in France were holy wars of the Right against the Left; the Second World War was depicted, in this country at least, as a war of freedom against tyranny; finally, all of these elements came together in the antagonisms of the Cold War, together with other elements like the strong distinctions often made between capitalism and Communism and between Christianity and Communism. Many other instances could be noted. In the United States, this general atmosphere of ideologically-based mistrust of those on the other side of the boundary of ideas, faith, politics, or economics has had its complement in the characteristic attitude towards war

29 *War and the Christian Conscience, passim.*
30 See his " Short of Nuclear Madness," 15 *Worldview*, Nr. 4 (April 1972), pp. 31–37.

described earlier in this paper. It is fair to regard the doctrine of massive retaliation, especially in the apologetic of Dulles, as the climax of these tendencies: a doctrine of " just war " defined by Americans so as to justify the annihilation of their ideological enemies, if such became necessary. The result was not unlike what obtained in the post-Reformation era, when holy war doctrine was developed to justify unlimited warfare by Protestants against Catholics and vice versa. There difference of religion provided the definition of one's ideological enemy.

Détente symbolises the waning of emphasis on ideological differences among nations as a possible justification for war, and with it comes the end of strategies for utter and total destruction of the enemy. When ideology becomes the highest end to be fought for, strategies must involve unlimited force, because an ideology makes an infinite claim. But when national purposes are defined by less ultimate claims, their strategies can be less ultimate also, and more important, they can now be conceived in terms of the classic just war criteria of proportionality and discrimination. Since the ends are finite, the means, also finite, can be gauged against them in terms of good and evil, profit and loss.

The re-targeting of nuclear missiles away from cities and towards military installations is a strategic symbol, alongside the political symbol of *détente*, for the passing of the 20th century's era of ideological warfare. As such, this re-targeting is an extremely important development, pointing to the realisation once again that war should be made to serve reasonable purposes.

Although this element of the Nixon Doctrine appears at this juncture to hold some promise for the development of a military posture in accordance with the standards of morality embodied in classic just war thought, the most important factor governing such a possible development is the general United States attitude towards the purposes of war. So long as the " all-or-nothing " attitude identified by Potter, Tucker and Weigley persists, national policy and the shape of strategy will reflect that attitude and will, thus far, be morally undesirable.

Perhaps Americans could benefit from the recollection that the post-Reformation era saw *two* doctrines of war emerging from the classic just war doctrine. Concurrently with the development of doctrine justifying the wars of the 16th and 17th centuries in terms of the ideological differences between Catholics and Protestants, and partially in reaction against such justifications, there developed a version of classic just war doctrine which explicitly disallowed war for religious, that is to say ideological, reasons. (This latter-day, just war doctrine first appears in the thought of theologians like

Vitoria and later moves into modern international law through theorists like Gentili and Grotius.) One feature of this new casting of just war doctrine was its stress on what could be done in war, the *jus in bello*, so as to exclude the tactics of terror and atrocity directed against civilians which had characterised the post-Reformation wars of religion. It is this latter doctrine, and not that of holy war, which outlived the post-Reformation period. By analogy with the movement which produced this doctrine, a serious attempt needs to be made to move United States attitudes towards war away from the norm described by Potter, Tucker and Weigley and towards attitudes which will support legal and other attempts, including the shaping of appropriate military policies and strategies, to limit the destructiveness of war in the nuclear age. This, in turn, implies the development of a new United States military policy and strategy more moral than the present Nixon Doctrine.

THE WORLD COUNCIL OF CHURCHES
AND RACISM

By

DARRIL HUDSON

THE World Council of Churches and its " diplomatic arm," the
Commission of the Churches on International Affairs (CCIA),
have been the subject of papers in this *Year Book* which have
discussed the international role of these bodies.[1] Although those
officially engaged in international affairs have regularly come across
World Council or CCIA studies or statements on the issues before
them—for example, on refugees, economic development, apartheid,
disarmament or East-West relations—it would be safe to say that
the man in the street or in the board-room has hardly been conscious
of this ecclesiastical activity. It remained an esoteric bit of knowledge of devoted Christians and academics until one World Council
action erupted into headlines in the major European newspapers:
in 1970, the World Council Executive Committee allotted grants
to organisations representing oppressed racial groups, a few of
which were engaged in armed struggles in southern Africa. The
debate thereby engendered was more often bitter and emotional
than considered and rational; however, it served to bring to the
attention of a vast public the World Council's international concerns.
The General Secretary at that time, Dr. Eugene Carson Blake,
admitted that some World Council programmes had been temporarily damaged by the controversy, but that the advance of the
anti-racism programme gave other advantages to the Council in
many parts of the world and especially to the victims of racism.
The Programme to Combat Racism will be described, discussed
and evaluated as an example of a major effort by a normative
non-governmental organisation to influence world affairs.

I—THE EARLY INTEREST IN RACISM
OF THE ECUMENICAL MOVEMENT

The organisations which gave way to the World Council of Churches
(WCC) include the World Alliance for International Friendship
Through the Churches, the International Missionary Council, and

---

[1] J. Duncan Wood, " The World Council of Churches " in this *Year Book,*
Vol. 26 (1972), pp. 218–234, and Sir Kenneth Grubb and A. R. Booth, " The
Church and International Relations," *ibid.* Vol. 17 (1963), pp. 219–235.

the Universal Christian Council on Life and Work.[2] The World Alliance, like the League of Nations, was primarily a European organisation; its interest in racial matters was limited to the ethnic minorities of Europe created by the Treaty of Versailles. The International Missionary Council and its members, on the other hand, ministered to a constituency which was primarily non-white. The records of its international conferences—as well as of the League of Nations itself—offer evidence of the concern of the mission leaders for the ill-treatment of the black peoples of the Congo and of several East African colonies, of the Assyrians and of the Armenians, and indeed, of everyone who was inhumanely treated. Life and Work was aroused by the blatant anti-Semitism of the Nazi Party in Germany; this led to a consideration of " The Church and Race " at the 1937 Oxford Conference on Church, Community and State, sponsored by Life and Work. Although racism throughout the world was included, in general terms the discussion and report focused on Nazism. Indeed the extent to which racism was still narrowly defined was only imperfectly realised by many who assumed a European superiority in functional areas.[3] Throughout the conference, the term racism was used by most delegates to refer to ethnic differences between white groups and to areas where laws and force segregated peoples of different colours.

The World Council of Churches existed in provisional form from 1938 to 1948. During this time it was preoccupied with the questions of war and peace and of relieving the suffering of war both during and immediately after hostilities. When the First Assembly of the World Council met in Amsterdam in 1948 to formally create the organisation, the question of race was on its agenda. It considered the issue in several sections, and condemnations of racism appeared in the reports,[4] where reports were addressed primarily to the churches, urging them to remove this scandal from their own lives. Basically, however, it was not an issue which excited passionate speeches or emotional debates, and Dr. W. A. Visser 't Hooft, the

---

[2] J. Duncan Wood, in *op. cit.* in note 1 above, repeated a view put forward in Ruth Rouse and S. Neill (eds.), *A History of the Ecumenical Movement 1517–1948* (1967), that the entire ecumenical movement and the World Council descended from the World Missionary Conference of 1910. In fact the activities leading up to the founding of the World Alliance in 1914 had already begun at the Hague Peace Conference of 1907, and Life and Work was created through the World Alliance. The correspondence and discussion in these early years indicate the lack of influence by the mission societies on the lay readers of the World Alliance. See this author's *The Ecumenical Movement in World Affairs* (1969), Chapter 2.

[3] W. Moberly *et al.*, *The Churches Survey Their Task, Report of the Conference at Oxford, July 1937, on Church, Community and State*, Vol. VIII, *The Church, Community and State Series* (1937), *passim*.

[4] W. A. Visser 't Hooft (ed.), *The First Assembly of the World Council of Churches: The Official Report* (1949), pp. 9–11, 51–56, 74–82, 88–100.

General Secretary, in his post-Assembly report commented on the lack of emphasis on this problem at Amsterdam.

The year 1948 saw not only the founding of the World Council but the election of the National Party in South Africa on a platform of apartheid, a then ill-defined doctrine of racial segregation. The international questions which this raised were discussed in the early CCIA Executive Committee and World Council Central Committee meetings. It is trite, but nonetheless true, to say that churchmen are children of their times and are no wiser than their contemporaries. The divisions within the World Council bodies on any topic were similar to those found in the secular world. So it was in regard to racism; some wanted immediate action against this evil, while others counselled restraint so as not to alienate the South African Christians.

The subconscious racial attitudes of white Europeans and Americans towards the prompt eradication of racism is illustrated by the debate within the Central Committee where those urging action were primarily non-white, led by Dr. M. M. Thomas of India, and those urging caution were primarily white, led by Dr. Visser 't Hooft.[5] The caution led to nought. In spite of every conciliatory gesture possible, the Dutch Reformed churches of South Africa officially held to their doctrine of racial superiority, though they were, and are, voices within these churches which disagree with the official policy. The World Council maintained a dialogue with the Reformed churches in which it hoped to convince them of the error of their ways. The CCIA with its representation at the United Nations did not actively support anti-apartheid resolutions for fear of jeopardising the uneasy relationship.

By the Second Assembly, held in the United States at Evanston, Illinois, in 1954, reaction against racism throughout the world was becoming more pronounced and attracted the attention of the delegates. The racial issue was considered thoroughly, racism *eo ipso* was condemned, and the establishment of a World Council department on racism was authorised.[6] It is unfortunate that this resolution was not put into effect for several years; the urgency of the problem of international racism was not yet realised by white liberals.

The Sharpeville massacre of 1960 brought the English-speaking South African churches into conflict with the Dutch Reformed churches, and the World Council took the opportunity (upon invitation of the churches) of sending a fact-finding team headed by

[5] See, for example, the debate in World Council of Churches Central Committee, *Minutes* (1949), pp. 17–19.

[6] World Council of Churches, *The Evanston Report* (1955), pp. 6, 158.

Dr. Robert S. Bilheimer. This visit resulted in the Cottesloe Consultation in that country the following December, with interracial
delegations from the Protestant churches in South Africa and officials
from the World Council participating. A majority of the delegates
there felt that apartheid was not consistent with the Christian gospel;
this finding was not acceptable to two of the Dutch Reformed
churches, both of which subsequently withdrew from the World
Council. The Consultation did act as a catalyst in public discussion
in South Africa; *Die Burger*, the influential Afrikaner newspaper,
on the basis of the Cottesloe Statement, editorially urged the ending
of the no-compromise stand on apartheid by the Verwoerd
government.[7]

The holding of the Third Assembly in a non-white land, in New
Delhi in 1961, insured greater Third World participation. Naturally
a great deal of attention was devoted to considering the racial issue.
In spite of urging the churches to strive for racial justice by all
means short of violence, no programme was offered to guide the
churches and the World Council in so doing.[8] In spite of all good
wishes and good resolution, racial conditions did not better themselves: indeed, repression grew in southern Africa as the Central
African Federation broke up and Rhodesia prepared for a unilateral
declaration of independence.

The World Council's Department on Church and Society, in
conjunction with the South African Institute of Race Relations and
the Mindolo Ecumenical Centre in Kitwe, Northern Rhodesia
(shortly to become Zambia), convened a consultation on racism
from May 25 to June 2, 1964, to consider what the churches as
a group could do to alleviate this intractable problem. Participants
included individuals from several Protestant denominations in
Northern and Southern Rhodesia, Malawi, the Congo, South Africa
and the then-High Commission Territories. Various aspects of social
problems engendered by apartheid were discussed as well as the
more general issue of Western cultural values being imposed as
Christian ethics on Africans and ignoring, or more usually condemning, certain African cultural traits, such as circumcision,
polygamy, and honour of ancestral spirits.

Violence as a legitimate means of attaining racial justice was also
broached there. The whites in Southern Africa, it was noted, de-
pended for their security on military power prolonging the *status
quo*. To counteract this, freedom fighters were being trained in
various parts of Africa. The participants in the consultation conceded that after all lawful means to attain economic equality had

---

[7] As reported in *The Sunday Times* (London), December 18, 1960.
[8] World Council of Churches, *The New Delhi Report* (1962), pp. 93–115.

been tried, then Christians would be justified in supporting boycotts, general strikes, and—as a last resort—planned industrial disruption, to achieve justice. Violence was not to be encouraged but neither was it to be condemned. Some members of the consultation dissociated themselves from this viewpoint.[9]

By the time the Fourth Assembly convened in Uppsala, Sweden, in 1968, race had become a burning issue throughout the world. In the United States the Civil Rights movement had heightened the consciousness of white and black alike. The independence of nearly all of Africa north of the Zambesi increased the membership of race-conscious churches in the World Council as it did of race-conscious States in the United Nations. Race, thereby, not only continued to be of concern to the World Council but became an issue of major proportions at Uppsala, made all the more poignant by the absence of a principal speaker, Dr. Martin Luther King Jr., who had fallen victim to the assassin's bullet two months prior to the Assembly. In addition to committee work, a special plenary session was devoted to a discussion of " White Racism or World Community? " in which the American black author Mr. James Baldwin made world headlines with his accusations of Christian betrayal of black peoples. Lord Caradon addressed the same audience with words of warning and words of hope: " Coupled as it is with the world problems of poverty and population and youth . . . , race is the most explosive and most dangerous issue which the world must face. . . . In such an international campaign we have a right to look for courageous leadership to the World Council of Churches." [10] Race was discussed at length in the reports of three sections. The Assembly as a whole was ready to adopt a statement on racism, but objection was made by Dr. D. T. Niles of Ceylon that the statement was too general. On his motion, the issue was remanded to the 1969 Central Committee meeting.

In accordance with the recommendation of the Committee on Church and Society of the Uppsala Assembly that the World Council undertake a crash programme to guide the churches and the Council in combating racism, the Department on Church and Society convened the International Consultation on Racism at Notting Hill, London, on May 19, 1969, chaired by United States Senator George McGovern, a prominent Methodist layman. This Consultation suffered some disorderly disruptions from black militant groups demanding the churches pay reparations, but neverthe-

[9] A full report of the Consultation is found in WCC, Department on Church and Society, *Christians and Race Relations in South Africa* (1964).
[10] N. Goodall (ed.), *The Uppsala Report 1968* (1968), pp. 29–30. Verbatim reports of the speeches are found in " White Racism or World Community? " in 20 *The Ecumenical Review* (October 1968), pp. 371–384.

less managed to produce recommendations for a more detailed programme to fight racism than theretofore. A little too active for the ecumenical " curia," the Ecumenical Programme to Combat Racism presented to the Central Committee meeting at Canterbury in 1969 was greatly modified from that proposed at Notting Hill, although it still proved too strong for some of the white ecclesiastics.

The five-year anti-racism programme as finally adopted by the Central Committee focused on white racism as the most dangerous form of racism, based as it was on the overwhelming economic, political and military might of white States. The programme consisted of the investigation of specific and selected racial programmes, consultations on problems common to all areas of racism, studies on possible means for achieving racial justice, strategies for churches to eliminate racism within their own countries, and the creation of an International Advisory Committee (on racism) from among members of the Central Committee.[11] The commitment became more than purely *pro forma* when a $150,000 budget was requested and a special fund created with $200,000 from World Council reserves and $300,000 from a special appeal. The special fund would dispense grants to organisations of oppressed racial groups for support of victims of racism, upon advice of the International Advisory and Executive Committees. Dr. E. A. Payne of the United Kingdom, supported by Dr. Robert J. Marshall of the United States and Dr. Adolf Wischmann of Germany, attempted to delete the latter provision, but the proposal was overwhelmingly defeated 62 to 7 with 11 abstentions. The World Council of Churches realised a whole-hearted commitment to the cause of human equality.

II—The Grants to Oppressed Racial Groups

To General Secretary Blake and other Council functionaries, the simple press release of September 3, 1970, seemed merely the culmination of their rather extended labours in developing an anti-racism programme. The members of the " curia " were shocked when they realised that they had themselves dumbfounded the world, or more accurately the white élite of the industrialised North, with the announcement of the disbursement of $200,000 to 19 organisations combating racism throughout the world.

This furor was caused by more of a public relations *faux pas* than any change of commitment or direction on the part of the World Council. Several ecumenists felt that the General Secretary should have better prepared the public for this announcement, or at least have elaborated on the grants and their purposes simultaneously with the press release. One British member of the Central

---

11 WCC Central Committee, *Minutes* (1969), pp. 35–40.

Committee expressed the view to the meeting of January 1971, that he himself had been " taken aback " by the off-hand nature of the announcement.[12] For the careful, or even careless, reader the press release clearly stated the authority for the grants and their objectives, namely to raise the level of awareness in the world to the existence of suffering of racially oppressed people and to strengthen the organisation of groups combating racism.

The grants were intended to support activist groups rather than welfare organisations; the latter simply alleviate symptoms—for example, the hunger of a family whose breadwinner has been arrested or executed—while the former prepare society for change through their programmes of propaganda and education. Some groups had engaged in constitutional activities for change—for example, voter registration drives—while similar groups had found that such " legal " activities led to jail in South Africa, Rhodesia and the Portuguese colonies. Therefore, many had already progressed to subversive activities, some even to the point of taking up arms. In the abstract there could be no Christian objection to raising the level of consciousness, that is making known in the countries which practised discrimination, and throughout the world, the conditions which racism fostered. In the concrete, rage and fear in the white establishment was the reaction to the priority given southern Africa: a total of $120,000 went to militant organisations called " liberation movements " or " guerrilla terrorists " depending on the political orientation of the speaker.

These grants were *not* given to carry on war; they were given expressly for humanitarian and educational purposes to groups responsible for large numbers of people. The People's Movement for the Liberation of Angola (MPLA) and its rivals, the Revolutionary Government of Angola in Exile (GRAE) and the National Union for the Total Independence of Angola (UNITA), as well as the Mozambique Liberation Front (FRELIMO) and the African Independence Party of Guinea and the Cape Verde Islands (PAIGC), all claim to control territory on which they carry out educational and health programmes among their peoples. There is good evidence that they do so. These organisations as well as the Zimbabwe African National Union (ZANU) and the Zimbabwe African People's Union (ZAPU)—both of Rhodesia—the African National Congress (ANC) and the Pan African Congress (PAC)—both of South Africa—and the South West African People's Organisation (SWAPO) try to support refugees from among their peoples who had fled to neighbouring States. The educational, medical and

---

[12] WCC, Programme to Combat Racism (Untitled), September 3, 1970 (4 pp. Mimeographed).

humanitarian demands are far greater than the resources of these organisations can meet.

The public debate following the announcement of the grants was carried on entirely within the frame of reference enunciated by the white minority régimes rather than in the terms of the donors of the grants. The churches gave humanitarian aid to victims of racism who needed various types of physical help; South African Prime Minister Vorster accused the churches of " subsidising murder in the name of God." [13] Indeed, the *New York Times* wrote that Mr. Vorster's verbal outbursts were part of a political offensive brought about by his own domestic problems of, primarily, a labour shortage and the inability to achieve genuine economic progress along racially separate lines.[14] This postulate is supported by Mr. Vorster's rather restrained initial reaction which was to describe the grants as " to put it mildly, shocking," [15] followed by a continual escalation to the most outrageous degree. The pronounced disarray among European and American church leaders, as well as the political and economic élites, reflected in leading newspapers was no doubt an encouragement for him to do so.

Among the élite newspapers, *The Times, The Daily Telegraph*, and *The Sunday Times* vociferously opposed the grants, while *The Guardian, Die Zeit* and the *Frankfurter Allgemeine Zeitung* wholly or partially supported them. The attacks as well as the defences, as reflected in the news reports, emanated from a preconceived white image of violence and justice. The Europeans perceived the African liberation groups as European armies, the military arm of the State, rather than as " governments " responsible for all the well-being of their peoples. They perceived budgets in terms of ability to shift from the educational sector to the military sector when outside gifts freed " obligated " funds, instead of recognising the existence of empty coffers requiring education, medicines and other " luxuries " to be simply forgone if funds are not available from outside sources. What is most amazing from the whole outburst is that the following September 1971, a further $200,000 was distributed to 24 organisations, and almost no comment appeared in the world press nor denunciations from the white ruling élites. In this distribution nine groups active in southern Africa received a total of $130,000.[16] In January 1973, a third allocation of $200,000 was made to 25 groups of which $101,000 was directed to southern Africa.

[13] *The Daily Telegraph,* September 7, 1971.

[14] E. R. Fiske, " Church in South Africa Defies Edict," *New York Times,* September 27, 1970.

[15] *New York Times,* September 5, 1971.

[16] For a complete breakdown of the grants for the three years, see this author's *A Voice for the Voiceless* (1975), Appendix 2.

One of the complaints lodged at the first granting was that no accounting for the funds was required; the only requirement was an assurance that the money would be used for the humanitarian purposes for which it was donated. Neither had any accounting been required from 1965, when the World Council contributed to white-administered legal defence funds for victims of discriminatory laws in South Africa and Rhodesia. The World Council wanted to show that it trusted blacks as well as whites. Some of the groups did, however, provide voluntary reports on the results achieved with the gifts. The Mozambique Institute of FRELIMO increased agricultural production in areas under FRELIMO control through the purchase of seeds and tools. It also began printing its own textbooks, trying to create an identity among the diverse peoples of Mozambique. SWAPO has increased care of its refugees in Zambia and Botswana and has opened illegal " bush-schools " in Namibia to educate its children for the world of tomorrow.

III—THE RED HERRING OF VIOLENCE VERSUS NONVIOLENCE

The white outcry was posed in terms of World Council, and thereby Christian, support for violence instead of love. That this was less a theological reaction than an emotional one based on subconscious racial feelings might be evidenced by the lack of similar theological concern among non-white theologians and church leaders. The Executive Committee of the All Africa Conference of Churches meeting in Lomé, Togo, on September 23, 1970, following the public announcement of the grants, unanimously supported the World Council action and welcomed " the revolution in the thinking of donors, in being prepared to trust people who are taking radical action against racism." [17] Dr. M. M. Thomas of India, chairman of the Central Committee, publicly defended the action in the presence of Emperor Haile Selassie, as " nothing more or less than the protest of the World Council of Churches against the *status quo* ideology of violence and an attempt to break the moral and religious sanctions behind it." [18] A former white Prime Minister of Southern Rhodesia, Mr. Garfield Todd, an astute politician well versed in the amount of violence innate in the *status quo* in Southern Africa, characterised the shock in Western Europe and white Africa as " a wave of pious hysteria." [19]

The question as formulated by its critics was whether the World Council of Churches could in good conscience support violence or whether the churches and their representatives ought always to be

[17] WCC, Department of Communication, Press Release, September 23, 1970.
[18] *New York Times,* January 11, 1971.
[19] *The Guardian,* September 7, 1971.

on the side of non-violent action. This was a bogus issue; the World Council did not support violence, it had never supported violence. It had never taken an official stand on the issue of violence, though some conferences sponsored by it, such as the 1966 World Conference on Church and Society, had considered the issue peripherally. As Dr. Blake replied to critical German church officials, " In the 200 years in which force was practised by whites, no one interested himself in this theme." [20] One World Council official stated before the United States Conference for the World Council of Churches: " White Christian laymen who had managed to remain silent while Africans were having the daylights beaten out of them at Sharpeville suddenly were moved to uphold non-violence as the one and only solution to the world's problems. . . . Church spokesmen who had little to say about the appalling violence exercised by whites on blacks over the years suddenly became vocal when blacks began to flex their own muscles; and it all added up to a splendid example of ethical double-think inspired by an ideology of dominant class defensiveness." [21]

The issue was framed in terms of the theological justification for the use of violence or non-violence in order to attain justice; the World Council felt it had to find a theological answer. Fulfilling an Uppsala Resolution, the 1969 Central Committee meeting requested a study [22] on non-violent methods of achieving social change which —naturally—included a consideration of the use of violence. This mandate took on a new urgency at the Central Committee meeting at Addis Ababa in January 1971, due to the controversy engendered by the grants, and the Department on Church and Society was charged with continuing the study with special reference to the use of violence in social change.[23] The Central Committee in 1973 received the report *Violence, Nonviolence and the Struggle for Social Justice*, not as the definitive Christian position on the topic but as a major step in its ongoing discussion and commended it " to the churches for study, comment and action." [24]

Church and Society noted that its distinctive role was especially in " helping white affluent Christians take seriously the perspectives of other parts of the Church." [25] For the main division of opinion among theologians was a condemnation of violence by those of the

[20] *Frankfurter Allgemeine Zeitung*, October 15, 1970.
[21] D. M. Gill, *Violence, Nonviolence and Christian Responsibility*, United States Conference for the WCC, Toledo, Ohio, April 17, 1972, pp. 3–4 (7 pp. Mimeographed).
[22] WCC, Central Committee, *Minutes* (1969), pp. 80–81.
[23] *Ibid.* (1971), p. 51.
[24] 25 *The Ecumenical Review*, Nr. 4 (October 1973).
[25] WCC, *Violence, Nonviolence and the Struggle for Social Justice* (1973).

industrialised North (except for a few who may be the precursors of change, such as Richard Shaull of the United States and Jürgen Moltmann of Germany),[26] in contrast to those of the non-white world who understood violence to be present in the unjust social order of racist societies. " The Third World is compelled to take its destiny into its own hands just as the Christians of Europe did when fighting Hitler," [27] is how Dr. Philip Potter, present General Secretary of the World Council from the West Indies, expressed his perception of the violence erupting in areas of the world where non-white peoples struggle for their freedom.

In spite of divisions of opinion on the topic of violence, there was a good deal of common ground among the thought of the Christian theologians. All agreed that Christians had the duty to help attain justice and freedom for all people, that governments had the duty to restrain private power in the interests of justice and public welfare and that Christians must stand with those oppressed by the unjust use of power; all agreed that the object of resistance must be not to destroy an enemy but rather to create a just social order for all.

The three major divisions of opinion, however, occurred, as is to be expected, on the use of violence to achieve justice. One view-point held that non-violence was the only option open to a Christian. Another group felt that violence could be justified in " extreme circumstances," while a third held that where Christians found themselves in situations of violence they had no choice but to react with violence. In any case, again there was agreement that the Christian duty was to humanise any means of conflict and to help to build just structures for peace. All were also in accord that some types of violence were prohibited to the Christian: the conquest of a people, deliberate oppression of a class or race, torture, the taking of hostages, and the indiscriminate killing of non-combatants.

It must be stressed that this is not an official position of the World Council of Churches. It is a report in the form of a statement of the major views of World Council members achieved as a result of conferences and correspondence. It has been commended to the member churches for study and comment; the inquiry continues.

IV—INVESTMENTS IN RACISM

Grants to victims of racism have been replaced in the headlines of the industrial world's newspapers by a further step in the Programme to Combat Racism (PCR), namely the withdrawal of church invest-

---

[26] R. Shaull, " Revolution Challenge to Church and Theology," 60 *Princeton Seminary Bulletin* (1966), pp. 25–32. Jürgen Moltmann, " Racism and the Right to Resist," 8 *Study Encounter* (1972).

[27] Peter Schmid, " The Clergyman and the Guerilla: A Conversation with Dr. Philip Potter," 39 *Encounter* (1972), pp. 58–61.

ment funds from corporations active in the economies of Southern Africa. The Uppsala Assembly had recommended the withdrawal of investments from " institutions that perpetuate racism," [28] and the PCR has been carrying out this mandate. It first considered alternatives to actual withdrawal: increased involvement in the economy thereby raising standards of living for all or reform of company policies in Southern Africa instituted by stockholders' meetings. The PCR holds that neither alternative is viable. It contends through the use of standard-of-living statistics that the primary argument for increased investment—that technology would raise the standards of living and this in turn would break down apartheid —was invalid. If the PCR interpretation of government-issued statistics is correct, then its argument is logically sound. However, the PCR has claimed on the basis of one case study that it is not possible to work through corporate boardrooms in the erosion of apartheid. This generalisation is based on the alleged failure of the American Polaroid Corporation's experiment in South Africa to raise the standard of living of its non-white workers within the framework of law prevailing in that country. The PCR holds that the white community would not permit corporation policies which would eventually overturn its way of life. This assumes no liberal thought either in South Africa or the rest of southern Africa compatible with gradual change.

The confrontation policy of the PCR dictates the only acceptable strategy to be total withdrawal of foreign capital in order to force the white South Africans to accept change. The PCR feels that if the World Council, all churches, and other sympathetic groups sold their shares in the corporations giving support to the southern African economies (and thereby to the racist régimes) forcing their withdrawal these governments would collapse. This thesis ignores the probability that those corporations would lose much more by withdrawing and having to leave capital investments in those countries than by the possible fall of their share prices. It also ignores the stock-market mechanism whereby the fall of shares to a certain point provides attractive bargains for morally uncommitted individuals who would go into the market and purchase them. In any event, no impact was observed on stock markets after the Central Committee adopted the resolution ordering its Finance Committee to sell holdings in such stocks. Nor did the actual divestment of the World Council's $1·5 million worth of stocks, as announced at an Executive Committee meeting in January 1973, cause a ripple in capitalist waters.[29]

28 *The Uppsala Report* 1968, p. 66.
29 *New York Times*, January 23, 1973.

The PCR pointed out in its report to the Central Committee at its summer meeting in 1973, that in spite of no observable stock market fluctuations, the corporate executives of American firms had been busy defending, explaining or obscuring their employment practices and policies in Southern Africa. This would seem to indicate a certain amount of managerial sensitivity to ecclesiastical probing. The British Council of Churches, for one, has not accepted the argument of total withdrawal of funds as a solution to racism, except in circumstances where boards of directors remain aloof from the pressures for information and change. Church bodies in Canada, Western Germany, the Netherlands, Norway, Denmark, Sweden, Belgium, France, Switzerland and Japan are studying the effects of their investments. At the 1974 Central Committee meeting, the German church officials proposed a resolution supported by American and British ecclesiastics to halt further implementation of the Programme to combat Racism until it can be reviewed by the Assembly meeting in 1975. These important sources of World Council funds could not be ignored.

The South African Council of Churches (SACC) is making inquiries into the pay policies of firms in South Africa. Some 150 foreign corporations active there have indicated their willingness to contribute to black-initiated projects. The SACC recognises the danger of " conscience money " being paid in order to continue unjust employment practices and is now wrestling with this problem. The self-justification by firms in the white, industrialised North of their activities in Southern Africa and their willingness to contribute to possibly unprofitable Black South African projects indicate that if the pressure can be maintained on corporations throughout the industrialised world through publicity and stockholder actions, more defensive actions may be taken, such as bettering employment conditions for black South African workers. In March 1973 the United Kingdom–South Africa Trade Association urged its members " to pay at least subsistence wages to blacks employed by their South African subsidiaries." [30] To guide sympathetic groups in their investment policies, the PCR has prepared a list of the firms in industrialised States doing business in South Africa; the World Council and its members are one source of unending pressure and propaganda needed to effect change.

V—Evaluation of the Programme to Combat Racism

Like other international non-governmental organisations (NGOs) the World Council of Churches acts much like a political interest group at the national level. Some NGOs attempt to achieve their

---

[30] " HMG Hints," *The Economist*, March 31, 1973, p. 66.

goals through power—for example, producing votes or campaign funds—while others rely primarily on the communication of information and ideas to the power-centres. The World Council has made use of both means in its activities throughout international affairs and, as the above illustrates, also in its campaign against racism. To attempt to evaluate the effectiveness of World Council activities is a difficult task, for few results can be attributed empirically to cause and effect. Nevertheless, there are some measurable results and in other cases, effects indirectly attributable to its efforts.

On many social and economic issues, especially new ones, the leaders of the World Council have no more of a clear perception of the problem and its solution than those in other fields. Once it is seised of an issue, however, its machinery engages its resources to think through the question, to understand all its aspects and to suggest stands compatible with Christian ethics. From the information given above, it can be seen that in its earlier years, the churches did not clearly perceive all of the economic and political ramifications of the social issue of inequality based on race. Nor did they comprehend the political importance which would in the future be raised by this emotional issue. The Amsterdam and Evanston Assemblies were cognisant of race as an issue which should disturb Christians; Evanston delegates even made recommendations for the establishment of Council machinery devoted to the solution of the problem, but the feeling of urgency did not exist in a white-dominated world.

The frequent condemnations of racism, even though it was primarily concerned with segregation within the life of the churches themselves, created and reinforced a norm of anti-discrimination. Naturally this norm was primarily diffused among the Christian constituents of the World Council. At the same time in secular institutions, such as labour unions and humanistic groups, as well as inter-governmental organisations, such as the United Nations, similar anti-racist norms were being promoted. By the time that World Council membership of non-white churches had increased substantially, there was a greater consciousness both within and without the Council of the magnitude, horror and urgency of racist oppression throughout the world. This was mirrored in the New Delhi Assembly, but it remained for the Uppsala Assembly seven years later to initiate a crash programme to eliminate racism. Among its constituents down to the parish levels, the new norms were being constantly reinforced.

Religion has had a recognised role in society since earliest time. In spite of increasing secularisation in this century, the church, synagogue, mosque or temple remains a recognised social institution.

That in the modern industrialised society it may have lost some of its immediately apparent influence does not detract from the fact that the religious élite is still prominent in the national societies. For the most secularised Englishman, the Archbishop of Canterbury represents a part of his heritage and is a symbol of the moral force in society.[31] Although there is still argument among the traditional élites as to what the limits of ecclesiastical interest in modern social, economic and political problems should be,[32] there is generally recognition of a legitimate role there.

The international system is often spoken of as though it existed apart from the inter-State and transnational actors. Men out of national societies act in and for intergovernmental organisations or take actions on international problems. These international civil servants are individuals who are also part of national societies, even when they act in and for intergovernmental organisations on international problems. They represent national bureaucratic and political élites, and there is a tendency for all élites, in order to retain their position within society, to foster its traditional order; this order includes a place for organised religion. The leaders of international religious organisations have access, due to their position, to the overlapping international and national élites. Obviously any suggestion or admonition addressed to either group will be only one factor affecting international decision-making.

The reporting of World Council statements and actions by the world's leading newspapers is another indication of recognition of the place in international society of religion in general and the World Council in particular. The fact that leading statesmen invoke the World Council, or curse it, illustrates the hold they perceive it has on their peoples or their élites. The strident execrations of Prime Minister Vorster indicate that he felt its actions needed countering. On the other side of the fence, President Kenneth Kaunda of Zambia remarked at a meeting in October 1970, attended by several Muslim African leaders, that World Council aid for African liberation groups had restored the credibility of Christianity

---

[31] Even *The Economist*—in essence a secular publication—notes: " The archbishop . . . is . . . a big man in English life because the churches have influence in the state and he is seen to be the chief representative of them, even by many of those who are not members of his own church." November 20, 1971, pp. 67–68.

[32] *The Times* welcomed the establishment of the WCC as a spokesman for the churches in the affairs of the world, September 4, 1948. *The Economist* more recently seems either not to know its own mind or does not understand the problem. It criticises the Council for " its ever deeper and . . . ever more reckless intervention in social and political issues at the expense of its more traditional religious concerns." In the same article it notes: " The idea of setting up a development agency under the council's auspices . . . is another indication of a more constructive trend . . . ," September 1, 1973, p. 30.

for many Africans.³³ The Director of the CCIA attributes the success of the Council's good offices in the Sudan conflict ³⁴ to the World Council putting its words into action through grants to liberation movements.

The World Council operates on several levels simultaneously to achieve its goals: the international, the national and the societal. Nationally it has felt free to contact government leaders. In the case of South Africa, the General Secretary, Dr. Visser 't Hooft, himself visited South Africa in 1952 consulting not only with ecclesiastics but also with leaders of business and government. On the problem of the Central African Federation, the British churches felt a particular responsibility; for supported by the World Council they initially foresaw strength in uniting the richer areas of Southern and Northern Rhodesia with the poorer Nyasaland and urged their African followers to co-operate in this political effort of the British government to end colonialism. When it became evident that the whites in Rhodesia would be the dominant group in government (and colonialism in another form would be continued), the British Council of Churches, with World Council encouragement, made continual representations to the British government to dissolve it.³⁵

At the international level, the CCIA made representations to delegations to the United Nations regarding acceptance by the General Assembly of the International Court of Justice's decisions regarding the status of South-West Africa. At first no official stand was taken on United Nations resolutions concerning apartheid, because of the hope of winning over the Dutch Reformed Churches —and thereby the Afrikaner government—through conciliation rather than confrontation; CCIA officials did state at that time that their views against apartheid were well known by United Nations delegates.

At the societal level, the World Council has acted through its own membership or through national councils of churches (which cannot themselves be members of the World Council) to effect change. When these members or national councils act at stockholders' meetings in accordance with World Council policy, this is an example of a transnational interaction ³⁶ at the societal level.

---

³³ WCC, " Commission on World Mission and Evangelism," *Bangkok Assembly 1973* (1973), p. 54.

³⁴ Slightly out of the purview of this paper, the conflict in the Sudan was regarded by some as a racial conflict between the lighter skinned Arabs of the north and the black Africans of the south. The World Council of Churches acted as an intermediary to bring both sides together, eventually resulting in a treaty of peace in a united Sudan. See this author's *A Voice for the Voiceless* (1975) Chap. 2.

³⁵ CCIA, *Annual Report* (1957–58), p. 16.

³⁶ The term " transnational " is used here in the sense in which J. S. Nye, Jr., and Robert O. Keohane suggested in "Transnational Relations and World

The World Council's own transnational interactions with multinational corporations through divestiture of stocks it recommends not to buy, were meant to influence directly corporate policies in respect of support for apartheid regulations. Whether the aid to groups of victims of racism, several of which claim to be governments in exile (and are so recognised by other African States), should be considered interaction at the national level (with governments) or at the societal level, only the future will tell.

In spite of some evidence of power, the World Council's main emphasis and role is as a moral spokesman. Its relative powerlessness may be compared to that of the newer, poverty-stricken States. Yet they are not without a voice, however small, in international affairs. In evaluating the " politics of the powerless," one scholar has pointed out that a major element in effecting changes of attitude on the part of powerful States by the less powerful has been argument. " The function of argument is to convince rather than to compel." [37] This scholar concludes that an important aspect of activities of lesser powers is to familiarise the world with the needs of the less powerful. This has been a self-appointed task of the World Council based on its interpretation of its God-given mission. As noted at the beginning of this section, the World Council's role has been seen to be one of argumentation, moral authority, and the communication of information.[38] But as national pressure groups use the power of their purses and vote-producing capabilities to clinch arguments based on logic, so the World Council in giving aid to liberation groups and in selling stock in corporations is also partially engaged in a power model of international relations.

It is obvious that the World Council has not achieved the end of racism in southern Africa, but then neither have all the independent States of Africa nor many of those from the industrialised world, both capitalist and communist. The World Council has achieved a heightened consciousness of the effects of racism throughout the world, a great deal of it through planned programmes to reach its constituents, and, fortuitously, through the publicity and public debate engendered by its first grants. It has strengthened the

Politics: An Introduction," in their edited work *Transnational Relations and World Politics* (1972), p. x. A transnational interaction is one between two non-governmental actors across state boundaries or between one non-governmental actor and a government.

[37] Carol J. Lancaster, *The Politics of the Powerless, Pressures in the United Nations for Economic Development 1945–1965* (1972). Unpublished Ph.D. thesis of the University of London, p. 291.

[38] In summarising the results of several studies concerning NGOs, Nye and Keohane distinguish four types of interaction, one of which is " communication, the movement of information, including the transmission of beliefs, ideas, and doctrines." *Op. cit.* in note 36 above, at p. xii.

organisations which were dedicated to fighting racism. It has ameliorated the conditions of poverty and ignorance, however slightly, of the victims of racism in southern Africa according to its resources. It has carried out its role as a partisan for the poor and the impoverished of the world who have no advocate.

INTERNATIONAL ORGANISATION
IN FOREIGN POLICY PERSPECTIVE

By

MARGARET DOXEY

THE proliferation of international organisation [1] in a rich variety of
forms must surely be reckoned as one of the most distinctive and
interesting phenomena of twentieth-century international relations,
and there exists today an almost bewildering array of institutions
with diverse structures and diverse resources, performing many
different tasks. [2] The first half of the century was notable for the
creation of organisations concerned with the provision of security
and welfare at the universal level. The United Nations, created
primarily as a conflict-controlling institution, is also involved in a
very wide range of economic and social activities; with it are
associated some fifteen agencies concerned with functional co-
operation in matters such as health, communications, finance, trade
and development. [3] In addition, since the Second World War, there
has been a marked propensity to develop regional organisations
and it is at this level that the greatest institutional proliferation
has occurred. The Charter itself assigns a subordinate role to
regional bodies in the maintenance of international peace and
security (Chapter VIII) and permits collective self-defence (Article
51); divisions in the world and particularly rivalry between the
super-Powers have meant, in practice, that alliances and regional
defence bodies can act independently of the United Nations. But
regional organisations are not concerned exclusively with defence;
for instance, the Organisation of American States (OAS) (which
grew out of the Pan-American Union), and the Organisation for
African Unity (OAU) are both multipurpose organisations, with
activities in political, economic and social fields. There has also

---

[1] The term "international organisation" is preferred to "intergovernmental
organisation" because, strictly speaking, States, not governments, are members of
international bodies. The United Kingdom, not the United Kingdom government,
is now a member of the European Economic Community. Non-governmental
forms of institutionalised international co-operation do not fall within the purview
of this paper, although their relevance to international relations is not in dispute.

[2] Detailed descriptions of the 200 international organisations in existence can be
found in numerous texts. P. E. Jacob et al., The Dynamics of International Organisation, revised ed. (1972) has a particularly good description of the United
Nations system in Appendix 1.

[3] Not all these agencies are of 20th-century vintage. The oldest is the International Telecommunications Union which dates from 1865; the Universal Postal
Union was established in 1875.

been a strong trend towards regional economic integration and in Western Europe the European Economic Community (EEC) stands out as a major achievement. In Eastern Europe the Soviet Union has promoted the Council for Mutual Economic Aid (COMECON), while the " common market " model of the EEC has been widely imitated in South and Central America, the Caribbean and East Africa. Most, though not all organisations with limited membership are regionally based; two exceptions are the Commonwealth, in which past relationships between the United Kingdom and the other members form the basis for the continuing association, and the *Agence de Coopération Culturelle et Technique* set up by francophone States in 1970.

Students of international relations have naturally devoted much attention to this phenomenon of burgeoning organisation and there is a considerable body of literature in existence.[4] In general, international organisation has been welcomed as both the product and harbinger of peaceful inter-State co-operation. There has been a tendency to assume that it is good *per se* and that more is better, and theories of federalism, functionalism and neo-functionalism have all looked for increased security and prosperity as a result of institutionalised integration.[5] Experience dictates reservations in this regard; in particular, expectations of automatic progression towards closer interdependence can underestimate the extent of control retained within member States. It is also important to recognise that the institutionalisation of international co-operation may not always be directed towards—or serve—the general good. Organisations with restricted membership may be a competitive as well as an imitative response to other organisations; they may also represent an attempt to internalise certain benefits which are denied to outsiders. What is good for the Organisation of Petroleum Exporting Countries (OPEC) is not necessarily good for the rest of the world. Moreover, membership of international organisations may be seen by the governments of certain States as a means of achieving their own policy goals or extending their influence, while in other cases, membership may be the product of duress. In a world of more than 130 sovereign States, with immensely disparate military and economic capabilities, such tendencies are no doubt inevitable, but they also merit critical analysis.

---

[4] See the excellent bibliographical survey by R. J. Yalem, "The Study of International Organisation, 1920–1965: a Survey of the Literature," 10 *Background* (1966), pp. 1–57.

[5] Leading exponents of these approaches are C. J. Friedrich, *Trends in Federalism in Theory and Practice* (1966); D. Mitrany, *A Working Peace System* (1966); E. Haas, *Beyond the Nation-State* (1964) and *The Uniting of Europe* (1958). For a critique of neo-functionalism, see C. Pentland, " Neofunctionalism " in this *Year Book*, Volume 27 (1973), pp. 345–371.

It is encouraging that recent scholarly work in the field of international organisation has contributed to the development of comprehensive frameworks which facilitate comparative studies and also have policy relevance.[6] Clearly, efforts to order the field and develop useful analytical perspectives must continue. Moreover, any set of perspectives on international organisation must take account of the dominant role played by States as members. These bodies may exhibit in varying degrees policy-making and policy-implementing capability of their own, and here what can be called the organisation-as-actor approach [7] is useful in distinguishing them from States and in recognising that they can be a source of influence both on individual States and on the international system. But international organisations remain, in our age, the creations and instruments of States and are dependent on their support [8]—and support is forthcoming in the interests of domestic and foreign policy. The organisation-as-actor approach can be misleading even when applied to a body such as the EEC which has certain supra-national features. In other cases it is clearly irrelevant. Equally, integrationist approaches are not relevant to all aspects of inter-national organisation—a fact which is, of course, recognised by leading writers.[9]

This paper views international organisations from a foreign policy perspective. It seeks to identify in broad terms the utility of inter-national bodies for States (and for their governments), going beyond general and recognised advantages of enhanced security or welfare to consider other relevant membership benefits of communication, role and status, participation and legitimisation of policy.[10] In this perspective, costs incurred through membership of international organisations are also illuminated; again not simply in terms of the financial or other material contributions which may be required, but taking account too of possible loss of national autonomy and of liability to sanctions.

Calculations of net benefit (or net cost) on a State by State basis

---

[6] *Cf.* E. Miles, " Organisations and Integration in International Systems," 12 *International Studies Quarterly* (1968), pp. 196–224; J. Nye, *Peace in Parts* (1971); D. Puchala, " Of Blind Men, Elephants and International Integration," 10 *Journal of Common Market Studies* (1972), pp. 267–284; R. W. Cox *et al., The Anatomy of Influence: Decision-making in International Organisation* (1973).

[7] See C. A. Cosgrove and K. Twitchett, *The New International Actors: the UN and the EEC* (1970).

[8] In a pioneering study P. B. Potter noted that " international co-operation . . . takes the nation-state as a permanent unit and expects neither its subjugation nor its disappearance by the sublimation of the principle of nationality." *An Introduction to the Study of International Organisation,* 3rd ed. (1928), p. 14.

[9] See J. Nye, *op. cit.* in note 6 above.

[10] R. E. Riggs has made a major contribution in this area. See *US/UN: Foreign Policy and International Organisation* (1971).

in respect of any international organisation would help to explain policies regarding membership and participation. In turn, these assessments would have significant implications for the vitality and effectiveness of the organisation, reflecting the level of support which it enjoys. For instance, divergent assessments of net benefit and net cost within the organisation would suggest that the foreign policy goals of one or more members are being served at the expense of others; moreover, if participation in some or all of the organisation's activities is seen by governments of key States as being too costly (in terms of compensating benefits), then their level of support may dwindle to the detriment of the organisation's work. On the other hand, organisations which do not place heavy demands on their members in terms of support costs may continue to function at a level where the rewards are small but useful.

No attempt is made here to elaborate on other relevant and important perspectives on international organisation which may be complementary. Among these, the focus on decision-making would seem particularly promising.[11] Nor is this paper presented as yet another new approach, but rather as an effort to stand back in order to gain better perspective.[12]

I—THE USES OF INTERNATIONAL ORGANISATION

At the time when an organisation is established, a set of purposes is usually spelled out, indicating the particular areas to which activity and effort will be directed.[13] One would therefore expect that the founding members see these general purposes as useful and the organisation as a means of achieving them. From the outset, however, and beneath the rhetoric, the organisation may also be perceived as having specific uses for members, and over time these uses may change. In some cases, the original purposes may be superseded, particularly if new members bring their own ideas about objectives. Changes in the scope of United Nations activity

---

[11] *Cf.* R. Cox *et al., op. cit.*; L. J. Cantori and S. L. Spiegel, "The Analysis of Regional International Politics: the integration versus the empirical systems approach," 27 *International Organisation* (1973), pp. 465–494.

[12] An undue proliferation of approaches to any subject must ultimately raise doubts about the value of pursuing something which is so elusive—which in relation to international organisation would be absurd—or about the skills of researchers. *Cf.* D. Puchala's comment that the degree of conceptual confusion reigning in integration studies should be "a source of embarrassment to students of international organisation," *loc. cit.* in note 6 above, p. 268.

[13] For instance, the Rome Treaty states that "it shall be the aim of the Community . . . to promote throughout the Community a harmonious development of economic activities, a continuous and balanced expansion, an increased stability, an accelerated raising of the standard of living and closer relations between its Member States " (Art. 2).

(*e.g.* pressure for decolonisation),[14] of Commonwealth activity (*e.g.* pressure on the United Kingdom over Rhodesia, emphasis on technical co-operation) [15] and of the activities of the specialised agencies (from peace and co-operation to aid and development) [16] are examples of this possibility.

This does not mean that the foreign policy goals of members are the only significant inputs to policy decisions taken within international organisations; for instance, new tasks may be developed in response to environmental needs (*e.g.* conservation of resources, anti-pollution measures), or because of initiatives originating largely within the organisation's own bureaucracy (*e.g.* the role of the United Nations Secretary-General in peacekeeping between 1956 and 1961). But authority for international organisations to undertake new tasks comes from national governments, and national governments also set limits to competence and provide the resources which make action possible. And national governments must justify their policies in terms of national interest.[17]

There is considerable reference to the foreign policy uses of international organisation in the literature. Inis Claude questions whether " the attribution of decisions, resolutions or actions to collective entities under their organisational labels can be properly regarded as much more than a rhetorical cover for the reality of actions taken by states, with varying degrees of consensus and contention, within the frameworks . . . provided by international organisations." [18] Why then should States use these frameworks? And to what extent do they use them? These are relevant questions of motivation and policy which a foreign policy perspective should help to explain.

In looking closely at the uses of international organisation, it is helpful to make a distinction between the pre-membership and the membership stage. In the former, a government decides whether or not to commit the State to membership; once inside the organisation there will be decisions to participate more or less actively—

---

[14] See R. E. Riggs, *op. cit.* in note 10 above; D. Kay, " The Impact of African States on the United Nations," 23 *International Organisation* (1969), pp. 20–47.

[15] See M. Doxey, " The Commonwealth in the 1970s " in this *Year Book*, Volume 27 (1973), pp. 90–109.

[16] See J. Harrod, " Problems of the United Nations Specialised Agencies at the Quarter Century " in this *Year Book*, Volume 28 (1974), pp. 187–203.

[17] See J. Frankel, *Contemporary International Theory and the Behaviour of States* (1973), at p. 77: " However vague, controversial and abused in political usage, the term ' national interest ' is still the most widely used and generally intelligible shorthand description of all the purposive elements in foreign policy."

[18] I. Claude Jnr., *Swords into Plowshares*, 4th ed. (1971), p. 11. See too R. E. Riggs, *op. cit.* in note 10 above at p. 2: " . . . international organisation is much less the voice of a genuine international community than an instrument by which states seek to promote their respective national interests."

and here multipurpose organisations like the United Nations and the Commonwealth permit different levels of participation in different aspects of their work; conceivably, at some stage, there may be a question of terminating membership.

In the pre-membership stage, *expectations* regarding the organisation's utility are relevant, and where a decision is made to join, it could be assumed that overall benefits of membership are expected to exceed costs, if only by a small margin. Conversely, a decision not to join would indicate that no benefits are anticipated or that costs are seen as likely to exceed them. Where membership is the product of coercion, it would seem reasonable to treat as a negative benefit the avoidance of penalties which would accompany non-membership; where coercion is exercised to prevent membership, penalties can be treated as a cost. In the membership stage, governments are concerned with perceptions of *realised* advantage, as well as with expectations of future advantage, and one might look for a greater measure of participation in areas where benefits are perceived as significant and outweighing costs. One might also expect a trend to non-participation where costs seem to exceed benefits.[19] There can be periodic or continuing reassessment of the utility of the organisation in the light of changing internal or external circumstances, and if a decision is made to terminate membership, the cost of staying in is presumably perceived as being excessive—though an alternative to withdrawal may be to remain a member at a minimal level of participation. Leaving an organisation suggests an element of salience in foreign policy and has an air of finality; as it may not be possible to resume membership at will, non-participation may be a safer option.

This foreign policy perspective is based on an assumption of the State (government) as rational actor.[20] Failure to join an organisation may be explained in some cases as the product of ignorance or inertia (and it may also represent a miscalculation of net benefit). Failure to leave could also be the result of inertia, though here one would expect continued membership to be characterised by a low level of participation. But in general, one expects foreign policy decision-making to have, or appear to have a quality of

[19] See F. A. Beer, *The Political Economy of Alliances: Benefits, Costs and Institutions in NATO* (1972), particularly pp. 33–34.

[20] See G. T. Allison, *Essence of Decision: Explaining the Cuban Missile Crisis* (1971), for identification of other models; see S. D. Krasner, " Are Bureaucracies Important?," 7 *Foreign Policy* (1972), pp. 159–179, for a discussion of their usefulness. In " Transgovernmental Interaction in the International Monetary System, 1960–1972," R. W. Russell convincingly demonstrates the value of the "image of rational, cohesive nation-states as actors " in seeking to understand international monetary policy: 27 *International Organisation* (1973), p. 463.

deliberation,[21] and the fact that *not* taking a decision may often constitute a decision does not seem particularly relevant to questions of joining, supporting or leaving international bodies. These are questions which have policy and cost implications to which the " collective mind of government " must be addressed.[22] Foreign policy decision-making is usually undertaken within the government system and the " balance sheets " are drawn up privately. On occasions, however, in democratic systems there may be considerable public and media involvement in policy decisions of this kind. Projections of costs and benefits were a continuing accompaniment to the series of British applications to join the EEC, with strong divisions of opinion persisting over the likely net advantages or disadvantages. The Government's need for public support for entry, which would have far-reaching implications for the country's future, as well as immediate effects on the economy, made such discussion and argument necessary and inevitable. Similar debates took place in Norway and Denmark and referenda were held in 1972 to determine the weight of public opinion in both countries. Government decisions regarding the level of participation in international organisations are not usually aired publicly, even in democracies, but the merits of continuing or terminating membership may be given some publicity. The Canadian government canvassed opinion on the merits of remaining in the North Atlantic Treaty Organisation (NATO) in the course of its 1969 foreign policy review, and argument was put forward, both pro and con, based on differing assessments of national interest.[23]

A suggested categorisation of the benefits and costs associated with membership of international organisations is given below:

Benefits	*Costs*
Positive	
Security	Loss of national autonomy
Welfare	Liability to sanctions within the
Communication	organisation

---

[21] Similar arguments were used by the writer to support a cost/benefit analysis of compliance with international norms. See M. Doxey, " International Sanctions: A Framework for Analysis with special reference to the UN and Southern Africa," 26 *International Organisation* (1972), pp. 527–550 and especially p. 532.

[22] The phrase is used by R. Robinson and J. Gallagher in *Africa and the Victorians* (1961), p. 19.

[23] See Canadian Institute of International Affairs, *Behind the Headlines*, Vol. XXVIII, Nrs. 1–6, 1969, for summaries of testimony given to the Canadian House of Commons Standing Committee on External Affairs and National Defence. The Canadian government rejected suggestions of a non-aligned posture for Canada and elected to remain in NATO as a full member. Commitment of Canadian forces in Europe was cut by 50 per cent.

Benefits	Costs
Positive—cont.	
Status and Role	Liability to penalties from non-
Participation	members
(a) in policy formulation	Contributions:
(b) in policy implementation	(a) Financial (and other
Legitimisation of national	material resources)
policy	(b) Personnel
Negative	
Avoidance of penalties	

Two points require emphasis before these categories are examined more closely. In the first place, they have been labelled for analytical convenience; in empirical situations there will be considerable overlap. For instance, in practice, the benefits of status and role and of legitimisation of policy may not be distinct from benefits of participation. Secondly, quantification of benefits and costs which are so mixed in character is neither possible nor necessary. At most it may be useful to indicate significance ratings such as low, moderate and high, and provide some overall assessment. What is important is to identify major components of the membership " balance-sheet " in order to clarify policies. On the question of participation Richard Gardner noted that " the central question is whether the credits exceed the debits, whether as a whole the institution is making a net contribution to the national interest." [24] In a pre-membership stage, the question is whether a net contribution to national interest seems likely.

II—BENEFITS

1. *Security*

The benefits of association for security purposes have been recognised and sought by individuals and groups throughout history. In international relations, alliances and coalitions have traditionally reflected the views of rulers that there was safety in numbers: while weaker Powers looked for protection, stronger Powers looked for the extension of their own influence and capabilities in the face of rivals, and the retention as allies of those who might otherwise be tempted (or coerced) to join the rival camp. But in the twentieth century, as noted earlier in this paper, a very much wider range of needs has led to the institutionalisation of links of all kinds. Defence is still relevant in the nuclear age and although collective security through the United Nations has not materialised, attempts to

---

[24] R. Gardner, *In Pursuit of World Order* (1964), pp. 119–120.

institutionalise security at the regional level have produced relatively durable alliance structures with little change in membership.[25]

Specific associational benefits which may increase members' security are well known. They include shelter under the nuclear " umbrella " of a super-Power; augmentation of manpower and material resources; securing of bases; use of overflying and port facilities; transit rights; access to technology and training; receipt of loans and grants for the purchase of military *matériel* of all kinds. A treaty obligation and an organisational framework make the furnishing of mutual support more, if not completely secure; the " front " is solidified and joint planning, joint manoeuvres, perhaps defence production sharing are made possible. In an international system characterised by the institutionalisation of defence arrangements, exclusion from such arrangements can mean increased vulnerability. One may cite the precarious position of Israel, and perhaps of South Africa, neither of whom can be assured of receiving assistance from other States if they should come under attack.[26]

2. Welfare

The second broad and familiar category of associational benefits has to do with economic and social welfare. Among the major objectives of the host of organisations in this field are: (i) benefits of improved services organised through agencies such as the International Civil Aviation Organisation (ICAO), the International Telecommunications Union (ITU) and the Universal Postal Union (UPU); (ii) benefits of shared experience and planning in economic and social fields through agencies such as the World Health Organisation (WHO), the Food and Agricultural Organisation (FAO) and the International Labour Organisation (ILO); (iii) benefits of orderly co-ordination of trade, tariff and monetary policy through agencies such as the International Monetary Fund (IMF) and the General Agreement on Tariffs and Trade (GATT); (iv) benefits of prosperity and growth through: (a) the establishment of free trade areas and common markets, and of economic communities such as the EEC whose members aspire to harmonise a whole range of economic and social policies and possibly, in the long run, to attain a degree of political union; (b) management or control of resources by bodies such as the Organisation of Petroleum Export-

---

[25] France remained a member of NATO but withdrew from participation in military aspects of its work in 1966. Iraq withdrew from the Baghdad Pact (re-named the Central Treaty Organisation) in 1959.

[26] M. Brecher notes Israel's " unremitting quest for a US guarantee or treaty of alliance." " Israel's foreign policy: challenges of the 1970s," 28 *International Journal* (1973), p. 749.

ing Countries (OPEC); (v) benefits of development aid and re-
distributive welfare through organisations such as the United
Nations, the Commonwealth, the United Nations Conference on
Trade and Development (UNCTAD) and the EEC-Yaoundé arrangements. These benefits are not limited to transfer payments, but
include improved or preferential access to capital, markets and
advanced technology, and the receipt of technical assistance.

General associational benefits, whether of a security or welfare
nature, correspond to the stated purposes of most international
organisations. Important questions are, first, whether they are being
realised and, secondly, whether benefit and cost are evenly distributed within the organisation. Where a preponderance of security
or welfare is enjoyed by a certain group or class of members, it is
clear that unless the organisation itself has independent sources
of financial support, there must be disproportionate costs for other
members. Multilateral philanthropy may be seen as its own reward
and the key word is probably " seen," in that assistance to less
affluent members of an organisation may offer role benefits to the
donors. If not, and there are no compensatory benefits of the kind
to be discussed below, one might expect a shrinking of support and
perhaps a preference for disbursing assistance on a bilateral basis
outside the organisation. This trend has been noted in recent years
with respect to United States and Soviet aid.

Suspicions or perceptions of unevenness of benefit can also arise
in organisations ostensibly serving the interests of all members.
For instance, France has been seen as the main beneficiary of the
Common Agricultural Policy within the European Economic Community (EEC). Such fears are not conducive to rapid progress
towards closer integration.[27]

3. Communication

A third major category of benefits relates to communication, and
here two main dimensions can be distinguished. In the first place
there is the dimension of inter-personal contact which results from
membership in international organisations. For politicians and
officials there are advantages and pleasures in travel to attend
meetings of organs of consultation and, periodically, in hosting
them; in getting to know their counterparts in other governments;
in discussing common problems on a formal and informal basis.
It is easier to talk or write of the value of this kind of inter-personal

---

[27] For an East African illustration of divergent interests and divergent policies
bringing a dilution of integration, see A. A. Mazrui, " Tanzania versus East Africa,"
3 *Journal of Commonwealth Political Studies* (1965), pp. 209–225 and especially
pp. 213–215.

contact than to bring evidence to prove it, but there would seem to be no doubt that it is a positive factor. The value of the United Nations as a centre for continuous diplomatic interchange is obvious, and regular meetings of the councils and assemblies of other organisations provide similar opportunities for private as well as public negotiation. Meetings at all levels of government are a feature of the contemporary Commonwealth which stresses informality and confidentiality. Officials may have no choice, but presumably if Heads of Government and senior Ministers found such meetings a waste of time, they would not attend them.[28] Indeed, it seems possible that the value to governments and government personnel (whether elected or appointed) of personal communication of this kind is at least as great as the oft-asserted value of international experience in " socialising " international bureaucrats. For instance, in a recent study of formal and informal exchanges within the IMF network, Robert Russell noted the pay-offs in terms of greater understanding of *national* viewpoints and strategies.[29]

The second dimension of the communication benefit is the service performed by the organisation in providing a framework within which differences can be negotiated and in acting as a channel for the dissemination of information among members. Although the information function may appear to be of subsidiary importance, it is by no means insignificant. A central secretariat, which is a feature of most international organisations, facilitates the transmission of information as well as performing other core services; conferences and meetings serve the same function, as well as facilitating negotiation and the settlement of differences.

It is interesting that resistance to the idea of a permanent Secretariat in the Commonwealth, which reflected members' concern about British dominance, changed to support in the mid-1960s. The Commonwealth Secretariat, which was set up in 1965, has taken over and developed the information and service role formerly handled by the British Commonwealth Relations Office and now plays a key role in the association.

A failure of communication may be a significant factor in bringing reassessment by members of the value of an organisation. One may cite the confusion in NATO over the United States Government's

---

[28] The Canadian Prime Minister told newsmen after the Heads of Government Conference in Ottawa in August 1973 that " academics spend half their time going to conferences or talking to each other and convincing each other that certain things are important. If it is true for them, it is certainly more true for Heads of Government." Quoted in *Commonwealth,* October 1973, p. 6.

[29] R. W. Russell, *loc. cit.* in note 20 above, pp. 457, 460 (emphasis added).

failure to consult its European allies before placing American forces on alert in the course of the 1973 Middle East War.

4. *Status and Role*

The two attributes of status and role are so closely intertwined that they are best considered jointly. Joseph Frankel comments that "role prescription in international politics is pronounced mainly within international organisations. . . ."[30] Here it is suggested that the status and role benefits which international organisations offer can be influential in government decisions to seek membership and to participate actively in an organisation's work.

One would expect these particular benefits to be of special importance to Powers of less than the first rank. As far as super-Powers are concerned, their "identity" is secure, regardless of organisational involvement; nevertheless, leadership roles can be prestigious at both the universal and regional level, and if hegemony is challenged in regional bodies, one might expect the super-Power to scale down its participation. Alternatively, it may exert pressure to retain its hegemonial position, which also carries legitimisation of policy possibilities and special costs—both of which are discussed below. For lesser Powers, however, there is little doubt that membership of organisations is perceived as strengthening the national image. This is particularly true of the many States which have emerged from dependence in the wake of decolonisation. Governments of such States have been concerned to assert their new status on the international scene by associating as equals with older and often much more powerful States, and also to improve it by organisational linkage with other States in the same rank as themselves. Not surprisingly, there is heavy stress on equality in both the OAU and the contemporary Commonwealth.

"Middle" or intermediate Power status can also be cultivated through membership in major political organisations. Canada in the St. Laurent and Pearson eras provided a good example of an "internationalist" foreign policy, heavily oriented to the United Nations and peacekeeping. Moreover, the change in policy emphasis announced by the Trudeau government in 1970,[31] which forecast less concern with middle Power status and the abandonment of the role of "helpful fixer," does not seem to have been implemented. Efforts to secure Canadian participation in the Middle East peacekeeping force in the autumn of 1973 reflected a continuing

---

[30] J. Frankel, *op. cit.* in note 17 above, p. 83.

[31] *Foreign Policy for Canadians* (Dept. of External Affairs, Ottawa), 1970, p. 8.

government (and public) concern that Canada should play a world peacekeeping role.

In confirming or conferring status and role, the large multi-purpose organisations are obviously the most significant; indeed United Nations membership has become an accolade of statehood. Ex-colonies have experienced few problems with admittance, but the application of Bangla Desh—a State seceding from an ex-colony and member of the United Nations—was vetoed by China. Bangla Desh was, however, admitted to the Commonwealth—from which Pakistan withdrew—in February 1972, and this served to reinforce its new status.

Attempts to exclude States from organisations are, in part, attempts to reduce their international status and role. Examples are the exclusion of the government of the People's Republic of China from participation in the United Nations from 1949 to 1971; the forced withdrawal of South Africa from the Commonwealth and numerous United Nations agencies in the 1960s; the exclusion of Cuba from the OAS from 1962 to the present. The universal non-recognition of Rhodesia's unilaterally declared independent status deprives it of any formal standing in the world community.

Most international bodies stress equality of status in spite of obvious inequalities of size and strength among their members. In the United Nations, however, inequality is reinforced by the position certain members are given within the Security Council, which alone has the power to make binding decisions. The pre-eminent status of five great Powers was recognised in their right to permanent seats and their veto power. Thus France and the United Kingdom enjoy the rank of great Powers alongside China, the Soviet Union and the United States. The rotation of the 10 non-permanent seats among other United Nations members gives an opportunity for temporary status, and the decision-making role which goes with it; but power to block action, should all permanent members favour it, depends on at least six of the non-permanent members forming a coalition to prevent a two-thirds majority. In the Assembly and other United Nations organs there is no system of privileged voting; all votes are of equal value and all members can derive role benefits from sponsoring, supporting or opposing resolutions.

It is interesting that the provisions of the Treaty of Rome for qualified majority voting in the EEC have been virtually negated by the 1966 Luxembourg Compromise which requires unanimity on any matter which touches the core interests of any members. The Compromise was a product of France's unwillingness to relinquish control of national decision-making power.

Status and role benefits obtained through membership of international bodies will support the national image which a government wishes to sustain in the eyes of its own public as well as in the world at large. A foreign policy which appears to yield international prestige will prove popular, particularly if it can be viewed as contributing to national sovereignty or national identity, or to world peace. These are intangible benefits, but most governments would see them as important. They contribute to national morale and purpose; in addition, they reinforce the government's standing within the country. This is desirable in any political system, but crucial where continuation in office depends on electoral process.

If the long-term economic benefits were seen as the prime reason for the belated British applications to joint the EEC, there was also heavy emphasis by Conservative and Labour governments on the status and role which membership would offer.[32] Jam the day after tomorrow is not necessarily a powerful incentive, and the prospect of a leading role in a re-invigorated Western Europe might be calculated to have a more direct appeal to the British public, aware of a marked diminution in Britain's world role.

5. Participation

The opportunity which membership of an international organisation gives for participation in policy-making and policy implementation can be perceived as useful for two reasons. In the first place, the chance to make an input to policy formation not only ensures the articulation of foreign policy goals of individual States, but also allows the possibility of persuading other States of the merits of these goals, and of seeing them collectively adopted. Participation may also allow governments to prevent the adoption of unacceptable collective goals either by individual vote, or by a coalition of votes. In 1950, as is well known, the Soviet Union discovered the risks attached to absenteeism from the Security Council where its presence would have enabled a veto to be cast on the Korean operation. Recently, a clear statement of the perceived benefits of participation was made by Mr. Heath in respect of British membership of the EEC. He commented that the strong voice which the United Kingdom now has in all EEC decisions is " the greatest benefit of all. . . . If we were to pull out . . . it would go on making its decisions, we would go on being affected by them, but we would have no part in taking them. . . . And on its own, our voice in world affairs would become increasingly ineffective." [33]

---

[32] See, *e.g.*, *The United Kingdom and the European Communities*, Cmnd. 4715, 1971, paras. 26–27 and 62–66.
[33] Interview with Hella Pick, *Manchester Guardian Weekly*, November 10, 1973.

Secondly, where the organisation adopts policies which are congruent with national policies, members can participate actively in their implementation (*e.g.* Canadians in peacekeeping). On the other hand, if unacceptable policies have been adopted, members can often work within the organisation to block their implementation. Non-participation may reduce the effect of decisions to zero: by failing to implement United Nations sanctions against Rhodesia, South Africa and Portugal have undermined the whole effort. Similarly, resolutions can remain aspirational; among many examples one may cite the United Nations General Assembly resolution which terminated the South African mandate over Namibia (South-West Africa).[34] This resolution has not had significant practical consequences because members are unwilling or unable to implement it.

The level of members' participation has a direct bearing on the effectiveness of an organisation, particularly if non-participating members are important contributors of resources, or are in a key position either to prevent decisions being taken, or to nullify their effects. Obviously, the United Nations security function has atrophied due to non-activation, while peacekeeping has only been attempted in certain areas, and with limited success. One may speculate whether the OAS would again rally to impose sanctions on a member State as it did in the case of Cuba. Jeffrey Harrod has noted the " declining prestige and power " of many specialised agencies, which raises " questions as to their purpose and utility." [35]

6. *Legitimisation of foreign policy*

Closely linked with status and role and with participation benefits, but of rather special character, are the possibilities of legitimisation of foreign policy within a major organisation which undertakes political and economic tasks. Robert Riggs, whose valuable study of the United Nations in relation to United States foreign policy has already been noted, emphasises that " the quest for legitimacy is a constant dimension of national policy at the UN," [36] and regional bodies can also be important in this context.

Legitimisation of policy is possible where a single power is able to dominate an organisation and its decision-making processes in

---

[34] General Assembly Resolution 2145 (XXI), October 27, 1966. The Security Council declared the continued presence of South African authorities illegal in Resolution Nr. 276, January 30, 1970.

[35] J. Harrod, *loc. cit.* in note 16 above, p. 189.

[36] R. E. Riggs, *op. cit.* in note 10 above, p. 211. I. Claude Jnr. notes that the United Nations " has come to be regarded, and used, as a dispenser of politically significant approval of the claims, policies and actions of states." *Op. cit.* in note 18 above, p. 73.

the interests of its own national policy, or where a group of Powers in coalition can exert a similar influence in the interests of shared goals. Such collective legitimisation of foreign policy (or policies) is valuable for both internal and external reasons.[37] It projects an image of world, or regional interest, rather than selfish national interest, strengthens a leadership role and de-legitimises opposing policies. It may also produce tangible benefits in the form of material contributions which assist in the realisation of national goals.

In the early years of the United Nations, the United States could rely on the support of the majority of members and was able to obtain collective legitimisation for its Cold War policies, either through the Security Council or through the Assembly, using the Uniting for Peace Resolution.[38] The Soviet Union never enjoyed this advantage. By the 1960s, however, new States made up the majority of United Nations membership and their concerns were decolonisation, self-determination, economic development and the end of racial discrimination in the form of white minority rule. Henceforth, the Assembly concentrated on these issues and was no longer amenable to United States direction, with the result that the United States increasingly dealt with major foreign policy issues outside the United Nations.

Both super-Powers have sought legitimisation of their policies through regional organisations. The United States has used the OAS as an instrument of policy legitimisation in the Western Hemisphere; the Soviet Union has used the Warsaw Pact to legiti-mise Soviet action in Eastern Europe.[39] In an era of heightened national sensitivity and resentment of super-Power hegemony, the question may be raised whether overt intervention authorised by regional bodies may not ultimately prove counter-productive. It seems unlikely that the United States leadership role in the hemis-phere was strengthened by intervention in the Dominican Republic in 1965.

In general, efforts to legitimise group policies within international organisations have been more productive of words than deeds. African States have persistently sought endorsement of their stand against white minority régimes in Southern Africa in the United

---

[37] See I. Claude Jnr., *The Changing United Nations* (1973), pp. 73–103.

[38] Riggs notes that between 1946 and 1954 there were 20 issues in which (a) the countries concerned were either communist or non-communist; (b) the United States supported United Nations intervention with legitimisation as the primary objective of its policy. *Op. cit.* in note 10 above, pp. 34–35.

[39] See T. M. Franck and E. Weisband, *World Politics: Verbal Strategy among the Superpowers* (1972); J. Slater, "The Limits of Legitimisation in International Organisations: the Organisation of American States and the Dominican Crisis," 23 *International Organization* (1969), pp. 48–72.

Nations, the Commonwealth and the OAU, and their efforts have been successful insofar as verbal condemnation is concerned. To date, however, apart from United Nations mandatory sanctions against Rhodesia (which are by no means fully implemented) one of the strongest United Nations moves has been to recommend that members should not sell arms to South Africa. Neither the resolution ending the mandate over Namibia nor the resolution recognising the independence of Guinea-Bissau [40] have been implemented in practical terms. It must be conceded, however, that the legitimacy of the African position is probably no longer in question; the fact that action has not followed does not necessarily erode its moral force. And if organisations like the United Nations and the Commonwealth did not exist, one might consider that African States would have found it much more difficult to obtain general and formal expressions of support for their position.

7. *Avoidance of penalties of non-membership*

In considering whether to join or leave international organisations, governments will certainly consider the likelihood of incurring penalties as a result of non-membership. Such negative benefits may weigh heavily, and may even be decisive. Experience suggests that the costs of non-membership of the Warsaw Pact for East European countries may be extremely high so that in practical terms they are really in a non-choice situation regarding membership. Coercion which *restrains* States from joining international organisations is dealt with on the cost side of the " balance sheet," to which the next section of this paper is devoted.

III—Costs

1. *Loss of autonomy in decision-making*

Loss of national autonomy in decision-making can be significant in bodies which have articulated substantive norms or where majority voting can commit members to carry out certain policies. The United Nations requires the renunciation of the use of force by members, except in self-defence, but in practice this has not proved a serious limitation on freedom of action. On the other hand, South Africa would have had to make significant modifications in its *apartheid* policy in order to remain in the Commonwealth as a republic; in other words, the autonomy of the South African government in domestic policy-making would have been diminished. In 1962, the Marxist-Leninist orientation of the Cuban government and its alignment with the Soviet Union was seen as incompatible

---

[40] General Assembly Resolution A/3061 (XXVIII), November 2, 1973.

with membership in the OAS: continued membership was contingent upon observance of the group norm of non-communism.

The effect on national autonomy is likely to be significant in regional organisations which have wide ranging authority over economic and social policy. The United Kingdom was not required to leave the Commonwealth in order to enter the EEC, but Commonwealth trade preferences had to be eliminated and the United Kingdom, like other members of the Community, is now bound to conform to its policies and procedures. There has been considerable concern in the United Kingdom over the possibility of a continuing erosion of sovereignty, with power passing from Westminster to Brussels, despite the fact that the United Kingdom now enjoys full participation in Community policy-making.[41] Perceptions will be all important here, as in all assessments of political and social benefits and costs, as there is no set of objective measures which can be used.

Once inside an organisation, a member can exert influence to block decisions which do not fit its own policies (as noted earlier in this paper) but if a constitutionally adequate majority rules against the interests of one State, there may be costs involved in adhering to the collective decision. The government of that State may decide to carry out the decision, regardless of cost; failure to do so, could mean liability to sanctions which are discussed below. Alternatively, it may decide to withdraw from active participation. The French government boycotted the organs of the EEC for several months in 1965 in order to limit the power of the Commission and to prevent inauguration of a policy of majority decisions in the Council.

2. *Liability to sanctions*

Failure to observe norms, or to carry out decisions made by international organisations, may carry a risk of sanctions, which must be reckoned as a cost, but experience has not established that intra-organisational sanctions are very compelling. At the universal level, a lack of consensus concerning their application has been matched by unwillingness to implement them; at the regional level, alternative sources of support have usually been available to targets of sanctions. International sanctions may take diplomatic, economic or military forms; if they are not feared, or if compliance would be

---

[41] See S. Z. Young, " Britain in the European Community: the view from Right and Left," *The World Today,* July 1973, pp. 300–306. G. Thomson noted two years earlier that " Undoubtedly . . . the main political argument against British entry is over sovereignty," " Britain and the Common Market: the political case," *ibid.,* July 1971, p. 282.

seen as very costly in terms of loss of national values, States may be prepared to run the risk of incurring them.[42]

3. *Liability to penalties*

In certain cases, membership of an international organisation might carry costs in the form of penalties applied by a disapproving third State. Faced with Soviet opposition, Czechoslovakia withdrew from the group of Western European nations which subsequently organised themselves to receive Marshall Aid. Finland found that membership in the European Free Trade Area (EFTA) did not threaten the delicate balance of its relationship with the Soviet Union, but did not attempt to join the EEC as a full member. Instead, it limited itself to negotiating a free trade agreement with the Community. Costs of this type are clearly significant in policy decisions regarding membership and require careful and accurate assessment. They reflect the same coercive dimension which was noted earlier in respect of forced membership.

4. *Contributions*

(a) *Financial (and other material resources)*. At the present time, virtually all international organisations are dependent on financial support from members in order to continue in existence and carry on their work.[43] Those financial contributions (together with other contributions of a material nature) constitute the most visible costs of membership and as they are susceptible to fairly precise calculation, they can often be used as a yardstick against which the value, or benefit of membership can be measured.[44] For rich nations, which see themselves as bearing the brunt of financial support of international organisations, a failure on the part of the organisation to meet expectations of advantage can result in pressure to scale down contributions. This, in turn, will affect the capability of the organisation to carry on its work.[45]

Regular contributions are often linked to Gross National Product (GNP); additional dues may not always be acceptable. The refusal of the French and Soviet governments to contribute to the expenses of the United Nations force in the Congo (ONUC) reflected their

---

[42] See M. Doxey, *loc. cit.* in note 21 above.

[43] The EEC is a partial exception in that its " own resources " system will eventually replace contributions from members. A progressively larger proportion of revenue will accrue to the Community from customs duties and levies on agricultural imports, but for some years contributions from members will continue to provide the main source of revenue.

[44] F. A. Beer, *op. cit.* in note 19 above, p. 31.

[45] The United States has now reduced its contribution to the United Nations to 25 per cent. of the organisation's total revenue, ostensibly because of the greatly enlarged membership. Formerly it contributed over 30 per cent.

opposition to the operation. The United States' attempt to invoke the penalties of Article 19 against the defaulters was unsuccessful,[46] and generally one might doubt the efficacy of sanctions in such cases.

In military organisations such as NATO and the Warsaw Pact, the major burden of providing security will fall on the hegemonial Power which makes the heaviest commitment of resources to collective defence. But its material contributions may not necessarily be greater in relation to its overall national resources than the contributions of other members are in relation to theirs, and for the major Power the financial cost will be offset by lower or negligible political costs in terms of loss of autonomy and liability to sanctions.

Financial burdens of membership of an elaborate economic system like the EEC are obviously substantial; they are also difficult to assess in advance. The White Paper published by the Labour Government in February 1970 noted that " the major uncertain factor . . . is the balance of economic advantage, particularly in the short run, where the assessments in this paper indicate a wide range of possible consequences of membership." [47]

(b) *Personnel.* Finally, it should be noted that international organisations must also recruit their personnel from nationals of member States and this can represent a minor cost to States who lose the services of talented diplomats, bureaucrats and experts of all kinds, either temporarily or permanently, particularly if the available pool of national talent is small and there are heavy competing demands in national government service.

IV—THE " BALANCE SHEET " REVIEWED

Not all these benefits and costs are applicable to all organisations at all times. Generally, however, in explaining a non-coerced decision to join an international body, one would look for expectations of net benefit encompassing security and/or welfare, communication and participation. Benefits of status and role, and of policy legiti-

---

[46] See J. G. Stoessinger, *The United Nations and the Super Powers* (1970), pp. 90–113. ONUC left the UN with a heavy burden of debt from which it has never fully recovered and its ability to undertake similar operations was clearly undermined.

[47] *Britain and the European Communities,* Cmnd. 4289 (1970), p. 46. Earlier in the White Paper it was noted that aggregation of the estimated costs of entry " in respect of agriculture, Community finance, trade and industry, capital movements and invisibles " was not practicable—a result could be an " overall balance of payments cost ranging from about £100 million to about £1,100 million " (p. 43). In 1971, the Conservative Government projected a possible United Kingdom net contribution rising from £100 million in 1973 to £200 million in 1977. *The United Kingdom and the European Communities,* Cmnd. 4715, Table. 2.

misation may be rarer, but where they promise to be significant, one would expect a positive commitment to the organisation. Some cost in the form of financial contributions will be usual, and obligations to provide security or economic benefits may be heavier for more affluent States, but in many organisations costs may be negligible in terms of loss of autonomy or liability to sanctions. Aggregation and comparison of benefit and cost may be difficult, but some kind of " balance sheet " must be struck in relation to membership decisions and where costs, of whatever nature, are expected to be high, benefits must also be rated highly. Where benefits are expected to be low, costs too must be low. One might also predict that the greater the anticipated cost, whether in terms of loss of autonomy or the amount of required contributions, the closer would be the calculation of the merits of joining. Thus much of the discussion about British entry to the EEC centred on whether the future benefits of economic growth and a new " European " role would *outweigh* the immediate monetary cost and the inevitable loss of sovereignty. In office, both Conservative and Labour governments concluded that they would, provided the right terms of entry could be negotiated. In contrast, in rejecting the case for joining the OAS, the present Canadian government concluded that costs of membership, in the form of possible limitations on Canada's freedom of action which would stem from adherence to the Rio Treaty and of obligations in respect of development assistance which " might absorb most available resources for a period of many years " would not be outweighed by the rather (nebulous) benefits of closer relations with Latin America, most of which could be realised outside the organisation through bilateral channels.[48]

For States who already belong to international organisations, the same relationships might be expected to hold between realised benefit and realised cost. High costs demand a high level of benefit; low benefits a low level of cost. Over time, changed circumstances may bring a change in perceptions of net benefit. For instance, an organisation may cease to contribute significantly to legitimisation of policy; the need for collective defence may seem less pressing; there may be heightened concern over national sovereignty. Members affected by such changed perceptions will be disposed to participate less enthusiastically and contribute less generously. And if disparities are perceived between overall benefits for some members and overall costs to others, there is likely to be pressure for redistribution of the cost burden, discussion of reduced levels of participation, even

---

[48] The " balance sheet " of decision is summarised in *Foreign Policy for Canadians: Latin America* (Dept. of External Affairs, Ottawa), 1970, pp. 20–24.

talk of withdrawal.[49] Although the organisation will not necessarily cease to exist, its efficiency in performance will obviously be lessened.

The proliferation of international bodies in recent years has obviously been a response to felt need, and there is no question that many problems today urgently require international co-operative action for their solution. But there may have been expectations of greater benefit at lower cost than have actually been realised; certainly the propensity to set up organisations has not been fully matched by their members' propensity to support them. What an organisation actually achieves is a function of who can move it, who pays, and whose foreign policy goals it serves. And in some cases, the coercive dimension must be recognised. By and large, however, States are eager to share in the increased benefits produced by international institutions, but reluctant to surrender national sovereignty. Moreover, willingness to shoulder disproportionate burdens, such as the United States undertook in the Marshall Aid programme, seems to be on the wane, particularly where the heavier burden is not accepted by other States as conferring a correspondingly dominant role in decision-making and leadership within the organisation, and where adjustment of burdens to meet changed circumstances is resisted.

High-cost/high-benefit organisations like the EEC reflect an intense preoccupation with issues of sovereignty and national well-being, and less concern with mutual assistance; low-cost/moderate-benefit organisations like the contemporary Commonwealth, which do not generally threaten sovereignty, may be in better shape, but their capacity to bring change is obviously more limited. Modest, low-cost/low-benefit organisations fulfilling a utilitarian service role, which do not occupy a salient position in members' foreign policy, may perform at a satisfactory level, and continue to do so, but one must question the likelihood of an extension of habits of co-operation into areas of greater political and economic importance.

This paper has sketched in outline what could be a useful policy-oriented research perspective. It should perhaps be stressed that the examples used to illustrate different costs and benefits in preceding sections are no more than indicative of the type of analysis which might be undertaken; nor are they necessarily " representative." In most instances, they were taken from organisations such as the United Nations and the EEC which offer a wide and fluctuating range of benefits to members and can also involve significant costs.

---

[49] Such reassessments have been characteristic of NATO in recent years. See F. A. Beer, *op. cit.* in note 19 above. See too G. Hadley, *CENTO: the forgotten alliance* (Institute for the Study of International Organisation, University of Sussex), Monograph Nr. 4, 1971.

Case studies of the overall organisational involvement of individual States, or of the overall membership of individual organisations could investigate relevant categories of benefit and cost in sufficient detail to provide useful insights into changing attitudes towards international organisations and the role which they play in the international system.

RECENT NORTH-SOUTH RELATIONS
AND MULTILATERAL SOFT LOANS

By

JOHN SYZ

IN the 30 years that have elapsed since the end of the Second World War the nature of the divisions which have separated members of the international society have undergone a profound change. In the years immediately following the cessation of hostilities, the most frequent source of conflict, whether physical or merely verbal, could be found in the ideological differences which existed between East and West under the respective leaderships of the Soviet Union and the United States. In addition to the several physical confrontations and engagements of that period, bipolarity, the Cold War, the arms and space races were additional manifestations of the mutual distrust and fear that existed between these two groups of States.

In the latter years of this period, which have been characterised by the spirit of *détente* and the growing universality of the United Nations and most of the Specialised Agencies, the shift in public attention and discussion has been away from the former East-West differences and towards what has come to be known in roughly accurate terms as the North-South split. This distinction divides the international society into the groups of richer and poorer countries and concentrates on the various elements of conflict between the two groups. Predominant among these elements are the following: the scope of an inclusion in preferential trading arrangements; distribution of the benefits arising from commodity agreements and stabilisation programmes; protection of private foreign investment; allocation of the recently created monetary reserves called special drawing rights (SDRs); the role of international capital transfers in the process of economic development and the terms on which such transfers should be made available.

This realignment of the world into groups of richer and poorer nations promises to be a more intractable problem than that arising out of the East-West differences for a number of reasons. In the first place, although a considerable number of countries remained non-aligned as to the earlier division, the issues now under discussion, by their very nature, involve every nation. Secondly, a high rate of population increase in the poorer countries, coming as it does prior to industrialisation, as contrasted to the now richer countries which were able to industrialise prior to substantial increases in population, has a dampening effect on economic development. To the extent that the escalating legitimate needs of the population in terms of all the various social and health services dictate priorities for the allocation of the limited funds available, they cannot be directed towards increasing the economic potential or output of a country. Thirdly, improved education at the lower levels and vastly improved media of communications have focused attention on the differences in living conditions among various nations within a very short period of time. This has come to be known as the problem of rising expectations. Fourthly and finally, to the extent that ideological conflicts have taken place within various of the poorer countries, they have tended to be reduced through the responsiveness of governments to popular pressures, or, in extreme cases, through the revolutionary removal of the former government. In the international context, however, due to the dependence of the poorer countries on the economies of the richer countries, neither the government nor the people of a poorer country have the power to respond unilaterally with similar effect.

In order to increase, redirect, and improve the terms and administration of international capital flows designed to accelerate development, a new type of international institution has come into existence during the period in question. These have generally been referred to as international development banks.[1] At the time of writing there exist at least ten of these institutions which share the following characteristics.[2] In the first place, they are all international organisations or creatures of international law. All of these organisations have treaties as their legal bases; and all these treaties confer upon them corporate personality. Secondly, all these organisations have as their main, or one main, purpose, the development of some or all of their member countries. Although some of the constitutive treaties are worded solely in terms of economic development, others include measures related to economic integration or for social development as well. The final common element is that all these institutions are banks. Very broadly this criterion may be considered to include two aspects. In the first place, their powers are operational

---

[1] For a comparative analysis of some of the institutional and operational aspects of this type of institution, see the present author's *The International Development Banks* (1974).

[2] International Bank for Reconstruction and Development (IBRD or World Bank), International Finance Corporation (IFC), European Investment Bank (EIB), Inter-American Development Bank (IDB), Central American Bank for Economic Integration (CABEI), African Development Bank (AfDB), Asian Development Bank (AsDB), East African Development Bank (EADB), Caribbean Development Bank (CDB), and the Andean Development Corporation (ADC). The study referred to in the previous footnote also includes the International Development Association (IDA) as essential to an understanding of the World Bank Group as a whole, but does not include the ADC.

rather than regulatory, being modelled on commercial rather than central banks. The second aspect of this banking criterion relates to their source of funds. These institutions have a fixed capital and rely on the financial markets for the major portion of their additional resources.

The need to compete in the capital markets for additional funds has largely dictated the terms on which these institutions have been able to make finance available. However, in times of extremely high interest rates, some of these institutions have been willing to lend on the basis of a negative interest rate spread which they have been able to afford because of their considerable paid-in capital and accumulated reserves. Despite this possibility of accepting a negative interest rate spread, the high levels of interest rates in the capital markets in the last several years have made these institutions feel compelled to increase their lending rates to levels which both they and the least developed of their borrowers have found to be excessive. In the most recent period, the interest rates charged on the non-concessional loans extended by these institutions have bunched in the range of 7–9 per cent., although certain exceptions both above and below this range can be observed.

I—THE RECORD SINCE 1950

In the 1950s and early 1960s, concern over the debt servicing capacity of a number of countries inspired the inclusion of a Fund for Special Operations (FSO) in the constitutive treaty of the IDB,[3] as well as the creation of the IDA as an affiliate of the IBRD.[4] Both the FSO of the IDB and IDA were designed as mechanisms for extending soft loans under certain circumstances.[5] In more recent years, others of the international development banks listed above have had significant amounts of funds made available to

---

[3] For the prehistory of the IDB, see IDB, *Banco Interamericano, Sus Antecenentes y Creacion* (1961). The Agreement Establishing the IDB, which came into force on December 30, 1959, can be found at 389 U.N.T.S. 72.

[4] For studies of the factors leading up to the creation of the IDA, see J. H. Weaver, *The International Development Association* (1965), and E. S. Mason and R. E. Asher, *The World Bank Since Bretton Woods* (1973), especially pp. 380–389.

[5] In the discussion that follows, the hardness or softness of loans will be considered to involve three factors; namely, the interest rate charged, the length of the period of amortisation, and the grace period allowed prior to the period of amortisation. Thus a loan with no or a very low interest rate, a long grace period followed by a long amortisation period would be considered to be a very soft loan. An explanation of the formula according to which these three variables have been integrated to compute the grant element of a loan can be found in OECD, *The Flow of Financial Resources to Less-Developed Countries 1961–1965* (1967), pp. 192–196. A further, although non-quantifiable aspect of softness can be observed when a loan advanced in convertible currencies may be repaid in non-convertible currency.

them for the purpose of permitting them to make soft loans. In some cases these funds have been extended, either by loan or under an administrative arrangement, by non-members (IDB, CABEI, AfDB, CDB) as well as by members (IDB, CABEI, AsDB, CDB) of the institution.

Throughout the decade of the 1960s, as well as more recently, concern has continued to mount over the problem of debt servicing capacity of many countries, both with regard to loans which represented suppliers' credits and as to those loans which could be extended on the ordinary terms of the international development banks. From within the World Bank Group, a number of studies documented the difficulties being presented to a number of member countries in this context.[6] Other studies showed the extent to which multilateral debt renegotiations had been required in a number of cases and appeared likely to be needed in the future.[7] Furthermore, it was also recognised that the rapid growth in Euro-currency borrowing by the less developed countries had been a clearly mixed blessing.[8]

Parallel to this growing concern over debt capacity, in the context of the types of development projects that had been financed in the past, emerged another, and probably more important trend. This, briefly, was a change in the nature of the concept of development itself and the appropriate role of international financing institutions in this process. At the time that the IBRD Agreement was being drafted during the Second World War, economic development was seen as primarily retarded by inadequate flows of foreign exchange to finance the import content of specific projects which, when completed, would contribute quantifiable additions to productive output, or which, being in the nature of economic infrastructure, would provide certain necessary inputs to the growth of production. This view, based on the non-directionist model of the pre-war and pre-Depression countries of the North Atlantic area, can be seen to have been more appropriate to those purposes of the IBRD concerned with reconstruction than with development.

Since the time of the drafting of the IBRD Agreement a number of changes have taken place in what is known about the process of

---

[6] D. Avramovic, *Debt Servicing Capacity and Postwar Growth in International Indebtedness* (1958); D. Avramovic and R. Gulhati, *Debt Servicing Problems of Low Income Countries 1956–1958* (1960); D. Avramovic and associates, *Economic Growth and External Debt* (1964).

[7] IBRD, *Multilateral Debt Renegotiations: 1956–1968*, Report Nr. EC–170 (1969).

[8] W. S. Gaud, Executive Vice-President of IFC, Speech in London on November 7, 1973 (mimeographed).

economic development, or more generally, development.[9] Among these the following should be noted: that a much larger role for the public sector than had previously been envisaged is often appropriate, both with regard to ownership of industrial enterprises and with regard to development planning; that the capital absorptive capacity of less developed countries is not static but can be greatly increased both through domestic structural and administrative changes and through the external provisions of technical assistance in many areas, including the identification and preparation of projects to be financed; that education in a relevant form and health related measures to improve human resources are among the most basic inputs for increasing economic productions, apart from being highly desirable from a social point of view; that the earlier capital-intensive bias of lending operations must be reconsidered with a view towards reaching more appropriate labour-intensive solutions to many of the problems of development, for both economic and humanitarian reasons; that local expenditures should be financed when local savings are inadequate in the cases of extremely poor countries; that, given an appropriate development plan—or at least confidence that the borrowing government has its priorities right and is capable of efficient management of loan funds—in many cases programme loans are more likely to hasten the process of development than are those for specific projects; finally, that the trickle-down effect is frequently ineffective towards raising the standard of living of the poorer segments of the population and that attention must be directed specifically towards income re-distribution and directly benefiting the poorest sector.

Various of the international development banks can be seen to be at differing stages of reconciliation of their policies with the present state of the art of economic development. Generally speaking, the institutions created earliest have found it somewhat more difficult to adapt to the most acutely perceived needs of their least developed members than have the newer institutions. This can be seen to be partly due to certain constitutional limitations included in the earlier treaties but omitted more recently, and partly due to certain precedents which had been established in the practice of the IBRD which have taken considerable efforts to overcome.

Thus, in recent years, these two main factors have tended to converge. In the first place there has been the increasing concern regarding the debt servicing capacity of a number of less developed

[9] For a useful summary of the evolution of the conception of the development process as seen by the IBRD, see Mason and Asher, *op. cit.* in note 4 above, pp. 457–487. Also instructive in this regard is a comparison between the sectoral distribution of loans in any early *Annual Report* of the IBRD with the recent IBRD publication *World Bank Operations—Sectoral Programs and Policies* (1972).

countries. Secondly, revised ideas about the nature of development and the appropriate role for international financing agencies have caused these agencies to become involved in financing a number of unconventional areas. Many of these are sectors in which the economic benefits created are unquantifiable and accrue to the economy over a longer time span than that envisaged by the terms of loans directed towards the more traditional sectors such as industry, electric power, and transportation. This convergence has increased the pressure for funds to be made available for making soft loans available for distribution through multilateral channels.

The insistence that a greater proportion of official development assistance (ODA) be made available on softer terms has been expressed from a number of quarters. The recommendation of the Pearson Commission,[10] that the terms of future ODA provide for interest of no more than 2 per cent. for maturity of between 25 and 40 years, and a grace period of 7 to 10 years was echoed in Resolution 60 (III) of the third Session of UNCTAD, which was held in 1972.[11] Elsewhere, in the United Nations General Assembly, Resolution 2626 (XXV), known as An International Development Strategy for the Second United Nations Development Decade,[12] and in the 1973 DAC Review[13] (to cite only the most recent in this series), increased soft loans, especially for the poorest of the less developed countries, have been called for.

One specific response which has been made to this increased appeal for soft funds has occurred with regard to Africa, the continent having the lowest *per capita* income. In the first few years of its existence the AfDB had directed much of its attention towards securing soft funds from non-regional countries. The search for these funds mainly took the form of visits by high officials of the AfDB to the capitals of most major capital-exporting countries as well as to the meetings of the DAC in Paris. For a number of years these efforts failed to produce any concrete results. One major obstacle, indeed the primary one, was the fact that the capital-exporting countries were unwilling to contribute these funds without having a continuing voice in how they were to be used. At the same time the AfDB has continued to oppose sharing control over its activities with non-regional countries, as would necessarily happen if these countries were admitted to full membership in the AfDB.

---

[10] L. B. Pearson, Chairman of the Commission on International Development, *Partners in Development* (1969), p. 164.

[11] United Nations Conference on Trade and Development, *Report of the Conference on its Third Session*, Cmnd. 5134, p. 103.

[12] Cmnd. 4568, p. 15.

[13] E. M. Martin, Chairman of the Development Assistance Committee, *Development Co-operation, 1973 Review* (1973), pp. 79–80.

An additional factor which made capital-exporting countries wary of contributing was the continuing bad record of many of the AfDB members with regard to payments of their capital subscriptions.

A solution was found in 1972, however, when it was decided to create the African Development Fund as a fully separate international institution in which the contributing countries would have a say in management. The Agreement establishing the African Development Fund [14] was signed on November 29, 1972. The signatories were the AfDB, the major European capital-exporting countries, Japan and Brazil. Enough of the signatories had ratified the AfDF Agreement so as to bring it into force on August 1, 1973. It is noteworthy that the United States has not chosen to avail itself of original membership, although it is entitled to do so.

In many respects the AfDF Agreement has been modelled on the IBRD format for international development banks (with the active assistance of a former member of the office of the General Counsel of the IBRD), although a number of interesting differences can be observed. The remainder of this paper will be devoted to comparing certain of the constitutional provisions applicable to the AfDF with those applicable to IDA and the FSO of the IDB, the two other multilateral sources of loans on soft terms referred to above. The practice of the latter two institutions will be introduced on certain points as well. It is believed that this comparison might prove useful to those responsible for operating the AfDF as well as to others contemplating the establishment of similar arrangements for the collection and allocation of this increasingly necessary type of international finance.

II—MEMBERSHIP

Of these three arrangements, it can be seen that IDA has by far the largest membership. Its more than 100 members, all of which must also be members of the IMF and IBRD, include both the major capital-exporting countries (apart from the Socialist States of Eastern Europe) and virtually all of the poorest of the less developed countries except for the People's Republic of China. A number of the capital-importing members of the IBRD have decided not to join IDA because their *per capita* income is too large to qualify them for receiving IDA credits. When one turns to an examination of the FSO of the IDB, which is not a separate international institution, but rather one of the several sources of funds available to the IDB, the participants are the members of the IDB. These are the United States, Canada, and all the independent States

14 Cmnd. 5230.

of Latin America and the Caribbean except for Cuba. Although, since 1972, membership has also been open to Switzerland and member countries of the IMF, the expansion of membership envisaged at that time has not yet taken place. Finally, the membership of the AfDF are the AfDB on the one hand, and the contributing non-regional States referred to in the previous section. Thus it can be seen that the member States of the AfDB, to whose territories the resources of the AfDF are to be allocated, are not members of the AfDF directly, but only indirectly through the membership of the AfDB.

III—AMOUNT AND DISTRIBUTION OF CONTRIBUTIONS

Compared to the present resources of the FSO and IDA, the initial resources of the AfDF are indeed modest. If all the signatories of the AfDF Agreement do become members of that institution, initial commitments to the AfDF will amount to somewhat more than 90,000,000 units of account (U.A.—defined as the gold equivalent of the United States dollar following the par value reduction of 1972). The amounts of these commitments vary from a high of 15,000,000 U.A. in the cases of Canada and Japan, to a low of 2,000,000 U.A. for Brazil, Finland, Spain, and Yugoslavia. The subscription of the AfDB is 5,000,000 U.A. On the other hand, the present level of quotas in the FSO amounts to almost $4,000 million while the total of subscriptions and supplementary resources committed to IDA amounts to more than $5,300 million. Both the FSO and IDA, came into being with much more limited resources, these being initially authorised quotas of $150 million for the FSO and subscriptions of $1,000 million for IDA. The increases of resources and replenishments which have built the assets of the FSO and IDA up to their present levels have not come easily but have been the result of most strenuous efforts designed to secure the necessary legislative approvals among member countries.

The initial quotas in the FSO were payable to the extent of 50 per cent. in gold or United States dollars, and 50 per cent. in local currencies. The four subsequent increases in the resources of the FSO, of which the share contributed by the United States varied from a low of two-thirds to a high of five-sixths, tended towards imposing a decreasing foreign exchange burden on the capital-importing members by permitting them to fulfil all but the first increase by payments of their national currencies. The United States continued to make all subsequent payments in dollars.

The progress of the IDA in establishing and replenishing its resources has followed somewhat of a similar course of imposing a lesser foreign exchange burden on the capital-importing countries than on the capital exporters. Thus, original IDA subscriptions were payable as to 100 per cent. in convertible currencies by the Part I, or developed, countries, and as to 10 per cent. in convertible currencies and 90 per cent. in local currencies by the Part II, or less developed, countries. The three replenishments which have gone into effect to date have involved mainly commitments by Part I members to contribute further convertible currencies and limited commitments of local currencies by the Part II members.

The AfDF Agreement requires all members including the AfDB to pay 100 per cent. of original subscriptions in freely convertible currencies. If the success of this institution in attracting additional resources is going to resemble that of the FSO or of IDA, it would seem likely that it will have to distinguish among members on the basis of foreign exchange capabilities and adopt a flexible approach to the question of what proportion of future contributions might take another form in certain cases. More particularly, as to the contributions of the AfDB, local African currencies, or payment in kind, such as the furnishing of technical assistance and administrative services should not be excluded.

IV—VOTING POWER AND CONTROL

With regard to voting power and the locus of control, considerable differences can be observed when one compares the AfDF to the provisions of the IDB Agreement relating to the FSO, and to IDA. The voting rights of members of the IDB and of IDA have been modelled, in principle, on those found in the IBRD Agreement. This common principle is that apart from a fixed number of votes which are distributed equally to all members, the remaining votes are distributed in direct proportion to the funds contributed by the member. In the case of both the IDB and the IDA, the amounts taken into consideration for this purpose are the amounts of capital or subscriptions allocated to each member. Contributions to the FSO and the furnishing of supplementary resources to IDA are not considered in determining voting power. Thus, the total voting power of any member can be seen to be the sum of its basic membership votes and its proportional votes. In these two institutions the relationship of basic votes to the total votes held by members differs greatly. The provisions of the IDA Agreement allocate a much higher proportion of total votes according to the principle of equality than do those of the IDB Agreement. Presumably this difference can be attributed to the strength of the bargaining position of the United States; originally the only capital-exporting member of the IDB.

The AfDF takes a different approach to the question of voting rights. There, both in the Board of Governors (consisting of the Governors of the AfDB plus one Governor appointed by each participating State) and in the Board of Directors (consisting of six Directors chosen by the AfDB and six chosen by the participating States), votes are so distributed that the AfDB, and the participating States as a group, shall each have 1,000 votes. Within the group of capital-exporting participants, voting power is proportional to the contributions made by each State. This principle has been adapted from that used in the international commodity agreements. In those agreements, the net importers of a particular commodity as a group are allocated the same voting rights as the group of net exporters.

When one compares these three arrangements in the context of the proportions of voting power required to take affirmative action, further interesting differences can be observed. With regard to the FSO, the IDB can only take decisions by a majority of two-thirds of the total voting power, as contrasted to the simple majority of the total voting power which is required for the other decisions of the IDB. Therefore, as the United States holds just under 40 per cent. of the total voting power, it can block decisions with regard to the FSO but not other decisions of the IDB. In IDA, the normal vote required is a majority of the votes cast. Finally, in the AfDF, the normal vote is taken by a three-quarters majority of the total voting power. Therefore, no action can be taken unless it is supported by the AfDB and half the voting power of the participating non-regional States, although no single State has enough voting power to block decisions.

This description of the schemes for weighting votes and of the majorities required for actions to be taken suggests that it is usual for decisions to be taken by these institutions through the procedure of formal voting. At least with regard to the IDB and IDA, however, it is believed that formal votes are taken only exceptionally; the more usual procedure, in meetings of both the executive and plenary bodies, is for the Chairman to ascertain the feeling of the meeting, although on occasion a dissent might be recorded. In ascertaining the feeling of the meeting, however, the Chairman must be constantly aware of the voting power represented by those present. Although this is believed to accurately reflect the usual manner in which decisions are taken, evidence of the precise extent of this more informal procedure remains locked in the internal records of these institutions.[15]

---

[15] An illuminating recent study of these and other issues raised in the context of the weighted voting arrangements of the IMF can be found in J. Gold, *Voting and Decisions in the International Monetary Fund* (1972).

V—ALLOCATION OF RESOURCES

The final area in which comparisons will be made is that of how these soft loan resources have been allocated among eligible borrowers by the FSO and IDA. When the demand for capital on soft terms exceeds its supply by as large a margin as has been the case in recent years, the question of allocation is basic. Briefly the two main alternatives are the following. On the one hand attention can be focused on member countries as units. Following this approach, a country would be considered highly eligible for soft loans if it were having difficulties servicing its existing foreign exchange obligations or would be likely to if further development were financed on the same terms as had been used in the past. The other main criterion relevant to the country approach is that of poverty. Thus, the countries with the lowest gross national product (GNP) *per capita* would be considered most eligible for soft loans. This approach has been adopted by IDA.[16] In that institution, it has been decided that for the most part, the same types of projects would be financed as have been financed by the IBRD, and they would be subjected to the same standards of preparation and appraisal as those financed by the IBRD. However, they would only be financed in countries where *per capita* GNP was below a certain level (originally $300 but now closer to $375) and where the country was having debt service problems. As the intention has been to use the benefits of very soft loans to benefit the country rather than the particular activity financed, all IDA credits are extended directly to the member concerned who then re-lends the funds on terms more closely approximating commercial terms to the entity whose activities are meant to be financed.

A rather different approach has been adopted with regard to the allocation of FSO funds. There, a comparison of the types of projects financed with the ordinary resources of the IDB with those financed by FSO funds would suggest that the main criteria applied are the extent to which the benefits flowing from the completed project are capable of being captured to amortise the loan, and the time periods by when, and over which, these benefits can be expected to accrue. However, this project approach has been modified to a certain extent by another type of country related criterion, namely, population. Thus, the four most populous recipient countries, Brazil, Mexico, Argentina, and Colombia have received the four largest volumes of loans from the FSO, in the same order. As their respective *per capita* GNP are $420, $670, $1,160 and $340, it can be seen that the FSO does not pay particular attention to the

---

[16] See Weaver, *op. cit.* in note 4 above, especially pp. 118–142.

poverty criterion in allocating its resources, at least with regard to its larger members.

Which of these approaches will be adopted by the AfDF is still an open question. As most of the members of the AfDB clearly satisfy the poverty criterion of IDA, this would not really be relevant to allocation decisions of the AfDF. Furthermore, most of these countries are already receiving soft loans on the basis of the poverty criterion from IDA. Therefore, it is suggested that perhaps the most appropriate basis for allocation would lie along the lines already chosen by the FSO of the IDB, which would permit the AfDF to specialise in projects of a type whose benefits may be unquantifiable or at least spread over many years.

THE ANDEAN COMMON MARKET

By

L. D. M. NELSON

THE idea of regional integration has been a *leit-motif* of international relations in Latin America almost since independence, and has from time to time been regarded as a panacea for the ills of the region. Some of the more notable achievements in this respect, particularly in regard to economic integration, have been taking place in Latin America since 1960—the results of such treaties as the General Treaty of Central American Economic Integration of December 13, 1960 (The Central American Common Market—CACM), the Treaty Establishing a Free Trade Area and Instituting the Latin American Free Trade Association of February 18, 1960 (The Latin American Free Trade Area—LAFTA)[1] and the Agreement on Andean Subregional Integration of May 26, 1969.[2] This last instrument, the Cartagena Agreement, is perhaps the most remarkable attempt ever staged in Latin America at furthering the development of the area within the context of a common market.

I—THE EVOLUTION AND GENERAL OBJECTIVES OF THE CARTAGENA AGREEMENT

The slow progress which LAFTA had been making was the cause of increasing discontent.[3] Moreover, the less developed member countries were realising with some concern that they were in danger of replacing foreign dependence by a new dependence on the most developed Latin American States—Argentina, Brazil and Mexico. Colombia, Chile, Peru, Uruguay and Venezuela were particularly concerned since their needs as countries with insufficient market were disregarded within the LAFTA system. On August 16, 1966, the Presidents of Colombia, Chile and Venezuela and the representatives of the Presidents of Ecuador and Peru signed the Declaration of Bogota which proposed a formula for hastening the economic integration of Latin America through the improvement of the existing integration systems—the Latin American Free Trade Association (LAFTA) and the Central American Common Market (CACM). To that end, also the Declaration recommended the

[1] The parties are Argentina, Brazil, Chile, Mexico, Paraguay, Peru, Uruguay, Colombia, Ecuador, Venezuela, Bolivia.

[2] For text, see 8 *International Legal Materials*, pp. 910–939.

[3] See 6 *Derecho de la integración, revista juridica latinoamericana*, Nr. 13 (1973), p. 9 (referred to hereafter as *Derecho de la integración*). This journal is published by the Institute for Latin American Integration which is a department of the Inter-American Development Bank.

conclusion of temporary subregional agreements in which only the countries of relatively less economic development and those of insufficient market will participate. This subregional approach to Latin American economic integration was later endorsed by the Declaration of the Presidents of America at Punta del Este on April 14, 1967,[4] and after prolonged negotiation on May 26, 1969, Bolivia, Colombia, Chile, Ecuador and Peru signed the Agreement on Andean Subregional Integration (The Cartagena Agreement). Venezuela had taken part in the negotiations but did not sign the agreement. She later acceded to the treaty on February 13, 1973.

The Cartagena Agreement has as one of its objects the creation of a customs union by means of the total liberation of intra-regional trade and the creation of a common external tariff. It was hoped that the operation of the subregional agreement will, in time, enable the member countries to face the challenge of their more developed LAFTA partners and thus create a climate favourable to the formation of a Latin American Common Market. In order to avoid any disequilibrium in the evolution of the subregional market considerable emphasis is placed on the notion of "balanced and harmonious development "[5] with preferential treatment, as a consequence, being given to the less developed member States—Bolivia and Ecuador.

What has given the evolving Andean Common Market its principal objective and its most characteristic features, however, is the determination of its members to raise the standard of living of their peoples by sharing in the benefits of technical progress. Industrialisation is seen as the principal mode of achieving progress and development and planned industrialisation plays a key role in the Andean system.[6] In fact it is "the fundamental machinery of the Agreement " (Article 48). The desire to see that the development of the area took place under national and subregional control constituted another pillar of the Andean market. In a sense the Andean experiment represents a bold attempt to solve the problems of under development through regional economic integration,[7] planned industrialisation and withal a firm subregional control of foreign investments.

---

[4] 6 *I.L.M.* (1967), p. 535. Resolution 179 of the Permanent Executive of LAFTA declared that the Cartagena Agreement was compatible with the Treaty of Montevideo. See Article 110 of the Cartagena Agreement.

[5] See Celso Furtado, *Théorie du développement économique* (1970).

[6] On which see "The Economic Development of Latin America and its Principal Problems " (1950), report prepared by Professor Raul Prebisch for the Economic Commission for Latin America. E/CN.12/89/Rev. 1.

[7] See United Nations: Report on multinational corporations in world development—an excerpt reproduced in 12 *I.L.M.* 1973, pp. 1109–1135 from U.N. Doc. ST/ECA/190.

II—THE INSTITUTIONAL FRAMEWORK

There are two principal organs of the Agreement: the Commission and the Junta and two auxiliary organs: the Advisory Committee and the Economic-Social Advisory Committee. The supreme organ of the Agreement is the Commission which is composed of plenipotentiary representatives of the member States. The Commission's main functions are, *inter alia*, to formulate the general policy of the Agreement, to appoint and remove members of the Junta and to approve the proposals of the Junta and fix the contributions of member States (Article 7). It is significant that as a general rule such decisions can be adopted by the affirmative vote cast by two-thirds of the member States. There are, however, certain exceptions where a right of veto exists: (i) in matters covered in annexes I and II of the Agreement; in the latter case, however, a member State cannot exercise its right to cast a negative vote more than once on the same subject-matter; (ii) in the appointment of members of the Junta and (iii) in matters relating to the preferential treatment to be accorded to Bolivia and Ecuador when either Bolivia or Ecuador must have voted affirmatively (Article 11).

The Junta consists of three members who may be nationals of any Latin American State and is the technical organ of the Cartagena Agreement. " Whereas the national interest of each member State is represented in the Commission, the Junta is the mouthpiece of the general interests of the subregion, that is to say, of the economic community which is being created." [8] The Junta is to receive instructions from neither governments nor any international entity and is responsible to the Commission. Its main functions are to present proposals for the consideration of the Commission and watch over the implementation of the Agreement of Cartagena and the Decisions of the Commission. The Junta passes Resolutions, while the Commission makes Decisions. There are no express provisions in the Cartagena Agreement whereby these Decisions may be incorporated within the municipal legal order. The divergence in practice among the member States in this matter has led the Junta to submit proposals whereby decisions of the Commission will be directly applicable within the territory of member States.[9]

III—THE FORMATION OF A CUSTOMS UNION

In order to achieve the economic integration of the region the Cartagena Agreement has provided for the liberalisation of intra-subregional trade and the establishment of a common external

---

[8] 13 *Derecho de la integración* (1973), p. 155, translated by the present writer.

[9] See Article 2 of the Bases de un tratado para la creación del tribunal justicia del Acuerdo de Cartagena, 13 *Derecho de la integración* (1973), p. 148.

tariff. The ultimate aim of the liberalisation programme is to effect
a complete liberalisation of intra-subregional trade not later than
December 31, 1980, through annual reductions of 10 per cent. The
mechanism is automatic and irrevocable. In fact the point of
departure for the annual 10 per cent. reductions (Article 52) was
agreed upon by Chile, Colombia and Peru on January 1, 1971.[10]
Bolivia and Ecuador were to comply with the demands of the
programme at a slower rate in accordance with the preferential
status accorded to these two countries by the Cartagena Agreement.

It must be noted, however, that for products included in the sectoral programmes of industrial development each of such programmes will contain its own mechanism for the elimination of
custom tariffs and other restraints.[11] Article 55 of the Cartagena
Agreement enabled the member States to present lists of exceptions
for certain " critical " goods thus excluding them from the programme of liberalisation.

The creation of a common external tariff was regarded as indispensable to the protection of the subregion's economic development
and also as a means of strengthening its negotiating position
with third States. The member States are under an obligation to
put the Common External Tariff into full operation by December 31,
1980. As an intermediate step there was to be established not later
than December 31, 1975, a Minimum Common External Tariff.

IV—NATIONAL AND SUBREGIONAL CONTROL
The Foreign Investment Code

Both the Declaration of Bogota (1966) and the Declaration of
the American Presidents (1967) stressed the important role that
private foreign investment could play in the economic development
of Latin America. The latter declaration expressly stated: " Foreign
private enterprise will be able to fill an important function in
assuring achievement of the objectives of integration within the
pertinent policies of each of the countries of Latin America."
Nevertheless the members of the Andean Pact were extremely
aware of the grave consequences of uncontrolled foreign investment.[12] During the last two decades foreign control of the manufacturing sector, for instance in the chemical, food and car industries,
had increased considerably with the import substitution policy

---

[10] Further see Final Act of the Negotiations on the Entry of Venezuela into the
Cartagena Agreement. 12 *I.L.M.* (1973), pp. 344–356.
[11] See below, p. 214.
[12] Mauricio Guerrero, " El régimen común de la inversión extranjera en el Grupo
Andino," 8 *Derecho de la integración* (1971), pp. 8–33.

embarked upon by several Latin American States. It seemed clear [13] that such a high level of foreign control of domestic industry was not compatible with a State's control over its own national economic activity nor indeed over its own general national development. There was also fear that the progressive " desnacionalizacion " of Latin American industries should not be further hastened by the process of regional economic integration.

The problem of foreign investment in Latin America should also be looked at within the context of the so-called transfer of foreign technology—the acquisition of which is considered to be of such paramount significance to the economic development of the region. The fact that contracts for the commercialisation of technology often contained export restrictive clauses, tie-in clauses making it obligatory for the recipient firm to buy intermediate goods and capital goods from the same source as that of the " know-how " and various other kinds of restrictive clauses made that type of transfer of foreign technology seem a formidable obstacle to industrial development.[14]

On July 17, 1971, the Commission of the Cartagena Agreement adopted Decision 24. The common régime of treatment of foreign capital and of trademarks, patents, licences, and royalties (The Andean Foreign Investment Code). There is no doubt that this instrument is a significant one.[15] First, it emphatically seeks to assert and maintain national and subregional control over the economic development of the area. In the second place it endeavours to posit clearly defined rules concerning direct foreign investments—an area of international law which seems in need of such rules; and, thirdly and finally—what is perhaps also important —it may seem an attractive model to certain States of the Third World in their struggle against underdevelopment.[16]

The Code classifies business enterprises into three types: national enterprises, mixed enterprises and foreign enterprises. A national enterprise is one where more than 80 per cent. of the capital belongs to national investors.[17] Where between 51 per cent. to 80 per cent.

---

[13] Further see Raul Prebisch, *Reflexiones sobre la cooperación internacional en el desarrollo latinoamericano* (1969).

[14] See United Nations Conference on Trade and Development—Transfer of Technology, a study by the Junta del Acuerdo de Cartagena, TD/107.

[15] On which see Covey Oliver, " The Andean Foreign Investment Code," 66 *American Journal of International Law* (1972), pp. 763–784. For text see 11 *I.L.M.* (1972), pp. 126–146.

[16] See F. Parkinson, " Power and Planning in the Andean Group," 29 *The World Today* (1973), pp. 527–536 on p. 530.

[17] The term national investor includes the State, national individuals and national non-profit entities. Foreign nationals of one year's residence in the recipient country who have renounced the right to repatriate capital or profits are also considered national investors.

of the capital is owned by national investors the enterprise is a mixed one and where there is less than 51 per cent. of the capital owned by national investors the enterprise is considered foreign. Not surprisingly, the controlling factor in the classification between national and mixed enterprises on the one hand and foreign enterprises on the other is the degree of real control exercised by the national investors over the enterprise in question.

The provision whereby foreign enterprises are under an obligation to transform themselves into mixed or national enterprises constitutes the centre-piece of the Andean Foreign Investment Code. Existing foreign enterprises must agree to a gradual transformation into national or mixed enterprises if they wish to enjoy the duty-free programme of the Cartagena Agreement, which means that an existing foreign enterprise may continue to operate in a member country, if it is prepared to forgo the benefits of the enlarged market. On the other hand new foreign enterprises, that is those coming into being after July 1, 1971, do not seem to possess that option, since Article 30 appears to make their transformation to mixed enterprises obligatory. Such an interpretation is in keeping with the general intention of the Code.[18] A further restriction on new foreign investments concerns the type of activities in which they are allowed to operate. New foreign investments are not permitted in certain sectors such as that concerning public utilities, insurance, commercial banking, transportation, advertising or commercial radio. In such industries existing foreign enterprises are under an obligation to sell at least 80 per cent. of their shares to national investors. Existing foreign banks which desire to continue accepting local deposits are under an obligation to sell at least 80 per cent. of their shares to national investors. This restriction was imposed upon foreign banking activities because they were seen as merely using the national savings to help foreign firms to the detriment of national companies.

It is of some significance that foreign enterprises engaged in the primary industries of exploration and exploitation of minerals of all kinds are exempt from the process of transformation but they cannot enjoy the benefits of the liberalisation programme of the Cartagena Agreement.[19]

The Code also seeks to control the repatriation of capital by defining " capital " more strictly and in particular stipulates that the right to transfer profits abroad should be limited to an annual 14 per cent.

The enormous importance which the Andean system attaches to

---

[18] *Op. cit.* in note 15 above.
[19] Further see Chapter iii of the Andean Foreign Investment Code.

the acquisition of foreign technology is reflected not only in the preamble of the Code but also in Article 22 which imposes upon national authorities the duty "to undertake a continuous and systematic task of identification of available technologies on the world market for the various industrial fields, in order to have available the most favourable and advisable alternative solutions for the economic conditions of the subregion," and to "forward the result of their work to the Junta." However, the Code regulates the transfer of foreign technology and patents by, for instance, prohibiting the restrictive clauses associated with such transfer and also forbidding the capitalisation of imported "know-how."

Latin American preoccupation with the tenets of the Calvo Clause found embodiment in Article 51 of the Andean Code of Foreign Investment. This significant provision declared that no instrument concerning investments or the transfer of technology may contain clauses attempting to remove possible disputes from the jurisdiction of the recipient country or "allow the subrogation by States to the rights and actions of their national investors." Such a provision is not surprising and is in keeping with Latin American tradition in this matter.[20]

Multinational enterprises

The Cartagena Agreement has given high priority to the creation of multinational enterprises. They are seen not only as a means of hastening the process of integration and helping in the balanced and programmed development of the Andean Common Market but also in contributing to the "strengthening of subregional entrepreneurial capacity in order to take fuller advantage of the expanded market." In December, 1971, the Commission of the Cartagena Agreement approved Decision 46, "Standard Code on Multinational Enterprises and the regulations with regard to subregional capital.[21] The principal objective of this decision is to accelerate subregional integration within the context of subregional control.

In order to enjoy the advantages accorded to multinational enterprises in Decision 46 a multinational enterprise has to comply with the following provisions: its principal domicile must be in the territory of one of the member States and it must have contributions from national investors from more than one member State. The crucial norm, however, is that foreign investors may not own more than 40 per cent. of the enterprise's capital and more importantly,

---

[20] See, for example, Article 9 of the Convention on the Rights and Duties of States (1933) and Article 7 of The Pact of Bogota (1948), and, generally, D. R. Shea, *The Calvo Clause* (1955).

[21] For text see 11 *I.L.M.* (1972), pp. 357–395 and for an extended exegesis see Gustavo Fernandez Saavedra, "El régimen uniforme de la empresa multinacional en el Grupo Andino," 11 *Derecho de la integración* (1972), pp. 11–38.

the majority capital of national and subregional investors must be
" reflected in the technical, administrative, financial and commercial
management of the enterprise." This requirement is the key to the
subregional control of these multinational enterprises. It has been
pointed out that the level of foreign participation is not the same
as that stipulated in the Foreign Investment Code because the risk
of foreign investors using national intermediaries increases in the
case of multinational enterprises where control becomes less easy.[22]
Finally, Article 52 of Decision 46 states that in cases where foreign
investors participate in a multinational enterprise, subregional shareholders shall appoint their own directors quite separately from those
of third countries. Here again the object was to maintain real control
in contradistinction to apparent control of the enterprise.

Multinational enterprises are to play an important part in the
Andean system. It is expressly stated that they are to aid in the
carrying out or developing of the sectoral programmes of industrial
development,[23] the infrastructure project and the joint agricultural
development programme. In a word their function is to participate
in projects of " subregional interest." Indeed member States are to
act as watch-dogs to ensure that multinational enterprises always
fulfilled the corporate purpose for which they are created.

Special treatment is accorded to multinational companies within
the Code. For instance, the products of multinational enterprises
shall enjoy the benefits of the liberalisation programme of the
Cartagena Agreement. The obligation, embodied in the Foreign
Investment Code, for foreign investors to sell shares to national
investors does not apply to investors in multinational enterprises.
More significantly multinational enterprises enjoy equal treatment
with national enterprises in respect of State purchases of goods
and services. When the main objectives of Decision 46 are recalled,
their special status within the national order of the member States
is hardly surprising.

The uniqueness of this scheme lies in the fact that it seeks to
create joint equity ventures among developing countries.[24] The
Andean multinational enterprises, if successful, can, in the words
of Gustavo Fernandez Saavedra establish " a veritable network of
shared interests and objectives " among the member States of the
Cartagena Agreement.

V—THE ROLE OF INDUSTRIALISATION

The Cartagena Agreement accords cardinal importance to the industrial development of the area. Under this Agreement the member

---

[22] *Ibid.* pp. 23–24.
[23] See below, p. 213.
[24] See 10 *Derecho de la integración* (1972), p. 8.

States " pledge themselves to undertake a process of industrial development of the subregion through joint programming in order to achieve," *inter alia*, greater expansion, specialisation and diversification of industrial production, maximum utilisation of available resources of the area, utilisation of economies of scale and an equitable distribution of benefits. It is this emphasis on planned industrialisation which is the most salient feature of the Agreement and which gives the Andean Common Market its most distinguishing feature.

The broad purposes of the industrialisation programme are to rationalise existing industries and more significantly to develop future industries by the use of sectoral programmes of industrial development. It is chiefly by means of these sectoral programmes of industrial development that it is hoped to realise the balanced and integrated development of the subregion. Each of such programmes is to identify the product which is to be subjected to it, assign industries to the various member States and establish its own norms for the Common External Tariff.

The first sectoral programme for the " metal-working industry "

The first sectoral programme for the metal-working industry [25] was approved by the Commission of the Cartagena Agreement in 1972 by Decision 57—a fact which in itself reflected the growing strength of Andean integration, given that the area covered by the programme is of such fundamental importance.

Decision 57 attempts to ensure the effectiveness of the sub-regional industrialisation programme by imposing certain constraints on the industrialisation policies of each member State. The member countries are obliged not to promote the establishment of industries similar to the ones already assigned to other countries by granting State subsidies or other forms of preferential treatment to new industries or increasing the privileges already granted to existing industries. It is to be noted that this programme does not stipulate an outright prohibition on establishing industries already located elsewhere. An observer has significantly remarked that the process of subregional integration has not yet reached the point where that type of obligation can be imposed.[26] Member States are, however, under the obligation not to authorise direct foreign investments in industries manufacturing products already assigned by the sectoral programme to other States.

---

[25] For text see 12 *Derecho de la integración* (1973), pp. 187–197; see also Mauricio Guerrero, " la programación conjunta del desarrollo industrial subregional y el primer programa sectorial de la industria metalmecánica," *ibid*. pp. 35–53.

[26] *Ibid*. p. 39.

In accordance with the terms of the Cartagena Agreement the first sectoral programme for the " metal-working industry " has established its own liberalisation programme. Member countries to which a particular industry has been assigned under the sectoral programme will maintain custom-tariffs on the import of goods manufactured by similar industries in other member countries in order to protect the internal market while the programme is being established. On the other hand, member countries to which a particular industry has not been assigned must eliminate the existing tariffs on the products of such an industry coming from the favoured country. Decision 57 has also established a process of automatic liberalisation between countries sharing the same industries under the programme. This sectoral programme also makes provisions for the creation of a customs union through the establishment of a common external tariff concerning products covered by it.

In keeping with the special status accorded to the two less developed member countries, Bolivia and Ecuador by the Cartagena Agreement, Decision 57 grants preferential treatment to these two countries. It assigns more industries to these two countries than could be accounted for on the basis of strict reciprocity. In addition the assignment of industries made to these countries are of an exclusive character—thus not exposing these countries to competition from their more developed partners. It is fair to state that it is in the industrial policy of the Andean system that the preferential treatment enjoyed by Bolivia and Ecuador seems most significant.

It is worth observing that Decision 57 expressly urges the member States to utilise multinational enterprises to fulfil the requirements of the sectoral programmes—a fact which reveals how mutually dependent is each part of the Andean mechanism.[27] Indeed the industrialisation programme itself depends on the success of the liberalisation programme, and the establishment of the common external tariff, with member States refraining from encouraging the manufacture of goods already assigned to others by the sectoral programmes. This interdependence is in a sense at once a weakness and a source of strength. The industrialisation plan constitutes the most conspicuous feature of the Cartagena Agreement and one which in fact differentiates it most clearly from other systems of integration in other parts of the world.

---

[27] In this respect the Andean Development Corporation whose main purpose is " the furthering of subregional integration " by, *inter alia,* " providing directly or indirectly the technical and financial assistance necessary for the preparation and execution of multinational or complementary projects " (further see Article 4 of the Agreement) is also of importance. See agreement establishing Andean Development Corporation, 8 *I.L.M.* (1969), pp. 940–958.

VI—THE SETTLEMENT OF DISPUTES

The present machinery for resolving disputes arising from the interpretation or implementation of the Cartagena Agreement is based on the 1967 LAFTA Protocol for the Settlement of Disputes.[28] In cases of disputes the Commission can execute procedures of negotiation, good offices, mediation and conciliation but, failing a settlement, the member States are to follow the procedure embodied in the LAFTA Protocol.[29]

The LAFTA Protocol for the Settlement of Disputes may have offered an appropriate dispute-settling machinery for the Free Trade Area established by the Treaty of Montevideo but it seems inadequate for resolving disputes arising in an economic union or during the formation of such a union.[30] Moreover, it must be noted that even among the parties to the Treaty of Montevideo the Protocol has never been resorted to and it has been remarked that, in spite of the presence of disputes, member States have not shown any intention of utilising it. Consequently disputes among the parties to the Treaty of Montevideo have generally been dealt with by direct negotiations with results that have been considered unsatisfactory.[31] Indeed only Bolivia, Colombia and Ecuador have ratified the Protocol—a fact which in itself reduces its significance as far as the Cartagena Agreement is concerned.[32]

There is increasing concern among the parties to the Cartagena Agreement that there is no judicial machinery for reviewing the Decisions of the Commission or the Resolution of the Junta and that, in other words, these organs are beyond judicial supervision and, as it were, are outside the law. The need to ensure that these organs act within the law becomes more apparent when one considers the system of voting in the Commission. It has already been stated that, as a general rule, the Commission adopts Decisions by majority rule. The absence of a veto in this political organ has thus thrown into relief the necessity for a subregional court of justice,[33] a judicial tribunal which can deal promptly and effectively with disputes

---

[28] For text see 7 *I.L.M.* (1968), pp. 747–756.

[29] The same type of provision is found in Article 51 of the Foreign Investment Code in regard to controversies arising between member countries in relation to the interpretation and implementation of the Code.

[30] " Informe de la Junta sobre el establecimiento de un organo jurisdiccional del Acuerdo de Cartagena," 13 *Derecho de la integración* (1973), p. 155.

[31] *Ibid.* p. 144.

[32] A provisional machinery for the settlement of disputes established by Resolution 165 is available to parties to the Treaty of Montevideo. For text see *Economic Integration in Latin America* (1968), Inter-American Institute of International Legal Studies, p. 333.

[33] 13 *Derecho de la integración* (1973), p. 143.

between member States and the controlling organs of the Cartagena Agreement, thus avoiding unnecessary political tensions.[34]

All such factors led the Commission of the Cartagena Agreement to accept the need for the creation of a Court of Justice which will settle disputes arising from the application of the Treaty, the Decisions of the Commission and the Resolutions of the Junta; and the Junta was entrusted with the task of submitting a report on the matter. The Junta's report of 1972 [35] gave strong support to the idea of establishing a judicial organ which will ensure the rule of law in the interpretation and application of the Cartagena Agreement. This report also contains a Draft treaty for the establishment of the Court of Justice of the Cartagena Agreement, which in fact is largely based on the European model.

The aim of the proposed court is to ensure the respect of law in the interpretation and application of the Cartagena Treaty.[36] Its main functions are: (i) to hear appeals for annulment, (ii) appeals against member States, and (iii) to give authoritative opinions by way of interpreting the provisions of the Cartagena Agreement and the executive acts of the controlling organs in the Agreement. In the first place, the court will have competence to decide on the legal validity of the Decisions of the Commission and the Resolutions of the Junta. The Draft therefore provides for what can be called a judicial review of the administrative acts of the executive organs of the Cartagena Agreement. Such acts can be challenged before the proposed court by member States, by the Commission itself in relation to the Resolutions of the Junta, by the Junta in relation to the Decisions of the Commission and by natural or legal persons.[37] The court will have power to annul the Commission's Decisions or the Junta's Resolution if there has been a violation of the legal norms embodied in the Treaty or there has been a misuse of power (*desviación de poder*). The period of time set for the challenging of a Decision or a Resolution is six months.

In the second place, an action can be brought before the court against a member State for failing to fulfil its obligations under the Treaty. Such action can be brought by the Junta or another member State. It must be pointed out that individuals will not have the capacity to bring such actions. In such cases they will have to rely on their national courts. If a member State does not comply with the judgment of the court any other member State which is affected

---

[34] *Ibid.* p. 141.
[35] *Ibid.* pp. 135–150.
[36] *Cf.* Art. 164 of the EEC Treaty.
[37] It will be recalled that individuals also had *locus standi* before the old Central American Court of Justice which functioned from 1908–1918. On which see Hudson, 26 *A.J.I.L.* (1932), pp. 759–786.

by this non-compliance may seek authorisation from the court to limit or suspend totally or partially certain privileges accorded to the delinquent State. Thirdly and finally, the court will also have power to give interpretative opinions at the request of the national courts to ensure uniform application of the Treaty.

It seems obvious to an observer that the type of subregional integration which the Cartagena Agreement has as its goal—a goal which in fact is being vigorously pursued—requires a dispute-settling machinery much more permanent and effective than is envisaged in the LAFTA Protocol for the Settlement of Disputes. In addition the very process of integration may be ill-served by the conflicting national interpretations put upon the Treaty and the regulations of its executive organs. In such a case only a judicial tribunal can ensure that uniformity of application which is a *desideratum* of the first importance to a developing common market.[38]

SOME CONCLUDING OBSERVATIONS

The evolving Andean Common Market faces and will continue to face some severe obstacles. Doubts have been expressed, for instance, as to whether the internal market is large enough to support " high technology " plants.[39] There is also the real possibility of member States abusing the safeguard provisions to be found in the Cartagena Agreement [40]—a criticism which has been made of the LAFTA countries. Given that balance of payments problems and inflation have become almost chronic ailments in Latin America, there is no reason to believe that the parties to the Cartagena Agreement will not use these safeguard provisions as indiscriminately as their LAFTA counterparts have done.[41]

The framers of the Cartagena Agreement were well aware of the importance of establishing the infrastructure for development, and the Agreement stressed the importance of the physical integration of the region by improving transportation, communications and so forth. Yet an educational programme was not seen as one deserving

---

[38] At their Lima Meeting in August 1973 the Ministers of Foreign Affairs of the Member States of the Cartagena Agreement declared that there was an " urgent necessity " for the establishment of a judicial tribunal. See *Acta Final de la cuarta reunion de Ministros de Relaciones Exteriores de los paises miembros del Acuerdo de Cartagena.*

[39] 25 *Inter American Affairs,* Autumn 1971, Nr. 2, p. 56. In this respect Venezuela's recent decision to join the Andean Group is of major importance.

[40] See Articles 78–81 of the Agreement. It should be noted that no saving clauses may be invoked for products incorporated in the sectoral programmes of industrial development. (Article 81.)

[41] On which see Bernardo Nun, *Integración subregional andina, estudio sobre el Acuerdo de Cartagena* (1971), pp. 204–205.

pride of place. It has always seemed to this writer that education —a well-designed educational programme—is the key to social and economic development in Latin America as elsewhere in the developing world. Bernardo Nun's observation on this point is very pertinent: " Every programme, project and agreement relating to economic, political and social development is destined to fail from its inception, if the problem of education is not taken into consideration. . . . Education in Latin America constitutes the necessary factor without which designs for social and economic advance will simply remain buried in paper formulas." [42] In the end it may be a matter of establishing priorities but perhaps education deserved a primordial role in the system created by the Cartagena Agreement.

Nevertheless the Andean Common Market remains a significant phenomenon. In attempting to effect the balanced and harmonious development of the member countries through the process of subregional integration and planned industrialisation, and through the control of foreign investment and the transfer of technology, the Andean Common Market is a significant experiment. The fact that this experiment is taking place in an area of the Third World very much enhances its importance.

---

[42] *Ibid.* p. 130. See also Dell, *A Latin American Common Market?* (1966), p. 4.

THE ECONOMIC SYSTEMS
OF SOCIALIST EASTERN EUROPE:
PRINCIPLES, DEVELOPMENT AND OPERATION

By

A. NUSSBAUMER

THE partition of the world between two super-Powers, attached to different ideologies and representing different political and economic systems, as well as their competition for non-aligned countries and uncommitted population groups, has generated widespread interest in both theoretical and empirical comparative studies of the two economic systems ever since the end of the Second World War.

Theoretical analysis had already started in the 1930s on the basis of the earlier contributions of such notable economists as L. v. Mises,[1] E. Barone,[2] and F. M. Taylor.[3] Meanwhile, a general discussion concerning the possibility of central planning without market prices was being led by the prominent Liberal sceptic, F. A. v. Hayek,[4] and by the Socialist, O. Lange,[5] while, in addition, an analysis of the main features of economic systems permitting theoretical classification was being presented by W. Eucken,[6] the founder of neo-liberal economic thought in Germany. Economists also made some of the most important contributions to the political discussion after the Second World War: for example, F. A. v. Hayek,[7] J. A. Schumpeter,[8] M. Dobb,[9] and K. Schiller,[10] a Socialist deeply convinced of the superiority of the market economic system, and subsequently German Minister of Finance and Economics. During the same period a number of books, dedicated to the study of comparative economic systems,[11] were published.

---

[1] L. v. Mises, *Die Gemeinwirtschaft* (1922).

[2] E. Barone, " Il mimistero della produzione nello stato collettivista," 37 *Giornale degli Economisti* (1968).

[3] F. M. Taylor, " The Guidance of Production in a Socialist State," 19 *American Economic Review* (1929).

[4] F. A. v. Hayek (ed.), *Collectivist Economic Planning* (1935).

[5] O. Lange, " On the Economic Theory of Socialism," 4 *Review of Economic Studies* (1936/37).

[6] W. Eucken, *Die Grundlagen der Nationalökonomie* (1939).

[7] F. A. v. Hayek, *The Road to Serfdom* (1946); *idem. Individualism and Economic Order* (1949).

[8] J. A. Schumpeter, *Capitalism, Socialism, and Democracy* (1947).

[9] M. Dobb, *On Economic Theory and Socialism* (1955).

[10] K. Schiller, *Sozialismus und Wettbewerb* (1955).

[11] See, *e.g.* R. H. Blodgett, *Comparative Economic Systems* (1947); G. N. Halm, *Economic Systems: A Comparative Analysis* (1951); Th. Suranyi-Unger, *Comparative Economic Systems* (1952); A. R. Burns, *Comparative Economic Organization* (1955).

I—The Theory of Macro-economic Organisation
and Political Reality

Economists distinguish today between theoretical and empirical economic systems, depending on the kind of approach chosen. Theoretical economic systems can be distinguished deductively in order to differentiate between them on the basis of the fundamental instruments used for co-ordinating the great number of isolated economic decisions which are taken continuously in every national economy: the market, the central plan, or a politico-economic bargaining process between powerful organisations under the supervision of the public authority.

Three kinds of theoretical economic systems exist: the competitive market economy, the centrally planned or centrally administered economy, and the oligopolistic market economy guided by strategic bargaining, not only between powerful firms at the level of the market, but even more so between officially recognised organisations representing economic interest groups and lobbies at the level of formulation and execution of public policy.

It is the latter kind of economic organisation which prevails in the developed industrial countries of the West and corresponds politically to their pluralistic social structures and multi-party democratic political systems. In the Socialist countries of Eastern Europe, however, the centralisation of economic decision by means of planning boards at the level of central governments and central secretariats of Parties, and their execution by using the techniques of public administration, correspond to their monopolistic social structures and autocratic political systems, providing for the dictatorship of the proletariat and generally referred to as " democratic centralism."

The interactions between economic and political systems indicated above and the complexity of the real world make it unlikely that a national economic system can be described adequately by means of one economic criterion only, *i.e.* the method emphasised for co-ordinating decisions. Thus, economists have also pursued an empirical approach to economic systems-analysis, trying to find out about the most important characteristics by which economic systems can be distinguished by means of abstractions from the complex realities of economic life and economic policies.

Already W. Sombart,[12] one of the most prominent economists of the younger German Historical School, pointed out that economic systems could be described adequately only if due attention was paid to the aims of economic policy and the instruments applied in their realisation, to patterns of human behaviour, economic and

---

[12] W. Sombart, *Der moderne Kapitalismus* (1927).

social institutions, and the stage of technological development, in other words to characteristics beyond the abstract principles of macro-economic organisation by which individual economic decisions were co-ordinated. Therefore analysis of economic systems had always to be concerned with the system realised in a specific country at a certain time and to a stage of its economic development.

A similar catalogue of important criteria has recently been developed and applied by a young Swiss scholar,[13] who distinguishes between the real factors—nature and natural environment, and the structure of the economy (*i.e.* the composition of production and consumption, the influence of technologies, the size of firms and economic organisation, and man's attitude towards economic life)— and between factors depending on ideals and ideologies, such as ethical convictions, aims, the position of private property, the choice between individual market competition and collectivist economic planning, and the political systems including the rôle attributed by such systems to the various social groups. When analysing the economic systems of Socialist countries in Eastern Europe which are generally founded upon the principles of central planning and State ownership of the means of production, their stages of social and economic development and political aims and mechanisms of control will have to be discussed as well as the methods of planning, in real or in monetary terms, by setting norms and targets in detail or by using incentives as stimuli for the activities of enterprises and individuals, the amount of decentralisation and the importance of individual contracts for markets, the regulation of foreign trade, the distribution of national income and the methods of financing investments.

II—Economic Systems, Political Systems, and Ideologies

At first sight, economic systems, political systems and social structures seem to be closely related. The only alternative which appears to exist is that between a free-market economy, combined with a liberal democracy, a pluralistic society and considerable social inequality, and a centrally planned economy, connected with authoritarian—one party—rule called " democratic centralism," a monolithic society and firmly established social equality. Yet, this strictly dualistic approach which finds its terminological expression in the simplified contrast between capitalism and socialism and of right or wrong in moral terms, does not provide for an adequate description of reality.

---

[13] K. Dopfer, *Ost-West-Konvergenz: Werden sich die östlichen und westlichen Wirtschaftsordnungen annähern?* (1970).

Even when considering merely the economic system and its leading characteristics, the antithesis between the market and the central plan, serving as alternative instruments of economic co-ordination, is not the only important one. In addition, the crucial difference may be seen in the distribution of income and property, above all the differences arising from private or public ownership of the instruments of production. Or does the most important difference consist in the control over the means of production whenever control and ownership do not coincide? Is not one of the most important features of capitalism that control can be exercised by monetary instruments whereas it is the technique of public administration which is typical for socialist central planning?

To believe that ownership of the means of production must be identical with control and give the owner the exclusive right to plan, and thus that the capitalist holds the most powerful position in society, is a typical 19th century prejudice, then justified by actual social and economic conditions. In the West, ownership without control, control without ownership, and power without property are today no longer exceptions. In Eastern Europe, Marxist theory and the political philosophy and practice founded upon it have helped to preserve this correspondence of social phenomena: State ownership, public control and central administrative planning. The unity of party and State also contributes to maintain this simple relationship.

In any discussion of economic systems in general, including those practised in Western Europe, one has to admit that various combinations of the crucial economic criteria, ownership, control, co-ordinative mechanism, distribution of income and property do exist, and that a wide variety of practical economic systems is possible. Besides, economic systems need not necessarily be tied to particular political systems or types of social organisation. Moreover, social criteria do not always have to be combined in the same way, as shown by parliamentary democracy and democratic centralism, multi-party system and one-party system, pluralistic and monistic society, class-struggle and classless society, social status determined by income and personal property and social status determined by service to society and public offices held, imperialism and internationalism.

Consequently economic systems should be analysed independently of political systems, at least initially. This is also demonstrated by the special terminology developed and used by economists and their scepticism against general political terms such as " capitalism " if employed to describe economic conditions. Also many political misunderstandings are due to an indiscriminate use and transfer of economic terminology to the political sphere. The most notable of these in recent times probably has been the belief that a convergence of instruments of economic policy used in Western and in Eastern European countries was indicative for, or even identical with, an assimilation of their political systems and tend to the disappearance of ideological controversies and the danger of political and military confrontation.

With reference to Socialist countries in Eastern Europe, the plurality of criteria available to describe a socialist economy has permitted the development of different concepts of socialist economic organisation in various countries. Due to the leading position of the Soviet Union, and the variety of systems practised in Eastern Europe it is not so great as in the " capitalist " West. Certainly the differences between the economic systems of these countries are greatest between the Soviet Union and uncommitted Yugoslavia. Yet variations can also be observed between the economic systems of the Soviet Union and those of the other members of the Council for Mutual Economic Assistance (COMECON) and the Warsaw Pact. It is by the degree of centralisation of economic decisions, the methods of financing investments, the kind of incentives used, the kind of practical control of the means of production, the existence of markets and market prices, and the continued or renewed consent to the operation of a private sector within the national economy by which these economic systems differ from one another.

III—Theoretical Approaches to Central Planning

Despite the fact that planning for development has been one of the main tasks and objectives of the Cameralists and Mercantilists in the 17th and 18th centuries, economic theory has not always been concerned with the problems of a planned economy. It was aimed above all to increasing government income from taxation. In the 19th century, virtually all economists were concerned with inquiries into the natural forces determining social and economic processes; the philosophical belief in the operation of an " invisible hand," and dedication to the values of individual free enterprise allowed for but insignificant stimuli to deal with the problems and methods of the State-administered economy. Even Karl Marx, while analysing and criticising vigorously the shortcomings of market-operated economies, believed that their economic performance was automatically determined by invariable laws, following from the private ownership of the means of production—a social criterium—and had little to say about the organisation of production in a collectivist State.

In this century, however, a fairly large number of contributions have been made to the theory of central economic planning, and several theoretical schemes have been developed.

Let us first consider the methods of planning founded upon direct and compulsory orders of central planning agencies. Already in 1908 the Italian born economist E. Barone [14] used the general equilibrium theory developed by his teacher, V. Pareto,[15] in order to show that, at least theoretically, exact planning of a national economy in all of its details by a government agency was possible. Pareto had demonstrated explicitly in which way and under which assumptions the market process led to general economic equilibrium, *i.e.* a situation of perfect co-ordination of all economic decisions, and which were the characteristics of this equilibrium. Barone turned the argument upside down and proved that, once a decision had been reached on the general goals of society, the objectives of planning were clear in all their details. Knowledge about the conditions of equilibrium permitted the construction of a situation of perfect harmony or co-ordination.

Although Barone, by doing so, was able to prove the theoretical possibility of central economic planning, he had nothing to say about the applicability of his method in practice, since knowledge about conditions of equilibrium will permit setting detailed objectives for planning only if there is complete information about present and future conditions (within the planning horizon), and since knowledge about the objectives of planning does not imply that practicable methods for calculating and realising plans exist or can be found.

Methods of direct central planning also had to be developed after the 1917 revolution in the Soviet Union, with their theoretical basis in the doctrines of Karl Marx about the creation of economic value, social ownership and governmental control of the means of production under socialism founded upon his rare remarks on planning. It was left to Lenin to devise the practical methods of collectivist social control.

The theory of planning also benefited from the experience with methods employed during the First World War. But its main task was to solve practical problems in line with the commandments of Communist ideology rather than to develop a universal and theoretically valid system of economic planning and techniques in accordance with it. The influence of capital accumulation and technological progress on production and productivity, differences in the qualities of labour and management, the productivity of

---

[14] *Op. cit.* in note 2 above.
[15] V. Pareto, *Manuel d'économie politique* (1909).

most services, income incentives for individuals and firms were neglected as well as the problems of subjective marginal utility, scientific social evaluation of methods and aims and frequently also relative scarcity; in the beginning even the necessity of money for social division of labour was ignored.

The system did not work too well. It had to be revised in the New Economic Policy (NEP) period by permitting the market mechanism to operate again on a limited scale and later by a concentration on the development of heavy industry, which by reducing the complexities of economic planning also helped to facilitate matters.

Fifteen years ago a new system of planning using direct controls was proposed for the Soviet Union. Starting with the economist Liberman [16] who pleaded for a decentralisation of decisions in production, neo-marginalist mathematicians, above all V. S. Nemčinov, supported these ideas and have concentrated efforts on the development of modern mathematical techniques of planning. These had already been used in the West by large corporations and many of them had been devised originally by Russian-born economists.[17] Thus, a new theory of central economic planning has been created, founded upon such mathematical tools as input-output analysis, linear programming, decision-models and game-theory. Developing better technical methods of central planning which served to improve the co-ordination and rationality of important decisions in a national economy thus was combined with decisions on decentralisation on less important issues. More power had to be given to individual companies to decide less important problems themselves so long as this was in conformity with the general plan, since even advanced technology does not allow increasing the capacity of modern processes of decision-taking beyond every limit and does not permit simultaneous handling of any number of problems.

For the same reasons, the central management of large corporations in the West has to decentralise decisions in order to allow for fast adjustment to new situations, to facilitate the use of all the information available at lower levels, to create incentives even for inferior ranks of the personnel, and to keep the amount of decisions to be taken centrally within manageable limits.

Central planners therefore have to consider taking fewer decisions

[16] E. G. Liberman, 10 *Kommunist* (1965); *idem.*, 252 *Pravada* (1962); *idem.*, " Problemy ekonomičeskogo stimulirovanija predprijatij," 11 *Voprosy ekonomiki* (1962), pp. 87–142.

[17] Input-output analysis has been developed by the Russian born American economist V. Leontieff and the techniques of linear programming can be traced back to the Soviet mathematician.

more accurately and effectively. Depending on the amount of decentralisation agreed on, central economic planning may even be reduced to relatively few macro-economic decisions about investment, foreign trade, and the distribution of income. But there are also limits to decentralisation; even if these decisions were mandatory it would be highly questionable, whether such a system of extreme decentralisation could meet the political needs and expectations of planners in Eastern European countries.

Other theories have been developed in order to show in which way a national economy could be planned by using instruments of indirect control only, such as accounting prices and other administered incentives, or how administered sectors of the economy and pocket of free enterprise could be co-ordinated. Already in the 1930s, the economists F. M. Taylor and O. Lange [18] proposed using accounting prices as instruments of central planning. Prices were not to be determined by the market process but were to be fixed by the planning board so as to create the demand and supply of individual commodities and services considered politically desirable. If these goals were not reached prices had to be changed by decree until the results aimed at could be realised by means of a process of trial and error. Unlike a market economy, production costs in such a system do not have to correspond to supply prices and prices paid by consumers do not have to be equal to revenue earned by companies, the difference being covered by transfer payments with the government, subsidies or indirect taxes respectively. Basically such a system is being used today to guide consumer demand and to plan the national pattern of consumption in the Soviet Union.

Finally, there have been attempts to combine centrally planned sectors and activities with others which are guided by a market process in the same national economy. Problems related to such systems also arise today in Western economies since a large number of services and even some commodities, generally referred to as " infrastructure," are provided for by government free of charge, or at moderate cost. In the Soviet Union private initiative was for the first time used to supplement the operation of the plan during the period of the New Economic Policy (NEP) from 1921–28, but was suppressed again later after the most pressing shortages had been overcome, due to increasing inequality in the distribution of income and property which was considered politically undesirable.

In the period since the Second World War, O. Sik, in particular, proposed in the Prague Spring of 1966–68 to introduce a new kind of economic decentralisation. This meant using fixed accounting

---

[18] *Op. cit.* in notes 3 and 5 above.

prices for key sectors of the economy only, while limiting government intervention in general by solely determining maximum and
minimum prices for most commodities by governmental ordinance,
and, furthermore, by allowing for the formation of free-market
prices in all cases in which this was not considered to be socially
harmful.[19] Sik also tried to justify his theory in ideological terms
by claiming it stemmed directly from an economic interpretation
of Marxism-Leninism.

Outside the immediate orbit of the Soviet Union, moreover,
Yugoslavia has formed a theory for a Socialist economic system
relying largely on the forces of the market for co-ordinating supply
and demand and is practising it quite successfully. In this system
central economic planning is, however, only of relatively limited
importance.

Economic planification in France cannot be considered a form
of central planning since governmental plans are not mandatory
and the government has to rely exclusively on setting incentives and
disincentives when trying to guide the economy towards established
aims.

IV—The Politics of Central Economic Control

Even the theory of central economic planning has not been concerned exclusively with systems of complete administrative control
exercised directly by a Central Planning Board. Much thought
has also been given to developing combinations of a variety of
different instruments, many of which operate through administered
prices, incentives, or monetary mechanisms.

Economic policies implemented by planners in Eastern European
countries also show that these economies have been guided in
practice by employing a great number of instruments. There are,
however, well defined patterns according to which the various
means of economic policy are being used and co-ordinated in order
to provide for far-reaching if not complete control of individual
economic decisions and actions.

In all Eastern European countries operating in close co-operation
with the Soviet Union these patterns are very similar. They are
organised on the lines of the Soviet model. After all, central planning
as the leading principle of economic policy was introduced in these
countries only after the end of the Second World War and it was
only the Soviet Union which could provide the Eastern European
States with the necessary experience and information.

---

[19] O. Šik, *Plan and Market under Socialism* (1967).

Planning the Various Kinds of Economic Activities

There are four kinds of economic activities which should be distinguished: allocation of the factors of production, the processes of production, the distribution of income, goods and services, and, finally, consumption.

According to Socialist ideology, all instruments of production should be owned by society. Control is being exercised by governments with the one exception of Yugoslavia where this is done by a system of workers' self-administration, set up for individual companies. Of the three factors of production, land, labour, and capital, two—capital and land—belong to the State which makes them available to the various producing units. There are only minor exceptions to this rule; for example, if small craftsmen are licensed to operate independently as has been the case in most countries during a transitory period when central planning was introduced, or if small independent farmers are allowed to continue as in Poland. But even then the principle of social ownership generally is being observed at least in so far as legal forms are concerned.

Collectivisation of land has been carried out either by expropriation of former private owners and by creation of State farms or by forced creation of farm co-operatives. As an intermediary measure frequently the land of large estates was handed over to small farmers, later to be incorporated into collective farms. Investment capital is being made available to the individual companies on the basis of a general investment plan by transfers of government funds. Often banks are used as intermediaries. Yet, these banks have no influence on the amount of capital supplied or on its distribution. They are merely serving as agents for the government. Besides, there are tendencies to entrust banks also with some decisions concerning the distribution of investment capital, for example, in Poland. In all countries of the Soviet bloc companies may also use part of their net returns for production if they exceed the goals of the general plan for financing extra investment. This method is similar to re-investment of profits in the West.

In general, labour is not allotted to the various companies and occupations by methods of direct control. People have a right to choose their own jobs unless there are special legal provisions compelling them to work in certain jobs or regions. In the Soviet Union, young university graduates, for instance, frequently have to work for a few years in Siberia. Many of these later decide to remain there voluntarily. In the past, inmates of detention camps also have been a major source of compulsory labour. On the whole, however, indirect methods of planning the labour supply are being used. The education system of the country is directed at producing the number of trainees needed in the various jobs and occupations. There are strict principles of selection, with the number of university students limited by the need for graduates. People are induced to move to development areas by the provision there of larger flats, special services or other advantages. Furthermore, income incentives may be used to influence job selection or stimulate extra work.

Like the allocation of capital and land, the processes of production are primarily subject to direct controls. Quantities and qualities of goods to be produced, in the past even down to minor technical details, suppliers of raw materials and semi-finished products, recipients of finished products, techniques of production used, wages and capital costs were determined by decisions of central planning agencies, with little room given for independent action on the part of company management. Beginning about 15 years ago, gradually a new system of controls has been developed providing for " decentralisation " by increasing responsibilities of plant managers.

This system operating today in the Soviet Union and in the other countries belonging to the Eastern bloc still provides for absolute control of all essential decisions by the central planning agencies despite the fact that the number of planning norms has been drastically reduced. Whereas in the Soviet Union individual companies have but little influence on the formulation of the general plan, in Poland plans are submitted to company managers so that they may voice opinions before final decisions are taken. Yet there is still strong opposition to transferring important decisions on production and sales to company managers, as has been shown by the reversal of the economic reforms introduced in Czechoslovakia under the Dubček régime.

Central economic plans also determine the macro-economic distribution of income between the public and the private sectors of the economy, between consumption and investment, as well as between the various groups of the population. They are founded upon political decisions concerning rates of economic growth, priorities between the satisfaction of public and private needs, and upon an evaluation of jobs by socio-political standards. Within the limits set by the plan, however, individuals are given a chance to increase their personal incomes by a performance above the average. Thus, on the micro-economic level, standards of relative efficiency are being introduced into the process of distribution of income, while, macro-economically, levels of income are determined by political evaluations of social utility.

The regional distribution of goods and services also is subject to direct control. Priorities are given to cities or rural areas according to the relative level of supply considered desirable for the technological, economic, and human development of the region.

The supply of individual consumers with goods and services is not regulated by direct control, for example, like rationing. Demand on markets for consumer goods and services is directed indirectly by fixing money incomes and commodity prices. By using such instruments of indirect planning, the individual may express his own economic preferences freely and satisfy his needs according to subjective considerations of personal utility. The authorities are, however, still in a position to determine macro-economically, which quantities of the various goods and services will be asked for. Should consumer demand not correspond to production targets fixed by the plan, retail prices will be changed accordingly, on the principle of trial and error. Since the general distribution of incomes also has been fixed by the plan, the authorities also determine indirectly which group of the population will be able to buy certain kinds of commodities. Thus general and individual consumption is being stimulated or discouraged, either by reducing consumer-good prices by means of subsidies or by increasing them by government levies, similar to indirect taxes in free-market economies.

The Instruments of Control

Central plans are developed and supervised by a Central Planning Bureau, called, in the Soviet Union, Gosplan. It operates as an instrument of central planning as well for the government as for the central committee of the Party. Hence there are also two channels of control, an administrative one and a political one.

Since there are no market prices serving as economic indicators, planning has to be founded upon national balances. These balances describe the actual state of the economy. They are therefore of a stationary kind, and take the form of input-output tables. The key balance is that of total production, showing the share of consumer goods and investment goods and also the use made of these products for replacing material inputs, for individual and social consumption, and for accumulation of capital. The balance of total production is supported by a system of additional central balances, such as a balance of capital invested in buildings and machinery, a balance of inter-industrial commodity supplies and final outputs, a balance of labour supply and occupation, a balance of inter-regional exchanges of commodities including transportation, and a financial balance, showing incomes, expenditure and financial transfers between the main sectors of the economy, groups of the population, and central governmental funds.[20]

Consequently plans have to be split up by sectors of industry. They are broken down further into plans directing the production of individual commodities and plants. For every sector of production a special ministry is in charge of preparing detailed plans and supervising their execution.

Compared with earlier stages of central planning in the Soviet Union, when a great number of norms were used in order to determine in detail the production of every single kind of commodity, individual enterprises themselves may take many more decisions today.

There remain only nine kinds of norms or plan-indicators. Yet, they permit the central authorities to maintain complete control of all important aspects of production. These plan-indicators concern the value of production sold, chief kinds of products, important technical qualities of products, the wages fund (sum total of money wages paid), the financial plan (financial transfers between the enterprise and the government, such as dues, taxes, investment credits), total investment, working capital, interest to be paid for capital held and, finally, the distribution of surpluses earned in production to be used for transfers to the government, self-financing of investments, premium wages, and social investments for the benefit of the community in which the enterprise is located.

The long-range economic development is guided by investment planning which uses transfers of investment funds by the State as its main instrument. Only a minor part of investments is financed by re-investing surpluses earned by the enterprises themselves. There are no capital markets, and banks serve only as agents for transferring government money and controlling financial transactions of enterprises. Even for very small amounts, enterprises are not allowed to make cash payments. Instead, they have to make use of the services of a bank determined by the authorities as an agent which also does all the necessary accounting. In contrast, banks in Socialist countries hardly have to perform banking services typical for banks in Western countries or Yugoslavia, such as collecting loan capital and giving commercial or investment credit, since incomes of households are supposed to be spent on consumer-goods and services, and savings should only provide for the necessary liquidity.[21]

---

[20] On the preparation of economic balances in the Soviet Union see M. Z. Bor, *Voprosy metodologii planovogo balansa narodnogo chozjajstva* (1960), and J. J. Tureckij, *Planirovanie e problemy balansa narodnogo chozjajstva* (1961).

[21] For further information on Soviet economic planning see: A. Nove, *The Soviet Economy* (1968); M. Kaser, *Soviet Economics* (1969); H. Köhler, *Economic*

Just as the internal operation of Socialist economies in Eastern Europe is not guided by the market but by a central plan, the principles of planning are also applied to foreign trade. Indeed, the purpose of international trade is to supply the national economy with all the commodities which cannot yet be produced within the country in sufficient quantity, for fulfilling plans, to sell surpluses, and to earn the amount of foreign currency needed for imports. It is not the price at which a product can be sold or the profits which can be earned which determine exports, but the need of the national economy for foreign currency. This creates serious difficulty if fair trading practices with Western partners—founded upon the principle of competitive buying and selling—are to be established. Generally, foreign trade is not handled by the producing firms themselves but by companies specialising exclusively in foreign transactions with certain groups of commodities and enjoying a monopoly position. It is difficult, therefore, to apply international conventions providing for non-discriminatory trading practices—such as the General Agreement on Tariffs and Trade (GATT)—to trade with Eastern European countries, even if they have joined as members, as Czechoslovakia and, more recently, Hungary, Poland and Roumania have done.

Similarly, international economic integration between Eastern European countries between the members to the Council of Mutual Economic Assistance (COMECON) works in a very different way from the European Communities (EEC) in the West. It is not one large market which has to be created on the basis of originally independent national markets. The task is to co-ordinate the independent national economic plans of member countries and to agree on imports and exports of member States as well as on targets for their economic development which can serve as guiding principles for future national planning. Since international payments in such a system can be made to balance by adjusting the volume of exports and of imports as well as by changing import and export prices, terms of trade become subject to political decisions. Similarly, the free convertibility of currencies is less important than for countries exporting and importing according to the international competitiveness of their firms. On the contrary, planners may use monetary restrictions to influence trade, whenever such restrictions seem to be more promising than other measures.

Additional Problems for Central Planners

When the economy of a country is guided directly by a central

Integration in the Soviet Bloc (1965); M. Bornstein, "The Soviet Price-Reform Discussion," 78 *The Quarterly Journal of Economics* (1964), pp. 15–48; W. Markert (ed.), *Sowjetunion. Das Wirtschaftssystem* (1965).

planning authority some additional problems have to be solved.
Planners must have complete information on all relevant facts. Lack
of information or the impossibility to report it correctly in quantitative terms may be an important reason for letting subordinate
bodies, which are closer to the original sources of information,
participate in central decision-making. In Poland, for instance, company management is asked by the central planners to comment
on the national plan before a final decision is taken.

Even if complete information should be available, the goals to
be achieved had been decided upon, and all the mathematical and
statistical problems involved in determining exact data and calculating the plan had been solved, planners will still have to start
from theoretical assumptions on the general operation of the
economy which cannot be empirically proved. The functional
relationship between economic variables used in macro-economic
decision-models also depends on theoretical assumptions, taking the
form of systems equations, which have to be introduced *a priori*.
These theoretical structures also determine how the empirical
material is to be organised.

Of necessity, plans are concerned with the future. Most techniques
for planning are, however, of a static nature. Just like input-output
analysis, they are suited well to explain the present state of the
economy and to plan for the immediate future, as long as no important conditions have changed. Some modern techniques such
as linear programming permit tracing the lines of future development, but even these cannot help to overcome the fundamental
handicap, that there will always be uncertainty on some aspects of
future economic and political conditions which have to enter as
assumptions into prediction and planning models. The standard
assumption of these models—" everything else remaining constant "
—may prove to be just as disastrous as it is unavoidable. Finally,
since all economic processes take time, time-lags have to be estimated
correctly, if economic plans are to be realised without difficulty.
This is why so much pressure has to be brought to bear upon
workers and management, to deliver the commodities ordered not
only completely and in good quality but also in due time.

But there are still the problems involved in realising a plan. Due
to the vastly larger number of products, suppliers and consumers,
national plans are more complicated than the plans even of giant
corporations. Also, the central planners cannot rely on the development of prices as objective indicators, if they desire to find out
whether their plans still correspond to actual conditions. Finally,
there is the human element: there may be errors in the transmission
of orders, there may be a lack of motivation to act up to the plan

exactly and promptly, there may not be enough incentives for workers and managers to do their best in order to overcome unexpected difficulties or surpass the norms set. Can plans ever be perfect enough and planners be powerful enough to replace the drive exercised by the self-interest of man in improving his personal economic and social status?

Do all COMECON Countries Adhere to the Soviet Methods of Planning?

It is not surprising that the economic systems of COMECON countries by and large are very similar to the one practised in the Soviet Union. This is not only due to their common membership of economic and political organisations and similar social and political objectives. In all Eastern European countries with the exception of the Soviet Union central planning as a permanent instrument of economic control has only been introduced after the Second World War. The Soviet Union has not only supported economic and political change, her system also has served as an example for the new kinds of economic and social organisation introduced by her new allies. There are, however, some national differences too, generally due to different stages of economic development, different traditions, and different social and economic conditions prevailing in the individual countries.

In Poland, for instance, agriculture on the whole continued to be privately operated. Even in the manufacturing sector, private craftsmen continued and co-operatives expanded, while the majority of enterprises today is owned and operated by the State. Besides the five-year plan, long term plans covering 20 years, and one-year plans are drawn up, enterprises participating in the process of central planning by giving advice to the authorities. As of January 1, 1974, decisions on investment finance have been transferred from the ministries to the banks, which now administer funds within the limits of the general plan according to micro-economic criteria of efficiency.[22]

Reforms discussed and partially introduced in Czechoslovakia would have led to a far more decisive deviation from Soviet practices. Directed by O. Sik,[23] a scholar and politician, central plans were to be reduced to determining macro-economic aggregates, all other decisions having to be taken by the management of enterprises. Prices would have to be flexible and depend upon demand; even-

---

[22] Theoretical problems have been discussed above all by M. Kalecki, *Introduction to the Theory of Growth in a Socialist Economy* (1970), and by M. Laski, *The Rate of Growth and the Rate of Interest in the Socialist Economy* (1972).
[23] O. Šik, *The Problems of Commodity Relations in a Socialist Economy* (1964).

tually only minimum and maximum prices for basic commodities would exist and all other prices would be determined by a free market; individual efficiency would have a wider influence on the distribution of income, and competition would replace central planning as an instrument of co-ordination in many economic relationships.[24] Sik also believed that fundamental differences of interest between the individual and organised society would continue to exist even in a Socialist society, and that more importance should be attached, therefore, to utility as experienced by individuals.[25] Yet, the transformation of these ideas into political practice was stopped by military intervention of the Soviet Union in August 1968.

While the other Eastern European countries, especially the German Democratic Republic continued to adhere closely to the methods of planning used by the Soviet Union and made only minor attempts to introduce flexible prices and new kinds of decentralised decision-making,[26] a comprehensive reform of the economic system of the country was introduced in Hungary on January 1, 1968. Methods applied in the central planning and control of the national economy have been completely transformed and much wider autonomy is being given to State-owned enterprises and other microeconomic units.[27] Plans now have to rely increasingly on economic and technical conceptions, and they are being supplemented by the functions of a socialist market.

Despite administrative controls on prices of products and services, they now have to be roughly proportionate to the amounts of socially necessary labour embodied in them. This formulation comes close to Western concepts of marginal productivity.

Much attention is being paid to interests associated with enterprise profits. Accordingly, preference is being given to economic regulators working indirectly. The new Code of Labour of 1967 facilitates the discontinuation of employment by the employer and the employee. Investments are not simply being financed by government funds, but enterprises may retain up to 60 per cent. of all depreciation allowances and also a part of their profits for investment purposes. Investment will be supplemented by bank credit. Only large projects are subject to decisions of the government. Investments for improving the quality of production and for introducing

[24] For a comparison of the projects for economic reform with the methods used in Czechoslovakia hitherto, see K. Hensel, *Die sozialistische Marktwirtschaft in der Tschechoslowakei* (1968).

[25] *Op. cit.* in note 23 above, at pp. 360, 365.

[26] S. Schauer, "Die Stimulierung des wissenschaftlich-technischen Fortschritts der Erzeugnisse durch die Preise," in *Autorenkollektiv. Zu aktuellen Fragen der Ökonomie* (1966).

[27] I. Friss (ed.), *Reforms of the Economic Mechanism in Hungary* (1969).

new products may be financed altogether from their own resources of the enterprises or by raising credits.

Giving more independence to enterprises and introducing more flexibility of prices has increased the danger of inflation. Despite this, reform has continued, aiming at alleviating bureaucratic restrictions and prescriptions, at creating economic incentives for the masses of the population, and at widening the number of persons interested and participating in economic decisions.

V—MARKET AND PLAN IN YUGOSLAVIA

Yugoslavia is the only Socialist country in Eastern Europe which today combines Communist one-party rule with an economic system founded on the principles of a competitive market economy. This has not always been so: after the Second World War, war-time planning was continued, and controls even were tightened after 1948, when Tito politically separated from Moscow. It was only after 1952, that a completely new and original economic system was gradually introduced. It is the economic manifestation of Yugoslavia's own and independent way to Socialism.

Central planning, regarded as being a form of economic organisation typical for State-capitalism, has been replaced by methods of government allowing for the direct participation of the population on every level at which decisions are taken. Even the Communist Party was reorganised so as to permit for more than one line of Socialist thought and was given the name " Association of Communists." Local self-government was strengthened, the size of administrative districts on the community level was increased considerably so as to enable them to assume more responsibilities, and the importance of the various Republics was increased as compared to the Federation.

The corresponding form of economic organisation was considered to be a system of workers' self-administration of their enterprises. Workers' councils take all important decisions, including those concerning investment policy, sales, prices, and the distribution of revenue. Enterprises have to finance their own investments by re-investing profits or by taking bank credit. If they run into difficulty due to bad management, they cannot rely on government support. Therefore workers representatives co-operating with emissaries of local government also choose the director. Naturally, his standing with the Communist party will also be taken into consideration.[28]

The activities of individual enterprises are co-ordinated by the

---

[28] For a detailed discussion going into all details see M. J. Broekmeyer (ed.), *Yugoslav Workers' Self-management* (1970).

mechanisms of a competitive market. Within the limits of fair trade laws, enterprises are free to set their own prices. This has contributed sometimes to relatively high rates of inflation, due to excess demand creating sellers' markets, and to the oligopolistic structure of Yugoslav industry. Foreign trade with countries not belonging to the Socialist bloc also has been organised according to the rules of international competition. There are no foreign trade monopolies, and Yugoslav producers may engage directly in exports and imports. Official exchange rates do not differ essentially from unofficial prices paid for the Yugoslav Dinar in Western Europe, and Yugoslavia hopes soon to introduce convertibility.

There is also a free labour market, permitting the individual to select his job freely, thereby stimulating considerable migration from the relatively underdeveloped to the economically advanced areas of the country. Yugoslavs also may take up occupations abroad. At times, this has even been considered desirable by the authorities, since it assists in reducing unemployment and improving the standards of professional and occupational training, and contributes to the country's reserves of foreign exchange.

As mentioned before much of the investments in Yugoslavia is financed by banks. Banks may be created by agreement between local communities and enterprises acting as founders; they may give commercial credit, handle foreign transactions and finance investments. The founders influence all decisions taken by the bank's assembly according to their relative share in the credit fund of the bank, which also determines the distribution of bank income. Founders are held fully responsible for all liabilities of the bank, but credits are determined by a professional bank management. There is still another similarity to Western and capitalist forms of organisation: shares may be sold to other enterprises but not to banks or political communities. This provides for direct financial ties in the productive and financial sector of the economy. Instruments of Central Bank policy are similar to those practised in the West.

There is also a relatively large private sector of the economy. 91·4 per cent. of arable land is owned and cultivated by private farmers. Many small crafts, restaurants, and other small businesses are operated by private owners, but these may not employ more than five salaried employees.

Public Finance, too, is organised on lines similar to those of Western countries. Government takes its income mainly from taxes: there is a retail tax of 20 per cent., customs duties amount to 20 to 32 per cent., enterprises have to pay a tax on their capital of 4 per cent., officially defined as an interest payment to the State and, finally, there is a proportional income tax of 12·5 per cent.

leading to a progressive scale for higher incomes. The income of the federation is spent on administrative services, including defence, the development of the infra-structure of the country, and transfer payments to development areas. Hardly any government money is spent on financing directly industrial investment.

Annual central plans which are mandatory have had no existence since 1965. Planning has been reduced to establishing global input-output accounts, these being above all a valuable source of information.[29]

But are there not tendencies today which indicate a shift towards the political practices of " democratic centralism," and if so, will the consequences for the economic system not be inevitable?

---

[29] For further details see: D. Milenkovitch, *Plan and Market in Yugoslav Economic Thought* (1971).

THE SOVIET CONCEPT
OF "SOCIALIST" INTERNATIONAL LAW

By

IVO LAPENNA

THE question of a separate "socialist" international law is very old: it has been on the agenda of the Soviet doctrine of international law since the October Revolution up to date. The idea was first launched by Professor Ye. A. Korovin in the '20s, but later it was rejected, particularly by Vyshinsky in 1938, as "ultra-leftist" and harmful to the interests of Soviet foreign policy. After the Second World War, the concept of a "socialist international law" was revived by Professor F. Kozhevnikov in 1948, when it had become clear that the so-called "people's democracies" will survive as independent States and when, after a rather long hesitation, they had been officially classified as "countries on the road towards socialism."

At present the concept of a "socialist international law" as allegedly applied in the international relations of the so-called "socialist" States or inside the "socialist camp" is generally accepted by the doctrine, but there are some differences in the approaches of various authors to the problem. According to the Soviet doctrine, "socialist international law" is based on the "higher" principle of "proletarian" (or "socialist") international-ism as distinct from "peaceful co-existence," which is regarded as the fundamental legal principle of general international law. G. I. Tunkin, among many others, explains that the principle of peaceful co-existence, "being the guiding principle of contemporary international law, influences the content of all other principles and rules," but, on the other hand, "it must be naturally borne in mind that the world socialist system is a system with new international relations of the highest type which, conforming to the requirements of peaceful co-existence, are based on higher principles—the principles of proletarian internationalism." [1] V. M. Shurshalov asserts that "the socialist states and their Communist and Workers' Parties have worked out correct principles of relations among the socialist countries and peoples, principles based on Marxism-Leninism and

---

[1] G. I. Tunkin (ed.), *Contemporary International Law* (1969), pp. 27–28 and 18. For a critical analysis of the Soviet concept of co-existence see I. Lapenna, "The Legal Aspects and Political Significance of the Soviet Concept of Co-existence," 12 *The International and Comparative Law Quarterly* (1963), pp. 737–777.

proletarian internationalism." [2] He emphasises that the first and most important of all these principles is the principle of socialist internationalism " which constitute the basis of the diverse forms of co-operation among socialist states . . ." and reflects " the community of the vital interests of the workers all over the world." [3]

As can be seen, " proletarian " or " socialist " internationalism constitutes the foundations of this so-called " socialist " international law, and therefore deserves special attention.

I—ORIGINS OF PROLETARIAN INTERNATIONALISM

The final words of the *Communist Manifesto* read: " Let the ruling classes tremble at a communist revolution. The proletarians have nothing to lose but their chains. They have a world to win. Working men of all countries, unite! "

Naturally, these words are not empty phrases or mere slogans formulated for some temporary political aims, but constitute one of the fundamental elements of the revolutionary theory of Marxism. Although, according to the *Communist Manifesto*, the struggle of the proletariat against the bourgeoisie is—if not in substance, yet in form—at first a national struggle, and " the proletariat of each country must, of course, first of all settle matters with its own bourgeoisie," nevertheless modern industrial labour and the subjection of that labour to capital are the same in England as in France, in America as in Germany, in all capitalist countries. This fact has stripped the proletarian " of every trace of national character." To those who reproached communists with desiring to abolish countries and nations, the *Manifesto* replies: " The working men have no country " and therefore " we cannot take from them what they have not got." For all these reasons the communists " point out and bring to the front the common interests of the entire proletariat, independently of all nationality." [4]

Marx strongly criticised that point of the *Gotha Programme* which relates to the emancipation of the working class " first of all *within the framework of the present day national state* " (italics in the original) and made the reproach that this was nothing but an imitation of Lasalle, who conceived the workers' movement from the narrowest national standpoint. He also criticised the passage concerning " the international brotherhood of peoples," because in the context of the Programme it was " intended to pass as equivalent

---

[2] V. M. Shurshalov, " International Law in Relations Among Socialist States," *op. cit.* in note 1 above, pp. 62–63.

[3] *Ibid.* p. 63.

[4] All quotations from the *Manifesto of the Communist Party* are according to K. Marx and F. Engels, *Selected Works in One Volume* (1968), pp. 31–63, esp. pp. 44–46, 51 and 63.

to the international brotherhood of the working classes in the joint struggle against the ruling classes and their governments." [5]

In the Inaugural Address on the occasion of the founding of the First International in London on September 28, 1864, Marx again dealt with the " brotherhood which ought to exist between the workmen of different countries." At the end he repeated " Proletarians of all countries, unite! "

From the whole Marxist doctrine it follows that for Marx and Engels proletarian internationalism was understood as international solidarity of the world-wide proletariat in its class struggle against the bourgeoisie, against the entire capitalist society all over the world. The proletariat, according to Marx and Engels, must organise itself in each individual country in order to fight most successfully on its immediate battleground, but even thus " nationally " organised it is a part, a detachment, of the world-wide proletariat. The revolution can fully succeed only as a result of the common efforts of the entire proletariat of all countries.

The international class solidarity, based on proletarian internationalism, is not only a mere organisational requirement, but a requirement determined by the capitalist mode of production which necessarily, in conformity with the dialectics of historical materialism, leads mankind towards internationalism. National differences and antagonism between peoples—asserts the *Communist Manifesto* —are vanishing owing to the development of the bourgeoisie, to freedom of commerce, to the world-market, to uniformity of the mode of production. All these factors cause corresponding changes in the conditions of life and therefore also in the way of thinking. The authors of the *Manifesto* expected that " the supremacy of the proletariat will cause them to vanish still faster." They also expected that parallel with the abolition of " the exploitation of one individual by another," the " exploitation of one nation by another " will also be abolished. Furthermore: " In proportion as the antagonism between classes within the nation vanishes, the hostility of one nation to another will come to an end." [6]

The international class solidarity of the workers throughout the world was to replace national solidarity or, at least, to take precedence over it in case of conflict between international class solidarity and national loyalty. From class solidarity thus conceived was to follow reciprocal help among the workers of various lands, the prevention of wars based upon national interests, and the creation— as the final result—of a world-wide classless society. Marx and Engels expected that the revolution, having succeeded in one or

---

[5] K. Marx, " *Critique of the Gotha Programme,*" *op. cit.* in note 4 above, p. 327.
[6] *Op. cit.* in note 4 above, p. 51.

several of the most highly developed countries [7] as a result of the international proletarian solidarity, would spread like wildfire to the others until the world capitalist system was overthrown and finally, following a transitional period characterised by the "withering away of State and law," a classless society was established in full communism, when State and law ought to be replaced by the administration of things, direction of the processes of production, high communist self-discipline and rules of communist morality.

II—SOVIET DOCTRINE IN THE TWENTIES

In the first decade of the Soviet Theory of State and Law, approximately up to the end of 1929, a strong impact of genuine Marxist philosophy was felt in the writings of all authors. There existed, both concerning State and law generally and in respect of individual law branches (including international law), various concepts which differed on many points, or even contradicted one another, but they were all united by the common effort to explain State and law in Marxist terms.

As regards especially the doctrine of public international law, the idea of proletarian internationalism played a decisive role. During the Revolution and for a short period after it many events in Russia itself, in the foreign policy of the new Soviet authority and in reactions from abroad seemed to support the correctness of Marx's expectations.

Inside the Soviet Union, among the first decrees and declarations of the Soviet authorities were the proclamation " To the People " of November 5 (18), 1917, the " Declaration on the Rights of the Peoples of Russia " of November 3 (16), 1917, and many other enactments dealing with the class solidarity of workers, peasants and all working people, on one hand, and with the rights of all nations of Russia to self-determination, on the other. These decrees —whatever their name in Russian [8]—were followed by deeds: the independence of the Ukrainian Republic was recognised on Decem-

---

[7] For reasons which cannot be analysed in the framework of this paper, Marx and Engels believed that the revolution would break out in one of the highly developed capitalist countries, or in several of them simultaneously, and that it would quickly spread throughout the entire world. As is well known, this did not happen. Neither Marx nor Engels ever imagined that a "socialist revolution" could first succeed in backward agrarian countries, mostly illiterate, at the very beginning of their industrial development, and therefore with a very weak proletariat and even weaker capitalist class. Russia of 1917, as well as Yugoslavia of 1941–45, or Albania, Roumania, China and other so-called socialist countries, was in no way ripe for a *socialist* revolution in the Marxist sense of the word. This is one of the reasons why the October Revolution generated very soon not socialism, but a new form of State capitalism formally still disguised under Marxist slogans.

[8] The term "decree" was used at that time not only for legislative enactments, but also for various declarations, simple decisions or orders.

ber 4 (17), 1917; that of the Finnish Republic on December 18 (31), 1917; and that of Turkish Armenia on December 29, 1917 (January 11, 1918), etc. Georgia was recognised as an independent State on May 7, 1920, by a treaty between Georgia and the Soviet Government. In the same year the Soviet Government signed peace treaties with the Baltic States and recognised their independence.[9]

The first Soviet Constitution—that of the R.S.F.S.R. of July 10, 1918, which served as a model for the constitutions of the other independent Soviet Republics in existence on the territory of Imperial Russia between 1917 and the two documents (Declaration and Treaty) on the formation of the Soviet Union of December 30, 1922 —was based on the fundamental idea of class rule, two blocs and the international class solidarity of the working people. Article 3 explicitly mentioned as the main task of the Soviet authority not only " the abolition of the exploitation of man by man " and the complete elimination of the division of society into classes, but also " the victory of socialism in all countries." The same article stated that the Soviet decree on annulment of all foreign debts was " the first stroke against the international bank and financial capital," and that the Soviet authority will continue on this road " until the full victory of the international revolt of the workers against the yoke of capital." Again: " Proceeding from the solidarity of workers of all nations," Article 20 of the Constitution granted full political and other rights to all workers of foreign citizenship residing in the Russian Republic.[10]

The Constitution of the Union of Soviet Socialist Republics of January 31, 1924, emphasised even more the idea of " two camps." Section One declared in the very first sentence that since the formation of the Soviet Republics, " the states of the world have been split into two camps: the camp of capitalism and the camp of socialism." It continued by characterising the two camps: " there, in the camp of capitalism, national hatred and inequality, colonial slavery and chauvinism, national oppression and pogroms, imperialist brutalities and wars; here, in the camp of socialism, mutual

---

[9] The subsequent fate of all these new States is well known: in 1924 the independent soviet socialist republics finally formed the U.S.S.R. on the basis of a treaty contained in Part Two of the U.S.S.R. Constitution of 1924, whereas the Baltic States, Lithuania, Latvia and Estonia, were forcibly incorporated in the U.S.S.R. (Soviet Union) in 1939–40 in flagrant violation of the non-aggression pacts between these countries and the Soviet Union. In November 1939, the Soviet Union unilaterally abrogated the non-aggression pact with Finland and invaded this country without declaration of war. By the Peace Treaty of March 1940, Finland was forced to cede substantial parts of her territory to the Soviet Union.

[10] S. S. Studenikin (ed.), *Istoriya Sovetskoy Konstitutsii (v Dokumentakh) 1917–1956* [History of the Soviet Constitution (Documents) 1917–1956] (1957), pp. 143 and 146.

confidence and peace, national freedom and equality, peaceful co-existence and fraternal co-operation of peoples." [11]

Soviet foreign policy appeared to be in line with the same principle of internationalism. The decree " On Peace " of October 26 (November 8), 1917, was directed to " all peoples and their governments " and invited them to begin immediate negotiations for a just and democratic peace " without annexations or indemnities." The Decree declared aggressive war to be " the greatest crime against mankind " and announced the end of secret diplomacy. It also appealed to the conscientious workers of England, France and Germany—" the three most advanced nations of the world "—to support the efforts of the Soviet Government for peace and " at the same time for liberation of the working people and the exploited masses of the population from any kind of slavery and exploitation." [12]

This decree was followed by a number of other foreign policy acts of a similar character, such as the " Appeal to the Toiling Moslems of Russia and the East " of November 20 (December 3), 1917 (denunciation of the secret tsarist treaties regarding Constantinople and the partition of Turkey and Persia); publication in December 1917 of the secret treaties concluded by the tsarist and provisional governments and later annulled by the Soviet Government and others. Worth mentioning is the treaty with Turkey of March 16, 1921, which contained provisions on the rights of nations to self-determination, abolition of capitulations and solidarity in the struggle against imperialism. Identical clauses regarding the renunciation by the régime of capitulations were formulated in other treaties of the Soviet State with Eastern countries.

Under the influence of the misery caused by the war and the revolutionary movement in Russia there were other revolutions in a number of European countries, particularly in Germany (November 1918) and Hungary (1919). The revolutions in these two countries resulted in the emergence of the Bavarian Soviet Republic in Germany and the Hungarian Soviet Republic, both in 1919. The two new Soviet republics were warmly greeted by the Soviet authorities. Already in November 1918, the Soviet government issued a decree on sending bread to the German revolutionaries. In March 1919, it promised full support by the working class of Russia, together with the workers of all countries, to the Hungarian Republic.

On the other hand, the " international character of the class struggle " received further confirmation by the foreign intervention

---

[11] *Op. cit.* in note 10 above, pp. 458–459. The term " peaceful co-existence " has nothing in common with the meaning given to " peaceful co-existence " in the contemporary Soviet doctrine of international law. For details, see I. Lapenna, *op. cit.* in note 1 above, p. 745.

[12] *Op. cit.* in note 10 above, pp. 44–47.

during the civil war in Russia, on one side, and the positive reaction of workers in many countries, including the United Kingdom, on the other. The support to the Soviet régime was given in the form of " hands off Russia " committees, strikes, refusals to load cargoes of military material for the interventionist forces, participation of foreign volunteers in the civil war on the side of the soviets, pressures for recognition of the Soviet government and the like.

All these factors contributed to the climate of internationalism [13] in which the first Soviet theory of a " socialist international law " was worked out, especially by Professor Ye. A. Korovin in his books *International Law of the Transitional Period* and *Contemporary Public International Law*.

Korovin explained international law mainly on the basis of class struggle, but with the possibility of co-operation in the field of trade. His starting point was that wherever there is any kind of community, there is also law. For this reason some of the relations between States in the so-called " international community " are governed by legal rules. This is valid also for the world in which the Soviet republics play a part, but, precisely because of their participation, international law possesses certain specific qualities, at least as far as it governs the relationships between these republics and the rest of the world. Investigating the character of these relationships, Korovin asserted that their basis was to be found in two main groups of interests of States: the interests of an intellectual (ideological) nature and economic interests. As regards the first group of interests, Korovin stressed in 1924 that co-operation in the intellectual field was impossible owing to lack of unity in legal, moral and ethical concepts between the two worlds: " Needless to prove that the fact itself of the existence of the Soviet State is the strongest negation of the whole bourgeois order as such and a permanent menace to its tranquillity, Is it necessary to recall the international solidarity of the working masses, the International of Workers, the factual and economic impossibility of a lasting existence of the socialist oasis, the passage concerning the world revolution—those cornerstones of our domestic and foreign policy? . . . . We think that the conclusion obtrudes itself: *communication on the basis of intellectual unity* (*solidarity of ideas*) between countries with bourgeois and socialist cultures is excluded in

---

[13] Of course there were also many signs of genuine internationalism at that time. For instance, in the twenties tens of thousands learnt the International Language (Esperanto) and developed numerous contacts with foreign countries; Moscow was one of the first radio stations to broadcast in Esperanto (in 1923); official stamps and post cards with parallel texts in Russian and Esperanto were issued by the Soviet postal authorities, etc. See also note 28 below.

principle, and the corresponding body of legal norms becomes without object. . . ." [14]

In support of his views—as a matter of fact fully in conformity with those of Lenin—Korovin mentioned a number of examples, such as the treaty with Turkey of 1921, the Genoa Conference of 1922 and especially the Constitution of 1918 which, as shown above, explicitly mentioned " the abolition of exploitation of man by man " and " the victory of socialism in all countries."

On the contrary, again fully in conformity with the policy formulated by Lenin and expressed by G. V. Chicherin at the Genoa Conference (1922), Korovin insisted on the possibility of co-operation " on the basis of material interests in the narrow sense of the word (economic needs, trade and the like)." [15]

Consequently, the field in which norms could be found for the relationships of the States in the two systems (" camps ") was limited to a narrow sphere, and this, according to Korovin, was an important characteristic of the international law of the transitional period. [16]

Korovin, however, could not fail to notice that international law did not function only as between the States of the two systems. This led him, some years later, to the " pluralistic " theory of international law which, in his opinion, was nothing but an aggregate of various and almost completely separated juridical spheres (circles): first of all the so-called " contemporary international law " (general) comprising, in fact, only " the circle of the mutual relationships of a group of European states," especially of the great Powers; and then, parallel with it, a number of other " circles," *i.e.* the system of American international law, the body of rules governing the relationships with second rank States (for instance the régime of national minorities), the completely separated juridical régime for the relationship " of the capitalist states with the colonies or quasi-colonies (unequal treaties, protectorates, mandates and the like)," and, finally, an even more special and limited juridical circle of the international law of the transitional period " regulating the modalities of the relationships between the socialist state and its bourgeois counter-partners." [17] In Korovin's opinion, this " circle " is the most important for the further development of international

---

[14] Ye. A. Korovin, *Mezhdunarodnoe Pravo Perekhodnogo Vremeni* [International Law of the Transitional Period], second edition (1925), pp. 13 and 16. (The first edition was published in 1924.)

[15] *Op. cit.* in note 14 above, p. 16.

[16] According to Marxism the transitional period is that of " the revolutionary transmutation " of society, of transition from the capitalist system to the communist, classless organisation of society.

[17] Ye. A. Korovin in the review 1 *Mezhdunarodnoe Pravo* [International Law] (1928), p. 52.

law, but it has, as its name implies, a provisional character—" during the co-existence of the bourgeois and socialist types of state "—and its norms must be " sufficiently elastic to embrace the two opposed legal systems." [18] It will disappear on the day when " the last columns of the bourgeois half of mankind " fall to give way to " inter-soviet law " which will expand to world dimensions." [19]

In 1926 Korovin defined international public law as " an aggregate of legal norms in force which determine the rights and obligations of collectives of ruling classes participating in international relations." [20] In the same book he emphasised again that the international law of the transitional period was one of the separate systems of international law.[21] He was even more explicit in respect of the State as an organisation of class domination in the section dealing with the question of the juridical personality of the State. " If the bourgeois theorist," he wrote, " defending the doctrine of solidarity and co-operation between the classes, is able to treat the state, though only in words, as an incarnation of that doctrine, and the state power as a factor above the classes and beyond them, with the corresponding expression of the state personality and its personified unity (Esmein), a juridical scheme of this kind, applied to the U.S.S.R., that is, to a state constructed from top to bottom on the principle of class dictatorship, immediately demonstrates its total failure." [22]

Korovin's pluralistic theory based on class struggle and negation of the State as a unified legal entity implied a number of far-reaching consequences. For instance, he asserted that the Soviet authority did not represent at all " the parasitic and exploiting classes of its own country " but, on the contrary, it was " the champion of the class interests of the Russian and international proletariat both inside the U.S.S.R. and abroad." [23] Therefore, a Soviet diplomatic representative, whatever his title, was regarded by Korovin as nothing else but a " plenipotentiary of the ruling class in the Republic." [24] In case of war, he wrote, the Soviet authorities should

---

[18] Ye. A. Korovin in the review 6 *Sovetskoe Pravo* [Soviet Law] (1925), p. 26.

[19] Ye. A. Korovin, *op. cit.* in note 14 above, p. 139.

[20] Ye. A. Korovin, *Souremennoe Mezhdunarodnoe Publichnoe Pravo* [Contemporary Public International Law] (1926), p. 5.

[21] *Op. cit.* in note 20 above, p. 8.   [22] *Op. cit.* in note 20 above, p. 23.

[23] *Op. cit.* in note 20 above, p. 23. In support of this view Korovin mentioned " comrade " Trotsky's Appeal to the Workers of Europe of December 6, 1917; the fact that in the Address of July 17, 1919, the Soviet Government directly explained its policy and " peaceful intentions " directly to the workers' organisations in France, England and Italy, etc. Marshal Timoshenko's Proclamation to Polish soldiers after the Soviet invasion of Poland in 1939, could be added to Korovin's list. Of course, owing to the changed political situation, neither this nor Trotsky's Appeal is ever mentioned in present Soviet writings.

[24] *Op. cit.* in note 14 above, p. 63, and *op. cit.* in note 20 above, p. 82.

treat prisoners of war differently according to rank: superior officers belonging to the exploiting class as enemies, soldiers and officers of lower ranks as comrades, and so on. Korovin believed at that time that only his " socialist " class theory could justify the annulment of foreign debts by the Soviet government (as " *res inter alios gesta* "); he tried, further, to attribute the quality of subjects of international law to various international organisations, in the first place to workers' organisations as the most important of all, and then to others.[25]

The transition from the so-called New Economic Policy (NEP) to the planned economy, the conclusion of a number of treaties with the neighbouring countries and especially Stalin's absolute dictatorship, very far indeed from the Marxist " dictatorship of the proletariat," caused radical changes in the Soviet doctrine of State and law, particularly as regards the question of " withering away " of State and law in the transitional period and their full disappearance in communism. Already in April 1929, Stalin attacked the " Bukharinist " attitude towards the State; one year later, in June 1930, he gave a new interpretation of the Marxist thesis on this question when he declared: " The highest possible development of the power of the state, with the object of preparing the conditions for the dying out of the state: that is the Marxist formula." [26] He repeated the same new " formula " on several occasions, especially in the Report on the Results of the First Five Year Plan, in which he explained that the State will wither away not as a result of weakening the State power, but " as a result of strengthening it to the utmost " in order to crush " the remnants of the dying classes " and to organise " defence against the capitalist encirclement." [27] Stalin's new political line provoked immediate discussions in the Institute of Soviet Construction and Law of the Communist Academy, and later led to the purge in Soviet legal theory as a part of the great purges and terror. All the theories of the first period had to be condemned and a single new doctrine had to be built up on the basis of Vyshinsky's theses accepted in 1938 by the Institute of Law of the Academy of Sciences of the Soviet Union. " Proletarian internationalism," too, was redefined very soon and transformed into one of the instruments of Russian imperialistic policy. Except for the external appearance of the word itself, it has nothing in common with that concept as formulated by Marx and Engels. Under Stalin's rule, internationalism in the ordinary sense

---

[25] For further details, see I. Lapenna, *Conceptions Soviétiques de Droit International Public* (1954), especially pp. 71–74 and 173–179.

[26] Joseph Stalin, *Leninism* (1933), vol. II, p. 223.

[27] J. V. Stalin, *Works* (1952–1955), vol. XIII, p. 215.

of the word was designated " bourgeois cosmopolitanism," and was considered as a serious deviation with grave consequences.[28] On the contrary, the " correct " internationalism was defined by Stalin in 1927 as follows: " An internationalist is he who unreservedly, unhesitatingly, unconditionally, is ready to protect the U.S.S.R., because the U.S.S.R. is the basis of the world revolutionary movement, and to protect, to forward that revolutionary movement is not possible without protecting the U.S.S.R. For he who thinks to protect the world revolutionary movement apart from and against the U.S.S.R., goes contrary to the revolution, and of necessity slides into the camp of the enemies of the revolution." [29]

Already in 1928 Vyshinsky passed judgment on the Soviet doctrine of international law as the most undeveloped branch of Soviet legal theory.[30] Vyshinsky's criticism and the discussions which followed reflected Stalin's alarming speech of December 1927, his redefinition of " proletarian internationalism," his thesis that " the period of ' peaceful co-existence ' is receding into the past " and other statements.[31] A meeting of Soviet internationalists, held at the Moscow University in 1930, discussed the question of " the bourgeois impact on Soviet literature of international law " and attacked Korovin's theory as bourgeois, anti-Marxist and harmful to the interests of the Soviet State. Professor Korovin promised to correct his errors. In the same year Professor F. Kozhevnikov called Korovin's writings " pseudo-revolutionary phraseology," " anti-Marxist," " especially harmful," and expressed the view that every attempt to set up a separate legal system which should govern the relationships between the Soviet Union and the other States was pure Utopianism.[32] A Resolution adopted by the Congress of Marxist Legal Theorists in 1931 characterised the attempts to construct a

---

[28] Among the many victims of the great purges there were about 30,000 persons speaking the International Language exiled and some 2,000 executed. They were listed in " group five " of suspected anti-Soviet elements (" citizens having contacts with foreign countries ") together with those who had any relatives or friends abroad, and corresponded with them. See also note 13 above.

[29] J. V. Stalin, *Sochineniya* [WORKS] (1946–1951), vol. X, p. 51.

[30] A. Ya. Vyshinsky in the review, 1 *Meshdunarodnoe Pravo* [International Law] (1928), Preface.

[31] Soviet theory of state and law, which has to follow the political line of the party and state rulers, has always been behind the changes in Soviet policy. On the other hand, Soviet doctrine of international law must be " the most undeveloped branch "—a judgment repeated afterwards on many occasions—because the character of international law forces the doctrine to wait for the new formulations in the general theory of state and law. Therefore, in Soviet conditions, some time necessarily elapses before a new political line is reflected in legal theory. (See also I. Lapenna, *op. cit.* in note 1 above, p. 744.)

[32] F. Kozhevnikov in the review 3 *Sovetskoe Gosudarstvo i Revolyutsiya Prava* [Soviet State and Revolution of Law] (1930), pp. 147–148.

socialist system of international law as "petty-bourgeois radicalism
. . . disguised under Marxist phraseology."

Thus, Korovin's theory of circles, including especially his concept
of a "socialist" international law was condemned. In 1935 Korovin
himself published a letter in the main Soviet legal periodical *Sovetskoe Gosudarstvo*,[33] in which he denied all value to his former books
and articles, admitted his deviations from Marxism-Leninism, condemned his "ultra-leftist attempt to construct a separate international law, *i.e.* the socialist international law of the transitional
period," recognised all his errors and again promised to correct
them in future.

In July 1938, at a further conference of theorists on questions
of State and law, A. Ya. Vyshinsky, then already President of the
Institute of Law of the Academy of Science of the Soviet Union,
delivered a report "On the Main Tasks of Soviet Socialist Law"
with instructions on some essential points. On July 19 the Conference accepted twelve theses concerning international law.[34] Thesis
Nr. 1 treated generally the very notion of international law and
positively declared that "international law is a special branch of
law, which is applied in the relations between states," thus decisively
taking a stand in the long controversy in the Soviet doctrine concerning the question whether international law was law at all. In
the twelve theses there was no mention of any "socialist" international law, and this was its end in the first period. At the same
time it was the end of the sole attempt in Soviet legal science to
work out a comprehensive doctrine of socialist international law in
accordance with the original Marxist concept of proletarian
internationalism.

III—REVIVAL OF THE QUESTION

Professor K. Grzybowski connects the revival of the issue of
"socialist" international law with Stalin's intervention into the
theoretical controversy regarding linguistics in 1951 (in fact already
in June 1950).[35] He says that the new protagonist of a separate
international law governing the relations between socialist countries
was Professor Kozhevnikov and mentions Kozhevnikov's article,
"Some Questions Regarding International Law in the Light of the
Work of J. V. Stalin: Marxism and Questions of Linguistics,"
published in 6 *Sovetskoe Gosudarstvo i Pravo* (1951), pp. 25 *et seq.*[36]

---

[33] 4 *Sovetskoe Gosudarstvo* [Soviet State] (1935), p. 171.
[34] 5 *Sovetskoe Gosudarstvo* (1938), p. 119 *et seq.* For an account of all the
12 theses and their significance, see *op. cit.* in note 25 above, pp. 112–122.
[35] Review 12 *Bol'shevik* (1950). See also *op. cit.* in note 25 above, pp. 41–42 and
157–159.
[36] K. Grzybowski, *Soviet Public International Law* (1970), p. 15.

As a matter of fact, the first attempt to revive the doctrine of "socialist" international law occurred as early as 1948, when Professor Kozhevnikov—the same who in 1930 attacked Professor Korovin's theory [37]—explained that "the principles of Socialist law, the principles of socialism" find their expression in the struggle of the Soviet Union for new principles and new forms of general international law. Since these principles, he added, are applied to the relationships between the Soviet Union and the countries of people's democracies, "it is already possible to speak about the birth of elements of the socialist international law." [38]

This idea, expressed rather cautiously by Kozhevnikov in 1948, was later developed at length by V. F. Generalov in an article published in *Sovetskoe Gosudarstvo i Pravo* (1950). He said that the first part of the formula "struggle and co-operation" (a formula given by Vyshinsky in 1938 as the basis of public international law) applied only to the relationships between capitalist countries, whereas its second part was valid for the relations between the Soviet Union and the countries of people's democracies, whose "political and economic mutual interests by their very nature are not opposed to each other." [39] Generalov asserted that the fundamental principles of "socialist" international law were first established at the time of the formation of the Soviet republics after the October Revolution, but that these principles have received their full recognition and application only in the framework of the relationships between the Soviet Union and the countries of people's democracies. The article ended with an appeal to Soviet scholars to study all problems and aspects of this "socialist" international law.

Such an appeal, published in the main Soviet legal periodical, at that time edited by F. Kozhevnikov who himself had earlier put forward the same idea, could not but encourage Korovin to return to his cherished theory. He certainly believed that he could do this without fear of serious and unpleasant consequences for himself. In the book *Mezhdunarodnoe Pravo* (International Law), published under the auspices of the Law Institute of the Academy of Sciences

---

[37] See note 32 above.

[38] F. I. Kozhevnikov, *Sovetskoe Gosudarstvo i Mezhdunarodnoe Pravo 1917–1947* [Soviet State and International Law 1917–1947] (1948), p. 24. In the same year Professor Korovin criticised Professor Krylov and Durdenevsky for their statement in the manual *Mezhdunarodnoe Pravo* [International Law] that "a socialist international law could come into being only in relationships among socialist states, but that such relationships actually do not exist." (8 *Sovetskoe Gosudarstvo i Pravo*, 1948, p. 75.) In "exoneration" of Krylov and Durdenevsky it is necessary to say that in 1947, when their book was published, it had not yet been "officially" established that "people's democracies" had stepped "on to the road of socialism."

[39] V. F. Generalov in the review 7 *Sov. Gos. i Pr.* [Soviet State and Law] (1950), p. 17.

of the Soviet Union in 1951, Korovin asserted that there existed three separate régimes of international law: one for the system of capitalist States, the other for the system of socialist States, and the third for the reciprocal relations of states belonging to the two opposed systems. According to Korovin, the " socialist " international law was not a " regional juridical system analogous to the so-called American international law," but a completely " new, socialist international law consisting of new economic and political forms of co-operation between peoples and states " unknown in the capitalist exploiting society.[40]

Although both Kozhevnikov and Generalov had said essentially the same thing, it was again Korovin who was to suffer the main reproaches. His concept of two systems of international law (bourgeois and socialist) with the simultaneous existence of " coincident norms " universally recognised, was criticised as incorrect. It was explicitly said that " there is only one general international law binding upon all states, and two opposed policies." [41] As a result of several criticisms by the Nineteenth Congress of the Communist Party regarding all branches of Soviet legal science, *Sovetskoe Gosudarstvo i Pravo* of January 1953, condemned Korovin's book. Both Korovin and Kozhevnikov were also dismissed from the editorial board of this periodical.[42]

Fortunately for Korovin, Kozhevnikov and others, the death of Stalin in 1953 considerably relaxed the general political climate. The discussion regarding the existence of a separate system of " socialist " international law went on for years and is still going on with many ups and downs following the changes in the political line. The present situation will be dealt with in the following section.

IV—PRESENT THEORETICAL CONSTRUCTIONS

(1) " *Socialist internationalism* " *as a legal principle.* The principle of " proletarian " internationalism, at present usually called " socialist " internationalism by the great majority of Soviet authors, is regarded as the fundamental principle of " socialist " international law. The application of this principle went through three different stages: before the October Revolution of 1917, after the Revolution and since the establishment of the " world socialist system." According to V. M. Shurshalov,[43] prior to the October Revolution it was " the militant slogan of the international labour movement."

---

[40] Ye. A. Korovin (ed.), *Mezhdunarodnoe Pravo* [International Law] (1951), p. 12.

[41] D. A. Gaybukov in 7 *Sov. Gos. i Pr.* [Soviet State and Law] (1952), p. 69.

[42] For further details, see *op. cit.* in note 36 above, and in note 25 above, pp. 153–154.

[43] *Op. cit.* in note 2 above, pp. 63 *et seq.*

As there was no socialist State, " this principle could not be implemented in interstate relations." After the Revolution, while remaining the " militant slogan " of solidarity of the workers, it also became " one of the most important principles " of Soviet domestic and foreign policy.[44] " The establishment of the world socialist system," states Shurshalov, " considerably expanded the sphere of operation of the principle of proletarian internationalism " which " has thus become the basic legal principle governing relations between the socialist countries." Other Soviet scholars give practically identical explanations with the same conclusion that the principle of " socialist " internationalism, as interpreted by the official political line, is a legal principle. G. I. Tunkin, for instance, asserts that it " has become an international law principle as well " or, putting it in another way, " the moral and political aspects of this principle are joined by the legal aspects, the moral and political obligations are joined by legal obligations." [45]

(2) *Subordinate principles.* Precisely as the principle of " peaceful co-existence " is regarded by Soviet doctrine as the basic legal principle of general international law, so the principle of " socialist " internationalism is considered to be the highest legal principle from which all other principles and norms of " socialist " international law follow. Again, precisely as Soviet doctrine is not unanimous in respect of the number and character of legal principles covered by the principle of peaceful co-existence," [46] so there are differences in listing " socialist " legal principles subordinate to " socialist " internationalism. Tunkin, for instance, enumerates only three principles: full equality, respect for sovereignty and non-interference in the internal affairs of socialist States.[47] Korovin lists five prin-

---

[44] This principle, as shown above in Section I, was not a mere slogan, but constituted one of the essential elements of the Marxist revolutionary doctrine. As regards the use or misuse of this principle in Soviet domestic and foreign policy, see comments in Section II above.

[45] G. I. Tunkin, " V. I. Lenin i Printsipy Otnoshenii Mezhdu Sotsialisticheskimi Gosudarstvami " [V. I. Lenin and The Principles of Relations among Socialist countries] in *Soviet Yearbook of International Law* 1969 (1970), pp. 21 and 30. Tunkin expressed the same opinion as to the legal character of this principle in 51 *Novoe Vremya* [New Times] (1957), p. 10 and on several other occasions, including his book *Teoriya Mezhdunarodnogo Prava* [Theory of International Law] (1970), pp. 8 and 489. Identical views were expressed by M. D. Kudryashev and V. I. Morozov in 10 *Sov. Gos. i Pravo* (1960), p. 23; V. M. Shurshalov in 7 *Sov. Gos. i Pravo* (1962), p. 96; E. T. Usenko in L. A. Modzhoryan and N. T. Blatova (eds.) *Mezhdunarodnoe Pravo* [International Law] (1970), p. 86, etc.

[46] In Soviet doctrine the number of these allegedly subordinate international law principles goes from one (just " peaceful co-existence ") up to the whole body of contemporary international law characterised by Korovin in 1961 as " the international code of peaceful co-existence." See also I. Lapenna, *op. cit.* in note 1 above, pp. 762–767.

[47] *Soviet Yearbook of International Law* 1969 (1970), pp. 25 and 30–31.

ciples: complete equality, respect for territorial integrity, State independence and sovereignty, and non-intervention in each other's internal affairs.[48] Shurshalov speaks about the principles of "fraternal mutual aid," equality, "voluntary co-operation in the building of socialism and communism," democratic nature of treaties, sovereignty and independence. He also states that the principle of non-aggression does not apply to relations between the socialist countries, because "inherent in the new-type international relations is the principle of perpetual peace which ensues directly from the principle of socialist internationalism." [49] Finally, the authors of a book published in 1967 say that "socialist internationalism fills with new contents all international law principles which socialist states apply in their mutual relationships." [50] This means that all the principles of general international law are transformed into "socialist" principles when applied to the "socialist" bloc of States and therefore radically modified by the principle of "socialist internationalism."

All these principles, whatever their number, allegedly follow from the identity of the economic basis, political structure, ideology and the common aim: building of communism, V. M. Shurshalov emphasises that "these factors constitute the basis of the social economic and political community of the socialist countries, the basis of their monolithic unity and invincibility." [51]

(3) *A separate system of international law.* According to the Soviet doctrine the principle of "socialist" internationalism and the subordinate principles and norms arising in the relations between States belonging to the "socialist camp," and applied to these relations, are international legal principles and norms: they form the new "socialist international law." In his books *Ideological Struggle and International Law* and *Theory of International Law* Tunkin explicitly uses the term "socialist international law" [52]; in the article on "V. I. Lenin and the Principles of Relations Among Socialist States" he says that these principles "present now a single system of international law principles of proletarian internationalism" [53]; in the six-volume *Kurs Mezhdunarodnogo Prava* the phrase

---

[48] Ye. A. Korovin in F. I. Kozhevnikov, *Mezhdunarodnoe Pravo* [International Law] (1957), p. 17 (English translation p. 20).

[49] *Op. cit.* in note 2 above, p. 67; identically: Usenko, *op. cit.* in note 45 above, p. 94; etc.

[50] F. Kozhevnikov *et al.* (eds.), *Sovetskoe Gosudarstvo i Mezhdunarodnoe Pravo* [The Soviet State and International Law] (1967), p. 25.

[51] *Op. cit.* in note 2 above, p. 60.

[52] G. I. Tunkin, *Ideologicheskaya Bor'ba i Mezhdunarodnoe Pravo* [Ideological Struggle and International Law] (1967), p. 188 and *op. cit.* in note 45 above, p. 503.

[53] *Op. cit.* in note 45 above, pp. 25 and 31.

" socialist international law " re-appears [54]; Korovin speaks about " developing socialist international law which has a great future " [55]; etc. Now, whatever the expression used, it is clear that Soviet authors regard these principles and norms as a separate body of " socialist " international law rules regulating *now* the legal relations between the so-called " socialist " States. It is true that some of them are inclined to avoid the expression itself " socialist international law," but this does not affect the general view of the doctrine as to the legal character of this separate body of rules. It is also true that in his article on Lenin and the principles of relations among socialist States Tunkin considers this body of rules also " the basis of a new type of international law, a socialist international law of the future." [56] Although Tunkin in the same article states very clearly that these " socialist " legal principles are at present (" now ") operative, and emphasises this even more explicitly in his *Theory*,[57] W. E. Butler argues that " Tunkin appears to go to some length to make clear that he is not suggesting the existence of a separate system of ' socialist international law ' . . ." (" which Tunkin implies is not yet the case ").[58] In fact not only Tunkin, but the whole Soviet doctrine of public international law, following the present political line of the Communist Party of the Soviet Union, unanimously claim the existence of a separate " socialist " international law, now in force inside the " socialist bloc." This is one thing; the future is a different matter. Whenever Tunkin or any other Soviet author refers to the " socialist international law of the future," they have in mind the *general* international law which will be " socialist " in character, but only after " the victory of socialism " in all countries of the world. This reflects the old Leninist-Stalinist dogma of the " two diametrically opposed camps " [59] and the belief contained in the 1961 Party Programme that capitalism is weakening and at the end must be defeated, as an " historical necessity," by the growing forces of socialism, *i.e.* by the Soviet system of government all over the world.[60] Thus,

---

[54] V. M. Chkhikvadze *et al.* (eds.), *Kurs Mezhdunarodnogo Prava v Shesti Tomakh* [Course of International Law in Six Volumes], vol. i (1967), pp. 99 and 101.

[55] *Op. cit.* in note 48 above, p. 18 (English translation p. 22).

[56] Tunkin, " V. I. Lenin . . . ," *op. cit.* in note 45 above, p. 28. He expressed the same idea in his *Teoriya* . . . , *op. cit.* in note 45 above, p. 503. So did Korovin in *op. cit.* in note 48 above, p. 17, and many others.

[57] Tunkin, *Teoriya* . . . , *op. cit.* in note 45 above, p. 503.

[58] W. E. Butler, " ' Socialist International Law ' or ' Socialist Principles of International Relations '? " 65 *The American Journal of International Law* (1971), pp. 798–799.

[59] See Section II above.

[60] *Cf.* with Korovin's pluralistic theory, especially with his views regarding " inter-Soviet " law of the future (at note 19 above). Perhaps it is worth mentioning

Soviet doctrine of international law clearly distinguishes three different things: (i) the general international law, allegedly based on " peaceful co-existence " as a legal principle and containing some progressive subordinate principles thanks to the participation of the Soviet Union in international relations and her impact on its development; (ii) the " socialist " international law—a separate system but, according to the present doctrine, not opposed to the general international law [61]—operative today in the " socialist camp " of States; (iii) a future transformation of the present " general international law of co-existence " into a single, general " socialist " international law as a result of the complete victory of " socialism " (of course, Soviet type " socialism ") all over the world.

(4) *Sovereignty and connected principles.* All Soviet authors agree that, in addition to the basic principle of " socialist internationalism," the subordinate principles of sovereignty, full equality and non-interference into the domestic affairs of other States are the most important principles of " socialist " international law. Tunkin explains that these " socialist " principles of respect for sovereignty, equality and non-interference " drastically differ from the principles with the same name of general international law which are general democratic norms." [62] What is, then, the difference?

During the entire existence of the Soviet State, sovereignty has been regarded as a fundamental principle of Soviet policy and of international law, but the concept of sovereignty has altered several times. In the '20s Korovin defined it as " the right of every nation to dispose of itself," and recognised that the Soviet State, because of its weakness in the post-revolutionary period had to play the role of " champion of the classical doctrine of sovereignty." Alongside with the consolidation of the dictatorship, Korovin's concept of " national sovereignty " lost its significance, and by 1930 Kozhevnikov wrote that " to everyone possessing a minimum of Marxist culture it is obvious that the proletarian masses do not march under the slogan of ' national sovereignty,' but under that of the dictatorship of the proletariat." [63] However, far from being discarded, the concept of national sovereignty was thereby given a new role.

---

that from a Marxist point of view—and the Soviet doctrine still claims to be the sole true interpreter of genuine Marxism—the idea of a general (universal) " socialist " international law is nonsense, because " after the victory of socialism in world dimensions " state and law should wither away and disappear in full communism, which means that the existence of any kind of international law would be impossible.

[61] D. B. Levin and G. P. Kalyuzhnaya (eds.), *Mezhdunarodnoe Pravo* [International Law] (1960), p. 6; G. I. Tunkin, *Ideologicheskaya . . . , op. cit.* in note 52 above, p. 119; F. I. Kozhevnikov, *op. cit.* in note 38 above, p. 25; etc.

[62] G. I. Tunkin, " V. I. Lenin . . . ," *op. cit.* in note 45 above, pp. 26 and 31.

[63] *Op. cit.* in note 32 above, p. 149.

L. Ratner concisely formulated it in 1935 when he wrote: "Let us take, for example, the principle of sovereignty, which is definitely not a socialist principle, but which we nevertheless support because it assists us in mobilising the forces of the oppressed peoples in the common struggle against imperialism, and because it is an important slogan in the struggle for national liberation in the East.[64]

This is the reason why Soviet doctrine preserves, in addition to the concept of State sovereignty, that of *national* or people's sovereignty as well. "Respect for people's sovereign rights . . . is not an empty formula; the peoples are potential subjects of present day international law," affirms R. L. Bobrov.[65] This does not apply to peoples in the "socialist camp," because they have already established their "socialist" States and therefore consummated this right.

As distinct from "national" or "people's" sovereignty, State sovereignty is defined at present "as the independence of a state expressed in its right freely and at its own discretion to decide its internal and external affairs without violating the rights of other states and the principles and rules of international law."[66] State sovereignty is regarded as one of the main weapons "in the struggle for peace and against imperialist aggression."[67] Since aggression is impossible between "socialist" countries, this weapon cannot be utilised in the relations inside the "socialist community of states," based on the principle of "socialist internationalism" and the "drastically" different "socialist" principle of sovereignty formulated by L. Brezhnev.

In his speech of November 12, 1968, in Warsaw, Brezhnev again connected sovereignty with "socialist" internationalism. He said that "the socialist states stand for strict respect of sovereignty of all countries," that the defence of sovereignty of socialist States is "of particular importance for us Communists," and therefore: "When internal and external forces that are hostile to socialism seek to reverse development of any socialist country in the direction of restoring the capitalist system, when a threat to the cause of socialism in that country appears, and a threat to the security of the socialist community as a whole, that is no longer only a problem for the people of that country but also a common problem, a matter of concern for all socialist countries."[68]

This doctrine of "collective sovereignty of socialist countries" or, better, limited sovereignty, whose consequences obviously contra-

[64] 6 *Sovetskoe Gosudarstvo* [Soviet State] (1935), pp. 131–132.
[65] Tunkin, *loc. cit.* in note 1 above, p. 49.
[66] *Op. cit.* in note 50 above, p. 90 (English trans., p. 93).
[67] *Op. cit.* in note 50 above, p. 95 (English trans., p. 98).
[68] English translation according to *Soviet News*, November 19, 1968.

dict the solutions given in the United Nations Charter, has been accepted by the Soviet theory of international law (without, however, being mentioned by its true name). V. M. Shurshalov explains that " a socialist country's right to receive all-round assistance in accordance with the principle of socialist internationalism presupposes its obligation to help its partners economically, politically, and, if need be, militarily when their independence is threatened by the imperialist aggressors." [69] E. T. Usenko explicitly mentions the armed intervention (called by him " events ") in Hungary (1956) and Czechoslovakia (1968) as " striking examples " of " mutual assistance of socialist states in the struggle for peace and in offering resistance to the intrigues of imperialism, as well as in the suppression of its attempts to export counter-revolution." [70] Tunkin asserts that the " activities of the five socialist states in August 1968, were aimed at the protection of socialism and of the socialist sovereignty of the Czechoslovak state, fully in conformity with the principles of proletarian internationalism." [71]

Thus, obvious interference in domestic affairs of other countries, or even armed aggression, which are regarded by the Soviet doctrine, too, as gross violations of general international law (based on the principle of " peaceful co-existence "), are classified under the principle of " socialist internationalism " not only as mere acts of " mutual fraternal assistance," but also as legal obligations. It is not surprising that Yugoslavia—and certainly many in the " socialist camp " dominated by Moscow—prefer to be treated according to the rules of " peaceful co-existence " rather than those of " socialist " internationalism.

Tunkin is angry at the " bourgeois press " for using the expression " doctrine of limited sovereignty " in connection with " the events of 1968," and regards this as a further action in the ideological struggle of imperialism against socialist co-operation." [72] Well, S. Avramov, a professor in the University of Belgrade, *i.e.* in the capital of a country which is at present again recognised by Moscow as a " socialist country," said in a remarkable criticism of the new Soviet doctrine that the Soviet intervention in Hungary and Czechoslovakia are two " disgraceful examples " which show " violence, and not tolerance and socialist spirit " in settling problems peacefully.[73] She firmly denies the existence of a " socialist " international

---

[69] *Op. cit.* in note 3 above, p. 65.

[70] E. T. Usenko, *op. cit.* in note 45 above, p. 93.

[71] G. I. Tunkin, " Lenin i . . . ," *op. cit.* in note 45 above, p. 27 (omitted in the English summary).

[72] *Ibid.*

[73] S. Avramov in 1–3 *Anali Pravnog Fakulteta ou Beogradu* [Anals of the Law Faculty in Belgrade] (1972), p. 14.

law in present "historical conditions" and states that co-operation of "socialist" countries is possible only through procedures envisaged partly by general international law, and partly by the constitutions of individual countries.[74]

It is worth mentioning that the treaty between the Soviet Union and Czechoslovakia of May 6, 1970, states that "the defence of socialist achievements is a common obligation of socialist states," but the treaty with relatively independent Roumania of July 7, 1970, does not contain such a formula.

(5) "*Socialist bloc.*" Following the theses of the 1961 Party Programme, Soviet doctrine divides all States into three main groups: 1. States belonging to the "socialist camp"; 2. capitalist States; and 3. non-committed States which, to use the formula from the Programme, "do not belong either to the system of imperialist states or to the system of socialist states," and form "the third force in the world, in the main a progressive revolutionary and anti-imperialist force."

This classification remains valid, although individual States may be shifted from time to time from one group to another depending not on the "socialist" or "non-socialist" character of their socio-economic structure,[75] but on the degree of their subordination to Moscow and the extent to which the Soviet Union is actually able to exercise power over them in the world political situation at a given time. For instance, in 1961, when the new Programme was passed, China and Albania were considered as members of the so-called "socialist camp" or "socialist community of nations," and Soviet authors generously quoted Mao Tse-tung.[76] At the same time Yugoslavia was regarded, owing to the "revisionist policy" of its leaders, as opposed to this camp. Sometime later Yugoslavia and its leadership—the same as in 1961—were praised as "socialist," whereas the Albanians and Chinese were—and still are—attacked as "anti-Marxist" and "revisionists."[77] Then came a period when Yugoslavia was again a "revisionist," non-socialist country. At present she is once more classified as a "socialist" country, but Yugoslavia, although now an associate member of the Council for

---

[74] *Op. cit.* in note 73 above, pp. 18 and 20.

[75] If these States were really socialist in the Marxist sense of the word, as their leaders claim them to be, and if the Marxist concept of society is correct, as the doctrine asserts that it is, then "socialist internationalism" as conceived by Marx and Engels (see Section I above) would automatically function as a regulator of their mutual relations. This is not the case. In fact, the antagonisms dividing these "socialist" States and nations are often considerably stronger than the antagonisms between States and nations in the world of Western democracies.

[76] For instance Ye. A. Korovin in *Soviet Yearbook of International Law* 1958 (1959), pp. 53–54.

[77] For instance *op. cit.* in note 50 above, p. 8.

Mutual Economic Aid (CMEA), is certainly not included in the " socialist camp," and its doctrine firmly rejects the idea of " socialist internationalism " as a *legal* principle and the whole Soviet concept of " socialist international law." China is excluded as well. Albania is not taking part in the Council for Mutual Economic Aid; she also ceased to participate in the Warsaw Treaty Organisation at the end of 1961 and formally withdrew her membership in September 1968. In November 1971 Enver Hoxha said that the theory of " limited sovereignty is the theory of chauvinism and great power expansionism, the theory by whose help the new Soviet imperialists are trying to stifle all sovereignty of other peoples. . . ." [78] Thus Albania, too, is excluded.

It appears that the subjects of this " socialist international law " would be limited to the seven members of the Warsaw Treaty Organisation in the field of military " fraternal aid " and, in addition, to Mongolia and Cuba as members of CMEA, which is unanimously praised by the Soviet doctrine as an outstanding example of unselfish socialist co-operation for mutual economic benefit. However, Roumania, although a member of both organisations, carefully re-jects the doctrine of limited sovereignty. Her military forces did not intervene in Czechoslovakia, and Roumanian scholars insist that the principle of sovereign equality and independence of States is of paramount importance for Roumania's relations both with " socia-list " and " non-socialist " countries.[79] Cuba is too far to be offered " fraternal military assistance " of the kind given to Czechoslovakia in 1968 without most serious risks of military confrontation with the United States. It is doubtful whether even Mongolia could be treated in the same way without provoking China and widening the already wide rift between the two " socialist " countries. North Korea and North Vietnam are excluded for the same reasons. What, in fact, remains, is the group of five " socialist " countries in Europe to which the Soviet Union tries forcibly to apply " socialist " international law, *i.e.* a body of principles worked out by the Soviet doctrine and aimed at justifying any political *fait accompli* or any possible future action undertaken by the Soviet political leadership. All this in the name of " proletarian " internationalism, at present most concisely defined in this single sentence addressed both to the " leftist " and " rightish " revisionists: " Those who at present attack the U.S.S.R., in fact weaken all peoples struggling for social progress and national liberation." [80] A formula not very far from that given by Stalin in 1927.

---

[78] Quoted according to Peter R. Prifti, " Albania's Expanding Horizons," xxi *Problems of Communism* (January–February 1972), p. 35.
[79] V. Duculescu and D. Popescu in 2 *Studii si Cercetari Juridice* (1971), p. 236.
[80] *Op. cit.* in note 50 above, p. 9; Stalin's definition at note 29 above.

The Soviet doctrine of international law, has always been a docile
servant of Soviet foreign policy. At present it reflects the two main
political instruments of Soviet expansionism: the double-faced
" peaceful co-existence " and the equally double-faced " socialist
internationalism." The Soviet doctrine of " socialist " international
law justifies the exclusive and absolute domination of the Soviet
Union in the " socialist camp," whereas the parallel doctrine of
" peaceful co-existence " enables the Soviet Union to interfere in
various ways in domestic affairs of all other countries. A skilful
combination of the two is a powerful tool for promoting Soviet
expansionist policy, because words, even when completely deprived
of their original meaning, are still attractive for many who do not
distinguish between empty slogans and deeds.

EQUALITY AND DISCRIMINATION IN INTERNATIONAL ECONOMIC LAW (V):

THE EUROPEAN COMMUNITIES AND THE WIDER WORLD

By

PETER GOLDSMITH AND FRIEDRICH SONDERKÖTTER

This is the fifth contribution to the series on *Equality and Discrimination in International Economic Law*, initiated by Professor Schwarzenberger's paper under this title in the 1971 Volume of this Annual, and continued in the 1972 Volume by G. G. Kaplan on *The UNCTAD Scheme for Generalised Preferences* and B. G. Ramcharan on *The Commonwealth Preferential System*, and in the 1974 Volume by the writers of this paper on *The European Communities—Managing Ed., Y.B.W.A.*

IN a previous paper in this *Year Book*,[1] the present authors endeavoured to illustrate the importance of the principle of non-discrimination in the internal relations of the member States of the European Economic Community. The formation of a Common Market, centred on a customs union, affected, however, not only the relations between the member States themselves, but also had a vital impact on their relations with third States. The elimination of customs duties within the European Economic Community (EEC) has meant that an American firm trading in the Dutch market has found itself in a worse position than its French competitors. This is the intention of all customs unions, which are " discriminatory by their very nature." [2] But there is no general prohibition of discrimination in *customary* international law, so that these adverse effects which the EEC may have on third States are not, *per se*, illegal. Nevertheless, all the member States of the EEC had, before 1958, undertaken obligations towards third States both by bilateral and by multilateral treaties. At first blush, certain of the provisions of the three Treaties establishing the Communities might seem in conflict with some of these international obligations. It is the purpose of this part of this paper to examine these possible conflicts.

---

[1] P. Goldsmith and F. Sonderkötter, " Equality and Discrimination in International *Economic* Law (IV): The European Communities," in this *Year Book*, Vol. 28 (1974), p. 262 *et seq.*

[2] K. Hyder, *Equality of Treatment and Trade Discrimination in International Law* (1968), p. 7.

Two preliminary points should be made. First, we do not seek to deal with the wider political and economic implications of the external policies of the EEC, but merely examine the legal basis of its relations with the rest of the world. Secondly, the paper has been written without the benefit of the result of three current rounds of negotiations which may yet resolve some of the problems raised below.

The course of discussions among the member States of the General Agreement on Tariffs and Trade (GATT) may lead to a change in certain aspects of the General Agreement, for example in the provisions relating to non-tariff barriers, safeguard clauses and agriculture. Moreover, international monetary reforms are still under discussion. The interrelation of the problems of trade negotiations and monetary reform seems clear, and so long as the international monetary system suffers from the uncertainty that causes periodic strains and imbalances, the benefits of, for example, tariff reductions, must be reduced. Finally, the negotiations between the EEC and more than forty developing countries, among them a number of Commonwealth States, may give birth to a new form of Association Agreement with the EEC.

I—THE IMPACT OF THE ROME TREATY
ON BILATERAL AGREEMENTS
CONCLUDED BY THE MEMBER STATES

In the Treaty of Friendship, Commerce and Navigation between the United States of America and the Federal Republic of Germany, concluded prior to the formation of the EEC, each party had accorded to the other most-favoured-nation treatment regarding customs duties. Other treaties concluded by the United States with, for example, Italy and the Netherlands, contained similar provisions. Is the effect of these most-favoured-nation clauses to oblige these countries to accord to the United States the same favourable treatment they undertook to accord to each other under the Rome Treaty? In the particular cases cited the answer must be in the negative, for all three treaties specifically exclude from the ambit of the most-favoured-nation clauses advantages accorded to a third State by reason of membership of a customs union or free trade area.[3]

In the absence of such specific exclusion, would the answer have been different? It may be argued that a customs union is of no higher order than a simple trade agreement, and that, therefore, a most-favoured-nation clause should operate, regarding the benefits

---

[3] See also J. J. Allen, *The European Common Market and the GATT* (1960), p. 57 *et seq.*

conferred by a customs union, in the same way as it operates regarding the benefits conferred by a trade agreement. Yet again it has been suggested—for example, by Professor O'Connell [4]—that entry into the EEC is " akin to State succession, so that it could be argued that incompatible treaties lapse, not so much because the Treaty of Rome is a document of higher normative order as because there has been a modification of economic sovereignty." However, whether such an argument be right or not, it does not seem necessary to go so far in order to conclude that the benefits accorded by the Rome Treaty need not be extended to third States. The legal régime established by the Treaty, or indeed that of any customs union, is one based on the reciprocal assumption of burdens as well as the mutual conferment of benefits. The economic purpose of the EEC would be frustrated if a third State could take such benefits of membership as, for example, tariff reductions on the importation of its products, without at the same time assuming the burdens of, for example, a reduction of its own customs duties or a certain degree of subordination of its own economic sovereignty to the Community.

This is the attitude taken by the original signatories of the Treaty of Rome. While Article 234 [5] provides in Paragraph 1 that rights and obligations arising under agreements concluded by member States before the entry into force of the EEC shall not be affected by the Rome Treaty, Paragraph 3 exhorts the member States, when observing their obligations under such agreements to have regard to the fact that the advantages accorded under the Treaty of Rome " form an integral part of the establishment of the Community and are thereby inseparably linked with the creation of common institutions, the conferring of powers upon them and the granting of the same advantages by all the other member States." In other words, the benefits mutually conferred under the Rome Treaty are not intended to be extended to non-member States through the mechanism of most-favoured-nation clauses. Indeed, the Treaty goes further, and obliges member States to take all appropriate steps to eliminate any incompatibilities between their EEC obligations and other Treaty obligations, if need be by adopting " a common attitude."

II—THE EEC TREATY AND GATT

Perhaps of even greater importance than the effect of the formation of the European Communities on bilateral agreements is the question of the compatibility of the Communities Treaties with the pro-

---

[4] *International Law*, Vol. 1, 2nd ed. (1970), p. 276.
[5] And see Art. 5, Act of Accession, Cmnd. 4862, in relation to the new member States.

visions of the General Agreement on Tariffs and Trade, to which all the member States of the EEC are parties. The lynchpin of GATT is contained in Article I which obliges the Contracting Parties to accord most-favoured-nation treatment to all the other Contracting Parties. Standing on its own, this would be a strict prohibition of any customs union. Yet it was recognised that it would be a mistake to inhibit the development of such unions or other regional integrations. Paragraph 5 of Article XXIV of the GATT Agreement, therefore, provides that the provisions of GATT " shall not prevent, as between the territories of contracting parties, the formation of a customs union or a free-trade-area," *provided* certain specified criteria are met. The history of the interpretation of these criteria in relation to the EEC is a chequered one.

Already in 1952 the European Coal and Steel Community (ECSC) was the subject of discussion in GATT. This discussion, however, offered little guidance on the interpretation of Article XXIV, for this article only applies in relation to unions in which duties are eliminated with respect to " substantially all the trade between the constituent territories." The ECSC, applying as it does only to steel and coal production, could not be regarded as fulfilling that criterion. The only way that the ECSC could be set up without the constituent members being in breach of their obligations under GATT was for the other Contracting Parties to grant a waiver under Article XXV (5) of the GATT Agreement. This article provides that " in exceptional circumstances not elsewhere provided for in this Agreement the Contracting Parties may waive an obligation imposed upon a contracting party under this Agreement." In November 1952, the necessary waiver was granted. The Contracting Parties stated that the realisation of the aims of ECSC could benefit other parties to GATT by increasing the production of coal and steel products, and by providing increased markets for the commodities used by the coal and steel producers. In addition, the political importance attached to any plan for the integration of Europe, of which the ECSC was seen as the first step, was regarded as forming the exceptional circumstances envisaged by the Agreement.[6] By virtue of this waiver, the six members of ECSC were permitted to grant each other advantages which they did not extend to the other Contracting Parties. GATT had suffered its first major breach. But actually, the other members of GATT could not have prevented this. It was preferable to keep the Six within GATT by stretching the rules than to cause a rift which might easily have destroyed GATT itself.

---

[6] See GATT, BISD, First Supplement (1953), p. 17 *et seq.*; Hyder *op. cit.* in note 2 at pp. 69–75; G. Patterson, *Discrimination in International Trade, the Policy Issues 1945–1965*, (1966) p. 126 *et seq.*

The foundation of the European Economic Community and Euratom in 1958 threatened an even greater breach of the spirit of GATT. The status of the EEC was hotly disputed.[7] The Six argued strongly that their Community fulfilled the conditions laid down in Article XXIV. Yet a substantial number of GATT members pointed out that some provisions of the Rome Treaty and of the Association with Overseas Territories were incompatible with GATT. In particular, they denied that the Community fulfilled the relevant conditions of Article XXIV, and that, therefore, the Six were obliged to ask for a waiver, either under Article XXV or Paragraph 10 of Article XXIV, which permits approval by a two-thirds majority of proposals not complying fully with the letter of Article XXIV. No agreement could be reached on this basic question of compatibility, and finally, with political considerations again outweighing all others, the two sides agreed to disagree. For the time being questions of law were put to one side, and the members of GATT decided to concentrate instead on practical problems. It was agreed that consultations should be held between the EEC and those Contracting Parties who felt that their economic interests were adversely affected by the EEC.

Thus, the legal problems concerning the compatibility of the EEC and GATT have remained unsolved, and no final decision was taken on what, in retrospect, was the crucial test of Article XXIV.[8] Indeed the way in which the Rome Treaty was discussed within GATT has been heavily criticised: " A lawyer cannot read the reports, for example of the subgroups appointed to study the EEC Treaty without a sense of despair at the absurdly legalistic quality of some of the discussion. One carries away from such a reading more than a fleeting impression of diplomats playing at being jurists." [9]

The EEC has now been in existence for more than fifteen years, and a repetition of the arguments about compatibility with GATT would be a sterile exercise.[10] The Contracting Parties to GATT have established normal relations with the institutions of EEC, a substantial number of them have concluded trade agreements with the

---

[7] See GATT, BISD Seventh Supplement (1959), pp. 24, 69–71.

[8] K. W. Dam, *The GATT—Law and International Economic Organisation* (1970), p. 292.

[9] *Ibid.*

[10] See, for example, J. J. Allen, *op. cit.* in note 3 above, at p. 217 *et seq.*; G. Curzon, *Multilateral Commercial Diplomacy* (1965), p. 275 *et seq.*; Dam, *op. cit.* in note 8 at p. 274 *et seq.*; Hyder, *op. cit* in note 2, p. 105 *et seq.*; Patterson, *op. cit.* in note 6, p. 157 *et seq.*; D. Vignes, " La clause de la nation la plus favorisée et sa pratique contemporaine—Problèmes posés par la Communauté Economique Européene," *Recueil*, Hague Academy of International Law, 1970 (II), pp. 251–263.

EEC, and the Community has become a party to agreements reached within the framework of GATT.[11] In practical terms, therefore, the Contracting Parties, despite divergent views on the question of compatibility, have come to accept that the member States of the EEC discriminating against them notwithstanding Article I of GATT, while reserving the legal position to avoid precedents in the future. The problems arising out of Article XXIV of the GATT Agreement have shifted away from the EEC itself to the question whether the various association and trade agreements concluded by the EEC with third States are compatible with the provisions of GATT. The Court of Justice of the Communities has pointed out that the abolition of customs duties among EEC members does not interfere with the rights which non-member States hold under GATT.[12] This decision, however, was not intended to exempt the EEC from GATT obligations nor to infringe the rights of third States being parties to GATT. This was made clear in *International Fruit Company* v. *Produktschap voor Groenten en Fruit*,[13] where it was held that in so far as the EEC has assumed in connection with the GATT powers previously exercised by the member States, the Community is itself bound by the provisions of GATT. By taking this view the Court has held that the validity of the acts of Community organs will be examined not only according to Community law but also according to international law where it is applicable.[14]

III—REDRESSING THE BALANCE

Notwithstanding treaty obligations, the effect, indeed the intention of the EEC, is to discriminate against non-member States and in favour of each other. What remedies are open to those States who consider themselves adversely affected by such discrimination, or who wish otherwise to enjoy some, if perhaps not all, of the benefits of the EEC?

1. *Accession to the EEC*

The most thorough-going remedy for any such *European* State is to seek, as did the United Kingdom, Denmark and Ireland, to accede to the Communities in accordance with Article 237 of the Rome Treaty. British experience has demonstrated the obstacles that such a State may experience in making such an application.

---

[11] See, for example, *Journal Officiel des Communautés Européenes* (J.O.) (1968), L305/1.

[12] *Commission* v. *Italy* (10/61)—1962 C.M.L.R., p. 187 at 204; see also *Advocate General Lagrange in Italy* v. *Commission* (13/63)—1963 C.M.L.R., p. 289 at 307.

[13] (21–24/72) XVIII Rec. (1972), p. 1219.

[14] See P. Pescatore *et al.*, Z.A.Ö.R.V. Vol. 32 (1972), p. 239 at p. 246.

However, little need be said about this possibility in this paper; the effect of a successful application is to put the new member in the same position as the old members subject only to the negotiated provisions of a transitional period.

2. *Free Trade Agreements with EEC*

Those members of the European Free Trade Association (EFTA) who, for political reasons, did not wish to accede to the EEC, at least at this stage, have concluded bilateral treaties with the Community.[15] The objective of such agreements is the formation of free trade areas between the parties; for example the barriers to " substantially all the trade " with Austria are to be eliminated by 1977. Free trade agreements, particularly with non-European States, are dealt with in more detail below, but it should be noted at this stage that the legal basis of these agreements has not been Article 238, dealing with Associations, but Article 113 which empowers the Community to conclude trade agreements.

3. *Compensatory adjustment of tariffs*

Articles XXIV (6) and XXVIII (1) of GATT entitles countries having " a principal supplying interest " or a " substantial interest " in such concessions, to negotiate with the community over tariff concessions and to claim adjustment of tariffs on certain products to compensate for the increases of tariffs on other products as a result of membership. A number of third countries, including the United States, New Zealand and Australia, have invoked this Article regarding the higher external tariffs of the United Kingdom, Denmark and Ireland, after the accession of these countries to the EEC.

The crucial question in such negotiations arises from the second sentence of Article XXIV (6): " In providing for compensatory adjustment, due account shall be taken of the compensation already afforded by the reductions brought about in the corresponding duty of the other constituents of the union." It has been argued that this provision entitles the EEC to say that the losses certain third States may incur in the agricultural sector are more than off-set by the increased industrial trade resulting from lower industrial tariffs.[16] However, the value of this interpretation may be of some doubt, at least for those countries who, because of their economic structure,

---

[15] Austria, Finland, Iceland, Norway, Portugal, Sweden, Switzerland; see, for example, J.O. (1972), L300 and L301; see further, E. P. Wellenstein, " The Free Trade Agreements between the Enlarged European Communities and the EFTA Countries," 10 C.M.L.Rev. (1973), p. 137.

[16] See, for example, *The Times*, March 20, 1973, p. 21.

are not in a position to compensate losses in one sector of the economy by gains in another.

4. *Association Agreements*

States that seek a higher degree of participation in Community objectives and a higher degree of institutionalisation of their relations with the EEC than are provided by a normal trade agreement, while not being prepared or entitled to assume the full benefits or burdens of Community membership, may endeavour to conclude Association Agreements with the EEC pursuant to Article 238 of the Rome Treaty: " The Community may conclude with a third State, a union of States or an international organisation agreement establishing an association involving reciprocal rights and obligations, common actions and special procedures." [17]

Two main categories of Association Agreements may be distinguished. Such an Agreement may be used in relation to a European country as a precursor to full membership of the Community. In this category are the agreements with Greece [18] and Turkey.[19] The other broad category consists of Association Agreements with the developing countries. In these cases it has been realised that a simple trade agreement providing primarily for tariff reductions can do little to improve effectively the trade position of these emergent States, and that, therefore, a more sophisticated relation with the EEC is required.[20]

Even within these two categories, the underlying motives, purposes and circumstances differ so that it is often difficult to make statements of universal application about the many Association Agreements already concluded. Nonetheless, these Agreements deserve detailed examination. Comparable with these Association Agreements are the provisions of the Association of Overseas Countries and Territories, set out in Part 4 of the Treaty of Rome, which are intended to continue and extend the relationship of former colonies and overseas territories of EEC members with the EEC itself. Indeed, it has proved necessary in respect of some of those territories to conclude further Association Agreements as a result of their attainment of independence since 1958.

---

[17] See H. P. Ipsen, *Europaisches Gemeinschaftsrecht* (1972), p. 168; and E. U. Petersmann, " Struktur und aktuelle Rechtsfragen des Assoziationsrechts," Z.A.Ö.R.V. Vol. 33 (1973), p. 266 *et seq.*

[18] J.O. (1963), p. 294.

[19] J.O. (1964), p. 3687.

[20] Memorandum from the Commission on a Community Policy on Development Co-operation—Programme for Initial Actions, *Bulletin of the European Communities*, Supplement 2/72, p. 9.

IV—TYPES OF ASSOCIATION AGREEMENTS
The question of discrimination and equality in relation to Association Agreements calls for a twofold review. First, the relative positions of the constituent parties have to be examined. Secondly, the impact of these Agreements on non-participant States has to be explored.

1. *The Yaoundé Conventions*
On July 20, 1963, 18 African States signed an Association Agreement at Yaoundé. This was superseded by a further Convention, also signed at Yaoundé on July 29, 1969, by the same parties.[21] This association, originally necessary to continue the provisions of Part 4 of the Treaty of Rome once these States had attained independence, has been stated by the Commission of the Communities to be " in the first place a political option, which aims at the maintenance and development of privileged relationships of every kind between Europe and Africa. . . . [T]hey have deliberately preferred the Community as their first foreign partner in their development." [22] Indeed, it may be argued that the Convention goes further than the Association Agreements envisaged by the Rome Treaty in the sense that it was necessary for the members of the EEC themselves also to sign the Convention in view of certain provisions for financial aid which the Community itself had no competence under the Rome Treaty to undertake. As perhaps the most important Association Agreement, at least with the Third World, certain aspects of the Yaoundé Convention call for special attention.

The central object of the Convention is the creation of a free-trade area between the EEC and the Associated States. To this end, provision is made for the abolition of customs duties and quantitative restrictions between the two areas, and for the reciprocal grant of most-favoured-nation treatment. But there are important exceptions to this basic principle. First, certain important exceptions are made regarding agricultural products of the Associates. Secondly, the Associated States are entitled to retain or introduce customs duties or quantitative restrictions which are necessary because of their development requirements or to finance their budgets. Yet, in so doing these States are not permitted to discriminate between the different members of the EEC who must be granted the same treatment, express provision being made, for example, to deal with *de facto*, as opposed to *legal*, discriminations

---

[21] J.O. (1970), L282/1.
[22] Commission Memorandum on a Community Development Co-operation Policy, *Bulletin of the European Communities*, Supplement 5/71, p. 11.

which arise from the application of a State import-monopoly. This non-discrimination between the various members of the Community is of particular importance to prevent those members who formerly had colonial or other special relationships with Associated States from gaining thereby preferential treatment. Thirdly, and of particular interest, is the right of the Associated States to derogate from the most-favoured-nation clauses in the Conventions in order to facilitate the development of regional economic integration among themselves. The Community is prepared to grant to others the rights it retains for itself. However, the Convention does lay down certain conditions of compatibility with Association with the EEC. These conditions vary according to the type of State with which integration is intended, and relate in particular to rules of product origin. The EEC is not prepared to permit third States to gain advantages accorded to the African States by exporting products of such third States through Associated States into the Community.

The Yaoundé Convention also provides for a certain degree of non-discrimination in the areas of the right of establishment, and the free movement of services and capital. The basic principle in these areas is that the member States of the EEC shall be accorded most-favoured-nation treatment, and, in particular, there shall not be any discrimination against any such member States. Two important reservations are, however, made. Advantages accorded to third States as a result of regional integration by an Associated State need not be granted to the Community members. The Associates are also entitled to restrict advantages to those member States who accord them reciprocal treatment in a particular economic sphere. This provision finds its rationale in the historical relationship between the Associated States and the member States.[23] France, in particular, had concluded far-reaching agreements on establishment and the like with its former colonies. It would have been unreasonable and impracticable to have expected these former colonies to have opened their countries immediately to a great influx of foreign enterprises from the other member States without obtaining reciprocal or at least equivalent advantages. Moreover, none of the parties to the existing agreements wanted their abolition.

At least lip-service is paid to the principle of equality in the institutional arrangements under the Yaoundé Convention. In the Association Council, the Association Committee, the Parliamentary Conference and the Court of Arbitration, the EEC and the Associates have equal representation. But the economic gulf between Europe and Africa cannot be denied, nor the factual inequality that

---

[23] Chr. von Arnim, "Der Stand der Assoziationsverhaltnisse der EWG mit aussereuropaischen Staaten," Z.A.Ö.R.V., Vol. 30 (1970), p. 482 at p. 494.

results from this state of affairs. It is true that the EEC has had to buy its benefits by the provisions of economic aid contained in Title II of the Convention, but it has been strongly argued that the Association has merely revived the old colonial system under a new name. This problem was carefully considered in a previous article in this *Year Book*.[24] Its authors concluded: " In point of fact the issue is not colonialism or neo-colonialism—there are many who would say that these are pejorative labels given to perfectly respectable instruments of international co-operation such as aid and trade preferences—but the discrimination involved in the Yaoundé system, which links such a large part of Europe with such a small part of Africa."

2. *Other Association Agreements*

The other Association Agreements concluded by the EEC remain below the level of integration established by the Yaoundé Conventions. The Arousha Convention,[25] for example, signed with Kenya, Tanzania and Uganda, does not provide for financial and technical co-operation, and the agreements with Morocco[26] and Tunisia[27] have been described as " in effect little more than preferential trade agreements with a slightly more sophisticated institutional system than usual."[28] Nevertheless, all the agreements seem to have four basic principles in common: their objective is at least stated to be the establishment of free-trade-areas; the Associates are not entitled to discriminate between the members of the EEC[29]; they are entitled to a certain measure of derogation from the first of these principles, however, where it is necessary for their development[30]; they are also entitled to derogate from the principle of equality of treatment in order to facilitate their own regional integrations.[31]

3. *Enlargement of the EEC and the Association Agreements*

The new member States of the EEC have not become automatically bound by the provisions of the existing agreements on their accession to the Community. Article 109 of the Treaty of Accession provides that the Yaoundé and Arousha Conventions

---

[24] G. and V. Curzon, " Neo-colonialism and the European Economic Community," in this *Year Book*, Vol. 25 (1971), pp. 118–141 at p. 139.
[25] J.O. 1970, L282/55.
[26] J.O. 1969, L197/5.
[27] J.O. 1969, L198/5.
[28] A. Parry and S. Hardy, *EEC Law* (1973), p. 453.
[29] See, for example, Article 3 (3), Arousha Convention.
[30] *Ibid.* Articles 3 (2) and 6 (2).
[31] *Ibid.* Articles 9, 10 and 11.

shall not apply to the relations between the new members and the Associates. Products originating in the countries associated with the EEC by these Conventions are, on importation into the United Kingdom, subject to the Arrangements applied to these products before accession.[32]

4. *The Commonwealth and Association*

The accession of the United Kingdom to the Community would have a profound effect on certain Commonwealth countries if these were denied a continuation of the special relations previously existing with the United Kingdom. With this in mind, Protocol 22 to the Treaty of Accession offers a choice of three different types of agreement to the Commonwealth members listed in Annex VI to the Treaty. These are basically the African and West Indian members, excluding the white Commonwealth States and the Asian developing nations.

The first option, and the one that the Community would prefer these nations to adopt, is that they should accede to the new Convention which will govern the relations with the African and Malagasy States when the Yaoundé Convention expires on January 31, 1975.

The second option is the conclusion of special Agreements of Association, comprising reciprocal rights and obligations, particularly in the field of trade. These would probably follow the Arousha Convention in many ways.

Thirdly, these States may conclude trade agreements " with a view to facilitating and developing trade between the Community and those countries."

As far as the other Commonwealth countries are concerned, the EEC has declared its readiness to examine trade problems with Sri Lanka, Malaysia, Pakistan and Singapore,[33] while in the meantime, a trade agreement has already been concluded with India. The problems of New Zealand's exports to the United Kingdom have been resolved, at least for the time being, by transitional arrangements set out in Protocol 18 to the Treaty of Accession, which is to expire by the end of 1977.

5. *A new type of Association Agreement?*

The possibility of association with the developing Commonwealth nations, and the necessity for a further agreement with the Associated States of Africa and Malagasy raises the possibility of a new type of association agreement. There are a number of possible

---

[32] See also Act of Accession, Articles 110–115.
[33] Joint Declaration of Intent, Cmnd. 4862–I, p. 117; see also B. G. Ramcharan,

aspects of such an agreement which, in the context of this paper, are of interest.

(a) *Reverse Preferences.* The existing association agreements provide for a reciprocal grant by the Associated States of tariff preferences to the EEC in return for tariff preferences granted by the Community to them. Whether such "reverse preferences" should be included in new agreements has for some time been a subject of controversy not only among the members of the EEC but also among the developing nations themselves. Some Associated States believe that reciprocity of this kind preserves their dignity and self-respect by demonstrating their equality with the European States.[34] Others, especially a number of Commonwealth countries, have argued that the EEC should not expect reciprocity, and point out that "reciprocity between those who are unequal in economic strength is a contradiction in economic terms." [35] While it is true that, according to Paragraph 1 of Article 238 of the EEC Treaty, association involves "reciprocal rights and obligations," it would not, at least in theory, be impossible for the EEC to grant certain unilateral advantages to the Associated States, perhaps by applying a standard of "relative reciprocity," [36] related to the level of development in the particular country. If the sole purpose of Associations is, as is stated in the Article 3 (k) of the Treaty of Rome of 1957, "to increase trade and to promote jointly economic and social development," it should be permissible, it is argued, to take such steps as are in fact necessary for the promotion of this aim, even if it means abandoning the principle of reciprocity.

(b) *Agriculture.* The Associates have argued also that the benefits of association should include free access of their agricultural products to the Common Market, at present an important right denied them. The effect that such a policy would have on present Community agricultural policy would be of the highest significance.

(c) *Insurance of export earnings.* Another important change in the system of association might be the inclusion of a system of insurance to stabilise the export earnings of those associated countries whose economies are dependent on the production of primary

---

"Equality and Discrimination in International Economic Law (III)," in this *Year Book*, Volume 26 (1972), pp. 286–313.

[34] See, for example, President Leopold Senghor, in Europa Nr. 3, *The Times* (Supplement) December 4, 1973: "We have always insisted in the conclusion of an agreement based on overall reciprocity. . . ."

[35] S. S. Ramphal, Foreign Minister of Guyana, *The Times*, July 27, 1973, p. 6.

[36] E. U. Petersmann, "Das Neue Recht des Nord-Sud-Handels," Z.A.Ö.R.V. Vol. 32 (1972), p. 339 at p. 389.

products—for example, the sugar producers of the Commonwealth. It is impossible to say at this stage what precise form such a scheme would take. Although such a scheme might be a valuable experiment for the rest of the world, it is almost inevitable that many will regard it as yet another preferential and discriminatory act by the EEC and its Associates.

Other changes in the new type of Association agreement may include changes in the EEC rules on the origin of products and on the right of establishment in order to permit the Associates greater freedom in the development of their own areas of economic integration.

V—TRADE AGREEMENTS

Before passing on to examine the Association Agreements in the light of GATT, some reference should be made to a series of trade agreements concluded by the Community.

A Common Market with a common external tariff needs a common commercial policy.[37] The Rome Treaty, therefore, confers powers on the Council to adopt and effect such a policy, including the power to undertake contractual obligations of a purely commercial nature towards non-member States.[38] It is true that some of the agreements concluded pursuant to these powers differ little from trade agreements, commonly found between two states, yet there are others which are closer to Association Agreements. The Agreement with Argentina [39] is an example of the first category; it provides for reciprocal most-favoured-nation treatment and certain tariff advantages. Agreements with Israel [40] and with Egypt,[41] however, provide for a higher degree of co-operation. The eventual aim is the establishment of a free-trade-area and, as a precursor to that, substantial tariff reductions are stipulated. The EEC is to be accorded at least most-favoured-nation treatment.[42] The member States of the Community are to be treated with equality.[43] Mixed Committees are to be established.[44] This narrow distinction between some Association Agreements and some Trade Agreements should be borne in mind, therefore, not only because the Trade Agreements

---

[37] G. Le Tallec, "The Common Commercial Policy of the EEC," 20 I.C.L.Q. (1971), p. 732; see also B. R. Bot, "Negotiating Community Agreements: Procedure and Practice," 7 C.M.L.Rev. (1970), p. 286.

[38] *Commission* v. *Council* (22/70)—1971 C.M.L.R., p. 335 at pp. 354–355.

[39] J.O. (1971), L249/19.

[40] J.O. (1970), L183/2.

[41] J.O. (1973), L251/2.

[42] See, for example, Articles 5, Agreements with Israel and Spain.

[43] *Ibid.* Article 4.

[44] See also the agreements with Iran, J.O. 1963, 2254; Spain, J.O. 1970, L182/2; Lebanon, J.O. 1968, L146/2; Yugoslavia, J.O. 1970, L58/2; and note 15 above.

might be mistaken otherwise for an orthodox trading agreement, but also because the legal régimes established by the Association Agreements might otherwise be mistakenly supposed to create a higher degree of integration than in fact they do. This is a crucial point when considering the applicability of Article XXIV of GATT to these agreements.

VI—ASSOCIATION AND TRADE AGREEMENTS AND ARTICLE XXIV OF GATT

It was stated above that the critical debate in GATT had shifted from the question of the compatibility of the EEC itself with the obligations of its members under GATT to an examination of the Agreements between the EEC and other States in the light of the general principle of non-discrimination contained in Article I of GATT. There is no question of incompatibility when those agreements go no further than merely to grant most-favoured-nation treatment to third States. The problem arises when third States are not only given the same treatment as the other parties to GATT, but when they are granted *preferential* treatment.

It cannot be denied that the Association Agreements do *in fact* lead to preferential treatment for the Associated States and in many cases for the EEC itself. This can only be justified by reference once again to Article XXIV of GATT. The Contracting Parties were unable to agree that even the high level of integration created by the Rome Treaty among the Six fell within GATT rules. Thus, inevitably, some of these States have argued even more strongly that the much lower levels of integration which were established by the Association and Trade Agreements cannot possibly justify the invocation of Article XXIV. The Agreements have been described as " a severe threat to the entire trading system, and a clear violation of the letter and spirit of GATT." [45] But despite these strong words, the Contracting Parties have been unable to reach any conclusions or solutions.[46] The Working Parties established to report on the agreements with Israel and Spain, for example, both concluded their reports with the words: " Having regard to the difference of view expressed on the legal issues involved, the members of the Working Party reserved their rights under the General Agreement." [47]

Certainly, there have been differences of opinion on the legal issues involved.[48] A customs union, we have already noted, must eliminate customs duties with respect to " substantially all the trade between the constituent territories." In an organisation which has

---

45 *The Times*, March 3, 1973, p. 19.
46 See generally, D. Vignes, *op. cit.* in note 10 above, pp. 307–338.
47 GATT, BISD, Eighteenth Supplement (1972), pp. 166, 174.
48 See generally K. W. Dam, *op. cit.* in note 10 above.

no tribunal to decide conflicts between its members save for those conflicting members themselves, a phrase such as this is open to as many different interpretations as there are interested parties. The requirement that an interim agreement leading to a customs union or free-trade area must include a " plan and schedule " of when that customs union or free-trade area will be formed has also been a fruitful source of dissension when considering agreements that do no more than set out the parties' desire to consider further agreements in the future,[49] and so the list of other interpretative difficulties continues.

It is not proposed, however, to consider these legal issues. To do so would mean missing the two fundamental points to which this discussion must inevitably lead to; first, appreciation of the fact that GATT was intended to operate more as an instrument of diplomacy than as an inflexible and enforceable code of international conduct. To condemn the EEC could only lead, in the end, to a widescale renunciation of GATT.

Secondly, the realisation that the ideal of an international community of States bargaining on a free, equal and non-discriminatory basis—the ideal on which the original General Agreement was founded—no longer accords, if indeed it ever did, with the economic realities of the international situation. This is now apparent from Part IV of GATT which, in itself, raises certain further interesting legal points. Thus, if the less developed nations are entitled to " special measures to promote their trade and development," as Article XXXVI suggests, does this enable the EEC to enter agreements which, while not complying strictly with the requirements of Article XXIV, nevertheless are designed to provide such " special measures? " [50] In other words to what extent does Part IV modify the earlier Parts of the General Agreement?

VII—THE EEC AND UNCTAD

A study of this subject would not be complete without some reference to the resolutions of the United Nations Conference on Trade and Development (UNCTAD). At UNCTAD I, preferential arrangements between the EEC and the developing countries were criticised in so far as they involved discrimination against other developing countries.[51] The close link between this criticism and the fear that the Community's policy towards the Third World is merely a perpetuation of colonial relations under a new disguise is clear.

---

[49] See, for example, the agreements with Tunisia, Morocco, Egypt, Israel and Spain.

[50] See E. U. Petersmann, *op. cit.* in note 36 above, pp. 381–382.

[51] See Final Act, Annex A III, Proceedings of UNCTAD I (1964).

Against this criticism the Community has argued that the economic expansion caused both in Europe and the Associated States—and only possible with the protectionist and geographically concentrated associations exemplified by the Yaoundé Convention—in the long run benefits everybody. Nevertheless, it has made concessions to Third-World feelings at least on paper by the introduction from July 1971 of the system of generalised preferences,[52] and by the call made at the first summit of the Nine in October 1972 for a " worldwide policy towards the developing nations."

Whatever becomes of the latter proposal, the system of generalised preferences can hardly be said to go very far on the road indicated by UNCTAD.[53] While the principle of such a scheme—to discriminate against the developed nations in favour of the developing nations but to do so on a basis that does not prefer some developing nations to others—is valuable, the limitations of the present scheme must be noted. The products covered by the tariff preferences granted by the EEC are essentially manufactured and semi-manufactured goods, the sensitive areas of agriculture and primary products being generally excluded, and a limit put on the amount of goods that can come within the scheme, coupled with a quota system to prevent the sole beneficiaries of the scheme being a handful of semi-developed nations. In any event, at least a part of the benefit of the whole scheme must be in some doubt now that many of the competitors in the type of goods covered by the scheme are European States which are now linked together on even more preferential terms than the developing nations can obtain, either because these competitors have now joined the enlarged Community, or because of new trading arrangements between the EEC and the members of EFTA.[54]

Conclusions

Is it possible to draw any formal conclusions from the foregoing study? It is probably too early to do more than to take stock of the existing situation and to note the trends and changes that appear to be taking place. The principle of *formal* equality through a universal or universalist application of the most-favoured-nation standard, as embodied in Article I of GATT has certainly been

---

[52] J.O. 1971, L142/1.

[53] See generally Petersmann, *op. cit.* in note 36 above, p. 387; G. G. Kaplan " The Unctad Scheme for Generalised Preferences," in this *Year Book*, Volume 26 (1972), pp. 267–285; R. Krishnamurti, " Tariff Preferences in Favour of Developing Countries," 4 J.W.T.L. (1970), p. 447.

[54] See J. Murray, " UNCTAD's Generalised Preferences, An Appraisal," 7 J.W.T.L. (1973), p. 461, at pp. 467, 468.

eroded by the establishment of regional economic organisations like the European Economic Communities and the associations which at least the EEC has formed. Whether this will result in a re-interpretation of Article I of GATT in the light of the principles laid down in Part IV of GATT remains to be seen.

Such an interpretation would lead to a novel double-standard of non-discrimination, where the classic most-favoured-nation might continue to apply in general to relations between the developed nations, while no longer applying in their relations with the developing nations. Nevertheless, this would not necessarily mean that the struggle through GATT to establish a system of equality and non-discrimination in international economic relations would have been lost.

In the first part of this paper a distinction was drawn between formal and material discrimination. A particular act may appear on its face to be discriminatory because two situations are treated differently. Yet, *in fact*, this is not so because the two situations are not comparable. The vast gulf between the economic power of the developed and the developing nations, which has shown no signs of narrowing and perhaps has increased, may well mean that it is only by taking measures that, in form, are discriminatory that equality in fact can be achieved.

THE INTERNATIONAL LAW COMMISSION

By

B. G. RAMCHARAN

THE International Law Commission [1] is charged with the task of assisting the General Assembly to codify and progressively develop international law.[2] Its task includes suggesting modifications and changes in the law to bring it in line with present-day international society, and suggesting new law where none existed before or where the law has hitherto been unclear. The Commission reached its 25th anniversary in 1973. Between 1967 and 1973, there took place in the Commission and in the Sixth Committee of the United Nations General Assembly, a review [3] of the approach, programme and

---

[1] From the diverse literature on the Commission, the following sample may be mentioned: United Nations Office of Public Information, *The International Law Commission* (Revised ed., 1972); *The Yearbooks of the International Law Commission* (1949–1973); H. W. Briggs, *The International Law Commission* (1965); B. Cheng, "The International Law Commission," 5 *Current Legal Problems* (1952), pp. 250–272; Y. Daudet, *Les Conferences des Nations Unies pour la codification du droit international* (1968); R. P. Dhokalia, *The Codification of Public International Law* (1970); A. E. Gotlieb, "The International Law Commission," 4 *Canadian Yearbook of International Law* (1966), pp. 64–80; R. Y. Jennings, "The Progressive Development of International Law," 24 *British Yearbook of International Law* (1947), pp. 310–329; R. Y. Jennings, "Recent Developments in the International Law Commission: Its Relation to the Sources of International Law," 13 *International and Comparative Law Quarterly* (1964), pp. 385–397; D. H. N. Johnson, "The Preparation of the 1958 Geneva Conference on the Law of the Sea," 8 *International and Comparative Law Quarterly* (1959), pp. 122–145; H. Lauterpacht, "Codification and Development of International Law," 49 *American Journal of International Law* (1955), pp. 16–43; L. T. Lee, "The International Law Commission Re-Examined," 59 *American Journal of International Law* (1965), pp. 545–569; Yuen-li Liang, "Le développement et la codification du droit international," 73 *Recueil des Cours* (1948, II), pp. 411–527; A. P. Movchan, "Significance of the Codification of Principles of International Law in the Framework of the United Nations" (in Russian), 35 *Sovetskoe Gosudarstvo i Pravo* (Moscow) (1965), pp. 46–55; M. K. Nawaz, "Future Work Programme of the International Law Commission," 12 *Indian Journal of International Law* (1972), pp. 71–83; S. Rosenne, "The International Law Commission 1949–1959," 36 *British Yearbook of International Law* (1960), pp. 104–173; S. Rosenne, "Relations Between Governments and the International Law Commission," in this *Year Book*, Vol. 19 (1965), pp. 183–198; M. Sahovic, "The General Assembly and Progressive Development of International Law," 13 *Medunarodni Problemi* (Belgrade) (1961), pp. 87–99; G. Schwarzenberger, *Manual of Public International Law* (1967), pp. 380–388; H. W. Thirlway, *International Customary Law and Codification* (1972).

[2] See Article 13, para. 1 (a) of the Charter of the United Nations; and United Nations Document, Reference A/CN/4/4: "Statute of the International Law Commission and Other Resolutions of the General Assembly Relating to the International Law Commission."

[3] The following issues were raised in the course of the review: the shortage of working time available to the Commission; lack of resources; need for a quicker

283

methods of the Commission and of co-ordination between its work and legal development taking place through other United Nations bodies. In its report for 1973, the Commission included a review of its work during its first 25 sessions [4] and submitted a list of topics [5] put forward by members of the Commission for inclusion in a programme for the next 20 to 25 years. The Commission decided to give further consideration to these proposals in the course of future sessions. It also requested additional staff for the Codification Division of the United Nations Office of Legal Affairs, which serves as the secretariat of the Commission, to enable it to give more assistance, especially in the area of research and studies.

In the Sixth Committee in 1973, the Commission's decision to press on with the five topics on its current active programme [6] received widespread support and its decision to continue the review of its long-term programme during future sessions was welcomed. Among the topics suggested by representatives, the following, listed in order of support received, were the most important: international responsibility for injurious consequences arising out of the performance of activities other than internationally wrongful acts—responsibility for lawful activities or for hazards or risks [7]; legal problems relating to the non-navigational uses of international watercourses,

---

rate of work; determination of the present and future needs of international society for the codification and development of international law; bringing international law to bear upon the important issues in international society such as economic development, maintenance of peace and security, and the pacific settlement of disputes; determining the approach and perspectives which should guide the Commission during the next 25 years; determining suitable criteria for the selection of topics; selecting a programme for a 20 to 25 year period; reviewing the work methods of the Commission, reconsidering whether its work should take the form of draft conventions only or whether it could also include the preparation of restatements or model rules the question of a possible extension in the term of office of members of the Commission; the need to strengthen the secretariat services available to the Commission; the problem of lack of ratification of codification conventions; the revision and up-dating of codification conventions; and the co-ordination of its work with legal development taking place through other United Nations bodies.

[4] See I.L.C. Report, 1973, U.N. Doc. A/9010, Chapter 6. See also, Doc. A/CN. 4/245—Survey of International Law prepared by the Secretary-General.

[5] The topics were: State immunity; unilateral acts; treatment of aliens; liability for damages from acts not yet prohibited by international law; the law relating to the environment; the law relating to economic development; extradition; the law relating to international organisations; succession of governments; peaceful settlement of disputes; recognition of States and Governments; and the right of asylum. The Commission is at present actively engaged on the following topics: Succession of States in respect of treaties; State responsibility; Succession of States in matters other than treaties; the most-favoured-nation clause; treaties concluded between States and international organisations or between two or more international organisations; and the non-navigational uses of international watercourses.

[6] Listed in note 5 above.

[7] This topic received support from the collective committee, which included in its draft resolution subsequently adopted by the General Assembly, the recom-

with special reference to the pollution of such watercourses [8]; international environmental law [9]; jurisdictional immunities of foreign States and their organs, agencies and property [10]; treatment of aliens [11]; unilateral acts [12]; international criminal law [13]; and the right of territorial asylum.[14] A number of States [15] stressed the necessity for the Commission to give attention to improving its methods of work. There were differing views on the Commission's request for a 14-week session in 1974, the majority being against any extension in the regular annual session beyond the present period of 10 weeks.[16] The Committee put forward a compromise by recommending a session of 12 weeks for 1974.

On November 30, 1973, the General Assembly adopted Resolution 3071 (XXVIII), in which it welcomed the decision of the Commission to give further consideration to the proposals and suggestions made in connection with the review of the Commission's long-term programme of work, and recommended that the Commission continue work on " Succession of States, State Responsibility, the Most-Favoured-Nation Clause, Treaties Concluded Between States and International Organisations or Between Two or More International Organisations, and Legal Problems Relating to non-Navigational Uses of International Watercourses," giving priority to the first two of these. It also recommended that the Commission should commence its work on international watercourses at its 26th session in 1974.

At the end of the first quarter century of the Commission, it is

mendation that the Commission should undertake at an appropriate time a separate study of the topic of international liability for injurious consequences arising out of the performance of activities other than internationally wrongful acts. Internationally wrongful acts are receiving attention in the current work of the Commission on international responsibility.

[8] The importance of this topic, which is already on the programme of the Commission, was emphasised by Argentina; Bulgaria; Cyprus; Finland; Ghana; Iraq; Indonesia; Kenya; Mexico; Nigeria; Thailand; United States; United Kingdom, and Zambia.

[9] Proposed by Canada; Cyprus; Ghana; Iraq, and Nigeria. Several delegations also proposed that the Commission should look at the problem of pollution in its consideration of the legal problems of international watercourses.

[10] Proposed by Ghana; Indonesia; Iraq; Nigeria and Zaire.

[11] Proposed by The Netherlands; Nigeria and Ghana.

[12] Proposed by Iraq.

[13] Proposed by Zaire.

[14] Proposed by The Netherlands.

[15] The Byelorussian Soviet Socialist Republic; The German Democratic Republic; Bulgaria; The Soviet Union; Czechoslovakia; Tanzania and India. See generally, A/C.6/SR. 1414–1416, Summary Records of the Sixth Committee, 1973, *General Assembly Official Records, Sixth Committee,* 1973.

[16] This carries the clear implication that any suggestion for making the Commission a full-time body will still not be accepted by Governments. A recommendation to this effect made by the Commission in 1951 was not accepted by the General Assembly.

opportune to step back from it, set it in perspective, examine the nature of the process in which it is engaged, and the lines along which the law is developing.

I—GENERAL PERSPECTIVES

The study of the work and functioning of the Commission comes under that branch of international law known as the science of international legislation, on which it has been observed: " International law-making by means of treaties has assumed such a scale as to make necessary not only the creation of an international legislative drafting bureau but also of another new branch of international law: that of international legislation. One of the chief tasks of this branch might be to concern itself with the factors which, at any time in the evolution of international law, determine the functional frontiers of the law of nations. . . . The factors which condition the functional scope of international legislation may be called field-determining agencies. Three of these agencies may claim to be of special significance: the degree of integration of international society or any of its segments; the measure of structural uniformity of States; the value of their ethical common denominator." [17] In addition to these one might add the political condition of international society and the adequacy (or inadequacy) of the organisational, methodological and general approaches of the body or bodies entrusted with the task of law-making.

There are four main sets of patterns [18] for the development of international law: (1) The *object* may be either restatement or reform; (2) The *technique* may be either the codification or the common-law pattern [19]; (3) The *scope* may be either universal or non-universal; and (4) The *agencies* may be either official or unofficial. The International Law Commission combines the restatement and reform patterns and employs the codification, universal and official patterns.

Among the agencies for the development of international law in international society the Commission is unique. The International Court of Justice is used infrequently,[20] and the trend is away from third party settlement to more direct, political forms of settlement of disputes. The future role of the United Nations General Assembly

---

[17] G. Schwarzenberger, " Scope and Limits of International Legislation," in *The Frontiers of International Law* (1962), p. 88. See also, *ibid.*, *Power Politics* (1963), p. 548; *ibid.*, *The Inductive Approach to International Law* (1965); *ibid.*, *International Law and Order* (1971).

[18] See on this, G. Schwarzenberger, *Manual of Public International Law* (1967), pp. 380–388.

[19] The common-law pattern indicates the development of international law by international courts and tribunals.

[20] The General Assembly is currently engaged in a review of the role of court.

in the formulation of international law is not likely to be as potent as it was during the first 25 years of the United Nations. Although it will continue to be a forum from which practice capable of giving rise to international customary law will emanate,[21] the areas calling for great resolutions have very nearly been covered. There now exists basic régimes for the law of the sea and the seabed, and for outer space. The difficulties of ascertaining new rules of international customary law in an international society consisting of over 130 States,[22] combined with the slowness of the process of formation of international customary law, assign to international customary law a subsidiary, supporting role in supplying new rules needed for the conduct of international relations, though its importance in the system will continue to be very high owing to the weakness of lack of ratification from which international codification conventions suffer.[23]

When the International Law Commission has completed its reports on State Responsibility and State Succession to add to those on the Law of Treaties and Diplomatic and Consular Relations, the basic chapters underpinning modern international law will have been initially mapped out, and the first cycle or first round of law in the United Nations system will have been accomplished. The initial mapping-out of the legal terrain will have been achieved. In the second round the task will be to develop on the existing framework, to bring in greater precision, and to give expression to the general principles established in the first round. This task belongs to the domain of the Commission and is one for which it is uniquely qualified. In the first cycle it has played a significant role. In the second cycle its role [24] is likely to be even greater in providing that necessary blend between scientific codification and political realism. In the hands of the Commission rests the responsibility for the quality of the law.

Contextually, the Commission has to be seen in a three-fold perspective: as an agency concerned with the general development and growth of international law; as an agency within the United Nations system for the codification and development of international law [25]; and as an agency within the world-wide process of codifica-

---

[21] See, on this, R. Higgins, *The Development of International Law Through the Political Organs of the United Nations* (1963).

[22] See, on this, L. Henkin, *How Nations Behave* (1968), p. 119.

[23] See H. W. Thirlway, *International Customary Law and Codification. An Examination of the Continuing Role of Custom in the Present Period of Codification of International Law* (1972).

[24] See below, "VIII—Appraisal and Conclusions," for an enumeration of the tasks facing the Commission in the future.

[25] *Cf.* J. E. S. Fawcett, *The Law of Nations* (1968) (1971), App. I; I. Brownlie, *Principles of Public International Law* (1973), pp. 673–677; K. Skubiszewski,

tion and development of international law, including the regional bodies such as the Asian-African Legal Consultative Committee, the European Committee on Legal Co-operation and the Inter-American Juridical Committee. Independent of the Commission, multilateral conventions are concluded which add to the growing infrastructure of the international legal system. International Customary law is being created through State practice and the practice of international organisations. Judicial decisions and treatises by publicists assist in the determination of the law. The Commission features among the " sources " of international law in three ways: the conventions which are produced on the basis of its work are clearly sources of obligations in the strict sense and of international law in the looser sense.[26] The Commission's work as a whole also forms part of the practice which either creates or assists in creating new rules of international customary law.[27] The Commission as a whole, containing as it does, experts of the highest repute, qualifies as a high-ranking body of international publicists.[28]

These are complementary facets. The two law-creating facets: the Commission as an agency for the creation of conventions and as an agency for the creation of customary law, take precedence over the law-determining facet: the Commission as a body of publicists. However, as between the law-creating facets, the hierarchical position is not straightcut. The position may be viewed from four angles: bindingness, applicability, relative merits and volume.

From the point of view of obligation, as long as codification conventions are subject to withdrawable ratification, international customary law remains the highest form of development of the law, and part of the rationale of the process of codification is that, in time, the rules which have emerged through the codification process may concrete into, or lead to, international customary law.

From the point of view of applicability, a conventional provision will, as between two parties for whom it is in force, take precedence over a pre-existing rule of international customary law, in accordance with the hierarchical position under Article 38 (1) of the Statute of the International Court of Justice.

From the point of view of relative merits, conventions are the main vehicles for introducing new rules needed for the conduct of

---

" Forms of Participation of International Organisations in the Law-Making Processes," 18 *International Organisations* (1964), pp. 790–805.

[26] *Cf.* Sir Gerald Fitzmaurice, " Some Problems Regarding the Formal Sources of International Law," in *Symbolae Verzijl* (1958), pp. 153–176.

[27] See I. Brownlie, *op. cit.* in note 25 above, p. 2.

[28] *Cf.* R. Y. Jennings, " Recent Developments in the International Law Commission: Its Relation to the Sources of International Law," 13 *International and Comparative Law Quarterly* (1964), pp. 385–397.

international relations. They are also the natural instruments for setting out the rules agreed on in the process of clarification and adaptation of international law which takes place in the Commission. The rules contained in them may be observed despite the absence of ratification. Finally, one has to bear in mind the position of some States that the conventional form is the preferred method of regulating international affairs; these States often refuse to hold themselves bound by rules of international customary law to which they have not hitherto consented.

From the standpoint of volume, we have to weigh the number of conventions actually produced through the Commission, with the other forms of its work, such as studies and reports, which are capable of giving rise to international customary law. The number of conventions is actually outstripped by the number of studies and reports. However, one has to take into account the number of rules of international customary law (relatively few) which have actually emerged from the Commission's work, and bear in mind the time lag—the period which elapses before a rule of customary law crystallises.

Turning to the relationship between the conventional rules produced through the Commission and related rules of customary international law, the fear has been expressed that in the process of codification, rules of pre-existing customary international law are in danger of losing their status unless they are carefully safeguarded.[29] " This criticism is valid up to a point. It is, no doubt, true that the Commission may provide a platform and an opportunity, for those who find an existing rule of law inconvenient, to weaken that rule under cover of a scientific analysis of legal principles. On the other hand, it must also be remembered that in providing an opportunity for change and growth of the law, the Commission is in fact providing just those procedures of legislation of which the international community is so much in need, and which are implicit in the notion of the ' development ' of the law referred to in Article 13 of the Charter. Furthermore, there is great value in a procedure by which the rival interests of States must be expressed in a scientific framework and made to speak the language of law.

" Moreover, in so far as the Commission's debates and reports reveal different understandings on apparently clear rules of law, it

---

[29] K. Marek, "Thoughts on Codification," 31 *Zeitschrift fur Ausländisches Öffentliches Recht und Völkerrecht* (1971), pp. 489–520 at p. 496; J. H. W. Verzijl, *International Law in Historical Perspective*, Vol. I (1968), pp. 85–88; H. W. Thirlway, *op. cit.* in note 1 above.

should be borne in mind that the Commission may be doing no more than bring healthily into the open the true state of affairs." [30]

II—THE ROLE OF THE INTERNATIONAL LAW COMMISSION

The role [31] of the International Law Commission in international society is four-fold: (1) to serve the needs of the United Nations system and of member States of the United Nations; (2) to promote the further development of the United Nations system; (3) to strengthen international customary law; (4) to suggest appropriate policies for the law, and to codify and develop the law in accordance with these policies.

In international society organised under the United Nations system, the need for codification and progressive development of international law is as follows: (a) *International Law as a Discipline.* The need here is for certainty in content, systematisation, and regular review and up-dating. (b) *Political and Psychological.* The need here is for translating the main chapters of international law into writing, adapting and accommodating them to the needs of present-day international society; giving an opportunity to the new States to participate in the process of translation; and making changes in the content of the law to take account of modern developments and modern needs. (c) *Infrastructural and Regulatory.* The need here is for providing legal bases for the conduct of existing and future international relations; providing legal bases for the intercourse, co-operation and interdependency of States; facilitating and consolidating legal development in newer areas of international relations and providing new rules to meet new or changed situations; promoting the settlement of disputes and the general maintenance of international peace and security. (d) *Developmental.* The need here is to facilitate economic development among States generally and the less-developed States in particular. (e) *General Objectives of the United Nations.* The need here is to assist generally in promoting the objectives of the United Nations. (f) *Advisory and Drafting.* The need here is for the consideration of requests by the General Assembly or other organs of the United Nations for studies or for the Commission's views on matters of international law, and for the drafting of provisions at the request of the General Assembly or other organs of the United Nations. (g) *Formative.* The need here is to influence the development of emerging patterns and to suggest new patterns of international

---

[30] R. Y. Jennings, " The Progress of International Law," 34 *British Yearbook of International Law* (1958), pp. 334–355 at p. 345.

[31] See S. Rosenne, " The Role of the International Law Commission," *Proceedings of the American Society of International Law* (1970), pp. 24–36. Paper contributed to a Panel on " The United Nations and Lawmaking."

law and organisation. A matter which comes to mind in this regard is the legal regulation of multinational corporations.

Regarding the further development of the United Nations system, though this is not an area in which the Commission can take the initiative, its role should be to monitor political initiatives and to be ready to provide legal guidance.

Regarding the strengthening of international customary law, a body like the Commission, concerned with the development of international law, and noting the historical role of international law in unorganised international society, should always have at the back of its mind the necessity for strengthening and enhancing the authority of international customary law. The thought of a return to an unorganised state of international society is not inconceivable.

III—THE NATURE OF THE PROCESS

In codifying and developing international law, the Commission may do one of four things: (1) It may codify an existing rule of international customary law. (2) It may propose a new rule by modifying and/or supplementing an existing rule, for example, where there is need for change or where the present law or practice is scanty. (3) It may put forward a completely new rule of international law where none existed before. (4) It may disregard the distinction between codification and progressive development and draft provisions which are likely to be of practical use in international relations and which are likely to obtain the acceptance of Governments.[32]

The juristic methodology of the Commission consists of an admixture of empiricism [33] and inductivism.[34] In addition, there have been some instances of a policy orientation, a notable example of which is the doctrine of *jus cogens*. The Commission tries at all stages of its work to draft provisions which are likely to be of

---

[32] See the Statute of the Commission, A/CN.4/4, Arts. 15–23. M. Lachs (Poland), A/C.6/SR.494, para. 11, *General Assembly Official Records, Sixth Committee* (1956). S. Rosenne, *The League of Nations Committee of Experts for the Progressive Codification of International Law 1925–1928* (1972), Vol. I, pp. 24–25. U.N. Office of Public Information, *The Work of the International Law Commission, op. cit.* in note 1 above, pp. 10–12. H. W. Thirlway, *op. cit.* in note 1 above, pp. 16–19.

[33] See C. de Visscher, Remarks, in the League of Nations Committee of Experts, in S. Rosenne, *op. cit.* in note 32 above, Vol. I, pp. 24–25; J. L. Brierly, *ibid.*, pp. 15–16; Mr. Brohi (Pakistan), A/C.6/SR.468, para. 9, *General Assembly Official Records, Sixth Committee* (1955).

[34] See G. Schwarzenberger, *The Inductive Approach to International Law* (1965); A/CN.4/246, Third Report on State Responsibility by Mr. R. Ago, Special Rapporteur, paras. 13–14. *General Assembly Official Records, Sixth Committee*, 1973: Mr. Mukuna (Zaire), S.R. 1399; Mr. Castren (Finland), S.R. 1399; Mr. Bracklo (Federal Republic of Germany), S.R. 1402; Mr. Klafkowski (Poland), S.R. 1402; Mr. Ceausu (Romania), S.R. 1405; Mr. Miras (Turkey), S.R. 1406; Mr. Wisnoemoerti (Indonesia), S.R. 1406; Mr. Sahovic (Yugoslavia), S.R. 1401.

practical use in international relations and to gain the acceptance of governments. Within this framework, however, it employs the inductive method to ascertain the status of particular rules of international law. Its policy-orientation is an *ad hoc* one. There is a case for a more deliberate policy-orientation, and for the development of a methodology based on such an orientation. In the task of legal planning it is important to work out appropriate policies.

IV—THE POLITICAL PERSPECTIVE

The political perspective through which the Commission has to be seen stems from: (1) the political significance of the work of the Commission; (2) the importance of political factors for the success of its work; (3) the impact of political factors upon specific areas of the Commission's work; and (4) the political approach of the Commission.

The political significance of the work of the Commission lies in the objectives of the United Nations Organisation of which it is a part, the political nature of the General Assembly its parent body, the context of the codification and progressive development element in Article 13 (1) (a) [35] of the Charter of the United Nations, the political environment of international society in which the Commission functions, and political aspects inherent in the process of codification and development, which is partly a legislative process.

The direct impact of political factors upon the work of the Commission may be observed in the following areas: the nomination and election of members of the Commission; the distribution of seats on the Commission; the selection of topics; political disagreements occasioning deadlock in the Commission and resultant failure to put forward draft provisions on some aspect or aspects of a subject; political factors causing watered-down drafts; political factors causing some topics not being sent to the Commission as in the case of the preparation of the third conference on the law of the sea; and political factors inherent in some of the topics before the Commission such as State responsibility and State succession.

In the face of the political context and significance of the work of the Commission, it has been necessary for it to work out a political approach, though this has been done, for the most part, inovertly. The political approach of the Commission has encompassed: (1) Cognisance of the political significance of its work and of the importance of political factors for its success; (2) cognisance of, and derivation of guidance from, the political environment of

---

[35] See, *United Nations Repertory of Practice*, Supplement 3, Vol. I, p. 296, paras. 1–4.

international society and of the main trends therein; (3) exercising political appreciations of particular situations; (4) striving to work out acceptable compromises when confronted with contending legal doctrines of high political significance; (5) bearing in mind political factors when selecting topics for codification or when treating parts of specific topics.

V—THE PHILOSOPHY OF THE COMMISSION

Examination of its work reveals that there are present, underlying juristic and guiding philosophies. At the juristic level, a distinction must be made between the ultimate source of legal obligation in international law and the source of actual rules of international law. Regarding the ultimate source of obligation, the juristic philosophy of the Commission flows from its enunciation of the principle of the supremacy of international law over the sovereignty of States. The first instrument drafted by the Commission, the draft declaration on the rights and duties of States, contained the following provision: " Every State has the duty to conduct its relations with other States in accordance with international law and with the principle that the sovereignty of each State is subject to the supremacy of international law." [36]

This principle was maintained by the Commission in the following provisions either drafted by it or subsequently adopted by it: Principle II of the Principles of International Law Recognised in the Charter of the Nuremburg Tribunal and in the Judgment of the Tribunal; Articles 27, 46, 53, and 64 of the Vienna Convention on the Law of Treaties; and Article 4 of the draft on State Responsibility.

In enunciating the doctrine of the supremacy of international law over the sovereignty of States, the Commission has, by necessary implication, rejected the consent theory as an explanation of the basis of obligation in international law. This conclusion was recognised by the then Chairman of the Commission, Sir Gerald Fitzmaurice, who, during the 610th meeting of the Sixth Committee, stated: " On the question of consent as the source of the international law obligations of States ... it was not enough to say that consent . . . was the formal source of the obligatory force of the individual concrete rules to which the States conformed; one had to ask what it was that give to consent the power to create obligations. It could not be the actual consent of the parties, since in that case there would be a vicious circle. If obligations could arise from

---

[36] Art. 14. See also Art. 13.

consent, it was because international law already made consent a source of obligation." [37]

From the practice of the Commission of preparing drafts for the approval of States, we may eliminate the naturalist doctrine as being its philosophy as to the source of obligation in international law. As the Chairman, Sir Gerald Fitzmaurice, put it in the statement to which we have just referred, " on the question of . . . the source of the international obligations of States . . . it was unnecessary to have recourse to any doctrine of natural law in order to postulate the binding force of the rules of customary international law, whether or not they had been embodied in a convention." [38]

Having eliminated the consent and naturalist theories it follows that the Commission's view of the basis of obligation would lie in a sociological explanation, for the determination of which there is no evidence from the Commission upon which we may proceed. It suffices, however, to place the position of the Commission in this sociological area, for by eliminating the consent and the naturalist theories, we have eliminated the theories which are potentially strangulatory (consent) or could lead international law into disrepute on account of its imprecision and subjectivity (natural law).

Moving from the question of the ultimate source or basis of obligation, to the question of the source of the content of rules of international law, the practice of the Commission is basically positivistic. However, there are elements of eclecticism and the incorporation of natural law ideas such as the rights and duties of States or *jus cogens*. [39]

The guiding philosophy of the Commission encompasses: the guiding philosophy of international law as such; the principles of the United Nations Charter; the current trends and developments in international society; the desire to satisfy the needs of the international community with respect to the codification and development of international law and the philosophy of equity and justice. [40]

VI—THE DOCTRINAL APPROACH OF THE COMMISSION

The doctrines which emerge through the Commission are shaped

---

[37] A/C.6/SR. 610, para. 33, *General Assembly Official Records, Sixth Committee* (1956).

[38] *Ibid.* See also Sir Gerald Fitzmaurice, "The General Principles of International Law Considered from the Standpoint of the Rule of Law," 92 *Recueil des Cours* (1957, II), pp. 1–227.

[39] See C. de Visscher, "Positivisme et 'jus cogens,'" 75 *Revue Générale de droit international public* (1971), pp. 5–11.

[40] See G. Schwarzenberger, "Equity in International Law," in this *Year Book*, Vol. 26 (1972), pp. 346–369. J. Stone, "Approaches to the Notion of International Justice," in R. A. Falk and C. E. Black (eds.), *The Future of the International Legal Order*, Vol. I (1969), Chap. 8, pp. 372–460.

by one or more of the following factors: (1) technical considerations as to the quality and integrity of the law; (2) adoption of policies by the Commission [41]; (3) the desire to strengthen international law and the international legal order [42]; (4) the policy of giving expression to the principles of the United Nations Charter; (5) the application of the principles of equity and justice in the development and codification of the law [43]; (6) the retention of traditional doctrines of international law, in existing or modified form; (7) the necessity, on occasions, to work out compromises; (8) efforts to synthesise contending doctrines; (9) efforts to find consensus on the highest measure of common ground among contending doctrines [44]; and (10) efforts to codify and develop the law in line with the main trends in international society.

VII—ORGANISATION AND METHODS

The basic institutional characteristics of the Commission include its membership of the United Nations system, its status as a subsidiary organ of the General Assembly, its part-time nature, its size and representative composition—representing the main civilisations and principal legal systems of the world.

The basic organisational pattern of the Commission has met with the continuing approval of Governments and there is evidence that the General Assembly would oppose any basic changes. During the debates in the Sixth Committee, several States have affirmed that they do not want a full-time Commission; that they oppose an extension in the term of office of its members; that they want the present size and representative character of its composition maintained.[45]

The Commission's work methods have been criticised in the past for causing a slow rate and low volume of work; for its lack of flexibility; that it results in wastage and inefficiency; that it spends too much time on line-by-line discussions of drafts.[46] Suggestions offered for curing these ills have included: placing it on a full-time basis; increasing the length of its sessions; holding two sessions each year; holding two meetings per day instead of one; splitting it into sub-commissions working on different topics; that the secretariat should be strengthened to give increased assistance in research and preparation of studies.

---

[41] *Cf.* the doctrine of *jus cogens.*
[42] *Cf.* the doctrine of the supremacy of international law.
[43] See note 40 above.
[44] *Cf. Y.B.I.L.C.* 1966, Vol. II, Report, para. 33; *ibid.* 1968, Vol. I, p. 162, para. 22.
[45] See the Report of the Sixth Committee on the Report of the Commission A/7746 (1969), para. 99; A/8537 (1971), para. 12.
[46] *Loc. cit.* in note 15 above, p. 3.

There would seem to be no case for basic changes in the organisation or methods of the Commission. The following improvements may be suggested: (1) the Commission should hold two sessions per year, a long session in the summer and a short session in the winter; (2) inter-sessional meetings of working parties and committees should be held to relieve the pressure of time which constantly troubles the Commission; (3) the Commission should adopt a policy of activating its whole programme through one of the following processes: consideration by the plenary Commission, consideration by sub-committees or working parties, and preparation of studies by the secretariat; (4) its work should take five forms: discussion papers, studies, restatements or model rules, recommendation of General Assembly resolutions, and draft conventions. The first four may serve as intermediate stages leading in time to draft conventions. (5) The secretariat should provide studies on each topic on the Commission's programme as soon as possible after its inclusion; (6) in addition to the Commissioners who are serving as special *rapporteurs,* members of the Commission themselves should be assigned the task of preparing studies on topics in the Commission's programme or on other matters; (7) the Commission should give attention to using the assistance of bodies like the International Law Association, the Institute of International Law, the Harvard Research, and similar bodies in other parts of the world; (8) the Commission should also consider steps needed to ensure that it is supplied with adequate inter-disciplinary data [47] in the course of its work. The Secretary-General may, for example, set up an inter-departmental committee within the secretariat with members drawn from various disciplines, to which the Commission can turn for assistance; or the Commission may seek the assistance of the professional associations of the various disciplines; (9) the Commission should set up three permanent committees appointed on a termly [48] basis, to deal with planning, research and co-ordination of its work with legal development taking place through other United Nations or regional agencies.

VIII—APPRAISAL AND CONCLUSIONS

Taking the Commission as an agency for the ascertainment of international law, the impact of political factors, the admixture of empiricism and inductivism, the legislative element involved in the drafting of new rules or modification of existing ones, and the

---

[47] See on this, W. L. Gould and M. Barkun, *International Law and the Social Sciences* (1970); W. L. Gould and M. Barkun, *Social Sciences Literature: A Bibliography for International Law* (1972); M. S. McDougall and Associates, *Studies in World Public Order* (1960).

[48] For a term of five years rather than annually.

difficulty experienced by the Commission in distinguishing between codification and progressive development, require that each draft rule be assessed separately, in order to ascertain its status in international law. One cannot apply as a decisive test the fact that a provision has gone through the process [49] of codification. It will be necessary to examine each provision to see the extent to which the Commission has examined the inductively verifiable material and whether the conclusion which it has drawn from the material is accurate.

The "rule by rule" test, rather than the "process" test, is the one which was applied by the International Court of Justice in the North Sea Continental Shelf Cases, to determine whether certain rules had attained the status of international customary law by virtue of having gone through the process of codification and development. The court rejected the Netherlands and Danish argument that Article 6 of the Geneva Convention on the Continental Shelf, having gone through the process of codification and development, had thereby become a rule of international customary law, though it implied that this argument could apply to other Articles of the Convention. The court examined the article on its own merit by reference to the deliberations in the Commission, the observations of governments, and the deliberations at the Geneva Conference on the Law of the Sea, of 1958. [50]

As a legislative agency, the blending of legal expertise and political realism within the Commission makes it a very qualified body to work out rules likely to be of use in practice and to gain the acceptance of governments. The consensus which builds around acceptable syntheses also holds good for the eventual formation of customary law.

Turning to the Commission as a vehicle of change, the modernisation of international law holds special significance at the present juncture of international society, and will continue to be of major importance if international law is to continue to fulfil adequately the various calls which will be made upon it in the future. In the process of codification and development of international law, the Commission is the vital first stage. However, there are constraints on the ability of the Commission to innovate. It is restricted by how far States are prepared to go and, generally, can innovate

---

[49] The process includes the Commission, Comments by Governments and International Organisations, the General Assembly, and the deliberations of Codification Conferences.

[50] See *I.C.J. Reports 1969*, p. 3, Judgment, paras. 61 and 62; Declaration of Judge Khan, at p. 55. The court also laid down certain tests such as, the provision in question should be of "norm-creating character." See A. D'Amato, "Manifest Intent and the Generation by Treaty of Customary Rules of International Law," 64 *American Journal of International Law* (1970), pp. 892–902.

doctrinally only where the innovation is in accordance with the Charter of the United Nations or in line with the prevailing opinions or attitudes of governments. Similar constraints operate on the ability of the Commission to put forward new policies. Nevertheless, as, through the adoption of a policy of empiricism the Commission will soon have succeeded in setting down the basic rules of the main chapters of international law, it should in the future direct its attention to the suggestion and formulation of appropriate policies and goals for international law. It should also, as we stated earlier, give attention to ways and means of providing itself with adequate inter-disciplinary data and expertise, which will become increasingly important in its work in the future.[51]

Among the criticisms of the Commission which may be made, the following may be pointed out: Whilst the political element may be unavoidable, it has to be recognised that a politically influenced body is sometimes forced to depart from the position which, by applying objective criteria, it might otherwise have adopted.

The slowness of the Commission's work has deleterious consequences for international law. A law constantly lagging behind the society it serves presents an unwholesome picture. The Commission is unable to respond to current needs. Current problems by-pass it. It is confined to the traditional areas of international law. Its formative role has been minimal. In the latter respect, it should, in our submission, make use of the technique of issuing discussion papers on which non-governmental entities and experts are allowed to comment, as a stage before a topic is taken up at the exclusively inter-governmental level.

Insufficient use has been made of the assistance which universities and research institutes can offer. The Commission should indicate to them areas in which they can be of assistance and request their co-operation.

⎯ Nothing has been done to co-ordinate legal development taking place within the United Nations as a whole. Although this was one of the objectives of its long-term review, its report for 1973 contained no proposal on the point.

The view has been expressed to the writer that the overall quality of membership of the Commission has declined in recent elections and that this tends to lessen the overall quality and efficiency of the Commission. This is a matter which rests in the hands of Governments, which should, in nominating and electing candidates, bear in mind the need to elect suitably qualified persons.[52]

---

[51] See on this, " III—The Nature of the Process," above.
[52] *Cf.* M. Saunders, " The 1971 Elections of the International Law Commission," 66 *American Journal of International Law* (1972), pp. 356–362.

What, it may be asked, is the justification of the process in which the Commission is engaged. The present approach of the Commission is based, in part, upon the reasoning that it is necessary to get as many States as possible to agree to, sign and subsequently, ratify the drafts which it prepares. However, in the process, a price is being paid through generality and looseness in drafting, evasion of issues, and the weakening of certain parts of international customary law. The dividend hoped for in paying these premiums, is that States, having agreed to and signed a convention, will proceed to ratify it. However, ratifications have been very difficult to come by.[53] In the absence of this dividend of ratification, the process needs other justification. In the first place, the process of clarification, adaptation, improvement and extension of international law which takes place through the Commission, is valuable in its own right. Secondly, although an instrument has not been ratified by a large number of States, it may nevertheless influence the policies and practice of States and International Organisations. It may be taken as the point of departure, as representing the basic principles of the existing law or the desirable future law in its particular field.[54] This influencing of policy and practice is an important and positive contribution. Thirdly, the common points of departure, common principles and similarity in practice, may lead in time to the formation of international customary law. Fourthly, the rules, principles and standards laid down in the instrument may, notwithstanding their lack of ratification, be invoked as rules, principles and standards upon which international tribunals may base their judgments, not as representing binding law, but as principles and standards for testing conduct. They take their weight from the fact that, having evolved through the codification process, they represent what have been thought by international society as a whole to be appropriate principles for the conduct of international relations.

Finally, let us turn to the tasks to be fulfilled by the Commission in the future. These will be: (1) The continuation of its programme of work; (2) up-dating and revising its previous work and making appropriate proposals concerning conventions concluded on the basis of its work; (3) consideration of projects assigned to it by the General Assembly; (4) consideration of topics put forward by other organs or specialised agencies of the United Nations; (5) co-ordinating its work and the work of other United Nations bodies dealing

---

[53] See, C. Th. Eustathiades, *Unratified Codification Conventions*, Gilbert Amado Memorial Lecture, United Nations (1973). R. Ago, " The Final Stage of the Codification of International Law," Doc. A/CN.4/205/Rev.1, *Y.B.I.L.C.* (1968), Vol. II, pp. 171–178.

[54] *Cf.* Mr. Bailey (Australia), A/C.6/SR.1404, *General Assembly Official Records, Sixth Committee*, 1973.

with the development of international law; (6) further research and organisation of research in the field of international law; (7) generally promoting the objectives, purposes and principles of the United Nations and enhancing the role of international law in the United Nations system; (8) taking up and considering some of the areas of international law dealt with by *ad hoc* United Nations bodies or by resolutions of the General Assembly.

In the future, the work of the Commission should be guided by the following general perspectives: implementing the second round of codification and development of international law, striving, in this round, for greater precision and improved technical quality; further developing the international legal system to equip it to deal with the growth in international relations; enhancing the role of international law in the United Nations system; enhancing the authority of international customary law in the international system; relating international law to the important problems facing governments, such as the maintenance of peace and security and economic development; and suggesting and formulating appropriate policies and goals for international law in international society.

MULTINATIONAL ENTERPRISES
AND THE INTERNATIONAL LAW
OF THE FUTURE

By

IGNAZ SEIDL-HOHENVELDERN

AN enterprise may be qualified as being multinational according to any of several criteria.[1] It may be deemed to be multinational merely because its activities are spread over several States. However, this " operational " criterion is rather unsatisfactory. It would cover cases where a single company from its headquarters in its home State operates as such in a number of other States (host States) as well. From the point of view of any such host State the enterprise concerned would be merely a foreign juridical person to be governed by the host State's aliens laws and by the general rules of international law applicable to foreigners. There is no question of the applicability of these rules in cases where the owners and managers of the enterprise are citizens of its home State. In these circumstances no special problems would arise to justify such an enterprise being subjected to any special rules.

If the owners and/or persons controlling an enterprise, or the managers of that enterprise, are of different nationalities, this by itself would not be sufficient to change the position. Yet, some authors have defined a multinational enterprise according to this very criterion. However, from the juridical standpoint, multinational ownership, control and/or management does not change the character or nationality of the enterprise concerned in the light of international law as it now stands—apart from exceptional cases which justify even, *de lege lata*, a piercing of the corporate veil.[2]

To select a " structural " definition of a multinational enterprise recommends itself on account of the fact that new problems of international law have arisen mainly in connection with enterprises falling into this category. Hence, the United Nations Commission

---

[1] Annex II to the Study of the United Nations Secretariat Department of Economic and Social Affairs, *Multinational Corporations in World Development*, ST/ECA/190 (1973), pp. 118–121, contains a selection of definitions of multinational enterprises.

[2] *e.g.* the case of practically defunct companies and the case where a host State acts in an illegal manner against a foreign-owned company which had been forced to accept the nominal nationality of that State (" Calvo companies "); see Seidl-Hohenveldern, " Der Barcelona-Traction-Fall," 22 *Österr. Zeitschrift f. öff. Recht* (1971), pp. 284–287.

on International Trade Law (UNCITRAL),[3] as well as Professor
Goldman of Paris University, the *rapporteur* of the Committee on
multinational enterprises of the Institut de Droit International,[4]
define them as follows: " The term multinational enterprise is
used in a broad sense and includes enterprises which through
branches, subsidiaries or affiliates or other establishments engage
in substantial commercial or other economic activities in States
(' host ' States) other than the State or the States in which decision-
making and/or control is centred (the ' home ' State)."

I—MULTINATIONAL ENTERPRISES—FRIEND OR FOE

It is, if anything, an understatement to say that recently multinational
enterprises have had a bad press. They have been accused of almost
any crime under the sun—of undermining the world's currency
system, of corrupting the governments of host States and of foment-
ing civil war or even international hostilities. Some of these accusations appear to cancel each other out. I hold no brief for International
Telephone and Telegraph Corporation (ITT) and I dare not pro-
nounce on its guilt or innocence in respect to the fate of the late
President Allende. Yet, at the same time, when ITT was accused
of interfering with the domestic affairs of Chile it was also accused
of having continued to work in Hitler's Germany until the United
States entered into the Second World War,[5] that is of having minded
its business and affairs, while abstaining from interference in the
domestic affairs of its host State, the Third Reich. Be that as it may,
even progressive writers should not consider the institution of
multinational enterprises as an evil *per se*.

In spite of some sensational reports in the daily press at the time
of publication of the recent study by the United Nations Secretariat's
Department of Economic and Social Affairs, *Multinational Corporations in World Development*,[6] such a view finds but scant
support in this paper. The United Nations study informs us that
the Soviet Union has entered into business relations with Western
multinational enterprises and tries to enlarge these links,[7] that the

---

[3] LE 133 (11) of August 3, 1973.

[4] The work of this Committee will not touch on all aspects of the problem.
By priority it will deal with the international control of the activities of, and with
diplomatic protection of, such enterprises, with projects to establish them as United
Nations corporations (see text at note 36 below), with conflict of jurisdiction
problems and—possibly—with anti-trust aspects (see text at note 45 below). The
Committee will not deal with problems of disinvestment and taxation (see note
43 below) and with labour problems (see note 47 below).

[5] *Der Spiegel*, Nr. 26/1973, p. 106 *et seq.*, reviewing the book by A. Sampson,
Weltmacht ITT (1973).

[6] See note 1 above.

[7] *Loc. cit.*, p. 22.

member States of the Organisation of Petroleum Exporting Countries (OPEC) plan to establish multinational enterprises of their own [8] and that even such critical observers of Western economic practices as the United Nations Conference on Trade and Development (UNCTAD) came to the same conclusion as the study itself, " that there is considerable uncertainty about the effects of multinational corporations on home countries, the conclusions depending upon the assumption made regarding what the alternative to the multinational corporation's activities would be likely to be." [9] No matter, however, whether we consider multinational enterprises as good or bad for the host State, they are a reality of contemporary international life. Their very existence constitutes a challenge to international lawyers in many ways.

II—Protection for Multinational Enterprises

We have the support of the Judgment of the International Court of Justice (ICJ) in the *Barcelona-Traction* Case when we claim that the present rules on the protection of corporations are inadequate to cope with the expansion of the international activities of such corporations,[10] and we have Judge Padilla Nervo's statement in his Concurring Opinion in the same Case that it is not these corporations who are in need of protection, but rather the poorer or weaker host States who need to be protected against them.[11]

This same judgment refers us to bilateral and multilateral treaties having solved such problems between the States parties thereto,[12] but the network of these treaties leaves all too many gaps. What solutions, if any, could be found to solve on a more general basis these problems of the protection of corporations as well as of their host States?

Complaints concerning the lack of adequate protection of such corporations and of their shareholders are based on the fact that the nominal home State may be uninterested, unable or simply too weak (for example Liechtenstein) to protect these interests. The remedy hitherto proposed consisted in admitting the home States of any of the shareholders to protect the interests [13] thereof. This remedy was held unworkable by the ICJ as it would lead to a multiplication of claims arising out of a single international delinquency. I have doubts as to the weight and reasonableness of this

---

[8] *Loc. cit.,* p. 37.
[9] *Loc. cit.,* p. 58.
[10] *I.C.J. Reports 1970,* p. 47, paras. 88–89.
[11] *I.C.J. Reports 1970,* p. 248.
[12] *I.C.J. Reports 1970,* p. 47, para. 90.
[13] *e.g.* Riphagen's Dissenting Opinion, I.C.J. Reports 1970, p. 350, para. 21.

argument,[14] but it has to be accepted as a fact. I will not be so unrealistic as to propose a solution which would give such a corporation direct access to the ICJ, although this would do away with the multiplicity of claimants.[15]

The United Nations Secretariat's study suggests another solution. In many cases the home State of a multinational enterprise would be reluctant in any way to espouse the latter's claims. If so, a recognition of the Calvo doctrine by the home State of the multinational enterprise would not impose a great sacrifice on either the home State or the multinational enterprise.[16] In exchange " as a measure to reciprocate the acceptance of the Calvo doctrine by home countries, host countries could incorporate in their basic legislation guarantees of economic rights to foreign affiliates, such as procedures for compensation following nationalisation and even the use of a previously specified formula determining the level of such compensation." [17]

However, the history of international investments is full of broken promises to this effect.[18] An international adjudication would thus appear to be more attractive to the foreign investor. It may be that some sort of access to the International Court of Justice could be obtained, after all, in a roundabout way. One might consider applying to multinational enterprises, *mutatis mutandis*, the procedures established for bringing practically (irrespective of the legal niceties) the appeal of a United Nations official against the decision of the United Nations Arbitral Tribunal before the ICJ.[19] Some sort of

---

[14] *I.C.J. Reports 1970*, p. 48, para. 94, and p. 50, para. 98 *contra* Seidl-Hohenveldern, *loc. cit.* in note 2 above, p. 293.

[15] This would be the best way to protect the interests of the investors—but the political obstacles against the solution are too large. See Seidl-Hohenveldern, "Judicial Protection of Foreign Investments," *Mélanges Séfériadès* (1961), Vol. I, pp. 253–257.

[16] ST/ECA 190, pp. 80–81.   [17] *Ibid.* p. 82.

[18] See *e.g.* the flagrant breach of the Algerian-French Petroleum Agreements of July 29, 1965, extending also to its arbitration clauses, by the unilateral action of the Algerian Government of February 24, 1971. See Manin, "Le différend franco-algérien relatif aux hydrocarbures," *Annuaire Français de Droit International* (1971), p. 150, and the nationalisation without indemnity of United States copper corporations in Chile two years after these corporations had ceded 51 per cent. of their shares to the Chilean government in order to reach a compromise between the interests of the host country and the investors. The breach of this promise is rightly criticised by the decision of the Landgericht Hamburg of January 22, 1973, *Aussenwirtschaftsdienst des Betriebsberaters* (AWD) (1973), p. 164; see also XII ILM (1973), p. 277.

[19] Advisory Opinion of July 12, 1973, Application for Review of Judgment Nr. 158 of the United Nations Administrative Tribunal (*Re Fasla*), *I.C.J. Reports 1973*, p. 166. See Seidl-Hohenveldern, "*Der Zugang internationaler Organisationen zum Internationalen Gerichtshof*," 54 *Friedenswarte* (1957), p. 16 *et seq.* For a comment on the earlier Advisory Opinion of October 23, 1956, on Judgments of the Administrative Tribunal of the I.L.O. upon Complaints Made against UNESCO, see *I.C.J. Reports 1956*, p. 77.

United Nations panel could receive and sift the complaints of such multinational enterprises, and then submit in its own name the cases it deems worthy of protection to the ICJ for an Advisory Opinion. In this way such claims would be detached from any link with the national States of either the corporation or of its shareholders. The role of the panel would thus be reminiscent of that of the European Commission of Human Rights before the European Court of Human Rights.[20] This method would recommend itself even more, if the most ambitious proposal of the United Nations Secretariat's study became a reality—the establishment of multinational enterprises as United Nations corporations,[21] under the supervision and hence, presumably, also under the protection of the United Nations.[22]

III—PROTECTION OF THE HOST STATE BY A UNITED NATIONS CODE OF GOOD BEHAVIOUR

Let us now turn to the claims of the host State for better protection against powerful multinational enterprises. Such claims, too, are justified. The relationship of the host State to such a corporation may be compared with that of a lynx to a hawk. On the ground, in its own territory, even a weak State is supreme, yet, unless it catches the corporation unaware, the latter will always be able to disentangle itself from the State's grip, losing some feathers or—at the worst—some nest eggs. On the other hand, the corporation, acting from its foreign bases beyond the reach of the host State, may deal the latter crippling or even mortal blows.

If ever the theory of risks was justified, it should, by inversion, be applied in such a situation to the host State.[23] If a State fears the power of foreign capital, all it has to do to protect itself against the attendant risks is to do without such capital. If you do not have a cake, you do not risk getting sick by eating it. However, it should be a challenge to lawyers to propose solutions which may permit a State to obtain much-needed foreign capital, yet reducing the risks inherent in its importation especially in case of multinational corporations.

Recently the International Law Association (ILA) has again

---

[20] Golsong, "Implementation of International Protection of Human Rights," 111 *Recueil des Cours* (1963 III), pp. 126–128.

[21] ST/ECA/190, pp. 93–94.

[22] There exists a firm and logical link between allegiance and protection, as "Lord Haw-Haw" found out to his detriment. See *Joyce* v. *Director of Public Prosecutions* [1946] A.C. 347, ILR 15, pp. 96–97.

[23] Seidl-Hohenveldern, *loc. cit.* in note 2 above, pp. 282–283.

undertaken research in this field, my colleague Philippe Kahn [24] improving and continuing work to which I had been able to contribute as rapporteur.[25] These efforts are concerned mainly with establishing a code of good behaviour for foreign investors. However, the various policies pursued by the host States may conflict with each other. It is generally held desirable, especially by host States, that a multinational enterprise should offer participation to local capital.[26] Particularly in developing countries, only members of the ruling élite will be able to avail themselves of such offers. Owing to the participation of these new partners, the multinational enterprise concerned inevitably becomes entangled in the domestic politics of the host State. Any such entanglement is rightly held to be undesirable.

Even the most recent and most sophisticated participation plan, that is Articles 30 and 31, of the Andean Investment Code,[27] fails to overcome this difficulty. Under this code foreign ownership of, and foreign participation in, enterprises in the host State will fade out gradually according to a prearranged timetable—yet, during the time where foreigners and nationals of the host State are partners in such an enterprise, this difficulty subsists. The danger of entanglement in domestic politics becomes even stronger, if it is the government of the host State itself, rather than its nationals, which —step by step—takes up the role of the foreign investors.

We are on safer ground where such codes request that foreign enterprises in the host State should always act in conformity with the latter's economic plans.[28] Such conformity ought to go further than mere obedience to the host State's planning laws. It goes without saying that a foreign enterprise is not above the law of the host State and will, therefore, have to respect the latter's planning laws like all its other legislation. The problem lies in the fact that plans by their very nature do not lend themselves very well to being

[24] " Les contrats d'investissement: Étude des principales clauses et propositions pour un contrat-type d'investissement," ILA 54th Conference Report (The Hague, 1970), p. 469 *et seq.* and p. 531 *et seq.*

[25] Seidl-Hohenveldern, " Report of the International Committee on Nationalisation," ILA 48th Conference Report (New York 1958), p. 184 ss; *idem.*, Report of the Committee on the Juridical Aspects of Nationalisation and Foreign Property, ILA 49th Conference Report (Hamburg 1960), p. 213 *et seq.*; *idem.*, Draft Statutes of the Arbitral Tribunal for Foreign Investments, ILA 50th Conference Report (Brussels 1962), p. 132 *et seq.*

[26] International Chamber of Commerce (ICC), Guidelines for International Investment (1972), Guidelines II (1) a–c, Kahn, *loc. cit.*, pp. 469–499.

[27] ILM XI (1972), p. 126 *et seq.* and Oliver, " The Andean Investment Code: A new phase in the quest for normative order as to direct foreign investment," 66 *American Journal of International Law* (1972), pp. 774–779.

[28] ICC Guideline I (1) a.

couched in strict legal rules [29] and that planning laws themselves are subject to frequent changes.[30]

Even planning in developed States runs the risk of being rendered futile by decisions taken at the headquarters of a multinational enterprise, often thousands of miles away, by a multinational board and in the interests of its multinational shareholders. Such a decision may be perfectly justifiable from the point of view of the overall planning of the corporation—yet, it may wreak havoc with local plans in the host State (for example the decision of International Business Machines Corporation (IBM) not to build its Research H.Q. in Hanover FRG.[31] Participation of nationals of the host State in the local management of the corporation may prevent some such decisions. Participation in the multinational management may be even more effective. Yet, it will be more difficult to obtain and, moreover, it will not be a panacea.[32] By necessity, the nationals of the host State will constitute only a minority on such a multi-national board. Thus, the best way for a host State to protect itself against these risks is a challenge to the imagination and to the foresight of its government lawyers.

The United Nations study suggests that government lawyers may obtain advice on these matters from officials of regional or world-wide International Organisations.[33] When admitting a multinational enterprise such lawyers would have to spell out, without risks of misunderstanding, all the requirements the enterprise would have to comply with, so as to reduce the risk of conflict with development plans of the host State. Even if these terms were pretty stiff the establishment of such unequivocal rules might encourage rather than discourage foreign investors who would be rightly apprehensive of vague rules. Sometimes vague rules work like a trap. Desiring to attract an investor, representatives of the host State might give an interpretation of these rules favourable to the investor, while subsequently other such representatives would tend to stretch the interpretation of the words concerned in the opposite direction.

The practical importance of a code of good behaviour would be rather insignificant if the only sanctions ensuring its enforcement

---

[29] Ipsen, "Fragestellungen zu einem Recht der Wirtschaftsplanung," I *Planung* (1965), p. 61.

[30] In that case, a person having acted in support of the public purposes pursued by the original planning rules may have a claim to compensation; *cf.* Ipsen, "Rechtsfragen der Wirtschaftsplanung," II *Planung* (1966), p. 111.

[31] It was reported in *Der Spiegel* (Magazine) Nr. 31/1971, p. 32, that IBM had declared during the negotiations leading to the acquisition of the Hanover racing grounds as a building site for IBM that "in order to maintain its entrepreneurial flexibility IBM was unable to accept a firm contractual commitment to build the new factory as planned according to a determined schedule."

[32] As to the difficulties involved, see, *mutatis mutandis*, text at note 26 above.

[33] ST/ECA/190, p. 88.

were those which a host State could adopt against the local assets of the multinational enterprise. Even without such a code a host State has jurisdiction to prescribe to a multinational enterprise any rule of law (within the wide limits drawn by the general rules of international law on the treatment of foreigners). The host State has also jurisdiction to enforce such rules against the local assets of the multinational enterprise concerned. The real problem consists in making the tail wag the dog, that is, in ensuring that the entire multinational enterprise—the managing organs in its home State as well as its other subsidiaries in other host States—conform to such a code.

Arbitration appears to be able to solve this problem. The difficulties resulting from the fact that the parties to such a dispute are, on the one hand, a State and, on the other, a private person, a multinational enterprise, can be overcome most easily by having recourse to the services of the International Centre for the Settlement of Investment Disputes [34] (ICSD). However, Latin-American countries in particular are reluctant to avail themselves of such arbitration possibilities owing to the Calvo doctrine.[35]

In the absence of arbitration, the proposal of the United Nations study to establish multinational enterprises as United Nations corporations [36] may likewise ensure the good behaviour of all parts of a multinational enterprise established as a United Nations corporation. The study does not indicate in any detail how such a United Nations corporation could be formed. Reference is merely made to the efforts of the European Economic Community (EEC) to establish a European corporation.[37] Actually these EEC attempts had been preceded by the efforts of the ILA to establish rules for " universal or international corporations " [38]—not limited to the European scene. We cannot go as far as discussing in detail the advantages and disadvantages of these proposals—for example, the need to present such corporations in an attractive light by granting special privileges which, should they prove attractive enough, would lead to a transformation of all corporations established under a national law into this new type of institution.[39]

---

[34] ST/ECA/190, pp. 94–95, 103. On the ICSD Pirrung, Die Schiedsgerichtsbarkeit nach dem Weltbankübereinkommen für Investitionsstreitigkeiten (West Berlin 1972).

[35] Ibid., at p. 95, and Brandenburg, " Verträge der Bundesrepublik Deutschland über die Förderung und den gegenseitigen Schutz von Kapitalanlagen in Lateinamerika " (Cologne Thesis 1968), pp. 19–95.

[36] ST/ECA/190, p. 93.   [37] Ibid., p. 94.

[38] Govare, " Les sociétés universelles," ILA 43rd Conference Report (Brussels 1948), p. 269 et seq.; and Niboyet " Rapport préliminaire sure les sociétés internationales," ILA 45th Conference Report (Lucerne 1952), p. 61 et seq.

[39] Seidl-Hohenveldern, " European Companies," Journal of Business Law (1959), pp. 124–125.

Even more important is the problem of worker representation on the managerial boards of such international corporations. This latter problem has proved the stumbling block which up to now has prevented the realisation of any of the projects concerning the establishment of a European corporation.[40]

The failure of these European projects bodes ill for the far more ambitious dream of a United Nations corporation. However, should it become a reality, withdrawal of the status of United Nations corporation and of the privileges attached to this status would be a very effective sanction ensuring compliance with a United Nations code of good behaviour. Undoubtedly, the imposition of this grave sanction could be left to the discretion of neither the United Nations General Assembly and any of its Committees, nor the United Nations Secretariat. In one way or another the control of the legality of such sanctions should be entrusted to the International Court of Justice.[41]

IV—PROTECTION OF THE HOST STATE BY OTHER MEANS

Prior to the realisation of such ambitious projects requiring large scale international legislation, much can be done to counteract certain activities of multinational enterprises deemed obnoxious by their host States. Thus, multinational enterprises are often accused of putting too high a price on the goods they sell to their subsidiary in the host State, whereas the latter sells its products to the mother enterprise at a price below world market levels. In Austria recently the government has initiated legislation preventing any foreign multinational enterprise from selling its goods in Austria at a price higher than that in any other country—due allowance being made merely for higher transport costs.[42] Such a law will work only if Austria is able to obtain reliable and complete information concerning the multinational enterprise's price policy in its home State and in other host States.

Another quite effective remedy against such artificial displacement of profits may be the simple exchange of information between the tax authorities of the States concerned. Again, lawyers of the host State, possibly aided by United Nations experts, will have to devise machinery for such an exchange of information. The provision of such information may be within the discretionary power of the administrations concerned. Its exchange may simply be based on the realisation that, at least in the long run, such an exchange will be to the mutual benefit of both States. Where a legal basis is

---

[40] Goldman, *Droit commercial européen* (1971), pp. 632–636.

[41] *Cf.* text at notes 19–22 above.

[42] Draft of a Price Formation Law (Preisbildungsgesetz), Arbeiter-Zeitung October 28, 1973.

required it would be better to couch it—like all other rules on multinational enterprises—in a uniform law to be adopted by an international convention. The establishment of model rules that might be adopted in national legislation without the obligation of uniformity appears to be less appropriate in the case of multi-national enterprises. The latter's lawyers would have a better chance to find loopholes in such rules than in really uniform rules.

Today attempts to curb the above-mentioned artificial displace-ment of profits will be based mainly on the operation of classical double taxation treaties. However, as we look into the future, we might imagine that, some day, lawyers may be required to establish a ratio between the taxes of several countries to be imposed on a multinational corporation and its shareholders.[43] Any such solutions will require of the States concerned more insight than they show at present in advancing their claims. It is true that the difference between the value of the extracted minerals or oil at the place of extraction is dramatically lower than at the place of consumption. Yet, to leave all this profit to the taxing power of the extraction country would be disproportionate, as the value at the place of consumption is dependent also on the machinery of distribution and, last but not least, on the capital furnished by the shareholders.

The temptation may be great for multinational corporations to resort to monopolistic or cartel practices on a world-wide scale, especially if any risk of retribution is limited in each case only to actions undertaken by one of its host States and then, by necessity, only against the part of the corporation's assets located there. Similar steps undertaken by the home State of the multinational enterprise might prove more effective. However, such steps are hampered by the fact that any extraterritorial enforcement of anti-trust legislation raises the problem of its compatibility with inter-national law as it now stands.[44] The ILA has already devoted much of its time to the study of international cartel problems.[45] In the future the existence of multinational enterprises may compel us to

[43] A panel of United Nations experts is examining this problem; *cf.* also ST/ECA/190, pp. 89–90. It is believed that tax problems will form also one of the main topics of the activities of the ILA Committee on Multinational Corporations.
[44] Seidl-Hohenveldern, "The Limits Imposed by International Law on the Application of Cartel Law," 5 *International Lawyer* (1971), pp. 279–299; and Oehler, *Internationales Strafrecht* (1973), p. 231, and pp. 239–240.
[45] Reports by Jennings, ILA 51st Conference Report (Tokyo 1964), p. 354 *et seq.*; Riedweg, *ibid.* p. 357 *et seq.*; Ellis, *ibid.* p. 483 *et seq.*; Oliver, *ibid.* p. 511 *et seq.*; Haight, *ibid.* p. 565 *et seq.*; Riedweg, ILA 52nd Conference Report (Helsinki 1962), p. 61 *et seq.*; Jennings/Mann, *ibid.* p. 109 *et seq.*; and Baxter, *ibid.* p. 115 *et seq.*; Ellis *et al.*, ILA 53rd Conference Report (Buenos Aires 1968), p. 360 *et seq.*; and Joannou, *ibid.* p. 402; Ellis *et al.*, ILA 54th Conference Report (The Hague 1970), p. 178 *et seq.*; Baxter, *ibid.* p. 200 *et seq.*; and Hunter, *ibid.* p. 221 *et seq.* For United Nations and United Nations Conference on Trade and Development (UNCTAD) efforts in this field, *cf.* ST/ECA/190, pp. 91–92.

co-ordinate anti-cartel measures at an international level—with the necessary corollary that fines imposed by one State for participation in a cartel forbidden in several countries should be taken into account when other States also choose to prosecute this cartel.[46]

There is one more field where complaints have been voiced against multinational enterprises. By shifting its orders from its production centre in one country to its production centre in another country the multinational enterprise can escape or, at least, mitigate the consequences of labour troubles in its several host States. Labour unions have been quick to see this menace to their power and have initiated counteractions transcending the level of merely one of the host States. Again, it will be the task of the lawyers to invent machinery which would allow for the possibility of multinational collective bargaining replacing labour trouble on a multinational level.[47]

CONCLUSIONS

All lawyers can do to cope with the phenomenon of multinational enterprises is to invent legal machinery appropriate to the legitimate requirements both of the multinational enterprises themselves and of their host States. The few suggestions I submit do not pretend to be an exhaustive solution of the problems raised by these enterprises. Nor will legal rules by themselves, however appropriate they may appear in theory, be able to solve these problems. For their solution we need above all a spirit of mutual goodwill and confidence between the multinational enterprises and their host States. Lawyers will thus not only have to create rules capable of avoiding friction or at least of reducing it. They should also, at the same time, help to promote a co-operative spirit in their clients—be they governments or enterprises.

If they succeed in creating such rules and instilling this spirit, there will no longer be any question whether the multinational enterprise is a friend or a foe of mankind. Then, the advantage offered by the existence of multinational enterprises will clearly outpass the dangers and disadvantages inherent to them, on which we have dwelt so much in the present paper. Then, the multinational

---

[46] Seidl-Hohenveldern, *loc. cit.* in note 44 above, pp. 288–289, *contra* Oehler, *loc. cit.* in note 44 above, p. 606.

[47] ST/ECA/190, p. 79–80; the ILO has begun an intensive study of this problem (ILO, *Multinational Enterprises and Social Policy Studies and Reports,* New Series Nr. 79 (1973). Two forthcoming theses are also devoted to this problem: Manitakis-Kravaritou, "Le système de négociation collective dans les États membres de la CEE et négotiations au niveau de la firme multinationale" (Brussels), and Zaum, "Multinationale Unternehmen und internationale Gewerkschaften" (Cologne).

enterprise may rightly be praised as the most efficient means of harnessing capital in smaller quantities also, and from smaller developed States, to meet the needs of developing countries; of avoiding the hardships imposed on migratory labour forces by spreading the procurement of supplies needed in one or several developed States to factories located in many host States; and, last but not least, of promoting peace and reducing international friction. Where investors of various nationalities combine in a joint venture spreading their investment over several host States, they all stand to lose, should friction or strife break out between any of the States concerned. Thus, all such investors have a stake in the maintenance of peaceful relations between the States concerned. Finally, given proper safeguards to be devised by lawyers, multinational enterprises could become a factor beneficial to mankind.

IMPERIALISM: PAST AND FUTURE

By

STANISLAV ANDRESKI

IT is widely accepted (and not only by the marxists) that the prosperity of the highly industrialised nations as well as the poverty of the so-called Third World are the outcome of the exploitation of the latter by the former. Despite the torrent of condemnations, however, no conclusive evidence has so far been produced to show that the said exploitation really took place . . . which is not surprising in view of the extreme vagueness of the concept of exploitation: for how can you prove that something exists when you know not what it is? True, we can define " exploitation " as taking away goods and services without giving any in return; and we can easily find examples which leave no room for doubt. The Romans were clearly exploiting the Egyptians when, after robbing them of all the gold and jewels they could find, they continued to force them to deliver every year a large part of their crops without payment. Nor can there be much doubt that the Spaniards were exploiting the Indians in Peru when they were forcing them by atrocious punishments to dig gold for them. As soon, however, as an exchange of goods and services takes place, the concept of exploitation becomes difficult to apply because it presupposes that a certain rate of exchange is just, while other rates constitute exploitation; which raises the problem of how do we determine which rate is just.

Take an example: what does it mean when we say that the British have exploited India? It is true that in the early days of the company straightforward spoliation (thinly, if at all, veiled by a few quibbles) often occurred; but what about the later times when the administration became regular and extortion and bribery rarer than they have ever been in India before or since? Nobody can deny that some of the proceeds from taxation went into paying the British administrators, including the retired in Great Britain, or that interest accrued to British investors who put their money into the Indian railways; while many British businessmen made good profits from jute mills or tea plantations. The label " exploitation " implies that they did not deserve these payments. Maybe they did not; but why not?

Suppose the British had not put their money into India: the railways, the factories and the plantations would have been far fewer. Perhaps that would have been better, and the inhabitants might have been happier. At the beginning they certainly did not

313

want to be developed, although their descendants of today would not like to be without these accoutrements of industrial civilisation. Anyway, forcing people to change their way of life is not the same thing as exploiting them, although they may go together. Thus, we cannot substantiate an assertion that the British exploited India without showing that they received more than a fair price for their activities in reorganising the economy and financing the new ventures. Here again: by virtue of which criteria do we establish which price would have been fair?

The concept of exploitation becomes even hazier if we put some value on the function of maintaining peace. True, from a nationalistic viewpoint any form of rule by foreigners is bad, but this is a valuation which is quite distinct from the evils of exploitation. It is also true that peace may not be so desirable when it is accompanied by oppression and misery; but if a régime manages to maintain peace more effectively, while imposing less oppression and misery than either its predecessors or successors, then it ought to be rated as fairly beneficial. By all of these criteria (at least after the early buccaneering days) British rule in India was a great improvement on the Mughuls, and it placed a much smaller burden on the ordinary folk than do the political, administrative and military machines of independent India, Pakistan and Bangladesh. In *The African Predicament* I have shown that analogous assertions can justifiably be made about tropical Africa.

Although this would not be enough to clinch the argument because of the inevitable arbitrary assumptions, we could try to justify the imputations of imperialist exploitation by showing that more wealth went from the colonies to the metropolitan country than the other way round. This would not be easy because we would have to include such elusive items as the cost of bringing up and educating the metropolitan personnel who spent (and often ended) their lives in the colonies. If we decided that the general effects of the rule should be put on the positive rather than the negative side, we would have to include the costs of defending the colonies borne by the taxpayers in the metropolitan country.

On the other hand, even if a calculation of this kind had shown that the colonies received more than they delivered, it could be argued that the most essential feature of colonialism was the policy of keeping the colonial economies in a backward state as sources of raw materials, complementary to the manufacturing metropolitan economy, and that the losses thereby inflicted on the colonies were enormous, though not calculable with any precision. Arguments either for or against this contention must entail a number of counterfactual conditional propositions about what would have happened had this or that not happened. These would be fairly convincing in cases where a subjugation by a foreign Power was followed by a clear decline in the aggregate wealth, especially if accompanied by a decrease in the population as happened in Peru after the Spanish conquest or in Iran after the Mongol. If we look at the European colonialism of the 19th century it is difficult to find an instance where the aggregate wealth of a conquered country did not greatly increase. If in some instances the average income did not rise, this was due to an equally rapid growth of the population. To hold colonialism responsible for the backwardness of the colonies we must presuppose that these would be more developed had the colonial rule never come; this would be more plausible if, among countries which were in a similar stage at the outset of the era of industrial colonialism, the ex-colonies had been less developed at the time of decolonisation than the countries which managed to preserve their independence throughout this era or lost it only briefly. A comparison of Ethiopia with Kenya or of Liberia with Ghana might be to the point. Some light on this question can also be shed by comparing the rates of economic progress within the given territories before, during and after the colonial era, which evidence hardly supports unequivocal assertions about the connections between colonialism and backwardness.

It is only fair to add that the last-mentioned evidence lends no support to the view that the ex-colonial populations would be better off today had decolonisation never come; because it seems that, having triggered off the population explosion, the colonialists got out just in time to avoid having to step up coercion in an effort to keep down the teeming and increasingly miserable and discontented subjects. Furthermore, there are instances (such as the Ivory Coast) where economic progress gained speed after independence. Nevertheless, such examples do not prove that the colonial rule held the development back while it lasted, because we cannot assume that a similar spurt would have followed its demise in an earlier period, when there were fewer natives equipped with modern skills. In some cases (most notably the Belgian Congo, now named Zaire) strong arguments have been put for the view that the decolonisation would have been more beneficial to the masses had it been postponed and carried out more gradually.

One can claim that the colonialists should have renounced some of their profits or emoluments, allowed more favourable terms of trade, or steered economic development into channels more advantageous to the local populations and less to the metropolitan exporters or importers. Such opinions are perfectly tenable—and had the colonialists been motivated by altruism they would, no doubt, have done more for the populations they were ruling. But if, on these grounds, we apply to the colonial situation the label of " exploitation " we are using it as a moral concept equivalent to " selfishness " rather than one definable in economic terms. From the latter standpoint there was little during the last century of the colonial era that could be clearly diagnosed as " exploitation," with the exception of the cases where the extraction of irreplaceable natural resources such as oil and tin by foreign firms produced a depletion of these resources without adding much to the income of the natives.

In contrast to the colonialism practised during the era of rapid industrial progress, a drastic impoverishment of the conquered lands was the usual consequence of pre-industrial imperialism; and I fear that this might also be the feature of such imperialisms as will operate in the future. Let me now explain why this should be so.

Until technology began to advance fast, and wealth to grow, trade could bring benefits to all parties, but politically induced changes in the economic relations between ethnic or political units had the character of a zero-sum game where one player's gain would be another's loss. A conquest would seldom be followed by an improvement in the methods or the quantity of production because the conquerors would normally be better only in the art of war and could very well be more backward in the peaceful crafts. Neither the Persian, the Macedonian, the Roman, the Arab, nor the Turkish conquests of western Asia, for instance, led to any important improvements in the technology of production. In many instances—like the Mongol invasion of Persia or China—at least the organisation and the quantity of production, if not the technology itself, underwent a clear retrogression in the aftermath of the conquest. This seems to have been the outcome even in instances where an area inhabited by many warring tribes was unified under the rule of a complex polity as in the case of the Roman conquest of Gaul which nearly halved the population of that area. What is even more surprising, the Spanish conquerors—who knew iron-smelting, navigation, masonry, the horse, and the wheel and a number of other technical skills unheard of by the Amerindians—reduced, instead of increasing, the wealth as well as the population of the more advanced kingdoms in America.

In a pre-industrial civilisation a conquest occasionally resulted in a removal (either by extermination or by driving out) of the defeated population, but the usual outcome was a change of masters while the peasants and craftsmen continued to work in their customary ways. Apart from the change of the beneficiaries, the machinery

for extracting wealth was often improved, or at least altered, and
its rate of suction stepped up; although the latter was not always
the case, as there are instances where the fiscal burden was reduced,
as happened after the Arab conquest of the Byzantine provinces.
The only economic benefit which a conquest could bestow upon the
subjugated population under the conditions of a static and fairly
uniform technology was a widening of the area of trade; but, as in
these times the trade included mostly superfluities consumed by the
privileged classes, it could benefit the masses only to a very small
extent. In contrast to imperialism of the earlier epochs, colonialism
—as well as the informal forms of control known as economic
imperialism—of western European nations from about 1840 until
the present time was practised by the possessors of organisational
and technical skills immensely superior to anything known to the
victims. The enormous technical superiority gave the colonialists
such a military advantage that they were able to carry out extensive
conquests without their cultures becoming exclusively oriented to
war. Before the complex machinery began to determine the outcome
of battles, military superiority often went with a simpler rather
than a more advanced economy and civilisation, as even pre-literate
tribes were able to make the most effective weapons of the day.
Never before the 19th century were the conquering armies followed
by a mass of specialists in superior methods of peaceful production.

During pre-industrial centuries, natural resources were scarce—
utilised more or less as fully as the stagnant technology permitted.
The spurt of science-based technology after about 1840 gave mankind the knowledge of how to extract all kinds of new goods from
the same area, which had the same effect as if the natural resources
had suddenly and miraculously multiplied. The scarcest factor of
production in this situation was culture in the shape of the skills,
habits and customs needed for organising production on a new level.
Now these cultural resources were, by and large, concentrated in
the countries which were at that time the chief agents of imperialism.
The coupling of imperial expansion with enforcement of technical
and economic progress endowed the post-1840 colonialism with the
characteristics of a non-zero sum game in which not only the conquerors but also the conquered could be richer at the end than they
were at the beginning because the aggregate wealth vastly increased.

The foregoing analysis constitutes no proof of altruism on the
part of the carriers of imperial expansion, which was clearly motivated by the desire for wealth and power, albeit some individuals
and groups involved in it might have been prompted by humanitarian
or religious impulses. A one-sided extraction of weath did not
come to predominate in the colonial situation because under the

existing constellation of circumstances the biggest gains could be obtained by organising economic growth.

The ecological limits to growth which mankind appears to be reaching must, at least in some respects, push the politico-economic relations between the nations back towards the condition of a zero-sum game which they experienced before the era of great industrial progress: for, if the amount of wealth cannot be increased, then a gain for one entails a loss for another. Moreover, since the technical and organisational skills needed for utilising fully the available natural resources have spread around the globe—and there is no reason to suppose that this diffusion will not continue until they are available in sufficient dosage throughout the world—a subjugation of a territory could not be followed by a spurt of economic development, but could only lead to a transfer of wealth to the conquerors.

A very important aspect of the ecological crisis is that, even apart from the competition for scarce raw materials, economic growth within a country causes damage through pollution to the others who consequently have a strong interest in preventing it. Thus we have a zero-sum game on two scores. On the penalties side, however, the politico-economic international relations would be much more in the nature of a non-zero-sum game than ever because, although not all could gain, all could very easily lose—and in extreme cases, such as an all-out war, all would lose everything. The gain from (or, if you prefer the game-theoretic terminology, the pay-off of) co-operation—at least in the sense of refraining from hostile actions —would be the magnitude of the loss avoided. This combination of a zero-sum game on the positive side (that is, in respect of non-notional gains) with a non-zero-sum game on the negative side (that is, in respect of losses) would be analogous to a situation of the survivors of a shipwreck in an easily capsizable lifeboat who have a certain amount of iron rations each: no-one could increase his share without wresting it from somebody else; but if they started fighting, the boat would capsize and all would drown.

A constellation of this kind could lead to total immobility if all the States had equal power to upset the boat—that is, speaking less metaphorically, to cause lethal damage eventually to themselves by getting into a fight. In fact, only a conflict between highly industrialised States could have such consequences; and for some time yet such States could set upon the weaker with relative impunity. For example, no atomic fall-out would ensue if the oil-producing Arab countries were seized by force—which not only the United States or the Soviet Union but even a second-rate Power like the United Kingdom or Japan could do without great difficulty. The

Arabs' freedom of manoeuvre rests entirely on the stalemate between the super-Powers in that area. What is most likely to occur in the no-man's-lands like these is an intensification of underhand and indirect forms of conflict between the great Powers which stops short of an all-out war.

In the areas which are unambiguously subordinate to one of the super- (or even second-rate) Powers a resurgence of open imperialism, or of its veiled form known as neo-imperialism may well take place; and if it does, it is likely to be more rapacious than its analogues in the recent past. The accusations often levelled about holding back the development of the dependent areas, which were only partly (if at all) justified about the imperialism of the last century, may well come true in the future. On the basis of the ecological considerations, moreover, we can expect the domains of Powers well provided with natural resources (such as the Soviet Union) to fare better than the dependencies of less self-sufficient States. Given that so much will depend on shifting constellations of forces, it could be rash to offer confident prophecies. I would venture, nonetheless, to make a conditional prediction that, if there is a resurgence of imperialism, it will be accompanied by an economic process which will fit much better the label of " exploitation " than the just defunct imperialism of the last century.

Concerning the internal struggles which are an alternative to war as a mechanism for adjusting population to resources, I must point out that the ecological predicament has inverted the relationship between the generations in a way which is likely to exacerbate conflicts between them. In a progressing economy, a later generation had reasons to be grateful to the preceding for what it had accumulated and bequeathed; whereas in a situation where irreplaceable and indispensable resources are being used up, a higher standard of living of the earlier generation can be maintained only at the expense of a lower standard for the next. It may be accidental but is nonetheless intriguing that the disappearance of filial respect and gratitude as a general custom has coincided with the advent of the ecological crisis.

THE CONCEPT OF WORLD ORDER

By

RONALD J. YALEM

THE concept of world order is one of the most widely used in the literature of international relations.[1] Yet it is also one of the most ill-defined and inadequately conceptualised notions. The purpose of this paper is to present the concept of world order as it appears in the literature and to analyse the reasons for the plurality of definitions and the inadequacy of its conceptualisation. Definitional ambiguity is largely the result of the failure of scholars to explicate clearly the conceptual foundations of world order. Part of the difficulty also lies in disagreement on the relative emphases accorded to law and power as elements of order; it also stems from a heavy emphasis on the prescriptive or normative thrust of conceptualisation and neglect of the empirical aspects. I will approach the subject from the perspectives of international law, international organisation, and international systems analysis.

The concept of world order has been articulated largely in a normative sense: either the prerequisites for world order are stipulated abstractly or the details of future world order systems are described. As yet we do not have a systematic theory of world order that incorporates both normative and empirical elements.

World order has been defined in a number of ways, reflecting the diversity and ambiguity of the concept. Most definitions attempt to conceptualise " order "; none attempts to operationalise it. In a recent criticism of Myres McDougal's efforts, Oran Young makes the following apt comment: " the ambiguities imbedded in McDougal's concept of world public order are not peculiar to him; on the contrary, they exemplify a widespread inability to define

[1] The author wishes to express his appreciation for the financial support for this study provided by the Research Grants Committee of the University of Alabama. Following is a list of recent works that employ the concept often without any attempt at definition: R. Riggs and J. Plano, *Forging World Order* (1967); A. Vandenbosch and W. Hogan, *Toward World Order* (1962); M. S. McDougal and F. P. Feliciano, *Law and Minimum World Public Order* (1961); M. S. McDougal *et al.*, *Studies in World Public Order* (1960); R. Osgood and R. Tucker, *Force, Order, and Justice* (1967); R. J. Yalem, *Regionalism and World Order* (1965); Linda Miller, *World Order and Local Disorder* (1967); R. A. Falk and C. Black (eds.), *The Future of the International Legal Order* (1969); R. A. Falk and S. Mendlovitz (eds.), *The Strategy of World Order* (1966); A. Lepawsky, E. Buehrig, and H. Lasswell (eds.), *The Search for World Order* (1971); R. A. Falk and S. Mendlovitz (eds.), *Regional Politics and World Order* (1973); A. James (ed.), *The Bases of International Order* (1973), and S. Mendlovitz (ed.), *On the Creation of a Just World Order* (1974).

the concept ' world order ' in a genuinely fruitful fashion." ² What
follows is a series of definitions that illustrates the point.

Minimum world order. " A public order which establishes as
authoritative, and seeks to make effective the principle that force,
or highly intense coercion, . . . is reserved in community monopoly
for support of processes of persuasion and agreement and is not
to be used as an instrument of unauthorized change." ³

Optimum world order. " A public order which, beyond authoritative orientation toward the minimum of coercion and the maximum
of persuasion . . . is further designed to promote the greatest
production . . . of human dignity values among peoples." ⁴

World order as a War Prevention System. The study of world
order concentrates on " . . . the avoidance of war through the
creation of a war prevention system. To conceive of world order
as the strategy by which one system is transformed into another
. . . is the essence of the undertaking." ⁵ World order is conceived
only as a future preferred goal in the form of a warless system.
The definition therefore implies there is no world order in the
absence of such a system which is certainly a debatable assumption.

World order as the Negation of World Disorder. " The concept
of world order necessarily assumes a substantive differentiation
corresponding to the guidelines of the kind of order that is proposed.
This is manifest methodologically by taking such a concept and
contrasting it with the possible forms of its negation. For it lies in
the nature of things that our ideas of right and good are less exact
and definite than our notions of wrong and bad. Consequently, the
concept of disorder, with whose elimination we are concerned, is
always more easily defined; it facilitates the understanding of the
different meanings of order." ⁶ Definition by negation may be
useful, but only if the various forms of disorder are described.

World order as a Condition. International order may be defined
" . . . primarily by reference to the extent and frequency of political
violence." ⁷ While this is one of the few definitions that stress the
present rather than the future, it fails to indicate how the incidence

² O. Young, " International Law and Social Science: The Contributions of
Myres S. McDougal," 66 *American Journal of International Law* (January, 1972),
p. 72.
³ M. S. McDougal *et al., Studies in World Public Order* (1960), p. xi.
⁴ *Ibid.* pp. xvii–xviii.
⁵ R. A. Falk and S. H. Mendlovitz (eds.), *Toward a Theory of War Prevention*
(1966), Preface.
⁶ H. G. Gadamer, " Planning for the Future," 95 *Daedalus* (Spring 1966), p. 573.
⁷ R. A. Falk, *The Status of Law in International Society* (1970), p. 68.

and the scope of violence is empirically related to the conditions of world order.

World Order as a Value. " Order is not merely an actual or possible condition or state of affairs in world politics, it is also generally regarded as a value. A pattern or structure of human relations such as to sustain the elementary or primary goals of social coexistence among states." [8] The difficulty with this definition lies in its abstractness. What kind of structure is required to sustain the value of social coexistence among States?

APPROACHES TO THE STUDY OF WORLD ORDER

The normative emphasis in most of the preceding definitions may be accounted for by the fact that the approaches to the study of world order have been dominated by students of international law and international organisation. These disciplines tend to stress a normative orientation to political reality with regard to the problem of world order. While normative inquiry is legitimate in all of the social sciences, in the study of international relations it may lead to a neglect of political factors and even to the conviction that politics is stultifying to order and is an attribute of disorder.

For example, Richard Falk and Saul Mendlovitz describe the Clark-Sohn plan for limited world government as a model for " the kind of world order that is needed if the prospect of major warfare is to be eliminated from international life. The strategy of study is to clarify the nature of order in the existing international political system, to postulate the Clark-Sohn model as an alternative international system," and ". . . to analyse the techniques for transforming the one into the other and thereby achieve a transition to a warless world." [9]

Most world order students share to a greater or lesser degree the pessimism of Falk and Mendlovitz about the quality of order in the present international system. Yet there is a curious contradiction in an approach which deplores the inadequacies of the system but implies that it may be transformed into a more centralised one.

The systems approach to world order has the advantage of relating the roles of international law and international organisation to the power-political features of the international system. Its principal disadvantage is the propensity towards abstract conceptualisation of the requirements for order; its principal advantage is a greater

---

[8] H. Bull, " Order vs. Justice in International Society," *Political Studies* (September, 1971), p. 17.

[9] R. A. Falk and S. H. Mendlovitz (eds.), *International Law* (1966), prefatory note.

realism in the discussion of the possibilities for world order than is usually found in the normative approaches.

(a) *International Law as an Approach to the Study of World Order*

International law, especially in the 20th century, has been expanded into what Stanley Hoffmann calls the " law of the political framework " for the purpose of controlling and regulating international violence.[10] In theory, at least, international law has become an important ordering mechanism in international affairs, though it is widely recognised that its effectiveness is minimal in restraining determined States from employing force in defiance of international norms. Despite the fact that States continue to ignore the restrictions imposed by international law when their vital interests are at stake, students of world order still stress the role of law as a precondition for order in international relations.[11] McDougal and Feliciano regard order as the principal function of any legal system.[12] Percy Corbett, however, believes that a sense of community is a necessary prerequisite to a legal order.[13]

Disagreement over the relative importance of international law as an ordering mechanism may be partly attributable to the absence of linkages between international law and international political relations. Many international lawyers still treat law as an autonomous influence to the neglect of social and political factors. According to Oran Young, when this occurs the concept of world order is assimilated by definition into legal analysis.[14]

In recent years political scientists have discussed international law within the context of international politics as a subsidiary rather than primary influence on world order. In all probability they have done so as a reaction against the failure of both international law and international organisation to establish world order in practice. Young typifies this view as revealed in the following statement: " . . . it seems reasonable to conclude that world order is basically a political condition and the central problems of world order often rest in the final analysis on social and political relationships that are not ordinarily regarded as legal issues." [15] However, Young and other political scientists who take this position rarely explain the

[10] S. Hoffmann, " International Systems and International Law," *World Politics* (October, 1961), pp. 205–237.
[11] G. Schwarzenberger, however, suggests that historical evidence supports the view that order precedes law: see *International Law and Order* (1971), p. 1.
[12] M. S. McDougal and F. P. Feliciano, *Law and Minimum World Public Order* (1961), p. 121.
[13] P. Corbett, *The Growth of World Law* (1971), p. 7.
[14] Young, *op. cit.* in note 2 above, p. 71.
[15] *Ibid.*

kinds of political conditions conducive to order in international relations.

To the extent that the problem of world order is considered political rather than legal, there may be the temptation to rule out the importance of law as an element of order. Many social systems exhibit stable patterns of order in which order is maintained by the operation of social and political norms despite the absence of formal legal rules.[16] While this may be true for primitive political systems, it is unlikely that it has ever been valid for the international system where a set of legal norms and principles was needed to offset political conditions that were disruptive. That these norms and principles have sometimes yielded to the requirements of " reason of State " or the " national interest " is incontrovertible. But despite the deviations States continue to recognise that they are subjects of international law and legally bound by its precepts.

International law is not the only or even the most important factor for world order but one that cannot be denied. What is debatable is the extent of its importance. Other factors such as nuclear deterrence, technical aid, and regionalism may stabilise international relations and therefore contribute to the conditions of world order.[17] Yet D. P. O'Connell deplores the neglect today of the philosophical foundations of international law: " Just as world order cannot be discussed effectively until the philosophical differences concerning what is meant by ' order ' have been exposed, so international law as a system of ordination cannot be examined until the nature of law, its origin and its purposes, has been clarified." [18]

No doubt the philosophical foundations of international law and world order are important. A classic statement that links law and order in the international system has been offered. In explaining the binding character of international law in a system that lacks enforcement through central institutions, Brierly sought an explanation outside the law: " The ultimate explanation of the binding force of all law is that man, whether he is a single individual or whether he is associated with other men in a state, is constrained, in so far as he is a reasonable being, to believe that order and not chaos is the governing principle of the world in which he has to live." [19] Brierly clearly implies that law is an instrument for order and stability among States whereas political scientists might argue that the law can just as easily serve as a rationalisation for illegal behaviour. So however important philosophical foundations may be

---

[16] *Ibid.*
[17] D. P. O'Connell, " The Role of International Law," 95 *Daedalus* (Spring 1966), p. 627.
[18] *Ibid.* p. 635.
[19] J. L. Brierly, *The Law of Nations* (1963), p. 56.

for international law and world order, we must examine to what extent the law is able to operate in accordance with its moral or philosophical purposes in international relations. This is a question which ultimately depends on an empirical investigation of the influence of law upon State behaviour.

We turn now to the contributions of Richard Falk. While trained in international law, his main interest lies in creating a new discipline of world order which would draw upon the findings of the social sciences to supplement knowledge derived from political science. Those who have followed his work closely are well aware that he has shifted from a position of near utopianism with respect to the influence of international law on world order to a more realistic interpretation. However, the fundamental idealism which infuses all of his writing has not been abandoned.

Falk's early work on the relationship between international law and world order appeared in 1966 in *The Strategy of World Order*. In that series of readings which he co-edited with Saul Mendlovitz, the Clark-Sohn model for limited world government was suggested as an example of the most desirable kind of new world order system. In spite of their attention to international political factors as obstacles to world government, Falk and Mendlovitz displayed an unmistakable idealism in their commentaries on the various readings.

In the introduction to the volume on international law, Falk and Mendlovitz discussed the role of law as a basis for actual order and in terms of a system of ideal order, indicating some enthusiasm for systems analysis as a tool for clarifying the distance from the present war-prone system to a limited world government. Though they acknowledged the necessity for transitional arrangements to achieve the system hypothesised in the Clark-Sohn model, scant attention was devoted to the details of such transitional mechanisms. Nor was there any delineation of the relationship between law and power and how the tension between them affects the nature of world order. Is order a function of law alone? If not, is order a function of power, especially balanced military power? Or are both law and power reciprocally important factors in the attainment of order? Such complex questions ought to guide the quest for knowledge of the nature of world order. Falk's neglect of these questions has been remedied, however, in subsequent work that is still idealistic, but much less enthusiastic, about achieving the kind of supranational structure advocated in the Clark-Sohn plan.

Falk shifted his conception of international law and world order in 1970 with the publication of *The Status of Law in International Society* which demonstrated a sophisticated understanding of the role of power political and strategic factors and their influence on world order. A deeper sensitivity to the relationship between law and power was also discernible. The discussion of international law was juxtaposed in a setting which also included nuclear weapons, universal and regional organisations, and a concern for the militant nationalism of the new nations.[20] Falk evidences a preference for a legal order intermediate between the " pure theory of law " of Hans Kelsen, with its sharp separation of law and politics, and the policy-oriented jurisprudence of Myres McDougal in which law is politicised into a tool of national decision-makers rather than conceptualised as a binding norm.

Falk's position on the nature of international law and world order is further amplified in *The Future of the International Legal Order* in which he contributes an essay on the Westphalian and United Nations Charter conceptions of law.[21] In addition to the normative restraints that these two systems of law imposed upon States, Falk allows a role and function for such non-legal ordering mechanisms as deterrence, spheres of influence, and political norms or " rules of the game." International law functions as a quasi-dependent variable which reflects the political forces in the international system but which also may serve " as a strategy by which to participate in or transform the international system." [22] By quasi-dependent variable Falk means that international law is almost, but not completely, dependent on international politics for its substance. This is implied by his assumption that law may be a means for transforming the international system. How and by what means this is to be accomplished is, however, not disclosed.

The conceptualisation of international law as a quasi-dependent variable in the international system avoids exaggerating its role as an autonomous influence on State behaviour or dismissing it altogether in favour of the primacy-of-politics argument. But there is also an imprecision in Falk's usage of quasi-dependent variable that must be overcome if it is to serve as a middle ground between the aforementioned extremes. One possibility is to concede a modest role for law as a restraint on State behaviour in those areas of international life where it is in the interest of States to limit voluntarily their freedom of manoeuvre chiefly in what Stanley Hoffmann refers to as the " law of reciprocity " and to admit frankly the dependency of law on political factors where there is a conflict between legal norms and the requirements of the " national interest."

[20] R. A. Falk, *The Status of Law in International Society* (1970), p. xii.
[21] R. A. Falk, " The Interplay of Westphalia and Charter Conceptions of International Legal Order," in R. A. Falk and C. Black (eds.), *The Future of the International Legal Order* (1969), pp. 32–70.
[22] *Ibid.* p. 35.

Insofar as changing the international system is concerned, however, Falk's conception of international law as a quasi-dependent variable seems contradicted by the following comment: " The existing system of international legal order appears resistant to drastic change through conscious redirection, whether in the form of agreement by sovereign States or by a transnational political movement." [23] This view would seem to predispose international law to a distinctly passive dependent variable role.

In a further analysis of the problems of world order, Falk analyses five principal dimensions: the Westphalian conception of order; the United Nations Charter norms; a geopolitical interpretation of nuclear deterrence and spheres of influence; political " rules of the game "; and the modes of implementing legal and political norms.[24] It is another attempt to evolve an intermediate position on the nature of world order, but in the opinion of this writer it is not entirely satisfactory.

He shows that despite the deviations from the principle of sovereign equality promulgated at the Peace of Westphalia, the principle survives in many of the non-vital sectors of international relations. And although the Charter conception of international society introduces a limited centralisation through the constitutional authority of the Security Council to enforce international peace and security, it is clear that " the national government remains the most exclusive source of territorial authority and the decisions and agreement of national governments continue to provide the most important sources of international authority." [25] Thus the Westphalian conception of a decentralised approach to peace and security through the operation of the balance of power continues to be dominant.

If this analysis is valid, the prospects for radical change in the structure of international society are not bright. With the role of the nation-State still predominant, no other conclusion seems possible. Yet Falk has abandoned the cautionary approach that characterises his recent scholarly writings in a polemical attack on the nation-State and a series of prescriptive proposals for transforming " this endangered planet " into a more centralised world order system.[26] Although *This Endangered Planet* was written for the attentive public, it reveals that Falk has not basically altered his views on the possibilities for system change advanced in his earlier writing. The result of his writings on world order is an unsuccessful attempt at reconciling international law and power

---

[23] *Ibid.* p. 38.
[24] *Ibid.* pp. 42–69.
[25] *Ibid.* p. 48.
[26] R. A. Falk, *This Endangered Planet* (1971).

politics by means of an intermediate position gravely weakened by periodic excursions into a utopianism which assumes that what is desirable is also possible.

The preceding analysis establishes international law as a necessary but hardly sufficient component of world order, where order is defined as the expectation of stable and predictable relations among sovereign States. Although Professor Falk's conception of international law as a quasi-dependent variable is inadequately developed, it does offer a reasonable alternative to conceptions of order that either ignore the role of international law or conversely overstress its influence on the character of international relations. Further, the conception of law as a quasi-independent variable is not only intellectually reasonable; it conforms to the empirical reality of international relations.

(b) *International Organisation as an Approach to the Study of World Order*

In the 20th century a vital aspect of the search for world order is the universal international organisation symbolised by the League of Nations and the United Nations. Within the context of the universal organisations, order has been defined as the maintenance of international peace and security against those States that would disturb the peace by unauthorised violence. Both the Covenant and the Charter prohibited or sharply restricted the circumstances under which force could be utilised by member States. But in practice both institutions were not able to secure the capacity for enforcing these prohibitions. They also lacked the legislative authority to adjust situations of international injustice that often have precipitated aggression by one State against another.

As an approach to world order, international organisation has been referred to as a kind of international constitutionalism [27]: " The constitutional approach [to international organisation] apprehends the problem of international organisation essentially from the point of view of a constitution maker. It provides the legal and institutional framework for international order, on the assumption that the political, social, and economic divisions and conflicts of mankind can either be overcome by such an institutional framework or that they do not matter." Yet neither the League of Nations nor the United Nations has been able to function successfully as guarantors of international order in the manner assumed in their constitutional provisions. Nevertheless, the search for peace and security through international organisations continues.

With over 50 years of experience with universal organisations,

---

[27] W. Friedmann, *The Changing Structure of International Law* (1964), p. 6.

it is possible to reach certain conclusions regarding the adequacy of the theory of international organisation which assumes that such institutions can function to preserve international peace and security. In practice both the League and the United Nations have had success only in quelling minor conflicts whereas in major conflicts they have largely been ineffectual. Based on the assumption that States will voluntarily co-operate to inflict military and non-military sanctions against aggressors, the lessons of the past indicate that international organisations are unlikely to be effective as instruments of world order so long as they are largely based upon the principle of sovereign consent for organisational action.

It is not surprising, therefore, that many scholars and laymen are dissatisfied with the weakness of the United Nations. While it is logical enough to argue that the United Nations will be severely limited as an ordering mechanism until its authority base is expanded, the practical possibilities for increasing the authority of the organisation are extremely limited. Inis Claude captures the dilemma of the United Nations very well [28]: " . . . if the United Nations had worked exceedingly well in its early years, the campaigner for world government would have a weaker argument for the urgency of his project but a vastly stronger one for its feasibility; since the United Nations has had very limited success, it is easy to argue that much more drastic measures are necessary, but difficult to prove that they are possible."

Some years ago this writer undertook a study of the relationship between universal and regional organisations concerned with assessing to what extent such organisations promoted or impeded world order.[29] The problem was perceived in terms of whether an equilibrium of influence existed and, if not, to what extent an imbalance in favour of regional organisations affected international order. Concluding that the imbalance was a reflection of the ineffectiveness of the United Nations as a security-producing institution rather than the responsibility of a disorderly flight to regional co-operation, I deduced that regional security organisations had not enhanced the prospects for order but had themselves contributed to an intensification of international tensions.

World order was conceptualised as a condition of legal order which could be facilitated by the complementary operations of universal and regional organisations.[30] This implied that universal and regional organisations could contribute to the attainment of world order. While the existence of such organisations does reflect

---

[28] I. L. Claude, Jr., *Swords into Plowshares: The Problems and Progress of International Organization* (1971), pp. 419–420.
[29] R. J. Yalem, *Regionalism and World Order* (1965).
[30] *Ibid.* p. 1.

the pragmatic need for co-operation beyond the nation State in an increasingly interdependent world community, international organisations like international law are better analysed as quasi-dependent variables affected more by international political forces than the reverse.

In contrast to the assumption that international institutions can contribute meaningfully to international order, the realist holds that the only restraint on power is countervailing power with world order a function of the successful operation of the balance of power.[31] Consequently, the function of world institutions is to help to stabilise the balance of power by facilitating adjustment without resort to violence.[32]

Even if one is sympathetic with this point of view, the United Nations has not performed well in this regard. Outside of the *ad hoc* peacekeeping ventures in the Congo, along the Gaza strip, and in Cyprus, the organisation has not been able to stabilise or facilitate the adjustment of power balances in other parts of the world, much less affect the dominant system of world bipolarity. The performance of international organisations even as ancillary mechanisms of order bears out the judgment of Geoffrey Goodwin who recognises that there is no guarantee that such institutions will encourage the orderly exercise of power by nation-States.[33]

In a recent review of the performance of the United Nations in the field of peace and security, Stanley Hoffmann offers the following pertinent assessment[34]: " The role played by the United Nations in legitimising the nation-State helps safeguard national independence and integrity, but it also perpetuates all the obstacles which the traditional state of nature has accumulated on the road to peace and co-operation. . . . One can conclude that while the United Nations has been a significant factor in establishing world order based on the nation-State . . . it has also perpetuated the drawbacks of sovereignty and bought moderation at the cost of making resort to limited or subliminal violence endemic and the recurrent explosions of unsolved disputes inevitable."

(c) The Systems Approach to World Order

While there is yet no systematic exposition of the systems approach to world order, the fragments of such an approach may be deduced from the work of a few scholars who utilise systems

[31] G. L. Goodwin, " World Institutions and World Order," in Carol Ann Cosgrove and K. J. Twitchett (eds.), *The New International Actors: The U.N. and the E.E.C.* (1970), p. 62.

[32] *Ibid.*

[33] *Ibid.*

[34] S. Hoffmann, " International Organization and the International System," XXIV *International Organization* Nr. 3 (1970), pp. 399–400.

analysis to study world order problems. Systems analysts explore the question of how the structure of international systems influence the intensity of inter-State conflict and how the nation-States in turn influence the structure of the system in which they coexist. Structure is usually defined in terms of the number of major Powers that is assumed to affect the stability or instability of the system, defined as its propensity for serious conflict. Raymond Aron, however, considers the factor of homogeneity or heterogeneity in the ideologies of the nation-States of equal importance as system structure, on the assumption that the former facilitates mutual adjustment of differences while the latter is more conducive to conflict.[35]

As an analytical tool for discerning the nature of world order, systems analysis has certain strengths and weaknesses. It does provide a useful conceptual framework for accommodating the main variables that influence the conditions of order in the international community: international law, international organisation, and the configuration of the balance of power. The principal weaknesses of systems analysis are that its insights are suggestive rather than definitive, its assumptions theoretical rather than strictly verifiable, and its conclusions often asserted with a finality that may not be warranted on the basis of whatever empirical evidence is presented.

Both the strengths and weaknesses of systems analysis are reflected in the work of Stanley Hoffmann whose contributions will now be analysed. His principal thesis is that security, satisfaction, and flexibility are the requirements for order in any political system.[36] Hoffmann differentiates moderate and revolutionary international systems whose features are determined by the extent to which the above requirements for order are satisfied. In moderate systems order is achieved because nation-States find it easier to attain security, satisfaction, and flexibility while revolutionary systems reflect a fundamental disorder because insecurity, dissatisfaction, and inflexibility characterise the relations of States.

International law is considered a dependent variable whose effectiveness as an ordering mechanism is determined by the type of international system. Thus, the reduced influence of international law in recent years is to be explained by the uncertainties and anxieties associated with the revolutionary system of bipolarity and ideological conflict established after 1945. The United Nations has likewise been adversely affected by the revolutionary character of the system.

[35] R. Aron, *Peace and War* (1966), pp. 99–100.
[36] Hoffmann, "International Systems and International Law," *op. cit.* in note 10 above, p. 212.

The implications of this approach to world order become fairly obvious and of some importance. The degree of order in international relations is not determined by the influence of international law and organisation but by the moderate or revolutionary character of international systems. What makes an international system moderate or revolutionary, however, is the character of the States that comprise it as will be described subsequently. Thus the attainment of order among States becomes a political rather than a legal or organisational problem. Hoffmann has effectively documented these generalisations by contrasting the relative tranquillity of the moderate international system of the 19th century with the disturbed state of international relations since 1945.

However, a principal limitation of his analysis cannot be ignored. Hoffmann overlooks the possibility that international systems may be a composite of both revolutionary and moderate elements. By neglecting this possibility, his analysis of systems is subject to a kind of static bias which fails to allow for changing patterns of international relations within primarily moderate or primarily revolutionary systems.

Hoffmann identifies the following characteristics of revolutionary systems: a wide scope of national objectives; predominance of international over domestic politics for the main actors; inflexibility of alignments; and the pursuit of foreign policy goals by immoderate means.[37] Such features correspond to the bipolar system existing in the period following the Second World War, at least until 1962 when the Cuba missile crisis inaugurated a new era of restraint in Soviet-United States relations. Moderate systems would be just the reverse. They would be characterised by the limited scope of State objectives, flexibility of alignments, greater saliency of domestic over international politics, and the employment of moderate means to achieve national goals. The 19th century international system fits easily into this pattern.

By 1968 Hoffmann had apparently recognised the possibility of an admixture of revolutionary and moderate elements in the same international system. This dualism was produced by the emergence of bipolar nuclear stalemate inducing restraint and caution in an otherwise revolutionary system. According to Hoffmann, the contemporary system has become relatively moderate with regard to both the means and ends of the foreign policies of the major Powers despite the impact of revolutionary changes in the course of its evolution.[38]

---

[37] S. Hoffmann, *Gulliver's Troubles, Or the Setting of American Foreign Policy* (1968), pp. 17–19.
[38] *Ibid.* pp. 20–21.

Insofar as the role of international organisation is concerned, Hoffmann applies systems analysis to explain the difficulties of the United Nations whose success as a moderating element was doomed by the nature of the revolutionary system in which it was obliged to function. Yet this does not imply that its fate will be any better in a moderate system because order depends primarily on a broad consensus among the members of such organisations on the utilisation of such institutions for the management of conflict.[39] Then, and only then, will organisations like the United Nations perform major roles as moderating instruments in world affairs. Unfortunately, the history of the United Nations is not encouraging in this respect because the major Powers have preferred to deal with major conflicts and tensions outside of the United Nations where they may have greater secrecy and flexibility in negotiating the settlement of differences.

The systems approach offers perhaps the most useful orientation for the analysis of world order because it encompasses a large number of variable factors that influence the degree of order in international relations. Such factors as the distribution of power, the existence of ideological convergences or divergences, the nature of weapons technology, and the character of the means and ends of foreign policy assist in our understanding of the causes of order and disorder in the international system. Useful though these variables are, they have not yet been formally interrelated in a model with more rigorous properties than system analysis has offered. There remains the difficult task of demonstrating theoretical relationships between the variables and how they may be made more precise through operationalisation.

Hoffmann's typology of revolutionary and moderate international system does offer a more fruitful explanatory device than the traditional disciplines of international law and organisation. Yet the delineation of such systems is left largely to the subjective predispositions of the observer which may or may not be congruent with international reality. Additionally, the possibility for mixed international systems is only barely allowed in connection with the present system. Assuming that it may be possible to identify empirically the elements that are moderate and those that are revolutionary, international systems may be mixed rather than uniform.

Consequently, it may be desirable to analyse the nature of world order from an empirical perspective in an effort to formulate more precise indicators of order and disorder in the international system.

---

[39] Hoffmann, " International Organization and the International System," *op. cit.* in note 34 above, p. 390.

As Beres suggests, there is a genuine need to apply empirical-scientific standards to the study of world order comparable to trends in other areas of political science.[40] Discussion about future world order systems is apt to be sterile and unrealistic without an understanding of the orderly and disorderly features of the contemporary international system. The concept of world order has been discussed primarily as normative theory, but empirical analysis has been lacking. If the vagueness and ambiguity that often characterise such discussion is to be reduced, then the concept must be operationalised as far as possible. Only then will it be possible to analyse intelligently the prospects for altering the present international system in the direction of centralisation proposed by some students of world order.

CONCLUSIONS

The preceding analysis has demonstrated the variety of definitions of the concept of world order. This is to be explained by the fact that order means different things to different observers. But it also reflects the fact that international lawyers and political scientists are divided on the relative importance of law and power as components of order. Following are a number of conclusions based on an investigation of the usage of the concept of world order:

(1) An overwhelming number of scholars identify world order with the future rather than the present on the assumption that the conditions of international life today are inadequate for the realisation of the requirements of an effective world order.

(2) When the concept of world order is used to refer to a future state of affairs, it is usually defined in terms of an ideal set of conditions including among others the minimisation of international violence, the establishment of world institutions to restrain and control violence, and the development of procedures to insure that disputes among nations will be resolved peacefully. These definitions stress the strengthening of the normative components of international law and organisation. Associated with this approach is the conviction that revolutionary changes in the international system have outstripped the capacity of the available procedures to maintain minimum public order.

(3) The systems approach to world order correlates order with the nature of the international system, especially with its revolutionary or moderate character. The system is the independent variable and international law and international organisation the

---

[40] L. R. Beres, " On Teaching about World Order: A Plea for Systematic Inquiry," Prepared for presentation at the annual convention of the International Studies Association, Dallas, Texas, March 14–18, 1972, p. 1.

dependent variables. This approach is similar to the law and organisation orientation in treating order in international relations as the minimisation of violent conflict among States. The most important fact that affects system stability is the balance of power. Where the balance is multipolar, a moderation in the means and ends of foreign policy behaviour is likely to exist and order predominate. System instability and system disorder are brought about by a bipolar structure in the balance of power characterised by the absence of moderation in pursuit of the means and ends of foreign policy. The principal weakness of the systems approach is the failure to recognise the possibility of a coexistence of revolutionary and moderate elements within the same international system.

(4) For the realist scholar world order is fundamentally a political problem rather than a legal or organisational one. Essentially, this means that the best way to secure order is through the balancing of military power rather than by means of international law or international organisation. Instead of condemning military power, the realist believes that it can contribute to the achievement of order through the " extension of relatively limited and informal reciprocal restraints rather than to the kind of legal and institutional reforms that have promoted order within states." [41] The difficulty with this view is that within a system of autonomous nation-States there is no secure guarantee that military power will be used responsibly to safeguard order or that military capabilities can be permanently stabilised in an equilibrium of power.

(5) All of the preceding approaches to the study of world order stress either the normative conditions necessary for its establishment or the creation of an international system conducive to orderly processes among nation-States. The analysis of the concept relies heavily on what ought to be rather than what is.

(6) Normative writers have been unable to resolve the dilemma between the assumed disorderly features of the present system and a more desirable centrally organised system of world order. They do not explain how the obstacles associated with a system of sovereign States may be overcome to create world structures that more logically conform to the needs of world society. The dialectical struggle between the Westphalian conception of order based upon the nation-State and the antithetical conception of an international community postulated by the United Nations Charter has not yet produced a new synthesis of centralised world order structures.

(7) This writer believes that there is an urgent need to reverse the prevailing normative approaches to the study of world order. Systematic empirical analysis of the kind of world order that

---

[41] R. Osgood and R. Tucker, *Force, Order, and Justice* (1967), p. 38.

presently exists is required to balance idealism with realism. More fundamentally, the concept of world order should be reconceptualised. Rather than conceptualisation in terms of ideal conditions that are unlikely to exist until or unless world government is achieved, we should accept the concept as a relative rather than absolute condition. We should recognise that the international system is a complex amalgam of orderly and disorderly elements and that the character or nature of order depends upon the relationship between these constantly changing elements instead of fixed conceptions of order.

CIVITAS MAXIMA?

By

GEORG SCHWARZENBERGER

This is the revised English version of a paper first published under the same title in German as *Heft 413/414* (1973) of the Series *Recht und Staat* by J. C. B. Mohr (Paul Siebeck) Tuebingen—*Managing Ed., Y.B.W.A.*

I—Attempt at an Empirical Synthesis

RESEARCH tends towards synthesis. Thus it is the primary object of this essay to attempt once again to explore the relations between world society, world law and world order and examine whether the results of more recent inter-disciplinary studies confirm earlier inquiries [1] or lead to new insights.

Moreover, since these earlier efforts, I have experimented with further techniques, such as the historical models of international law and the distinction between international law and international order. The time has now come to test the potential relevance of these tools for purposes of a synthesis of world affairs.

It is a by-product of such an empirical synopsis as is here attempted that it makes possible a critical analysis of more speculative—or intuitive—overall evaluations of international relations. Without adequate evidence, they can command no more acceptance than any other non-proven hypothesis. These *a priori* notions find their most extreme formulation in Christian von Wolff's tempting concept of *Civitas Maxima* and ethical postulates derived from it, such as the fundamental norm of international law proposed by Hersch Lauterpacht: *Voluntas civitatis maximae est servanda* (Let the will of the world community be done).

This critical function of the essay determines the title. The question mark emphasises that the—at least on the surface—rapidly changing character of our world environment calls for renewed analysis.

II—Society and Community Models

In spite of unavoidable possibilities of abuse, the distinction between *community* and *society* offers a useful starting point for inter-disciplinary studies in the field of international relations.

---

[1] See, for instance, *The Misery and Grandeur of International Law* (University College London, 1963) or *The Inductive Approach to International Law* (1964), p. 165 *et seq.*

As with other " pure " types of conceptual models, social reality does not know of any groups which wholly represent the extremes of an undiluted society or a pure community (in the former, relations based entirely on fear; in the latter, relations based entirely on love). All existing groups occupy positions intermediate between these two poles.

In the last resort, the distinction between society and community is based on different but typical patterns of behaviour of those involved. It is difficult to examine directly the reasons for anybody's behaviour. Thus, it is advisable to subject such motives to a test that makes possible an, at least relatively, objective verification and may claim respectable theological authority : " For the tree is known by his fruit " (Matthew 12 : 33). The consequences of actions and omissions are better guides to the society and community character of particular groups than unavoidably complex motives.

The differences between the two types of social relations are not absolute but relative. Awareness of the relativity of the difference between societies and communities leads to a further insight : a society can be transformed into a community, and the process can be reversed. Yet freedom of choice in either direction is limited, and possibilities vary from group to group and from one historical situation to another. Moreover, any person or group may be simultaneously involved in relations in either category.

The distinction between society and community is as fundamental for international relations as for any other branch of social studies. It facilitates the understanding of international relations as relations in concrete social environments. It provides models which are as relevant for the study of international law as of national law. It leads to a relativist approach to problems of international planning and permits a critical analysis of " committed " proposals for the improvement of world affairs.

Consciousness of the limited but always open choice between the organisation of international relations on a society or community basis has also another beneficial effect. It makes possible a sharp distinction between the treatment of the material chosen in this essay and " realist " analyses such as Kautilya's *Arthasastra*, Macchiavelli's *Il Principe* and Hitler's *Mein Kampf*.

III—WORLD COMMUNITY?

International relations of the past and present may differ in some respects. Yet they have one feature in common : the pivotal position of power.

The place of power is half-way between influence and force. Influence is exercised by persuasion. Force means physically enforced subordination of another's will. In contrast to influence and force, power involves the imposition of one's own will on a group or the will of one group on another, if possible without, but, if it cannot be helped, by the application of the minimum of necessary force.

On the basis of overwhelming historical material, it appears appropriate—until the contrary is proved—to understand international relations primarily as society relations and present them as, in essence, systems of open power politics or power politics in disguise.

The multitude of consecutive and overlapping international societies throughout the centuries has three characteristic features in common. The members of such international societies tend to regard their own groups as ends in themselves, and not merely as means to higher and overriding community ends. In the last resort, they consider themselves entitled to defend their existence by all means, including force. The hierarchy between the members of these societies is determined by their power, that is, ultimately, their relative strength in terms of political, economic or military conflict. These basic motivations lead to typical patterns of behaviour: self-defence (if not self-aggrandisement) as the first duty of the State; alliances; counter-alliances; balance of power systems; neutralisation; neutrality and armed conflict. In such an environment, morality and law may exist but play a merely subordinate role.

The international societies of the pre- and post-1815 periods differ in two respects: the latter are world societies and are at least partly organised.

Contemporary world society is the result of a threefold process: *disintegration* of the European Christian community (with all necessary reservations regarding States in which the greater part of the population were little more than serfs), *expansion* of this European society since the sixteenth century into a world society during the periods of colonialism and imperialism, and *concentration* of power in a decreasing number of great and world Powers.

From the middle of the nineteenth century onwards, this unorganised international society was transformed under the influence of liberalist, pacifist and nationalist movements. It became a partly-organised international society, endowed with weak administrative international unions and *ad hoc* arbitration tribunals.

The First World War led to renewed attempts to develop the pre-war system of open power politics into an organised community. The goal of a true world community was to be reached by the outlawry of war, disarmament, collective security, the pacific settlement of international disputes and orderly revision of dated or unjust international engagements. The Russian October Revolution of 1917 and the danger of Communist revolts in other countries suggested an additional international experiment in the administration of anodyne: the creation of an International Labour Organisation with distinct representation of employers' and workers' unions in national delegations.

The League of Nations failed to achieve the object of even relative universality, that is, an expansion of its membership to all States whose membership would have been indispensable for the successful achievement of its programme. At every critical point, decisive great and middle Powers remained outside or ceased to be members. Thus it was convenient, if superficial, to explain the failure of the League of Nations by its non-universality. It required the repetition of the League experiment in circumstances in which, from the outset, the world organisation of the United Nations had attained relative universality, to reveal the inadequacy of this analysis.

It then became evident that the reasons for the failures of both Organisations in the sphere that mattered most—prevention of international armed conflicts and maintenance of world peace— were more fundamental than the non-attainment of universality.

The precarious equilibrium between the world Powers which exists at present—in spite of an increasing number of small wars and internal armed conflicts that tend to spill over into international confrontations—rests on foundations other than the seven Principles " enshrined " in Article 2 of the United Nations Charter (sovereign equality; good faith; the pacific settlement of international disputes; prohibition of the threat and use of force; collective action; extension of these Principles of the Charter of the United Nations to non-members in the interest of international peace and security, and prohibition, in principle, of United Nations intervention in matters essentially within the domestic jurisdiction of any State).

IV—WORLD LAW?

The distinction between society and community yields three models of Law: the law of a society which, as for example in the basic regulation of property rights, serves the interest of ruling persons or groups (*Law of Power*); the law of a community which, as, for instance, the canon law of the Roman Catholic Church, serves the interests of the group as a whole and primarily fulfils the function of rationalising generally accepted patterns of behaviour (*Law of Co-ordination*), and the law of hybrids between societies and communities which, as, for instance, the Roman or English law of contract, is based on formal or substantive reciprocity (*Law of Reciprocity*).

It contributes to the understanding not only of International Law but also of its social environment to examine this legal system in its sociological, historical and ethical perspectives.

International Law in Sociological Perspective

The inductively verifiable rules of international *customary* law can be reduced to seven legal principles: Sovereignty, Recognition, Consent, Good Faith, Freedom of the Seas, International Responsibility, and Self-Defence. The criterion for selecting these legal principles is negative and hypothetical. If one or more of the potentially relevant groups of legal rules were excluded from such a presentation of international law, would this still permit international customary law to be fairly represented?

In the abstract, an international legal system based on rules under the above seven heads would be compatible with both an international society and an international community.

In an international *community*, such a legal system would tend to work almost automatically. The absence of a procedure for the impartial determination of the law in case of conflict could be compensated for by the willingness of those subject to the law to obey it. Given this basic attitude, there would be hardly any need for an independent procedure for the enforcement of the law. Similarly, changes in the law could be attained with the consent of all concerned.

In an international *society*, such a legal system would restrict but little the freedom of action of the players. Armaments, alliances, agreed neutralisations of territories in dispute, the acquisition of territory by cession, the creation of international protectorates and other relations of dependence, unilateral incorporation of countries not recognised as subjects of international law, and resort to force in case of real or alleged self-defence would be possible within, and despite, the existence of such a legal system.

In fields which are peripheral from the point of view of power politics, it is possible to establish legal relations of a primarily consensual character on the basis of formal or substantive reciprocity. Diplomatic relations or co-operation in the spheres of economics and communication illustrate this point. In such relations it is also possible to sublimate sanctions of power into mutual interest in the fulfilment of one's own legal obligations.

By and large, this description of a society type of international law is probably a correct sketch of international law during the period between the Napoleonic Wars and the First World War. For the sake of completeness, it would be necessary to supplement the description by reference to the partial organisation of this international society through optional international institutions. Administrative international unions and the list of arbitrators of the Permanent Court of Arbitration which is neither permanent nor a Court, belong to this category.

In the League of Nations and the United Nations with its Specialised Agencies, this partially organised international society was transformed into organised world societies within the frameworks of loose world confederations. This was done in ways which permitted and permit all participants, with little hindrance, to continue the game of power politics.

At first sight, decolonisation and admission to the United Nations as " sovereign and equal " States of a multitude of politically and economically unstable and militarily, at most, marginally relevant States, appear to be notable counter-tendencies. They seem to point to a basic transformation of organised world society into an organised world community. Actually, these apparently novel features are probably more symptomatic of another change: the decline of salt-water empires in favour of geographically contiguous macro-political and macro-economic systems such as the United States of America, the Soviet Union, China, and, possibly, Western Europe, and of the atomisation of power in the areas between these centres of power.

In subordinate fields, systems of power politics in disguise entail changes in the superstructures of existing world society. Decisions against one of the world Powers or middle Powers by verbose majorities in organs such as the General Assembly and the Security Council of the United Nations—not to speak of the United Nations Conference on Trade and Development—are part of the game and are normally accepted by the losers with more or less good grace.

On this basis, it is also possible to pass off community versions of international morality as, for instance, the principle of national self-determination as a moral and legal principle of the organised world " community." By repetition of such claims in a mounting heap of resolutions, it may even be attempted to describe such postulates as a dynamically developing law of the United Nations.

If needs be, it is simple enough to switch back from such consensual arrangements to the level of power politics without any disguise. In matters other than those of a purely internal and especially organisational character, most of these international organisations are limited to the task of making recommendations. They are not allowed to make binding decisions.

In cases in which, for example, under Chapter Seven of the Charter of the United Nations, organs such as the Security Council are competent to make binding decisions, the world and great

Powers of 1945 have safeguarded themselves by the reserve right of an absolute veto against unacceptable majority decisions. Similarly, they control at least negatively the admission and expulsion of member States, the election of the Secretary-General and alterations in the Charter of the United Nations.

With few exceptions such as the functional representation of employers and workers and the freedom of voting of delegates in the International Labour Organisation, delegates in the organs of the United Nations and its Specialised Agencies are government representatives in the strict sense. Thus, normally, neither the United Nations nor its Specialised Agencies may establish official contacts, without permission from the central governments of member States, with subordinate governmental or administrative organs of such States, nor give instructions to individuals in member States. In these ways, the confederate world societies established since the First World War distinguish themselves from federations, which represent the weakest form of central government in the accepted meaning of the term.

The age of decolonisation and anti-imperialism favours also other significant types and legal forms of power politics in disguise. The techniques of hegemony, that is, the guidance of equals in law by leading Powers—first described by Thucydides—are refined in confederations of the League of Nations and United Nations type. Yet they are hardly less real than in systems of open power politics. Spheres of influence of the world Powers replace direct colonial control. Association agreements, such as those of the European Economic Community with the Mediterranean and African hinterland of the European Economic Community, are the West European variants of attempts to create macro-economic preference areas which are comparable to the internal markets of the United States of America, the Soviet Union and China.

Finally, it is necessary to recall the right of withdrawal from these confederate organisations and escape clauses in their constitutions, such as Article 51 of the United Nations Charter. Under this Article, members remain entitled to take all measures they consider necessary for purposes of self-defence or collective defence against armed attack. Provisionally, each member State itself decides on what falls under this rubric and may continue with its unilateral action until the Security Council finds otherwise. If a decision under Chapter Seven of the Charter of the United Nations concerns a permanent member of the Security Council, such a State need not abstain from voting but may itself veto the decision. If it does not belong to the exclusive category of permanent members of the

United Nations, it has to rely on a friendly or hegemonial Power in this most favoured class.

On a world scale, the international law of power politics in disguise distinguishes itself from the international law of open power politics less by its greater efficiency than by the additional opportunities it offers for ideological abuses. Conventions such as the Genocide Convention of 1948, the Convention of 1965 on the Elimination of all Racial Discriminations and the United Nations Covenants of 1966 on Civil and Political Rights and on Economic, Social and Cultural Rights are model illustrations of conventions which in many words say remarkably little. Even in relation to Contracting Parties, the exceptions and reservations are more important than the principles embodied in these conventions.

International Law in Historical Perspective

World history offers an abundance of material which suggests the interpretation of international relations as society relations and the classification of their correlated systems of international law in terms of society law. Conversely, any attempt to present such relations in terms of community relations and community law would be difficult to justify.

The basic historical hypotheses of these systems of international law are of dramatic and traumatic simplicity: non-peace as the normal state of affairs, rightlessness of foreigners and anarchy on the high seas. From these inauspicious beginnings developed the systems of international law of the past and present.

It makes little difference whether one investigates the international relations in the eastern Mediterranean at the times of Ramesses II or the compilation of the Old Testament; in East Asia, Europe and Asia Minor at the time of the Roman-Carthaginian rivalry, the Persian-Byzantine co-existence, the Christian-Islamic confrontation or any subsequent period. At any of these times, relations were governed decisively by power politics, with occasional excursions into power politics in disguise as with the Treaty of Eternal Peace and Alliance between Ramesses II of Egypt and King Hattusilis III of Hatti (1270–1269 B.C.) or the Treaties of Eternal Peace of A.D. 532 and 562 between the Byzantine and Persian Empires.

The relevant international law material confirms the working hypothesis of international law as, predominantly, a law of power and reciprocity in such systems of power politics. It also reflects clearly the society character of its political environment.

There is little evidence in practice of continuity between the international law of Antiquity and the present. It is, however, true that, with remarkable consistency, power politicians have again and again relied on types of international law that have altered but little in essentials during three millennia.

The results of such a comparative history of international law can be summarised in five models:

(1) *The Model of Omnipotence.* The object of omnipotence can be attained on a *de facto* basis. It may lead to a universal State or situation in which a " Middle " Kingdom such as China or a " world " empire such as the Roman Empire subjectively views itself in this light, while actually two or more of such empires co-exist side by side.

In such situations, international law tends to sink to the level of external public law as happened in the case of *jus fetiale* in Roman Law. It is only in exceptional cases, as with the treaties between Rome and Carthage, that the assumption of at least some embryonic rules of international law on a basis of legal equality between the contracting parties is made.

(2) *The jus strictum Model.* This model presupposes the co-existence of at least two entities neither of which is prepared to subordinate itself to the other. They may co-exist on a footing of *de facto* peace or war, or they may decide to recognise each other as sovereign and equal Powers.

The relations between England and Scotland before and after the recognition of Scotland in 1328 as an independent kingdom illustrate this model. It presupposes three legal rules:

First: A claim to territorial sovereignty must be founded on a State territory that is fixed in its essentials, and non-subjection of this territorial supremacy to the superior authority of any other sovereign.

Secondly: recognition of this situation may be demanded from other sovereigns, but the grant of such a request lies in their absolute discretion.

Thirdly: the request for such recognition presupposes at least tacit recognition of the unit from which recognition as a sovereign entity is demanded.

In the case of consensual obligations such as truces or armistices, good faith has, in case of doubt, merely its minimum content, that is, the exclusion of bad faith or deceit. At least in embryonic form, this model also presupposes legal rules on the consequences of the breach of legal obligations or, as an alternative, the relapse into a prelegal state of anarchy, the possibility of a state of war or the admissibility of the application of limited force by way of reprisals.

(3) *The jus aequum Model.* This model is characterised by good faith in the positive sense as *jus aequum*, especially in consensual relations. In other words, the rights and duties of the parties are to be exercised reasonably and equitably. This model may exist side by side with, or as a development of, the *jus strictum* model.

Especially between allies, the *jus aequum* model has been used since the dawn of history. Thus, the above mentioned Treaty between Egypt and Hatti was the result of a state of equilibrium between two of the great Powers in a triangular relation with Assyria, in which each of them was more afraid of the rising military power of Assyria than of the other contracting party. On this basis, the two hegemonial Powers found it possible to conclude a comprehensive treaty of peace and alliance with far-reaching reciprocal obligations and, in addition to the invocation of a thousand gods on either side as witnesses of the Treaty, to rely on the sanctions automatically built into such relations, that is, the loss of agreed and cherished rights.

The *jus aequum* model presupposes at least two legal rules beyond those of *jus strictum*:

First, the contracting parties regard all their consensual obligations as legally binding.

Secondly, they accept that the breach of any treaty obligation creates the duty to make reparation for such an illegal act.

(4) *The Oceanic Model.* With the exception of rules of contemporary international law which fall under the headings of the principles of the freedom of the seas and self-defence, the *jus aequum* model presupposes or contains all the key-rules of existing international customary law. The special characteristics of the legal rules which relate to the high seas—over two-thirds of the surface of the globe—justify the presentation of contemporary international customary law in a model of its own: the oceanic model.

(5) *The Unionist Model.* This model exists in four chief variants: hegemonial, confederate, federal and unitary sub-models. As this model makes it possible, on a consensual basis, to transform an eristic international society into an international community, it deserves to be treated as a model of its own. In Hegel's terminology, at this point quantity changes into quality.

The *hegemonial* sub-model is illustrated by the vassal treaties between the Hittite Great Kings and their little kings, the hegemonial treaties of the Greek city States with Athens or Sparta, the Roman *foedus iniquum*, the Anglo-Scots Treaty of 1174 and Prussian pre-eminence in Bismarck's German Empire.

The *confederate* sub-model exists on a treaty basis in the China

of the seventh century B.C., the Confederation of the Iroquois tribes
of 1675, the final period of the Holy Roman Empire since 1648,
the Germanic Confederation of 1815 and, on a universalist footing,
the League of Nations and the United Nations.

The *federal* sub-model has two variants of its own: that of
political federation such as the foundation treaties of the German
Empire of 1871 and the experiments with functional federalism in
the three European Communities of 1952 and 1957.

The *unitary* sub-model is exemplified on a treaty basis by *deditio*
in the law of the Roman Republic and the Union of 1707 of England
and Wales with Scotland.

International Law in Ethical Perspective

Already Plato explained the need for the existence of law side
by side with morality. Only if all of us were prepared at all times
to do everything we recognised to be right, would the need cease
for law, in addition to morality.

What is " right " depends more on the social environment of
morality and law than on either of these normative systems. There
are society ethics, such as Spinoza's proposition of *homo homini
lupus* in an unorganised society, and community ethics, such as
Christian von Wolff's postulate of the weal of the community as
the supreme " law " of his *Civitas maxima.*

In the form of the minimum standards of civilisation, pre-1914
international customary law incorporated such community values
in three fields: the limitation of recognition in State practice to
candidates which recognising States, rightly or wrongly, regarded
as being civilised; a minimum standard, observance of which, at
least in relation to foreign nationals, could be expected from civilised
States, and the laws of war applicable between civilised States.

In Article 38 of the Statute of the Permanent Court of International Justice of the League of Nations and the International
Court of Justice of the United Nations, the general principles of
law recognised by civilised nations are enumerated—after international treaties and general international customary law—as the
third of the law-creating processes of contemporary international
law.

It is legitimate to introduce norms of society or community ethics
into international law by one of the three above-mentioned law-
creating processes. Thus, for instance, the rules governing the
principle of good faith in the meaning of *jus aequum* have been
received into international customary law.

Attempts to smuggle rules of any system of morality into international law irrespective of such transformation constitute pre-

tensions which must be rejected. If such alleged rules of pseudo-international law fulfil the function of supporting an existing *status quo*, they are typical illustrations of a conservative natural law. In the reverse case, they fulfil corresponding functions of a revolutionary natural law.

In all cases in which the reception of ethical norms by international law cannot be inductively verified, such meta-legal norms remain what they are: self-cancelling postulates of society and community morality or self-neutralising natural-law ideologies and utopias.

In this context, the term " Common Law of Mankind " also deserves attention. By addressing the human substratum of national and international groups at large, proponents of this concept are able to skirt round any analysis of the actual international environment in which this Common Law is supposed to apply. Moreover, whenever it suits them, they can argue that this environment is, or ought to be, viewed as an international community in the technical sense. It then takes but one further step to indulge in any natural-law phantasies that, according to personal predilection, may be termed creative, imaginative or, perhaps more accurately, speculative or messianic.

V—WORLD ORDER?

The need for the distinction between law and order can be readily demonstrated by reference to the conquest pattern of the rise of the territorial State.

If an armed group establishes itself in a country and subjects the local population to its sway, such an order of force may dispense with law altogether. The conquerors may, however, prefer to organise the territory in question by means of schools, churches, administrative services and judicial institutions.

In such cases, as, for example, the Norman conquest of England or the establishment of a colonial régime overland or overseas, the law serves primarily the interests of the conquerors. If necessary, this law of power receives the requisite support from the background apparatus of overwhelming physical force in the shape of police forces, militias and armed services.

Analogous situations exist in totalitarian and authoritarian legal systems in relation to suppressed or outlawed groups. The treatment of Jews, gypsies or other " sub-human " beings in the Third Reich illustrates this proposition.

The more a legal system falls into the category of community law, the less need exists for the distinction between law and the factual order sustaining it. It may even happen that this factual order is fully integrated in the community law and subject to its control.

In other words, the more a legal system has the character of a society law, the more apparent are the functions of the dualism of order and law. There is a good reason for this. A law of power enjoys greater social prestige than a mere order of force. Without decisively altering the substance of such an order, the law of power contributes to at least some legitimation of the factual order of force that supports it.

In international societies based on power, territorial States have proved themselves to be the strongest units. By mutual recognition as sovereign States, these associations create for their own benefit normative legitimations of their monopolistic claims inside their territories. By co-operation with each other, they can control more effectively than would otherwise be possible horizontal cross-sections of an economic character, such as international and multinational companies and secure their territorial supremacy against such intruders and competitors.

The international *de facto* order of a system of open power politics is as precarious or stable as the equilibrium between the major Powers of any age. Yet, so far, any system of open power politics has ended in a major war. Thus these systems are less orders of peace than inter-war orders. It is therefore more accurate to describe them as international quasi-orders, rather than international orders with implied claims to an effectiveness they evidently lack.

The League of Nations period of world power politics in disguise proved that, in this respect, the confederate world society of the period between the First and Second World Wars differed but little from the preceding inter-war periods.

Bearing in mind the structural similarities between the League of Nations and the United Nations, and the experiences gained with the United Nations in action, it is advisable, until convincing proof to the contrary is furnished, to view also this confederate super-structure as merely an international quasi-order. It is precariously poised on the ever-changing equilibrium between the nuclear Powers, that is, the " overkill " capacity of two—and sooner or later, three or more—super-Powers. Between these agglomerations lie large military in-between spaces, occasionally misdescribed as the Third World. Here world Powers and middle Powers manoeuvre with and against one another.

On the propagandist plane, it pays even the world Powers to leave at least one illusion to the international proletariat of small States: their feeling of importance in the United Nations and its Specialised Agencies. In any case, the treatment as sovereign and equal members given in these organisations to the serried ranks of small and minute States at least helps to boost their self-respect.

Within the frameworks of such quasi-orders, the laws of un-organised, partly-organised and confederate international societies fulfil functions of their own. It is their task to legitimise such quasi-orders in a manner comparable to the law of power within the State.

In fields of reciprocity which, from the point of view of power politics, are peripheral, international law is even permitted to fulfil other than purely ideological functions. The same is true of relations between Powers whose equality of strength neutralises the back-ground threats of power politics.

This is even truer in exceptional situations as, for instance, when an international organisation for the care of earthquake victims is established. So long as a natural catastrophe takes place in time of peace and does not become an act of divine providence in time of war, the humanitarian altruism displayed in such contingencies is genuine enough. In such fleeting moments it is no illusion that an international law of co-ordination actually operates and fulfils its purported functions.

VI—Diagnoses, Remedies and Prognoses

Attempts at making articulate medium- and long-range trends and evaluating critically diagnoses, remedies and prognoses of others are open to three serious objections: the difficulty, if not the im-possibility, of making any value-judgments with more than a claim to relative objectivity; the need to answer questions in fields of which, the more remote they are from personal specialisation, any observer knows less than is desirable, and the inevitability of generalisations that are difficult to verify rationally.

To aim at perfectionism in these respects would be equivalent to renunciation altogether of such inter-disciplinary endeavours. It appears preferable to point out the risks of experiments of this type in a spirit of becoming self-criticism, but to undertake them in full awareness of these pitfalls.

Such investigations are needed for an additional reason. Any examination, however casual, of the literature of international law and relations yields an astounding harvest of subconscious or half-conscious value-judgments, made by academic writers. More or less charitably, these can be described as declarations of faith, ideologies or illusions. Yet they are hardly verifiable or better—with Karl Popper—falsifiable.

In this situation it appears to be the lesser evil neither to relapse into pre-scientific attitudes of unchecked value-judgments nor to take up a purely negative attitude of purist self-denial towards all value-judgments. There is an alternative that is probably preferable. It consists of undertaking such work in a manner that permits the reader the maximum of rational control and the opportunity to dissent, for reasons of his own, from any evaluation offered or to accept, with or without reservations, any diagnoses, remedies and prognoses suggested.

In this context, it becomes even worthwhile to examine critically past and present blueprints for international organisation the location of which may be considered to be left (or right) of reason (Lenin). The value of such schemes lies not so much in their positive contents as in the complementary analyses they suggest: Are such proposals utopias or ideologies in the technical meanings given to these terms by Karl Mannheim? In the former case, their realisation would presuppose a fundamental change, for instance, in contemporary world society. In the latter, such proposals are likely to serve on the international plane the purpose of hiding basic shortcomings of any existing *status quo* or of attempting to obtain tactical advantages in yet another exercise in one-upmanship.

The proposition that schemes for instant and complete disarmament or " world peace through world law," are utopian within the existing world system does not imply any negative judgment. Within the French feudal system, the slogans of the bourgeois revolutionaries of the 18th century were utopian. Yet the social and political Revolution of 1789 made them realities. Conversely, the bourgeois counter-revolution against Jacobinism reduced the social-revolutionary utopias of freedom, equality and fraternity to ideological covers of the newly-created bourgeois society in France.

Finally, it is necessary to underline yet more strongly the difference between the ideas advanced in this essay and the so-called realistic treatment of international relations. It consists of the awareness which academic exercises in *Realpolitik* appear to lack that there is an ever-present possibility of transforming personal and group relations from society relations into community relations, and to reverse this process. What was and what is need not so remain.

It is possible to put a higher value on community relations than society relations as, for ultimately metaphysical reasons, the writer does. Anybody who shares this attitude will be inclined to speak of the danger of a degeneration of a community into a society and, in case of doubt, react positively to opportunities of transforming society relations into community relations.

If such an attitude is to be more than unworldly idealism, it is not enough to realise that one has the choice of basing any social relation on a society or community footing. It is important to know that this freedom of choice is greater in small than in big groups and easier to attain in personal than in impersonal relations.

The more firmly any particular social system is established the more difficult it is to change its fundamental character. In such cases, even the strongest players have but a limited and, from the higher to the lower ranks of this power hierarchy, decreasing freedom of choice.

Moreover, irrespective of the degree of freedom of choice, the more fundamental and thorough a change is, the higher are its costs.

Decisive Realities

What, in a concrete historical situation, are realities, that is, circumstances that have to be taken into account—and even more so, what are decisive realities—depends on value-judgments on which wide disagreement is possible.

Perhaps the best attitude to value-judgments of others is to reflect on how often anybody who has to make judgments of his own has been wrong himself in his own past evaluations of situations and people. It is also rewarding to re-examine the writings of past decades from the point of view of how far the hypotheses, diagnoses and prognoses of distinguished authors of their times were confirmed or refuted by subsequent developments, and reflect on the difference if any which the implementation of their brain waves would have made.

In full awareness of these hard tests, a diagnosis of existing world society in fifteen guide-lines is offered:

(1) The doubling of world population within the next 25 years from three thousand million to six thousand million, especially in the world's poorest quarters, is likely.

(2) Continuation of the spoliation of the environment by *homo habilis*, who hardly deserves to be termed *homo sapiens*, is more probable than commensurate but expensive limitations of the present excessive exploitation of nature.

(3) In technologically developed countries with capitalist or State capitalist—frequently misdescribed as socialist or communist—forms of economic organisation, destructive tendencies towards ethical *laissez-faire* and nihilism are apparent. They favour anarchist threats to the State monopoly of legitimate force (Max Weber) and extreme —and probably more successful—authoritarian and totalitarian counter-reactions.

(4) This state has already been reached in most of the poor countries whose leading groups do not see any alternative but military or other one-party systems to maintain their privileged

positions. The growing abyss between the standards of living of the technologically advanced nations and the proletariat of the poor countries, which, especially in the countryside, tend to develop backwards rather than forwards, accentuates these difficulties.

(5) The tendencies noted under (3) and (4) strengthen the general trend of a relapse of world civilisation into a mechanical and materialist type of neo-barbarism with atavistic tribal and racial ideologies.

(6) In States which owe their independence to the process of decolonisation, a neo-colonialism by detribalised urban politicians or leading tribes towards minorities is developing.

(7) The reintegration of the poor countries in the hierarchy of world society within the framework of the United Nations and other international institutions takes place in varying ways: competitive " development " or corruption aid, military alliances, treaties of friendship and association agreements with individual hegemonial Powers or behind the façades of sectional blocs.

(8) These blocs are organised around hegemonial Powers and serve to create political, economic or military macro-spaces.

(9) Contiguous macro-spaces are symptomatic for the present phase of an accelerating concentration of power in few world Powers and a greater number of middle Powers. They are more significant than the counter-tendencies towards the atomisation and sublimation of the power of former overseas empires.

(10) The neutralism of small countries outside these blocs is little more than an ideology of middle and small States which find it increasingly difficult to convince themselves and others of the reality of their claims to leadership outside international organisations such as the United Nations and its Specialised Agencies.

(11) The state of armaments remains the most reliable barometer of international relations. Irrespective of whether absolute or relative standards are applied, the armaments of all States, and especially the super-Powers, have reached a cosmic scale. More convincingly than all protestations to the contrary, they demonstrate the strength of fear as the decisive motivation of international behaviour. This basic motivation has stamped international relations of the past and present as society relations which, essentially, are based on power.

(12) The existing world peace—in the sense of non-war—between the leading nations does not rest on the United Nations and its Specialised Agencies but on the background threat of nuclear

co-extermination of the world Powers and the ruin of the rest of the world.

(13) The instability of this state of society peace which has already lasted longer than the whole inter-war period between the First and Second World Wars, is aggravated by three factors: the fallibility of little men in high positions in front of coloured telephones and nuclear push buttons, perhaps even under the influence of potent drugs; the possibility of action based on false or falsely-interpreted information, and the growing danger that expanding nuclear conflicts will be triggered off by the increasing number of States with primitive nuclear equipment.

(14) Legal, moral and institutional superstructures of this world system of power politics in disguise offer opportunities for regular co-operation and manoeuvres by the Powers against one another on planes of sublimated power politics, with occasional excursions into genuine community politics, such as the United Nations Children's Fund.

(15) The analysis of multilateral treaties, " adopted " by international organisations—that is proposed for acceptance by them to their member States and others—provides reliable evidence of the significance of treaties such as the Genocide Convention or Human Rights Covenants of the United Nations. After the identification of the contracting parties, it still remains advisable to begin such investigations with a study of the reservations, contracting out provisions and exception clauses. Only then is it worthwhile analysing, if with becoming scepticism, the blaze of principles enunciated in the Preambles and chief articles of such humanitarian endeavours.

Ideologies, Utopias and Possibilities

What matters least in a sociological study of the successes and failures of a charitable organisation are the intentions of the operators. They can be taken for granted but, the Day of Judgment apart, are irrelevant. What matters is the help actually given, and the positive and negative effects of these efforts. The same applies to the ideologies and utopias of contemporary world society, offered in remarkable profusion.

Seven types of such efforts may be singled out from others:

(1) *Protection of Human Rights by International Law.* In international customary law, the legal personality of an entity depends on its recognition as a full or limited subject of international law by existing subjects of international law. In each case, the positive or negative answer to this question is not a dogmatic affirmation of faith but a question of evidence.

During the Second World War, it became evident that the Powers likely to be victorious were not prepared to subject themselves or, as after the First World War, some of their lesser allies to any international protection of minorities. Nor were the States subsequently created any more willing to accept comparable limitations of their newly acquired sovereignty.

Thus, the counsellors and spokesmen of minorities attempted to achieve the same end in more circuitous ways. If the protection of minorities was to be extended to all human beings, there would be no ethnic, linguistic, religious or other minority left that would not profit from such a generalisation of minorities protection. The international protection of human rights constituted a possible solution of an otherwise insoluble problem.

This argument was combined with a further thesis that was pressed for what it was worth and more: the individual as the direct bearer of rights and duties or, if not of rights, then at least of duties under international law. If accepted, this doctrine, which it would be hard to substantiate in international customary law, would have a desirable side effect. It would strengthen the claims for the automatic protection of human rights by international law beyond what was attained long ago by the protection of the minimum standards to be observed towards foreign nationals.

The heterogeneous character of the United Nations presents a major obstacle to the automatic protection of human rights by this world organisation. The United Nations must treat democratic States (in the Western sense), authoritarian States and totalitarian States on a footing of complete equality. Thus, it can hardly insist on maintaining that the denial of even the most primitive human rights by any member State to any of its subjects is incompatible with membership. This explains why, in the Charter of the United Nations, objects such as the protection of human rights have been formulated so as not to create any legal obligations that are automatically binding on member States.

This dilemma became evident in the discussions and vote on the Declaration of Human Rights, adopted unanimously in 1948 by the General Assembly of the United Nations. So long as it was clear that the Declaration was not legally binding but was merely standard-setting and limited to moral goal-values, members vied with one another in the widest possible formulation of these moral rules. Yet, when the United Nations began to formulate legally binding covenants in these fields, this became a protracted business, and every member State took it for granted that it would not be bound automatically by any of these Covenants. Moreover, the human rights to be protected were subjected to a rapid process of shrinkage and far-reaching exception clauses, such as the legality of discrimination against non-nationals. Finally, potential contracting parties were granted the widest immunity from any verification by impartial organs of compliance with their obligations under the Human Rights Covenants.

In spite of all these concessions to national sovereignty, neither of the two International Covenants on Human Rights of 1966 has, as yet, entered into force.

The typical behaviour of States on the universalist level of the United Nations in drafting conventions of this type is also demonstrated by the treatment of genocide in the post-1945 period. In the London War Crimes Charter of 1945, the punishment of crimes against humanity was limited to crimes which were connected with the preparation and conduct of the Second World War. In the Genocide Convention of 1948, genocide was limited to acts, committed with *intent* to achieve the destruction of national, ethnic, racial or religious groups. As an alternative to an international criminal tribunal, as yet not created, criminal proceedings against persons accused of such crimes are left to the courts of the country whose government or executive organs have ordered or carried out such mass murder. The chief effect of the Convention has been to make genocide a favoured invective for charging other States with unproven acts in a semi-legal terminology.

In the relations between States which have more ethical values in common than is the case on a global level, Conventions such as the European Convention on Human Rights of 1950 and its supplementary Protocols fulfil a more positive task. They contribute to the further integration of such sectional groupings and the creation of a common law, based on treaties and the practice of quasi-judicial and judicial organs.

(2) *Transnational Law.* Especially in the United States of America, the term *Transnational Law*, invented by Philip Jessup, has found a positive response. It is intended to describe legal relations which neither international nor national law is supposed to cover adequately.

In existing law, the purely negative character of this term limits its uses to systematic purposes. Even so, its existence encourages naturalist abuses: the deduction " from the nature of things " of legal rules which presuppose an inarticulate social environment of a community character and whose nourishing ground is usually one of the few systems of national law known to any particular transnational lawyer.

Related to these types of law-making under the counter are attempts to build a *Commercial Law of Nations* on general principles of law recognised by civilised nations. In such efforts, the operative incentive tends to be that of " finding " additional " transnational " legal rules for the protection of private property.

Actually, failures to achieve this object by way of multilateral conventions which proved unacceptable to capital-importing States might have suggested a different approach. It would probably have been academically less controversial and of greater assistance to private investors.

What is necessary is to face the unpalatable character of the prospects for private investments in poor countries. In contemporary world society, the export of private capital to countries other than the technologically most highly developed capitalist States or countries under their political or military control can be little more than lottery investments.

(3) *International Jus Cogens.* The international customary law of unorganised international society does not know of any *jus cogens.* The reason for this lies in the character of this type of international society. It lacks an order comparable to that of the State. Thus, there is little point in distinguishing between law that may be changed by agreement between the parties (*jus dispositivum*) and peremptory law that may not be so changed (*jus cogens*).

International systems of power politics have, at the most, quasi-orders of their own. This means a merely factual relation between the existence of such quasi-orders and the treaties strengthening and developing these systems. In case of doubt, the overthrow of any such political system also puts an end to the basic political treaties sustaining it.

On a consensual basis, subjects of international law may create as much *jus cogens* as they desire. Yet, such consensual *jus cogens* does not impose any legal obligations on third States. What is true is that the greater the number of parties to a treaty, the more difficult it is in fact to alter such consensual *jus cogens.* The seven Principles embodied in Article 2 of the Charter of the United Nations belong to this category.

The International Law Commission of the United Nations and the Vienna Diplomatic Conference of 1968–1969 incorporated the concept of international *jus cogens* in the 1969 Convention on the Law of Treaties. Yet neither the International Commission of the United Nations nor the Vienna Conference could agree on any binding list of rules of international customary law that were supposed to constitute *jus cogens.*

The fact that the concept of *jus cogens* has been embodied in the 1969 Convention is occasionally treated as a sufficient substitute for concrete evidence of the existence of *jus cogens* in international

customary law. The further difficulty that the Convention is not yet
in force is pushed aside with an assertion of similar evidential
cogency: that, at least on the issue of *jus cogens,* the Convention
is but declaratory of existing international law.

What makes the terminology of *jus cogens* politically attractive
are the opportunities it offers for purposes of ideological abuse.
Thus, already before 1939, the term was employed with the object
of discrediting the Peace Treaties of 1919–1920, and it is again
available for similar purposes.

Jus cogens also offers a welcome device to escape from burden-
some treaty obligations on the assertion of their incompatibility
with an alleged rule of a peremptory character. The "supreme
international interest" in the form of an asserted rule of international *jus cogens* also conveniently permits interference with
treaty relations between third parties.

(4) *International Criminal Law.* International customary law
knows as little of International Criminal Law as it does of rules
of *jus cogens* which are comparable to those of a national *ordre
public* or *public policy.* The reason is the same: in a world confederation, an overriding public order corresponding to those of
national orders is lacking, as are international organs with automatic
jurisdiction to apply and enforce such peremptory legal rules.

Apparent exceptions confirm the rule. The punishment of pirates
and war criminals constitutes the exercise of an extraordinary
national jurisdiction by States, in circumstances authorised by international customary law. A pirate ship which, at one time, may have
been entitled to fly a national flag loses this privilege when she
becomes a pirate ship. It may also be that such a ship was never
under the jurisdiction of any subject of international law. Thus, in
neither case, is there any State which is entitled to protest against
the application of the national law of another State against the
pirate ship or her crew.

Similarly, under international customary law, a belligerent or
neutral Power may not claim that the rules of the Law of Armed
Conflict which apply to prisoners of war are automatically extended
to war criminals. These rules exist for the protection of prisoners
who are entitled to carry arms and themselves observe the rules of
the Law of Armed Conflict. The laws and customs of war contain
but a single, and this merely an apparent, exception to this rule.
In trials of alleged war criminals and spies, belligerents must
observe minimum standards applicable in favour of any offender.
For instance, the accused must have a fair trial and must not be
subjected to any barbaric punishment.

Rules on the jurisdiction of national organs to apply internationally authorised—or, on a consensual basis, internationally prescribed—national criminal law are international criminal law in a but limited meaning of the term. The same applies to mutual assistance given to each other by State organs in proceedings leading to the extradition of accused or convicted persons.

On the confederate level, more far-reaching attempts to create international criminal organs have remained in the limbo of draft conventions. Even so, like other proposals for reform which go beyond whatever happens to be the degree of international integration feasible at any time on a global scale, such drafts have a symptomatic relevance. They stimulate reflection on the reasons why, at this particular phase of the evolution of world society, they are condemned to the shadowy existence of ideologies or utopias.

(5) *International Parliamentary Diplomacy.* Several features of contemporary international institutions prompt sanguine conclusions on the character and functions of these consensual superstructures. Among them may be enumerated the multitude of international institutions with organs in which all member States are represented; the wide scope of their jurisdiction; the length of their public sessions; the possibility offered by debates on procedure and other comparable exercises; the inundation of delegations with relevant and irrelevant material; the self-propagation of committees and sub-committees; the ministrations of international and national civil servants to the members of delegations and the contact with accredited correspondents of the world press and other mass media. The plethora of these activities, coupled with the needs of all concerned to convince themselves and others of their own relevance, can easily create the impression of a new phenomenon in the making: democratic and quasi-parliamentary forms of international diplomacy.

If, in addition, in exceptional cases such as that of the General Conference of the International Labour Organisation, at least half of the national delegations are nominated by their governments on the recommendation of the sectional interests concerned and, in voting, national delegates are free from government instructions, the illusion of international democracy in action is further strengthened. For reasons of formal universality and international *camaraderie,* it is also charitably overlooked that, in the United Nations and its Specialised Agencies, the majority of the delegates who are supposed to practise international parliamentary democracy represent authoritarian or totalitarian régimes.

Moreover, it appears far-fetched to apply the analogy of parliamentary representation to organs which, on almost all matters of substance, are limited to advisory functions but lack decision-making powers.

As with other ideologies and utopias discussed and to be discussed, this terminology has its dangers. It contributes to the mollification of a typical system of power politics in disguise and diverts attention from the constitutional weaknesses of its confederate superstructures.

(6) *International Functionalism.* As far back as the second half of the nineteenth century, the founders of the International and, subsequently, Universal Postal Union had a splendid idea. They realised that if the whole world could be organised as a uniform postal territory, this would assure the best postal services.

To everybody's benefit, this was done. Why should this experiment not be extended to other fields? There are many tasks which can be performed better in co-operation, with the aid of functional institutions, than in isolation and competition. In this way, it might even be possible to achieve indirectly another object: to outflank power politics. Before the guardians of national sovereignty became aware of it, a system of open power politics or politics in disguise might be irrevocably transformed into a functional world community.

At first sight, the creation of the Specialised Agencies of the United Nations may be viewed as a series of such attempts. They extend from areas covering the protection of labour and exchange parities via education and liberalisation of trade to development aid, the freedom of the seas and the international control of nuclear energy.

Functionalists tend to overlook but one small point. Irrespective of what the rest of the world wants—and it is improbable that most of the old, as well as new, middle Powers and small States want anything different—the governments and bureaucracies of the world Powers are little inclined to share their governmental and administrative monopolies with other government representatives and competing sets of international bureaucrats. They are, however, willing to create confederate international organisations with essentially consultative and prelegislative functions and, within a margin of tolerance, let them behave as if they were the organs of a functional international community.

The foundation of the German Customs Union (*Zollverein*) of 1833 and the three European Communities of 1952 and 1957 furnish reversals of this situation and, as regional or sectional exceptions, confirm the general rule. For the forces which, in the nineteenth century, aimed at German unification, the German Customs Union was but an economic means to a political end. Similarly, the fathers of the European Communities knew that, in the period immediately following the Second World War, any direct political union of

Western Europe was psychologically unacceptable to the victims and enemies of Nazism, if not Germany. They wanted this unification but were astute enough to seek this objective through the back door of international functionalism.

Wherever and to the extent to which the common will to attain such unity exists, functionalism is a realistic means of avoiding a waste of energy by competition between units which are no longer viable as independent entities or less powerful than they would be if they pooled their resources.

It is an open question whether this supranational *élan* in Western Europe has evaporated. Thus, only the future can tell whether these Communities amount merely to a West European Confederation, *l'Europe des patries*, or whether the infusion of new blood into the Communities will lead to a new advance in functional federalism.

Even if this common will proved stronger than at present is apparent and led to a federation of Western Europe, this would mean merely the creation of a new if artificial great Power in a world society that remains in character unchanged. It would hardly constitute a staging-post on the road to supranational functionalism on a world scale.

(7) *Reform of the United Nations.* There is an ambiguous way of formualting proposals for the mitigation or elimination of the shortcomings of the existing system of world power politics in disguise. It is to present such suggestions under the rubric of a reform of the United Nations.

In form, such proposals may appear to involve no more than changes in the voting patterns of organs of the United Nations. Suggestions for limiting or abolishing the right of veto of the permanent members of the Security Council belong to this category. Actually, any such change would make possible majority decisions against one or more of the world Powers and thus alter fundamentally the character of the United Nations as an essentially hegemonial world confederation.

This would apply even more to proposals of a similar hue regarding the pacific settlement of legal and political disputes and the peaceful change of any existing *status quo*. Formally, it would suffice to transform the non-binding or optional character of available procedures into a binding and obligatory jurisdiction of the relevant political and legal organs of the United Nations.

The same is true of a whole series of other proposals: the creation of economic organs with automatic power of decision regarding all members of the United Nations, and not only those who submit themselves voluntarily to the jurisdiction of institutions such as the Bretton Woods Organisations or the General Agreement on Tariffs and Trade; the establishment of *ad hoc* or permanent international police forces with delegated powers to act, or the abolition of national armaments by majority decisions.

Regarding such projects, two alternatives exist: either they mean but an apparent development of existing confederate organisations or organs which, as does the United Nations Conference on Trade and Development, make less impact than noise, or they constitute embryonic and surreptitious developments of a federal character.

Whether any such proposals can be realised in any particular historical situation or whether they are merely tactical moves in games of one-upmanship is easy to find out.

Two tests will assist in this task:

(1) Is it likely that, as would be required under the Charter of the United Nations, any of these blue prints are acceptable to two-thirds of the members of the General Assembly?

(2) Is it likely that any such changes in the Charter would be ratified by two-thirds of the members of the United Nations, including all permanent members of the Security Council? [2]

Observers and Actors

For a considerable period, our world has been dragged along by a quaint seven-tiger team: population explosion; spoliation of the human environment; growing inflation; increasing financial inequality between rich and poor countries; racial discrimination; cosmic armaments, and an inherently unstable nuclear equilibrium.

In a situation fraught with chronic dangers of this magnitude, observers of international relations and actors on the international scene fulfil different functions. In such an atmosphere of glaring contradictions between appearances and realities, observers alone can afford the luxury of calling a spade a spade. To indulge in euphemisms would not alter these realities. It would merely demean academic analysis to another propaganda service in aid of covering up these grim realities.

Actually, detached analyses may help the player to avoid anything that may contribute to the actual deterioration of the existing situation. Should any actor be able to do anything that actually improved this situation, he would deserve a Nobel Prize. If he and other statesmen succeeded in transforming the existing world society into a world community, those engaged in this truly noble task would deserve a super-Nobel Prize.

---

[2] Readers interested in the writer's relativist approach to problems of international planning and legislation may wish to consult Part Three of *Power Politics. A Study of World Society* (3rd ed., 1964), p. 519 *et seq.*, or *Manual of International Law* (5th ed., 1967), p. 375 *et seq.*

In any case, one thing only should be impossible for a generation which has survived two World Wars and, in one form or another, has already heard in previous pre-war, war and post-war periods all the slogans and patent solutions offered again as novelties in our time. It is to fall again for the siren songs of power politics in disguise and crown its bards in anticipation of deeds yet to be performed.

Is it not more appropriate to follow the example of doubting Thomas and believe only what one clearly sees? Even so, it is advisable first to ascertain whether what one sees or imagines one sees is more than a *fata morgana.*

SELECTED READINGS

I—Attempt
at an Empirical Synthesis

Augustinus: *De Civitate Dei* (c. 413–226)
Campanella, T.: *Civitas Solis* (1620)
Curtis, L.: *Civitas Dei* (1934)
Huber, M.: *Gesellschaft und Humanitaet* (1948)
Jenks, C. W.: *The Will of the World Community as the Basis of Obligation in International Law* in *Law, Freedom and Welfare* (1963)
Lauterpacht, H.: *The Nature of International Law and General Jurisprudence* (12 *Economica* 1932)
Lippman, W.: *The Good Society* (1937)
Verdross, A.: *Statisches und dynamisches Naturrecht* (1971)
Wallas, G.: *The Great Society* (1914)
Wolff, Chr. von: *Jus Gentium Methodo Scientifica Pertractatum* (1749)

II—Society and Community Models

Andresky, S.: *Social Sciences as Sorcery* (1972)
Burton, J. W.: *Systems, States, Diplomacy and Rules* (1968)
Carter, F. W.: *Dubrovnik (Ragusa). A Classical City State* (1972)
Collingwood, R. G.: *The New Leviathan* (1942)
Cobb, R. W., and Elder, C.: *International Community* (1972)
Cooley, Ch. H.: *Human Nature and the Social Order* (1902)
Deutsch, K. W.: *The Nerves of Government* (1966)
Durkheim, E.: *De la division du travail social* (1893)
Easton, D.: *A Framework for Social Analysis* (1965)
Gluckman, M.: *Politics, Law and Ritual in Tribal Society* (1971)
Jacoby, E. G.: *Die moderne Gesellschaft im sozialwissenschaftlichen Denken von Ferdinand Toennies* (1971)
Kropotkin, Prinz Peter: *Mutual Aid* (1904)
Lévy-Strauss, C.: *La Pensée Sauvage* (1968)
Lorenz, K.: *On Aggression* (1966)

Macmurray, J.: *Creative Society* (1938)

Maine, Sir Henry Sumner: *Ancient Law* (1861)

Marx, K.: *Zur Judenfrage (Deutsch-Franzoesische Jahrbuecher 1843/44*)

Merton, R. K.: *Social Theory and Social Structure* (1968)

Montagu, A. (ed.): *Man and Aggression* (1973)

Niebuhr, R.: *Moral Man and Immoral Society* (1934)

Northrop, F. S. C.: *Philosophical Anthropology and Practical Politics* (1960)

Olsen, M. E. (ed.): *Power in Societies* (1970)

Parsons, T.: *Societies: Evolutionary and Comparative Perspectives* (1966)

Popper, K.: *The Open Society and its Enemies* (1950)

Scherer, J.: *Contemporary Community* (1972)

Schwarzenberger, G.: *The Frontiers of International Law* (1962—Chap. 1: The Three Types of Law)

Spinoza, B. de: *Tractatus Theologico-Politicus* (1670)

Toennies, F.: *Gemeinschaft und Gesellschaft* (1887)

Toynbee, A.: *A Study of History*, Vol. 12: *Reconsiderations* (1961)

Weber, M.: *Wirtschaft und Gesellschaft* (1922)

Zimmern, A.: *The Greek Commonwealth* (1915)

Zweig, F.: *The Quest for Fellowship* (1965)

III—WORLD COMMUNITY?

Aron, R.: *Paix et guerre entre les nations* (1962)

Barston, R. P.: *The Other Powers* (1973)

Bell, C.: *The Conventions of Crisis* (1971)

Brandon, H.: *The Retreat of American Power* (1973)

Brow, N.: *European Security 1972–1980* (1972)

Buchan, A.: *An Expedition to the Poles* (29 *Year Book of World Affairs—* 1975)

———: *Power and Equilibrium in the 1970's* (1973)

Bull, H.: *The Control of the Arms Race* (1965)

Burton, J. W.: *World Society* (1972)

Butterfield, H. and Wight, M. (eds.): *Diplomatic Investigations* (1966)

Carr, E. H.: *The Twenty Years Crisis 1919–1939* (1939)

Claude, I. L.: *Power and International Relations* (1962)

Cox, R. W., and Jacobsen, H.: *The Anatomy of Influence* (1973)

Frankel, J.: *International Politics* (1973)

Harrod, J.: *Trade Union Foreign Policy* (1972)

Hexter, J. H.: *The History Primer* (1972)

Hinsley, F. H.: *Nationalism and the International System* (1973)

James, A.: *The Politics of Peace-Keeping* (1969)

Jouvenel, B. de: *Du Pouvoir* (1945)

———: *De la Souveraineté* (1955)

Joynt, C.: *The Analysis of Crises* (28 *Year Book of World Affairs* 1974)

Kissinger, H.: *The World Restored. Metternich, Castlereagh and the Problem of Peace 1812–1822* (1957)

Knorr, K.: *Power and Wealth. The Political Economy of International Power* (1973)

Kyellen, R.: *Die Grossmaechte der Gegenwart* (1914)

Lasswell, H. D.: *World Politics and Personal Insecurity* (1935)
Manning, C. A.: *The Nature of International Society* (1962)
Martin, L. W.: *The Sea in Modern Strategy* (1967)
Modelski, G.: *Principles of World Politics* (1972)
Morgan, R. (ed.): *The Study of International Affairs* (1972)
Morgenthau, H.-J.: *Politics in the 20th Century* (3 vols.—1962)
Owen, D.: *The Politics of Defence* (1972)
Pierre, A. J.: *Nuclear Politics* (1972)
Porter, B. (ed.): *The Aberystwyth Papers: International Politics 1919–1969* (1972)
Rosenau, J. N., and Others (eds.): *The Analysis of International Politics* (1972)
Russett, B. M. (ed.): *Peace, War and Numbers* (1972)
Ruyssen, Th.: *La Société Internationale* (1950)
Schwarzenberger, G.: *Power Politics. A Study of World Society* (1941—3rd ed. 1964)
——: *Ueber die Machtpolitik hinaus?* (1968)
Singer, H. R.: *Weak States in a World of Powers* (1972)
Spanier, J. W.: *Games Nations Play* (1972)
Sperlich, P. W.: *Conflict and Harmony in Human Affairs* (1971)
Tanter, R., and Ullmann, R. H. (eds.): *Theory and Policy in International Relations* (1972)
Thucydides (translated by Thomas Hobbes): *The Peloponnesian War* (1676) or *History of the Peloponnesian War* (translated by R. Warner—1972)
Ulam, A.: *The Rivals: America and Russia since World War II* (1973)
Vasquez, M. S.: *Zones of Influence* (27 *Year Book of World Affairs*—1973)
Wheeler-Bennett, J., and Nicholls, A.: *The Semblance of Peace* (1972)
Whitaker, B. Ch.: *The Fourth World* (1972)

IV—WORLD LAW?

Barkun, M.: *Law without Sanctions* (1968)
Brierly, J. L. (ed. Sir Humphrey Waldock): *The Law of Nations* (1963)
Cheng, Bin: *The General Principles of Law as Applied by International Courts and Tribunals* (1953)
Corbett, P. E.: *From International to World Law* (1969)
Delos, J. T.: *La Société Internationale et les Principes du Droit Public* (1950)
Deutsch, K., and Hoffmann, S. (eds.): *The Relevance of International Law* (1968)
Falk, R. A.: *The Status of Law in International Society* (1970)
Fawcett, J. E. S.: *The Law of Nations* (1968)
Guggenheim, P.: *Traité de Droit international public* (2 vols.—1953)
Henkin, L.: *How Nations Behave* (1968)
Jenks, C. W.: *A New World Law?* (1969)
Lauterpacht, H.: *The Function of Law in the International Community* (1933)
Niemeyer, G.: *Law without Force* (1941)
O'Connell, D. P.: *International Law* (2 vols.—1970)

Rousseau, Ch.: *Principes de droit international public* (*Recueil*, Hague Academy of International Law, Vol. 93—1958)

Schwarzenberger, G.: *The Fundamental Principles of International Law* (*Recueil*, Hague Academy of International Law, Vol. 87—1955)

——: *Historical Models of International Law* (25 *Current Legal Problems*— 1972)

Simma, B.: *Das Reziprozitaetselement in der Entstehung des voelkerrecht-lichen Gewohnheitsrechts* (1970)

——: *Das Reziprozitaetselement im Zustandekommen voelkerrechtlicher Vertraege* (1972)

Tunkin, G.: *Voelkerrechtstheorie* (1972)

Verdross, A.: *Die Einheit des rechtlichen Weltbildes auf Grundlage der Voelkerrechtsverfassung* (1923)

——, and Others: *Voelkerrecht* (1964)

Visscher, Ch. de: *Théories et Réalités en Droit International Public* (1960)

V—WORLD ORDER?

Alexandrowicz, Ch. H.: *The Law of Global Communications* (1971)

Aron, R.: *République impériale. Les Etas-Unis dans le monde 1945–1972* (1973)

Bocard, L.: *Le Massacre des Indiens* (1969)

Bowett, D. W.: *The Law of International Institutions* (1970)

Brown, E. D.: *The Legal Regime of Hydrospace* (1971)

Falk, A. R., and Mendloviz, S. H.: *The Strategy of World Order* (5 vols.— 1966–   )

Feller, A. H.: *United Nations and World Community* (1952)

Friedmann, W.: *The Changing Structure of International Law* (1964)

Goodrich, L. M., Hambro, E., and Simons, A. P.: *The Charter of the United Nations* (1969)

Gutteridge, J. A. C.: *The United Nations in a Changing World* (1970)

Haas, E. B., and Others: *Conflict Management by International Organisations* (1972)

Herz, J. H.: *International Politics in the Atomic Age* (1960)

Heydte, F. A. Freiherr von der: *Die Geburtsstunde des souveraenen Staates* (1952)

Higgins, R.: *The Development of International Law through the Political Organs of the United Nations* (1963)

Holbraad, C. (ed.): *Super Powers and World Order* (1971)

Kahn, H.: *On Escalation* (1965)

Kelsen, H.: *The Law of the United Nations* (1950–51)

Kohn, H.: *World Order in Historical Perspectives* (1942)

McDougal, M. S., and Associates: *Studies in World Public Order* (1960)

——, and Feliciano, F. P.: *Law and Minimum World Public Order* (1961)

Moore, J. N.: *Law and the Indo-China War* (1972)

Schiffer, W.: *The Legal Community of Mankind* (1954)

Schwarzenberger, G.: *The League of Nations and World Order* (1936)

——: *International Law and Order* (1971)

Stone, J.: *Aggression and World Order* (1958)

Touscoz, J.: *Le principe d'effectivité dans l'ordre international* (1964)

Tunkin, G.: *Der ideologische Kampf und das Voelkerrecht* in E. Menzel (ed.): *Drei sowjetische Beitraege zur Voelkerrechtslehre* (1969)

Zimmern, A.: *The League of Nations and the Rule of Law* (1936)

VI—DIAGNOSES, REMEDIES AND PROGNOSES

Black, C. E., and Falk, R. A. (eds.): *The Future of the International Legal Order* (4 vols.—1969–72)

Brierly, J. L.: *The Outlook for International Law* (1944)

Carr, E. H.: *Conditions of Peace* (1942)

Clarke, G., and Sohn, L. B.: *World Peace through World Law* (1966)

Fawcett, J. E. S.: *The Application of the European Convention on Human Rights* (1969)

Flechtheim, O. R.: *History and Futurology* (1966)

Frankel, J.: *Contemporary International Theory and the Behaviour of States* (1973)

Friedmann, W., and Others (eds.): *Transnational Law in a Changing Society* (1972)

Fromm, E.: *The Sane Society* (1956)

Hahlo, H. R., and Others (eds.): *Nationalism and the Multinational Enterprise* (1973)

Hamilton, A., Madison, J., and Jay, J.: *The Federalist* (1787–88)

Horkheimer, M.: *Eclipse of Reason* (1947)

James, A. (ed.): *Bases of International Order* (1973)

Jenks, C. W.: *The Common Law of Mankind* (1958)

Jessup, Ph. C.: *Transnational Law* (1956)

——: *Parliamentary Diplomacy* (*Recueil*, Hague Academy of International Law, Vol. 89—1956)

——: *The Present State of Transnational Law* in M. Bos (ed.): *The Present State of International Law and Other Essays* (1973)

Kahn, H., and Bruce-Briggs, B.: *Things to Come* (1972)

Kalmus, H.: *Living Together Without Man* (25 *Year Book of World Affairs* —1971)

Laski, H.: *Reflections on the Revolution of Our Time* (1943)

Lauterpacht, H.: *An International Bill of the Rights of Man* (1945)

——: *International Law and Human Rights* (1950)

Le Bon, G.: *The World in Revolt* (1921)

Lieber, R. J.: *Theory and World Politics* (1973)

Liebmann, H.: *Ein Planet wird unbewohnbar* (1973)

McNair, Lord: *The General Principles of Law Recognised by Civilised Nations* (33 *British Year Book of International Law*—1957)

——: *Hersch Lauterpacht* (10 *International and Comparative Law Quarterly*— 1961)

Mann, A. F.: *Reflections on a Commercial Law of Nations* (33 *British Year Book of International Law*—1957)

Mannheim, K.: *Ideology and Utopia* (1936)

——: *Diagnosis of our Time* (1943)

Mitrany, D.: *A Working Peace System* (1966)

Nostradamus, M.: *Les Prophéties* (1568)

Owen, H. (ed.): *The Next Phase in Foreign Policy* (1973)

Pentland, C. C.: *Neofunctionalism* (27 *Year Book of World Affairs*—1973)

Picht, G.: *Mut zur Utopie* (1969)

Plischke, E. (ed.): *Systems of Integrating the International Community* (1964)

Roeling, B. V. A.: *International Law in an Expanded World* (1960)

Russell, B.: *Has Man a Future?* (1961)

Schlochauer, H.-J.: *Die Idee des ewigen Friedens* (1953)

Schmitt, C.: *Der Nomos der Erde* (1950)

Schwarzenberger, G.: *Foreign Investments and International Law* (1969—Chap. 12)

——: *Equity in International Law* (26 *Year Book of World Affairs*—1972)

Sewell, J. P.: *Functionalism and World Politics* (1966)

Sorokin, P. A.: *Russia and the United States* (1950)

Vallat, Sir Francis (ed.): *Human Rights* (1972)

Vincent, R. J.: *The Functions of Functionalism in International Relations* (27 *Year Book of World Affairs*—1973)

Waltz, K. N.: *Man, the State and War* (1959)

INDEX

AFRICAN NATIONAL CONGRESS (ANC), 161
African States,
EEC, Yaoundé Convention, and, 273–276
United Nations, and NATO in, 47
Agence de Coopération Culturelle et Technique, 174
Albania, 56, 262
Algeria, 94
Allende, S., 72–87 *passim*, 302
Soviet Union (1972), visit to, 73
Trade Union Federation (CUT), calls mass demonstration in support of, 77
American Military Policy; Just War, the Nixon Doctrine and the future shape of, 137–154
American attitudes towards war, 139–144
Holy War Doctrine in post-Reformation England, 144–148
Nixon Doctrine, 148–154
Amnesty International,
Chilean coup, and, 82
Andean Common Market, 208–221
Cartagena Agreement,
evolution and general objectives of, 208–210
Customs Union, formation of, 210–211
industrialisation, role of, 215–217
first sectoral programme for the " metal working industry," 216
institutional framework, 210
national and subregional control, 211–215
multinational enterprises and, 214–215
settlement of disputes, 218–220
See also under Cartagena Agreement.
Andean Investment Code, 306
Anderson, J., 80
Andreski, S., 313–319
Angola,
Government in Exile (GRAE), 161
National Union for the Total Independence of (UNITA), 161
People's Movement for the Liberation of (MPLA), 161

ANZUK (Australia, New Zealand and UK force in Singapore), 118
ANZUS (Australia, New Zealand, United States) Alliance, 91, 94
Aquinas, St. T., 130, 132
Thomists, 127, 129, 135
Arab States, 17, 107
oil as a weapon, and, 44
Ardrey, R., 131–133
Argentina, 206
Chilean junta, recognition of, 84
economic co-operation in Latin America, and, 208
travail, in, 56–71
armed forces, 67–69
development, arrest of, 59–61
government investment, 66
industrialisation, 67–68
interregnum, 68–69
nationalisation, policy of, 64, 65
Peron periods,
first, 63–68
second, 69–71
Pinedo Plan, 61
Second World War, effects of, 61–63
standard of living, 56–59
inequitable distribution, 56–57
United States, trade with, 59
Aristotle, 135, 136
Aron, R., 55, 126, 127, 135, 136, 331
Arousha Convention, 275
Ashton, C., 101
Asian and Pacific Council (ASPAC), 116
Asian Development Bank, 89
Association of Southeast Asia (ASA), 118
Association of Southeast Asian Nations (ASEAN), 119
peace, freedom and neutrality, zone of, 119
Assyria, 346
Atlantic Alliance, new tasks for, 22–33
allies and rivals, 24–25
balance of power, 23–24
European co-operation, 31
stability, chances for a new, 22–23
United States and Europe, 25–30
defence and security, 25–26
energy policies, 29–30

Atlantic Alliance—*cont.*
United States and Europe—*cont.*
monetary policy, 26–27
European zone of stable ex-
change rates, 26
Soviet Union, and, 30
trade, 27–29
Augustine, St., 135, 363
Australia, 57, 88–105 *passim*, 108, 109,
116
ANZUK, and, 118
ANZUS, and, 91, 94
BBC television in, 92
China, People's Republic of, diplo-
matic recognition of, 93
EEC, and, 271
Indonesia, and, 113
military threat from Southeast Asia,
perceived, 99, 100
national anthem, new, 93
natural resources, development of,
104
Returned Servicemen's League (RSL),
99
United States military bases, 94
See *also under* Pacific Alliance,
towards a new.
Austria,
Argentina, trade with, 60
EEC, and, 271
multinational corporations, and, 309
Avramov, S., 261
d'Azeglio, T., 124

BACHELET, GENERAL A., 79
Balance of Power, 14, 23–24, 31, 38, 50,
53, 118, 335
balance of terror, 38
balanced military force ratio, 31
multipolar, 335
nineteenth century, in, 40
Baldwin, J., 159
Bangladesh, 185, 314
Commonwealth membership, 185
UN membership, 185
Barnard, L., 99, 100
Barnes, T., 146
Barone, E., 222, 227
Bearton, L., 9
Belgium, 167
Argentina, trade with, 60
Chilean *coup*, and, 84
Beres, L. R., 334
Bilheimer, R. S., 158
Bipolarity, 6, 7, 11
See *also under* Poles, expedition to.
Bismark, O. von, 346
Blake, E. C., 155, 160, 164

Bobrov, R. L., 260
Bogota (1966), Declaration of, 208, 211
Bolivia, 58, 63
economic co-operation in Latin
America, and, 209–211, 217, 218
Brandt, W., 94
Brazil, 13, 58, 202, 203, 206
Argentina, trade with, 60
Chilean junta, recognition of, 84
economic co-operation in Latin
America, and, 208
Brezhnev, L.,
Doctrine, 41n., 260–261
Nixon (1973), meeting with, 39
Brierly, J. L., 324
British Empire, 313–315
Commonwealth, evolution into, 5
Bruce-Briggs, B., 134–135
Buchan, A., 4–21
Bull, H., 4, 9, 12, 126
Burma, 108, 109, 115, 119
Butler, W. E., 258

CABOT LODGE, H., 49, 50
Calvo Doctrine, 304, 308
Cambodia, 94, 95, 108, 111, 114, 116
Cameralism, 226
Canada, 13, 56, 57, 59, 61, 88, 167, 179,
184, 185, 202, 203
Middle East peace-keeping, contribu-
tion to, 184
OAS, and, 193
oil resources of, 19
UN peace-keeping forces, and, 185,
187
Canning, G., 49, 50
Caradon, Lord, 159
Cartagena Agreement,
(Agreement on Andean subregional
integration), 208–221 *passim*
Andean Foreign Investment Code,
212, 213, 215
multinational enterprises, and, 215
Commission of, 212, 216, 218
Court of Justice, 219
Common External Tariff, 216
minimum, 211
multinational enterprises, and, 214–
215
standard code on, 214
See *also under* Andean Common
Market.
Castlereagh, Viscount, 48, 49
Chapman, C., 88
Chiang Kai-shek, 107
Chicherin, G. V., 249
Chile, 58, 63, 88, 209, 302
Anaconda Copper Corporation, 73

Chile—*cont.*
Christian Democratic Government (1966–69), 73
coup (1973), 72–87
aftermath of, 82–83
implications, wider, 86–87
repudiation of, 80
textbook, 78–82
United Kingdom,
press and BBC reactions, 78, 85–86
United States, role in, 79–80
economic co-operation in Latin America, and, 208, 209, 211
economy, internal, 74–76
Federation of Democratic Parties (CODE), 76
Helsinki Conference: "Solidarity with the People of Chile," 84
Independent Socialist Party (USOPO), 76
Kennecott Copper Corporation, 73, 74
Movimiento de Izquierda Revolucionaria (MIR), 77, 81
National Party, 76, 77
Patria y Libertad, 77, 78, 83
politics and its extension, 76–78
trade balance, external, 73–74
Trade Union Federation (CUT), 73, 81
Unidad Popular (UP), 76, 79, 81
China, People's Republic of, 7, 12, 14–16, 51, 88, 89, 91, 107, 116, 118, 138, 185, 202, 262, 342
Australia, diplomatic recognition by, 93
Bangladesh, vetoed UN membership of, 185
Indonesia, and, 116
New Zealand, diplomatic recognition by, 93
nuclear capability of, 7, 13
nuclear device, first detonation of, 9
oil, exports of, 19
Southeast Asia, and, 116, 118
proposed neutralisation of, 115
Soviet Union, and, 7, 9, 10
hostility between, 14, 15, 51–52, 110, 120
ideological ally of, 107
Taiwan, and, 116
United States,
rapprochement with, 34, 39, 42
trade with, 89
Western Europe, and, 14, 15
See also under Southeast Asia, Sino-American *rapprochement* and the new configurations in.

Churchill, Sir W. S., 91
Civitas Maxima?, 337–368
diagnoses, remedies and prognoses, 350–363
decisive realities, 352–354
ideologies, utopias and possibilities, 354–362
international criminal law, 358–359
international functionalism, 360–361
international *jus cogens*, 357–358
international parliamentary diplomacy, 359–360
protection of human rights by international law, 354–356
reform of the UN, 361–362
transnational law, 356–357
observers and actors, 362–363
empirical synthesis attempted, 337
selected readings, 363–368
diagnoses, remedies and prognoses, 367–368
empirical synthesis, attempt at, 363
society and community models, 363–364
world community? 364–365
world law? 365–366
world order? 366–367
society and community models, 337–338
world community? 338–340
world law? 340–348
international law,
ethical perspective, in, 347–348
historical perspective, in, 344–347
jus aequum model, 346
jus strictum model, 345
oceanic model, 346
omnipotence model, 345
unionist model, 346
confederate submodel, 346
federal submodel, 346
hegemonial submodel, 346
unitary submodel, 346
world order? 348–350
Clark, C., 56
Claude, I. L., Jr., 177, 329
Cobden, R.,
non-intervention, doctrine of, 51
Cold War, 12, 19, 51, 107, 110, 120, 138, 188, 196
Colombia, 206
economic co-operation in Latin America, 208, 209, 211, 218
Colombo Plan, 109

Commonwealth of Nations, 5, 174, 177, 178, 182, 190
  Bangladesh admitted, 185
  Commonwealth Relations Office, UK, 183
  Commonwealth Secretariat, 183
  Pakistan's withdrawal from, 185
  South Africa's withdrawal from, 185, 189
  sugar producers and EEC, 378
Communist ideology,
  See under Marxism-Leninism.
Companies, see under Multinational corporations.
Congo, 156, 158
  Belgian, 315
Congress of Vienna (1815), 46, 48
Corbett, P., 323
Corvalan, L., 83
Council for Mutual Economic Aid (COMECON), (CMEA), 174, 226
  economic systems of Eastern Europe and Soviet Union, comparison of, 237
  EEC, comparison with, 235
Cuba,
  Chilean rupture of diplomatic relations, 83
  COMECON, and, 263
  Marxist-Leninist orientation (1962), 189
  Missile Crisis (1962), 10, 332
  OAS, exclusion from, 185, 186, 188
Czechoslovakia, 263
  Dubček régime, economy under, 232, 237
  Marshall Aid (1947) and, 191
  Prague Spring (1968), 229
  Soviet intervention (1968), 20, 238, 260–261
  Soviet Treaty (1970), 262

D'ABERNON, LORD, 60
Darwin, C., 4–5, 132
  Darwinian models, 4–5
  "Socialist Darwinism," 132
Denmark, 167, 179
  Chilean coup, and, 84
  EEC, and, 270, 271
  International Court,
    North Sea continental shelf cases, and, 297
Détente
  Sino-American, 106, 110, 111, 117
  Soviet-American, 34, 38, 48, 152, 196
Developing World, see under Third World.
Dodd, M., 222

Doxey, Margaret, 173–195
Dulles, J. F., 137, 141–143, 146–150, 152

EASTERN EUROPE, 13, 22, 23, 33, 202
  Chilean coup, and, 84
  economic systems of Socialist, principles, development and operation, 222–241
    central economic control, politics of, 230–239
    control, instruments of, 233–237
    planning, 231–233
      Soviet methods, comparison of, with COMECON States, 237–239
    central planning, theoretical approaches to, 226–230
    economic and political systems, and ideologies, 224–226
    macro-economic organisation and political reality, 223–224
    market and plan in Yugoslavia, 239–241
  economies of, comparison with Soviet Union, 237
Eastern Germany,
  economic planning, method of, 238
Economic Commission for Asia and the Far East (ECAFE), 109, 114, 120
Ecuador,
  economic co-operation in Latin America, and, 209–211, 217, 218
Edelstam, H., 84
Egypt, 16, 17, 44, 110, 313
  Hatti, and, 345, 346
  Rome, and, 313, 316
Eisenhower, D. D., 137, 143, 149, 150, 151
  administration, 141
El Salvador,
  Chilean, junta, recognition of, 84
Engels, F., 244, 251
Espinoza, G., 77
Ethiopia, 315
Eucken, W., 222
Europe, 22, 24, 28, 107
  Concert of, 34, 37
    nineteenth century, 39, 45
      Gladstone's appeal to, 46–47
      Metternich's case for, 46, 48
  Mutual and Balanced Force Reductions (MBFR) Conference, 22

Europe—*cont.*
United States, and, 25–30
See also under Eastern, and Western.
European Atomic Energy Community (EURATOM), 269
European Coal and Steel Community (ECSC), 268
European Communities,
Court of Justice, 270
International Fruit Company v. *voor Groenten en Fruit,* 270
See also under EEC; *and* International Economic Law, Equality and Discrimination in: European Communities and the Wider World.
European Economic Community (EEC), 9, 13, 15, 28, 31, 97, 174, 175, 179, 181, 190, 192, 194, 265–282 *passim,* 343
African States, and, 29
Arousha Convention, 275
British application for membership, 186, 190, 193
Caribbean countries, and, 29
COMECON, comparison with, 235
Common Agricultural Policy (CAP), 128, 182, 277
energy policy, 29
European Union by 1980, 31
Mediterranean States, and, 29
multinational corporations, and, 308
oil crisis (1973), and, 29
Treaty of Rome, 185, 266, 267, 269, 270, 272, 273
United States, and, 28
Yaoundé Convention, 273–275
See also under International Economic Law, Equality and Discrimination in: European Communities and the Wider World.
European Free Trade Association (EFTA), 191, 270, 281

FALK, R. A., 55, 322, 326, 327, 328
Feliciano, F. P., 323
Fernandez Saavedra, G., 215
Ferns, H. S., 56–71
Fiji, 90, 105
Finland, 203, 246
Argentina, trade with, 60
First World War, 152, 227, 338, 341, 343, 348, 354, 355
Peace Treaties (1919), 358
Fitzmaurice, Sir Gerald, 293–294
Flores Labra, F., 75

Ford, H., 57
Foreign policy, *see under* International Organisation in foreign policy perspective.
France, 10, 16, 30, 68, 117, 167, 185
Argentina, trade with, 60, 61
Chilean junta, recognition of, 84
EEC (1965), boycott of, 190
Yaoundé Convention, and, 273–275
influence, decline of French, in 1950s, 6
nuclear forces of, 7
OPEC, and, 18
Soviet Decree on Peace (1917), and, 247
United States, criticism of, 10
Frankel, J., 184
Frei Montalves, E., 75, 83
Freud, S., 131
Fuentealba, R., 80
Functionalism, 127, 128, 129

GADDAFI, M., 52
Gallois, P., 13
Gardner, R., 180
General Agreement on Tariffs and Trade (GATT), 22, 28, 181, 235, 266, 267–271, 279–280, 361
ECSC, and, 268
EEC, and, 265–282 *passim*
EURATOM, and, 269
Generalov, V. F., 254, 255
Genoa Conference (1922), 249
Germany,
Democratic Republic of, *see under* Eastern Germany.
Federal Republic of, *see under* Western Germany.
Imperial, and Soviet Decree on Peace, 247
Nazi, 57, 58, 361
anti-Semitism in, 156, 348
Argentina, trade with, 60
multinational corporations, and, 302
Second World War, and, 62
Weimar, Bavarian Soviet Republic (1919), 247
Ghana, 315
Gladstone, W. E., 46, 47, 51, 54, 55
Goldsmith, P., 265–282
Gorton, J., 102
Gotha programme, 243
Gouge, W., 145

Greece,
  EEC, and, 272
  Greek City States, 346
Grotius, H., 125, 154
Grzybowski, K., 253
Guatemala,
  Chilean junta, recognition of, 84
Guinea-Bissau, 189
Guzman, General L., 79

HAILE SELASSIE, 163
Harrod, J., 187
Hauriou, M., 127
Hayek, F. A. von, 222
Heath, E., administration of, 92
Hegel, E. W. F., 346
Herz, J. H., 55
Hipolito Yrigoyen, 60
Hiroshima, 143, 146
Hitler, A., 57, 165, 302, 338
Hobbes, T., 123, 131
Hoffmann, S., 323, 326, 330–333
Holt, H., 90
Hooft, W. A. Visser't, 156, 157, 170
Horne, D., 91
Hot Line, 6
Howard, M., 122
Hudson, D., 155–172
Huerta, Rear-Admiral, 81
Hume, D., 122
Hungary,
  Hungarian Soviet Republic (1919), 247
  Soviet intervention (1956), 261
Hutchinson, G. W., 72–87

IMPERIALISM: PAST AND FUTURE, 313–319
  British Raj in India, 313–314
  Byzantium, 317, 344
  China (Imperial), 316
  "exploitation," examination of term, 313–319 *passim*
  Macedonia, 316
  neo-colonialism, 353
  neo-imperialism, 319
  Persia, 316, 344
  Rome (Imperial), 313, 316, 344, 345
    Roman law, 345
  "selfishness," 316
  Spanish exploitation of Peruvian Indians, 313, 315, 316
Independence Party of Guinea and the Cape Verde Islands (PAIGC), 161

India, 7, 13, 19, 107, 109, 314
  British Raj, 313
Indian Ocean,
  Soviet naval presence, 115
Indonesia, 18, 95, 108, 109, 112–113, 115, 119
  Australia and New Zealand, relations with, 97
  China, and, 116
  Soviet Union, and, 116
  UK, and, 118
Institut de Droit International (Paris), 302
Institute of International Law, 296
Integrated Missiles Early Warning System (IMEWS), 94, 95
International Centre for the Settlement of Investment Disputes (ICSD), 308
International Civil Aviation Organisation (ICAO), 181
International Court of Justice, 309
  Barcelona-Traction Case, 303
  International Law Commission, and, 286
  North Sea continental shelf cases, 297
  Statute of, 288
International Development Banks, 197
  African Development Bank (AFDB), 197, 199, 201–205, 207
    Fund, 204
  Andean Development Corporation (ADC), 197
  Asian Development Bank (AsDB), 197, 199
  Caribbean Development Bank (CDB), 197, 199
  Central American Bank for Economic Co-operation (CABEI), 197, 199
  East African Development Bank (EADB), 197
  European Investment Bank (EIB), 197
  Inter-American Development Bank (IDB), 197–199, 202
    Fund for Special Operations (FSO), 198
  International Bank for Reconstruction and Development (IBRD), 197–200, 202, 206
  International Development Association (IDA), 197, 204–207
    Bank, 204–206
  International Finance Corporation (IFC), 197
    Official development assistance (ODA), 201

International Economic Law, Equality and Discrimination in: European Communities and the Wider World, 265–282
  Association Agreements, types of, 273–280
  Commonwealth and, 276
  EEC, enlargement of, 275–276
  new type? 276–278
    agriculture, 277
    insurance of export earnings, 277–278
    reverse preferences, 277
    others, 275
    Yaoundé conventions, 273–275
  Bilateral agreements of member States,
    impact of Rome Treaty on, 266–267
  GATT, and, 279–280
  Rome Treaty, and, 267–270
  redressing the balance, 270–272
    Accession to EEC, 270–271
    Association Agreements, 272
    Free Trade agreements with EEC, 271
    tariffs, compensatory adjustment of, 271–272
International Labour Organisation (ILO), 181, 359
International Law, 323–328
  Conventions,
    Civil and Political Rights (1966), 344
    Elimination of all Racial Discrimination (1965), 344
    Genocide (1948), 344, 354, 356
    Social and Cultural Rights (1966), 344
  discipline, as a, 290
  ethical perspective, in, 347–348
  historical perspective, in, 344–347
  human rights, protection of, 354–356
  international criminal law, 358–359
  jus aequum model, 346
  jus cogens, doctrine of, 291, 294
    international, 357–358
  jus strictum model, 345
  law of armed conflict, 358
  law of co-ordination, 340
  law of power, 340
  law of reciprocity, 340
  seven legal principles, 341
  sociological perspective, in, 341–344
  See also under Civitas Maxima?;
    International Economic Law, equality and discrimination in;
    International Law Commission;
    "Socialist" International Law;
    World Order, concept of.

International Law Association (ILA), 296, 305, 308, 309
International Law Commission, 283–300, 357
  doctrinal approach of, 294–295
  general perspectives, 286–290
  Geneva Conference on Law of the Sea (1958), 297
  international law, codification and progressive development of, 290
    advisory and drafting, 290
    formative, 290
    general objectives of UN, related to, 290
    infrastructural and regulatory, 290
  nature of the process, 291–292
  organisation and methods, 295–296
  philosophy of, 293–294
  political perspective, 292–293
  role of, 290–291
International Monetary Fund (IMF), 181, 183 202, 203
International Order,
  Concert and idea of, 34–55
    Concert, definitions of, 34–35
    order, and, 37–46
    order, definitions, of, 35–37
    justice, 36
    " law and order," 35
    security, 36
    status quo, maintenance of, 35–36
    See also under World Order, concept of.
International Organisation,
  in foreign policy perspective, 173–195
    " balance-sheet " (cost/benefit), 192–195
    benefits, 180–189
      communication, 182–184
      foreign policy, legitimisation of, 187–189
      participation, 186–187
      penalties of non-membership, avoidance of, 189
      security, 180–187
      status and role, 184–186
    costs, 189–191
      contributions, 191–192
      loss of autonomy in decision-making, 189–190
      penalties, liability to, 191
      sanctions, liability to, 190–191
International Relations,
  natural law and the renewal of the philosophy of, 121–136

International Relations—*cont.*
 natural law and the renewal of the philosophy of—*cont.*
  aggression and the biological ideologies, 131–134
  antinomies in modern legal and political thought on international relations, 124–127
  Bull, " classical " ideology of, 126
  Christian-Machiavellian ideology in Niebuhr, 127
  legal versus extra-legal rationality, 124–125
  McDougal versus juridical positivism, 125–126
  neo-Machiavellian ideology in Aron, 126–127
  functionalist integration theory, ideological factors, 127–131
  futurology, ideologies in, 134–135
  liberal ideology, significance of, 122–124
International Telecommunications Union (ITU), 181
Israel, 7, 17, 184
 Gaza strip, 330
 October War (1973), and, 16, 149, 184
Italy, 18, 68, 266
 Argentina, trade with, 60
Ivory Coast, 315

JAGAN, C., 72
Japan, 7, 12–14, 19, 23, 25, 27–29, 34, 52, 88, 89, 95, 100, 105, 109, 115, 119, 167, 202, 203, 318
 Australia's trading partner, as, 92, 103
 defence policy, low profile, 100
 economic policy, 109
 energy policy, 29
 Greater East Asia Co-Prosperity Sphere, 107
 Southeast Asia (1945), retreat from, 107, 115, 119
 Trade Bill (1973), Nixon's, and, 28
 United States influence, 6
Jara, V., 82
Jessup, P., 356
Johnson, J. T., 137–154
Johnson, L. B., 11, 90, 13, 144, 149
 administration, 90, 112
 Vietnam War, and, 144
Judaeo-Christian revelation, 121

KAHN, H., 134–135
Kahn, P., 306
Kaplan, M. A., 5, 11

Kaunda, K., 169
Kautilya, 338
Kelsen, H., 326
Kennedy, J. F., 9, 137, 149
 administration, 90, 143
Kenya, 275, 315
Khrushchev, N. S., 6
King, M. L., Jr., 159
Kirk, N., 93, 96–98, 104
Kissinger, H. A., 9, 12, 15, 17, 88, 111, 149
 Middle East, and, 17, 44
Korean War (1950–1953), 138, 149, 150
Korovih, Ye. A., 242, 248, 250, 252–256, 258, 259
Kozhevnikov, F., 242, 252–255, 259

LANGE, O., 222, 229
Laos, 110, 111, 114
 Sino-American relations, and, 110
Lapenna, I., 242–264
Latin America, 193
 Central American Common Market (CACM), 208–221 *passim*
 Latin-American Free Trade Area (LAFTA), 208–331 *passim*
 Montevideo, Treaty of, 218
  See also under Andean Common Market.
Lauterpacht, Sir H., 124, 337
Law of the Sea (1958), Geneva Conference of, 297
League of Nations, 156, 328, 329, 340, 342, 347, 348
 Covenant of, 37, 42, 49, 328
  Ethiopia (1935–1936), case of, 42–43
  Manchuria (1931–1933), case of, 42–43
 Permanent Court of International Justice, 347
 United States, and, 49
Leighton, A., 147
Leighton, B., 80
Lenin, V. I., 249, 257, 258, 351
Liberia, 315
Liberman, Y., 228
Liechtenstein, 303
Little, Arthur D., Inc.,
 Southeast Asia, prognoses on, 89
Lon Nol, General, 94
Luxembourg,
 Argentina, trade with, 60

MACHIAVELLI, N., 126, 131, 146, 338
Mahajani, Usha, 106–120

Malacca Straits, 116
Malagasy States, 276
Malawi, 158
Malaya, 119
Malaysia, 96, 109, 112, 114, 115, 119, 276
  New Zealand forces in, 96
  Sabah, dispute with Philippines over, 118
Mannheim, K., 351
Mao Tse-tung, 262
MAPHILINDO (Malaysia, the Philippines and Indonesia), 119
Marshall Aid, 191, 194
Marshall, R. J., 160
Martin, W. O., 122
Marx, K., 226, 227, 244, 245, 251
Marxism-Leninism, 51, 189, 242, 253
  Communist Manifesto, 243, 244
  economic interpretation of, 230
  First International (1864), 244
  Marxism, 135, 243, 251, 259
  Marxist theory, 255
    proletarianism, concept of, 243–245, 253
  Soviet theory of State and Law until 1929,
    impact on, 245
McDougal, M., 125, 126, 320, 323, 326
McGovern, G. T., 159
McNamara, R. S., 9–11
Medlovitz, S., 322, 325
Mendoza, General C., 79
Menzies, Sir R., 90, 92
Mercantilism, 226
Metternich, K. von, 46, 47, 49, 51, 55
Mexico, 206
  economic co-operation in Latin America, and, 208
Middle East, 24, 34, 91, 109
  fragile peace, 44
  Kissinger negotiations (1974), 17
  October War (1973), 16, 18, 20, 52
  oil, World economy and, 29
  peace-keeping force in Gaza strip, Canadian role in, 184
  Security Council Resolution 242 (1967), 44
Midgley, E. B. F., 121–136
Mindola Ecumenical Centre, 158
Ministerial Conference for Economic Development for Southeast Asia (MEDSEA), 116, 117
Mises, L. von, 222
Model-building in International Relations, 4–5, 320–322, 334–338 *passim*
Moltmann, J., 165
Monetary system, world, 26–27

Mongolia, COMECON, and, 263
Monroe Doctrine (1823), 49, 50
Montagu, A., 131–134 *passim*
Montero, Admiral P., 79
Montevideo, Treaty of, 218
Morgenthau, H., 5
Mozambique Liberation Front (FRELIMO), 161, 163
Multinational corporations,
  American Polaroid Corpn., 166
  Austrian law, and, 309
  Cartagena Agreement (Andean Common Market), and, 214–215
  EEC, and, 265
  European Communities Court of Justice and, 270
  friend or foe? 302–303
  Hitler's Germany, and, 302
  host State, protection of, by UN code, 305–309
    by other means, 309–311
  International Business Machines (IBM) Inc., in Western Germany, 307
  International Centre for the Settlement of Investment Disputes (ICSD), 308
  International Court of Justice, Calvo Doctrine, and, 304–305
  International Law Commission, and, 291
  International Law of the future, and, 301–312
  International Telephone and Telegraph (ITT), role in Chilean *coup*, 80, 302
  OPEC, and, 302
  protection for, 303–305
  Rio Tinto Zinc, Papua New Guinea, and, 102
  Soviet Union, and, 302
Murray, C., 129
Mutual and Balanced Force Reductions (MBFR) Conference, 22, 30, 33

NAGASAKI, 146
Namibia, 189
Napoleonic Wars, 341
Near East, *see under* Middle East.
Nehru, Pandit, 48
Nelson, L. D. M., 208–221
Nemčinov, V. S., 228
Neruda, P., 82
Nervo, Judge P., 303
Netherlands, 167, 266
  Argentina, trade with, 60
  Chilean *coup*, and, 84

Netherlands—*cont.*
  International Court of Justice and
    North Sea continental shelf cases,
    297
New Caledonia, 90, 165
New Guinea, 90, 102, 105
  Papua, 101
  West Irian (1962), 109
New Zealand, 57, 59, 64, 88–105 *passim*,
    108, 109
  ANZUK, and, 118
  China, People's Republic of,
    diplomatic recognition of, 93
  EEC, and, 271, 276
  Japanese business interests and, 105
  Maori population, and, 104
  military threat from Southeast Asia,
    perceived, 99
  UK, trade with, 92, 276
    See also under Pacific Alliance,
    towards a new.
Niebuhr, R., 127, 135
Nigeria, 13
Niles, D. T., 159
Nixon, R. M., 14, 26, 34, 38–40, 106,
    110, 137–154 *passim*
  administration, 17
  Brezhnev (1973) meeting with, 39
  Guam Doctrine, 110–111, 138, 139,
    148–154
  Trade Bill (1973) of, 28
  Vietnam War, and, 93, 110, 144
    See also under American Military
    Policy: Just War, the Nixon
    Doctrine and the future.
North Atlantic Treaty Organisation
    (NATO), 16, 23, 31, 33, 179, 183,
    192
  EUROGROUP, 31
  France, and, 31
  United Nations, and African States
    in, 47
    See also under Atlantic Alliance,
    new tasks for.
North Korea, 10, 149, 263.
North Vietnam, 89, 94, 109, 110, 113,
    115, 263
North-South Relations and,
  Multilateral Soft Loans, recent, 196–
    207
    contributions, amounts and distri-
      bution of, 203–204
    membership, 202–203
    since 1950, 198–202
    voting power and control, 204–205
Northern Rhodesia, 158
Norway, 167, 179

Nuclear deterrence, 6
  balance of terror, 38
  co-extermination, threat of nuclear,
    354
  credibility of, 8
  massive retaliation, threat of, 143,
    146
  parity, strategic, 25, 138
  peace, 48
  sufficiency, strategy of, 38
  superiority, strategy of, 38
Nuclear   Non-Proliferation   Treaty
    (1968), 7, 39
Nuclear Test Ban Treaty (1963), 6
Nuclear weapons,
  multiple, independently targetable re-
    entry vehicles (MIRVs), 20
  Polaris submarine fleet, US, 94
    See also under SALT.
Nun, B., 221
Nuremberg, Military Tribunal, Charter
    of, 293
Nussbaumer, A., 222–241

O'CONNELL, D. P., 267, 324
Oil,
  Southeast Asia, potential resources in,
    88–89
  Washington   Energy   Conference
    (1974), 30
  World economy, and, 27, 29
    See also under OPEC.
Oppenheim, L., 37
Organisation for African Unity (OAU),
    173, 184, 189
Organisation of American States (OAS),
    173, 189–190
  Canada, and, 193
  Cuba's exclusion from, 185–186
  Rio de Janeiro Treaty, 193
  US instrument of policy, as a, 188
Organisation of Economic Co-operation
    and Development (OECD), 18
Organisation of Petroleum Exporting
    Countries (OPEC), 18, 27, 174, 181–
    182
  multilateral enterprises, plan to estab-
    lish, 303
  pole, considered as a, 18
  Riyadh agreement, 18
  Teheran agreement, 18

PACIFIC ALLIANCE,
  towards a new, 88–105
  ANZUS (Australia, New Zealand
    and United States) Alliance, 91,
    94

PACIFIC ALLIANCE—*cont.*
towards a new—*cont.*
Atlantic or Pacific World? 88–89
Australia's place in the sun, 90–93
cutting the strings, 93–95
defence or defencelessness? 98–107
future of region, 101–105
senses of difference, 95–98
Paine, T., 51
Pakistan, 10, 276, 314
Commonwealth, withdrawal from, 185
Pan African Congress (PAC), 161
Paracel Islands, 115
Paraguay, 58, 63
Pareto, V., 227
Pascal, B., 124
Payne, A. E., 160
Peaceful Co-existence, 252, 257, 264
Peron, E., 63
Peron, J. D., 63–68, 69–71
Peru,
Argentina, trade with, 60
economic co-operation in Latin
America, and, 208, 209, 211
Indians, Spanish exploitation of, 313
Phanomyoung, P., 118
Pinochet, General, 79, 81
Plato, 347
Poland, 231
agriculture in, 231, 237
company management, 236
Poles, expedition to the, 4–21
bi-multipolarity, 16–19, 20
bipolarity, erosion of, 10–12, 196
models, inevitability of, 4–5
multipolarity, 12–16, 20
OPEC, considered as a pole, 18
pole, properties of, 6–10
Soviet Union, pole of, 6, 10
unipolarity, 8
United States, pole of, 6, 10
Popper, K., 350
Portugal, 56
Chilean junta, recognition of, 84
Portuguese Africa,
Liberation movements,
World Council of Churches grants
to, 161–163
press comments, public debate
arising, 162
Potsdam Agreement, 108
Potter, P., 165
Potter, R. B., 139, 140, 141, 145, 153,
154
Power politics, 128
Prats Gonzales, General C., 77, 78
Punta del Este (1967) Declaration of,
209

RACISM,
World Council of Churches, and,
155–172
oppressed racial groups,
grants to, 160–163
Programme to Combat Racism
(1969), Ecumenical, evaluation of,
160, 167–172
racism,
ecumenical movement, early in-
terest in, 155–160
International Advisory Commit-
tee on, 160
international consultation on
(1969), 159
investments in, 165–167
violence versus non-violence,
red herring of, 163–165
Ramcharan, B. G., 283–300
Ramsey, P., 150, 151
Ratner, L., 260
Realpolitik, 351
Renard, G., 127
Rhodesia, 161, 177, 185
Unilateral Declaration of Indepen-
dence (UDI), 185
UN sanctions against, 186, 189
Riggs, R., 187
Rio Tinto Zinc Inc., 102
Robinson, P., 104
Rogers, W., 17, 111
Roman Catholic Church, 340
Roosevelt, F. D., 107
Roosevelt, T., 4
Rosencrance, R., 20
Roumania, 10, 263
Argentina, trade with, 60
Rousseau, J.-J., 131
Rusk, D., 11
Russell, R., 183
Russett, B. R., 152

ST. PAUL, 131–132
Santa Cruz, V., 84
Saudi Arabia, 18
Schiller, K., 222
Schmidt, H., 22–33
Schumpeter, J. A., 222
Schwarzenberger, G., 337–368
Second World War, 50, 137, 139, 152,
173, 196, 230, 237, 239, 242, 332,
354–356, 360
Seidl-Hohenveldern, I., 301–312
Shaull, R., 165
Shurshalov, V. M., 242, 255–257, 261
Sihanouk, Prince N., 94, 110
Sik, O., 229, 230, 237, 238

Singapore, 94, 109, 112, 115, 119, 276

Sioux Indians, 146

" Socialist " International Law,
  Soviet concept of, 242–264
    Congress of Marxist Legal Theorists
      (1931), 252–253
    Institute of Law of the Academy of
      Sciences of the Soviet Union, 251
    Institute of Soviet Construction and
      Law of the Communist Academy,
      251
    peaceful co-existence, and, 261
    present theoretical constructions,
      255–264
      international law,
        separate system of, 257–259
        socialist bloc, 262–264
        socialist internationalism as a
          legal principle, 255–256
        Sovereignty and connected
          principles, 259–262
        Subordinate principles, 256–
          257
    proletarian internationalism, origins
      of, 243–253
    revival of the issue of " socialist "
      international law, 253–255
    Soviet doctrine in the 1920s, 245–
      253
    UN Charter, and, 261

Somare, M., 102

Sombart, W., 223

Sonderkötter, F., 265–282

Souper Onfray, Col. R., 77

South Africa, 157, 181
  Commonwealth, withdrawal from,
    185, 189
  Cottesloe settlement, 158
  Die Burger, 158
  Dutch Reformed Churches, 157, 158,
    170
  Institute of Race Relations, 158
  Namibia, UN, and, 189
  National Party, 157
  South African Council of Churches
    (SACC), 167
  UN resolution: non-sale of arms to,
    189

South Korea, 149

South Pacific Parliament, idea of, 105

South Vietnam, 96, 111, 116, 138

South West African People's Organisation (SWAPO), 161, 163

Southeast Asia, 22, 27, 42, 53, 88–90,
  93, 100, 104, 113, 115, 116, 138, 139
  military threat to Australia and New
    Zealand, perceived, 99, 100
  neutralisation of, proposed, 115

Southeast Asia—*cont.*
  oil, potential resources, 88–89
  Sino-American *rapprochement* and
    new configurations in, 106–120
    period, 1945–1971, 107–110;
    1970s, 110–119
  region, profile of, 106–107

Southeast Asia League (1947), 118

Southeast Asia Treaty Organisation
  (SEATO), 96, 108, 111, 114, 118

Southern Ireland,
  EEC, and, 270, 271

Southern Rhodesia, 158

Sovereignty, principle of State, 41, 45,
  342
  EEC, question of British, and, 190
  liberty of small States,
    Gladstone's invocation of principle
      of, 47
  non-intervention,
    Brezhnev doctrine of, 41n., 260–
      261
    Cobdenite doctrine of, 51
  Soviet concept of, 41n., 259–262

Soviet Union, 14, 16, 19, 33, 38, 43, 88,
  91, 115, 118, 138, 152, 196, 226, 230,
  318, 319, 342
  Chilean *coup* (1973), and, 84
  China, People's Republic of, and, 7,
    9, 10
    hostility between, 14, 15, 51–52,
      110, 120
    ideological ally of, 107
  Civil War (1919–21), 248
  COMECON, and, 226
  Communist Party (CPSU), 258
    nineteenth Congress of, 255
    programme (1961), 258
  Constitutions (1918 and 1924), Soviet,
    246
  Czechoslovakia (1968), and, 20, 41n.
    Treaty with (1970), 262
  Declaration on the Rights of the
    Peoples of Russia (1917), 245
  Decree of Peace (1917), 247
  Eastern Europe, and, 23, 24
    sphere of influence in, 40
    troops in, 26
  economic planning, 228–230
    GOSPLAN (Central Planning
      Bureau), 233
    First 5-Year Plan, 251
    NEP (New Economic Policy), 228,
      229, 251
  Finnish Republic (1917), and, 246
  Georgia, recognition as independent
    State, 246
  Indian Ocean, and, 115

Soviet Union—*cont.*
  Indonesia, and, 116
  Middle East, and, 44
  multinational corporations, and, 302
  nuclear parity, strategic, 25
  nuclear weapons, acquisition of, 8
  October Revolution (1917), 227, 255, 339
  oil resources of, 20, 89
  Second World War, and, 62
  Southeast Asia, and, 115, 117
  Thailand, and, 117
  Turkish Armenia (1917), and, 246
  Ukrainian Republic, 245
  United States, and, 332
    détente with, 38
    SALT with, 30
    security interests, and, 31, 39
    See also under Eastern Europe, economic systems, of Socialist: principles, development and operation; Poles, expedition to the; " Socialist " International Law, Soviet concept of; Super-Powers.
Spain, 203
  Argentina, trade with, 60
  Chilean junta, recognition of, 84
  Civil War, 151, 152
  Peruvian Indians, onetime exploitation of, 313
Special Drawing Rights (SDRs), 196
Spinoza, B., 347
Sri Lanka, 276
Stalin, J., 109, 251, 253, 263
  " Bukharinist " attitude, attacked, 251
  death of, 255
  First 5-Year Plan, 251
  Soviet legal theory, and, 251
Strachey, J., 39, 40
Strategic Arms Limitation Talks (SALT), 30
  Agreement on the Prevention of Nuclear War (1973), 30, 38
Suharto, General, 112
Sukarno, R., 109, 116
Super-Powers, 6, 7, 9, 16, 19, 34, 35, 38, 40, 44, 48, 52, 181, 188, 319, 348
  concert and, idea of, 34–35
  deterrence, and, 6
  inter-bloc norms, 41
  spheres of influence, 40
  " hegemonial jurisdiction," 42
    See also under International Order, Concert and idea of; Poles, expedition to the; Soviet Union; United States.
Sweden, 53, 56, 167
  Chilian *coup*, and, 81, 83–84

Switzerland, 53, 56, 167
  Chilean junta, recognition of, 84
Syria, 16
Syz, J., 196–207

TAIWAN, 116
Tanzania, 275
Taylor, F. M., 222, 229
Thailand, 111–112, 116, 117, 119
  Soviet Union, and, 117
Third World, 6, 9, 47, 52, 53, 71, 103, 165, 212, 280, 281, 313, 348
Thomas, M. M., 157, 163
Thompson, Sir R., 137
Thucydides, 343
Todd, G., 163
Tomic, R., 80
Toribio Menno, Vice-Admiral, 79
Truman, H. S., 137, 143
  Doctrine, 138
Tucker, R. W., 141, 142, 143, 145, 146, 153, 154
Tunkin, G. I., 242, 256, 258, 259, 261
Turkey,
  EEC, and, 272
  Soviet Treaty (1919), 249

UGANDA, 275
Union of Soviet Socialist Republics. *See under* Soviet Union.
United Arab Republic. *See under* Egypt.
United Kingdom, 16, 30, 56, 57, 91, 108, 117, 118, 122, 167, 174, 177, 185, 248, 318
  ANZUK, and, 118
  Argentina, and, 64, 65
    Roca-Runciman agreement (1933), 60
    trade with, 59–60, 61–62
  Australia, and, 91, 103
    East of Suez policy, and, 92
    influence, decline of British in 1950s, 6
    trade with, 97
  British Council of Churches, 167
  British Empire,
    Indian Raj, and, 313
  Chilean *coup* (1973), and, 84
    junta, diplomatic recognition of, 84–85
    press and BBC reaction in UK, 78, 85–86
  EEC, 271
    accession, 275
    financial burden, 192

United Kingdom—*cont.*
  EEC—*cont.*
    membership, application for, 186, 190, 193, 270
    sovereignty, possible erosion of, 190
  Indonesia, and, 118
  New Zealand,
    trade with, 92, 97
  nuclear forces of, 78, 85
  OPEC, and, 18
  Southeast Asia, and, 118
  Soviet Declaration on Peace (1917), and, 247
  See also Commonwealth of Nations.
United Nations, 48, 176, 180, 194, 329
  African States in, 47
  Bretton Woods agreement, 361
  Charter of, 37, 42, 46, 173, 261, 292, 295, 298, 326
  Children's Fund (UNICEF), 354
  China, People's Republic of,
    admission of, 42
    vetoes Bangladesh membership, 185
  General Assembly, 47, 94, 185, 188, 201, 309, 342, 355, 362
    Declaration on Human Rights, 354, 355
    Sixth Committee and ILC, 283–300
  Korean War (1950–1953), and, 42–43, 138, 149
  Uniting for Peace Resolution, 188
  NATO, and, 47
  San Francisco Conference (1945), 50
  Secretariat, 309
    Department of Economic and Social Affairs, 302
  Secretary General, 177, 296, 343
  Security Council, 43–44, 188, 327, 342, 343, 361
    Korea (1950), and, 43
    Middle East (1967), and, 44
    permanent membership of, 185
  Specialised Agencies, 181–182, 196, 342, 348, 353
  UN Corporations as multinational enterprises, 308
    See also under International Law Commission; I n t e r n a t i o n a l Organisation in foreign policy perspective.
United Nations Commission on International Trade Law (UNCITRAL), 302
  EEC, and, 280–281
  multinational corporations, and, 303

United Nations Food and Agriculture Organisation (FAO), 181
United Nations Force in the Congo (ONUC), 191, 330
United States, 14, 15, 16, 19, 38, 56, 57, 68, 88, 95, 115, 118, 122, 185, 196, 202, 318, 343
  Argentina, trade with, 61–62, 65
  ASEAN, and, 119
  Australia, and, 103
    military bases in, 94
  Chile, and, 73
    coup (1973), 79–80
      CIA and ITT, possible roles of, 80
  China, People's Republic of,
    rapprochement with, 34, 39, 42
    trade with, 89
  Civil Rights movement, 159
  Dominican Republic (1965), intervention, 41n., 188
  energy policy,
    Washington Conference (1974), 30
  Europe, and, 25–30
    EEC, and, 271
  Latin America,
    OAS, an instrument of US policy, 188
    sphere of influence in, 40
  League of Nations, and, 49
  Marshall Aid Programme, 191, 194
  Middle East, and, 17, 44
  monetary policy,
    Europe, and, 26–27
  nuclear parity, strategic, 25
  role, reappraisal of, 24
  Soviet Union, 332
    détente, and, 38, 51–52
    SALT with, 30
    security interests, and, 31, 39
  Trade Bill (1973), 28
  Vietnam War, and, 11, 43, 53, 54
  Western Germany,
    Treaty of Friendship, Commerce and Navigation, 266
    See also under American Military Policy; Atlantic Alliance, new tasks for; Poles, expedition to the; Super-Powers; Southeast Asia, Sino-American *rapprochement* and the new configurations.
Universal Postal Union (UPU), 181, 360
Uruguay, 58
  Argentina, trade with, 60
  Chilean junta, recognition of, 84
  economic co-operation in Latin America, 208
Usenko, E. T., 261

VANDENBERG, A., 50, 51
Venezuela, 10, 18, 56
  economic co-operation in Latin America, 208
Vergara, S., 84
Vienna Diplomatic Conference (1968–1969), 357
Vietnam War, 8, 10, 11, 43, 53, 54, 88, 90, 91, 93, 108, 110, 112, 138, 144, 148, 151
Vincent, R. J., 34–55
Vorster, J., 162, 169
Vyshinsky, A., 242
  Soviet Doctrine of International Law, 252
  Theses (1938), 251, 253

WALSH, M., 95
Waltz, K., 9
War, Law of, 125
  Just, *see under* American Military Policy.
  limited, 140
  nuclear, 150
  religious, 144–148
Warsaw Treaty Organisation (WTO), 23, 24, 189, 192, 226, 263
Washington Post, Chile, *coup* in, 80
Weber, M., 27, 126, 352
Weighley, R. F., 138, 140, 141, 144, 149, 153
Wells, L. T., 102
Western Europe, 14, 15, 19, 22–25, 58, 70, 88, 94, 100, 342, 343, 361
  African States, and, 273–275
  banking in, compared with Eastern European practice, 235
  economic systems of, 225
  nuclear policy, future, 33
  oil crisis (1973), and, 29
  Trade Bill (1973), 28
  United States and, 25–30
Western Germany, 6, 7, 14, 27, 30, 167
  Chilean *coup*, and, 84
  United States,
    Treaty of Friendship, Commerce and Navigation, 266
Westphalia (1648), Peace of, 326, 327, 335
Whitlam, G., 93, 94, 96–98, 100, 102–104
Willkie, W., " One World," concept of, 50
Wilson, W., 49, 50
Wischmann, A., 160
Wolff, C. von, 337, 347

World Bank (IBRD), 89
  See also under International Development Banks.
World Council of Churches, 155–172
  All Africa Conference of Churches, 163
  Assemblies,
    First (1948), 156
    Second (1954), 157
    Third (1961), 158
    Fourth (1968), 159
  Commission of the Churches on International Affairs (CCIA), 155, 157
  Ecumenical Programme to Combat Racism (1969), 160
  International Consultation on Racism (1969), 159
  International Missionary Council, 155, 156
  Oxford Conference on Church, Community and State (1937), 156
  Portuguese Africa,
    National Liberation Movements, grants to, 161–162, 166
  Programme to Combat Racism, 155, 165–167
    evaluation of, 167
  Report: Violence, Non-Violence and the Struggle for Social Justice, 164
  Universal Christian Council on Life and Work, 156
  World Alliance for International Friendship through the Churches, 155
  See also under Racism, World Council of Churches, and.
World Health Organisation (WHO), 181
World Order, Concept of, 320–336
  Clark-Sohn plan for limited world government, 322, 325
  condition, as a, 321–322
  future, identification with, 334
  minimum, 321
  negation of disorder, as the, 321
  normative writer, and the, 335
  optimum, 321
  realist scholar, and the, 335
  study of, approaches to the, 322–334
    international law, 323–328
    international organisation, 328–330
    systems approach, 330–335
  value, as a, 322
  war prevention system, as a, 321
Wounded Knee, 146

YALEM, R. J., 320–336
Yaoundé Convention, 182, 273–276, 281

Young, O., 320, 323
Yugoslavia, 56, 203, 231, 261, 262
    banking in, 234
    market and plan in, 239–241

ZAIRE, 315

Zambia, 169
Zero-sum game, 6, 318
    non-zero sum game, 317
Zimbabwe African National Union
    (ZANU), 161
Zollverein (German Customs Union—
    1833), 360